A History of Christian, Jewish, Hindu, Buddhist, and Muslim Perspectives on War and Peace

A HISTORY OF CHRISTIAN, JEWISH, HINDU, BUDDHIST, AND MUSLIM PERSPECTIVES ON WAR AND PEACE

Volume II

A Century of Wars

J. William Frost

Studies in Religion and Society
Volume 65b

The Edwin Mellen Press
Lewiston•Queenston•Lampeter

Library of Congress Cataloging-in-Publication Data

Frost, J. William (Jerry William)
  A history of Christian, Jewish, Muslim, Hindu, and Buddhist perspectives on war and peace / J. William Frost.
     p. cm. -- (Studies in religion and society ; v. 65 a-b)
  Includes bibliographical references and index.
  Contents: v. 1. The Bible to 1914 -- v. 2. A century of wars.
  ISBN 0-7734-6561-8 (v. 1) -- ISBN 0-7734-6563-4 (v. 2)
  1. War--Religious aspects--Comparative studies. 2. Peace--Religious
aspects--Comparative studies. 3. Religions--History. I. Title. II. Studies in religion and
society (Lewiston, N.Y.) ; v. 65.

BL65.W2F76 2004
201'.72--dc22

2003071017

This is volume 65b in the continuing series
Studies in Religion and Society
Volume 65b ISBN 0-7734-6563-4
SRS Series ISBN 0-88946-863-X

A CIP catalog record for this book is available from the British Library.

The Edwin Mellen Press
Box 450
Lewiston, New York
USA 14092-0450

The Edwin Mellen Press
Box 67
Queenston, Ontario
CANADA L0S 1L0

The Edwin Mellen Press, Ltd.
Lampeter, Ceredigion, Wales
UNITED KINGDOM SA48 8LT

Printed in the United States of America

Table of Contents

A HISTORY OF CHRISTIAN, JEWISH, HINDU, BUDDHIST, AND
MUSLIM PERSPECTIVES ON WAR AND PEACE
Volume I: THE *BIBLE* TO 1914

Table of Contents

A HISTORY OF CHRISTIAN, JEWISH, HINDU, BUDDHIST, AND MUSLIM PERSPECTIVES ON WAR AND PEACE
Volume II: A CENTURY OF WARS

XIV.
World War I

Pundits are already characterizing the twentieth century as the Second Hundred Years War: a prelude and World War I, the Depression and World War II, a Cold War ending in 1989 followed by a period of adjustment. Our task in this and the following chapters is to assess the impact of this century of wars on organized religion. Emphasizing war as the determinate factor is correct, because religion neither caused nor had much influence on conduct before or during battle. Our primary focus is on the various roles of religion as supporter, critic, seeker of alternatives, interpreter of significance, and comforter of the bereaved. However, to understand the impact of the Great War or War to End Wars, as it was called at the time, we must understand its causes, influence on the peace movement, the nature of the fighting, why the United States felt it necessary to become involved, and results of the Allies' victory. The organization of this chapter follows classic Just War categories: the causes of war and the conduct of war, looking first at Europe and then America.

The assassination of Austrian Archduke Ferdinand and his wife in Sarajevo by a Serbian set off a chain of events in the summer of 1914 that led to World War I. The Archduke, heir to the throne of the Dual Monarchy of Austria-Hungary, had been visiting Bosnia-Herzegovina, an area recently annexed amid intense ethnic hostilities. The Austrians suspected the government of Serbia had supported the assassination and sought vengeance, so they presented to Serbian authorities a set of demands they knew would be rejected. The Austrians ignored the Serbian request for arbitration. The German Emperor promised in the so-called "blank check" to back his ally, the Austrians, who then declared war and invaded Serbia. The Russians, traditional defender of all Slavs, announced support for the Serbians and - knowing that their preparations for war would take longer than either Austria or Germany - announced mobilization.

How could a minor incident involving two weak powers lead to what became the world's most destructive war up to that time, a war that would claim ten million lives, eliminate dynasties in Austria-Hungary, Russia, and Germany, and destroy nineteenth-century beliefs in optimism and progress?[1] From its start, contemporaries saw the war as an avoidable tragedy and described it as a "descent into hell," "an abyss," or in words alleged to have been said by the English foreign minister, Edward Grey, "The lamps are going out all over Europe. We shall not see them lit again in our time."[2]

Historians proposed the following as underlying causes for World War I: a rigid alliance system, an arms race, imperial jealousies, economic rivalries, irresponsible leadership, jingoistic press, misunderstandings of the impact of industrialism on modern war, and glorification of military virtues.[3] The main indirect cause of the war was the deep insecurity felt by all the major powers of Europe. These nations, fearing their neighbors, had built enormous armies and navies, drawn up detailed plans for war, and come to believe that arms were the best guarantor of peace. However much in theory they espoused the values of the peace movement, in practice they followed the Roman dictum: to have peace, prepare for war.

Germany had long feared a two-front war and had attempted to compensate for the geographical weakness of having no strong natural barriers on either eastern or western frontiers. Since the Austrians, Germans, and Russians had carved up Poland, there was no buffer area dividing the three empires. The

---

[1]John Stroessinger, *Why Nations Go to War* (6th ed., 1993), ch. L, is a brief summary of the causes; popular narrative history at its best is in Barbara Tuchman, *The Guns of August* (1962). A more scholarly analysis is Henry Kissinger, *Diplomacy* (1994), ch. 7-9. There are several good reference works devoted to W.W. I: *The Marshall Cavendish Illustrated Encyclopedia of World War I* (1984) and *The European Powers in the First World War*, ed. Spencer Tucker (1996).
[2]Samuel Hynes, *A War Imagined: The First World War and English Culture* (1991), 3.
[3]Niall Ferguson, *The Pity of War: Explaining World War* (1999), 28, 33, 68, 70, 83-87, 91, is an excellent revisionist history arguing that Britain's irresponsible foreign policy was more important

North Sea and her navy protected Germany from the north, and the Austrian alliance provided security on the south. The danger lay from an invasion from France and Russia. The German plan in case of war was to attack first before the two neighbors could combine to crush her.

The French, since their crushing defeat in 1870, wanted revenge and to regain Alsace-Lorraine from the Germans. Since France had a smaller population and less heavy industry than Germany, she worked for alliances first with Russia and then with Great Britain. The French had a formal alliance with the Russians and an understanding, or entente, with the British government, who had promised aid in a defensive war. However, the Parliament had never been informed or voted on the entente and did not even know that the English and French had engaged in joint planning to put British troops on the continent in case of war. Britain had a defensive alliance with Russia, even though Britain had consistently opposed Tsarist expansion and the autocratic government remained unpopular. Her alliance with France tied England to Russia's aggressive Balkan policies.

After finding herself isolated and unpopular during the Boer War, Great Britain sought alliances after 1900. Germany's shipbuilding program threatened England's traditional supremacy on the sea, dominance that she felt the maintenance of empire required. England first dropped her policy of isolation by signing a treaty with Japan in 1902, a logical partner since both nations opposed Russian expansionism. Britain's next treaty with France was also logical because both nations were democracies with large colonial possessions. Germany now faced, in addition to hostile France, the largest navy and army in the world. Neither Germany, France, Great Britain, nor even Russia had a compelling strategic interest in Serbia, and the public had general sympathy with Franz Joseph, the elderly Habsburg monarch whose nephew and heir had been killed by a terrorist.

---

than business, nationalism, imperialism, or excessive arms spending in turning a minor crisis into a major war.

Ascribing Germany's victory over France in 1870 to Clausewitz's emphasis upon a quick attack of overwhelming mass on a critical objective, the general staffs of the armies planned for an offensive. The Germans had concluded that the only way for a victory was to mobilize an enormous army and strike first to the west, defeating France in eight weeks before Russia could field its massive armies. The Tsar believed that his army's size and the logistical difficulties in equipping and bringing so unwieldy a force to battle required an early mobilization. Allowing such a mobilization struck at the heart of the Prussian strategy. The German general staff concluded that striking at France through Belgium offered the best prospect of quick victory. The difficulty was that all major powers in Europe had guaranteed Belgian neutrality.

The war did not begin because European powers desired new borders; only France had a specific land grievance. In August 1914 the German government had no intention of incorporating new territory, but individuals did desire to expand the empire in the East and West. A Pan-German movement saw states as organisms, which during their period of growth had to increase territory. The French had elaborate plans to invade Germany and to re-conquer Alsace-Lorraine. So after the crisis erupted, when Germany began to mobilize, so did the French. Diplomats sought peace while their countries prepared to fight.

When personal appeals from the Kaiser to the Tsar failed and after Germany rejected the British plea for a conference of major powers to settle the dispute, the major states of Christendom - invoking the blessing of God and trusting in His help in what each defined as a defensive struggle - declared war on one another. A surprise attack without a declaration of war, as Japan had done to China and Russia, was not in keeping with the European way of war. There was little war fever among the various peoples, but in August 1914 the public rallied to their respective flags, confident of a short, glorious war. Military struggle would uplift the people, prove the value of honor, and vindicate the national culture. At the outset, governments found they had diverted rancorous discord into a surge of patriotic unity, almost a new birth, which they called a second Pentecost.

II. An Ideology for Total War

The Eclipse of the Peace Movement

The onset of war showed that the regnant religion was neither Christianity nor socialism, but nationalism. Whenever possible, nationalism reinforced Christianity or socialism to make an even more potent force, but any conflicts between patriotism and other sources of values ended with the primacy of the nation-state. The survival of the state and its distinctive culture and values served to justify the sacrifice of the blood of young men. Nationalism created a mystic unity of the people working together against an enemy who, during the course of the war, became subhuman. French Catholics and Protestants, or German Lutherans and Catholics, or Anglicans and Dissenters submerged religious differences in the common effort. Earlier struggles among farmers and factory workers, capitalist and socialist parties, democrat and aristocrats, could be postponed in the common effort to enlist the entire population.

The war proved either the irrelevance or bankruptcy of various agencies and ideals that intellectuals and reformers had declared would make a major war impossible. The program of the liberal or bourgeois peace movement - Hague conferences, treaties of arbitration, mediations, cooling-off periods, the skilled practice of diplomacy, which in retrospect seems greatly superior to what actually took place in the summer of 1914 - appeared during the war as naïve attempts to ignore the necessity of military preparedness.

The pre-war peace movement had stressed the importance of alternatives to war, but also a country's right to self-defense. In August 1914 the European peace movement's adherents in all the belligerent countries decided that only by supporting the war efforts of their respective states could world peace be created and maintained. They proclaimed that if the other side had not acted treacherously and threatened the security of their state, then peace would have continued. The peace movement, far from condemning the war, changed emphasis from stressing Christian harmony and the economic and social advantages of peace to using religion to differentiate the good from the bad and to justify the necessity to extirpate evil.[4] The God of battles replaced the God of love, at least so far as the enemy was concerned. A corollary was that the enemy's character had to be blackened sufficiently that his defeat became a prerequisite to reform the international system.

Those who opposed all war, almost always for religious reasons, were now termed conscientious objectors (COs). No belligerent country, including the United States after 1917, contained large numbers of COs. Neither Russia, France, Austria, Italy nor Germany recognized the rights of conscientious objectors to war. The French court-martialed and executed draft-age pacifist men who would not serve (a policy envied by some members of the English military) and compelled Catholic priests to serve. The British did not begin conscription until January 1916 and, although subjecting pacifist men to prison and various forms of cruelty, did recognize the right of not carrying arms as they sought to persuade or coerce the COs into ambulance work or another form of militarily necessary work. Those who refused to cooperate were imprisoned. The Americans also began the war assuming that all men who opposed the war could serve in the military in a non-combatant manner. The "absolutist" COs in Britain and America who refused to do any military service or even to wear uniforms were imprisoned. Eventually a few of the COs in England and America gained furloughs to work in France for civilian relief and reconstruction, a program justified by the pacifists as proving their patriotism while preserving their testimony against war and approved by the governments as helping to win the war. The small number of conscientious objectors posed no threat to the war effort of any country. Even so, whether motivated by religion or social philosophy, pacifist attempts to debate the necessity or morality of the war encountered censorship in all lands.[5]

---

[4] Sandi Cooper, *Patriotic Pacifism: Waging War on War in Europe, 1815-1914* (1991), ch. 8.
[5] Martin Ceadel, *Pacifism in Britain 1914-1945* (1980), 33-39; Charles Chatfield, *For Peace and Justice: Pacifism in America, 1914-1941* (1971), Part 1.

The Churches

Except for traditionally pacifist religious sects, the churches preached the necessity of military service. An Anglican priest would not recruit soldiers directly from the pulpit, but he would use his influence in the wider society to persuade men to volunteer. The Church of England managed to prevent priests from being conscripted, a policy also followed in Austria and Italy. But early in the war, a church directive forbidding Anglican priests from serving in the front lines served to discredit these men with the soldiers, and the policy was soon rescinded. There was no shortage of Anglican priests willing to volunteer for religious services in the front lines. Still, the press criticized the bishops for not allowing young priests to be drafted.[6]

Roman Catholic chaplains from the beginning served in the front lines. There was no tradition of support for lay conscientious objectors in the Catholic Church, so there was no religious protest against universal conscription. Throughout the war, the papacy officially took no position on war guilt, much to the disgust of the Allies who thought the failure to condemn the invasion of Belgium was an unneutral act, and Roman Catholic priests ministered to men in the trenches but did not carry arms or fight.[7]

The churches played little role in formulating the policies that led to war or in the crucial events of the summer of 1914. Statesmen often consulted religious leaders and sought reassurance that their conduct was not immoral, but they did not seek the counsel of religious leaders on foreign affairs and no ranking ecclesiastical officials offered public rebuke. The churches did not issue jingoist statements or whip up sentiments for war in July when the crisis developed. Rather, in services the clergy prayed for "peace in our time." The clergy during the summer was ineffective in opposing war because they remained essentially

---

[6]Albert Marrin, *The Last Crusade: The Church of England in the First World War* (1974), 189-195.
[7]Robert Graham, *Vatican Diplomacy: A Study of Church and State on the International Plane* (1959), ch. 2.

apolitical, at least in foreign policy, and assumed until too late that statesmen had the ability to avoid war.

All the initial belligerents, except France, had an official or state-linked church. (The Ottoman sultan, essentially reduced to a religious leader after a 1908 rebellion in Turkey, was induced to proclaim a *jihad*.) The Church of England, the Russian Orthodox Church, the Roman Catholic Church in the Dual Monarchy, and the Evangelical Church in parts of the German Empire were established churches whose clergy received salaries from governments that saw the churches as bulwarks against radicalism, supporters of the monarchy, and traditional defenders of the state. In spite of the heritage of Just War thought, there was no tradition of pacifism or even selective opposition to immoral war in any of these churches. Germany had a strong concentration of Catholics in its western areas who constituted about one-third of the total population. Owing to a pervasive anti-Catholicism in German ruling circles and anti-clericalism in republican France, relationships between the papacy and these governments remained strained.[8]

With Roman Catholics fighting on both sides, the pope refused to condemn either side, believing that a position of strict neutrality offered the only place by which mediation could occur. Even though the Catholic Church was a worldwide institution, cardinals and bishops supported the war efforts of their respective countries. So German and Austrian bishops prayed for victory for the Central Powers, while French, Belgian, and, after Italy entered the war, Italian bishops sought divine blessings for the Allies. When French Catholics tried to portray the war as an attack by Protestant Germany against Catholicism, German Catholics emphatically denied the charge. Catholic center parties headed the opposition to the socialists in Germany, France, and Italy. Because of anti-Catholic tendencies in the governments of France, Germany, and Italy, the papacy had encouraged the creation of Catholic center parties, devoted to protection of the Church's interests and a moderate social policy. Even though the papacy did

---

[8]Anthony Rhodes, *The Power of Rome in the Twentieth Century: The Vatican in the Age of Liberal Democracies*, 1870-1922 (1983), chs. 15-18.

not succumb to war fever, the Catholic parties wholeheartedly rallied behind their respective nations. The clergy of the Russian Orthodox and Church of England had throughout their history assured their country's politicians and generals that God was on their side. Even the few Anglican clergymen who had criticized the government's policies in the Boer War rallied to defend their country's conduct in 1914. Governments did not have to force religious leaders to support their war aims.

Patriotism did not mean that the clergy subscribed to the view that war was a good. The German and English clergy saw the war as a necessary evil, and distinguished among Russia and Austria - where the war was a crusade and holy - and Britain, France, and Germany where states initiated the war for strategic purposes. Still, bishops, cardinals, and pastors willingly identified religion with the aims of the government. German Protestants proclaimed that war was to defend their *Kultur* against Roman Catholic France and Russian Orthodoxy; French Protestants, a small minority in a Catholic country, rallied for French civilization against German barbarities. The churches of each belligerent admitted to no inconsistency between loving your neighbor and fighting him. From 1914-18, the Hebrews' wars, apocalyptic wars, and the Justified War traditions made preeminent the God of wars and a wrathful Jesus.[9]

The pre-war secular advocates of peace joined the churches' embrace of war. European socialists had stressed international workmen's solidarity and proclaimed the necessity of a general strike in case of a major war. The workmen would not become cannon fodder for the imperialist rivalries of the capitalist ruling class. Social democratic parties played a major role in the parliaments of Britain, France, and Germany and had long criticized the arms race, the secrecy of foreign policy decisions, and emphasis on war plans. Yet in August 1914 when

---

[9]John Williams, *The Home Fronts: Britain, France and Germany 1914-1918* (1972), 17, 68-69, 235; Ellen Evans, *The German Center Party 1870-1933: A Study in Political Catholicism* (1981), 203-206. Marrin, ch. 3-4; Bailey, "'Got mit uns': Germany's Protestant Theologians in the First World War," Ph.D. diss.

parliaments were asked to ratify the decision for war, the social democrats in all nations rallied to the flag almost without dissent. The socialists would not undermine this patriotic war.

A series of exposés, Randolph Bourne's *War and the Intellectuals* (1917), Ray Abrams' *Preachers Present Arms* (1933) about Americans, and Julien Benda's *Trahison des clercs* (Treason of the Intellectuals) (1927) about the French, showed how clergy, university professors, journalists, and writers jettisoned objectivity to support the war. A similar indictment could have been made against German and British thinkers. Churches, socialists, and intellectuals were like a thermometer, reflecting rather than changing the temperature of the society.

The socialists and religious peace advocates had warned against a coming general war but had not anticipated a specific war in the summer of 1914, and their surprise meant there was no effective planning against mobilization. Perhaps had they thought that war was probable, they would have taken more action against it, although it is likely that nothing they could have done would have altered the peculiar combination of planning, fear, nationalism, and irrationality that prevailed in the chanceries of Europe in the summer of 1914.

III. A New Kind of Battle

Surprised by its beginning, even more astonishing to politicians, churchmen, and to the military was the changed character of the war. The education of the generals would be paid for with the lives of soldiers. French and British incompetence almost cost them the war during the first weeks. The French high command assumed that patriotic soldiers could overrun heavily fortified German positions manned by machine gunners. The result was 329,000 killed in two months and half a million in six months.[10] Following Clausewitz (and misunderstanding him), the French stressed above all the importance of the attack and morale among men. Logistics were secondary to the quality of men.

University of Virginia (1978), 40, 50, 130-34; Ferguson, 207-210, 355-56.
[10]Ferguson, 341.

Both French and Germans believed that bringing overwhelming force to bear on a critical point was the key to victory. In their enthusiasm for attack they ignored or forgot Clausewitz's caution that even the simplest maneuver will become difficult in war and that the unforeseen will impede the best-laid plans. The Germans' advance into France bogged down because, as Clausewitz insisted, a successful offense will lose momentum as supply lines lengthen and troops get spread more thinly; at this point, the initiative tended to go to the defense. Ironically, World War I proved that Clausewitz's insights could be relevant in the conduct of a kind of war he had never envisaged.

Industrialization, technology, nationalism, science, planning, professionalization of the military, and universal conscription revolutionized war. Armies numbering in the millions (except in Britain), having already been trained, now had to be fed, clothed, armed, transported and directed. More soldiers died in the first month of World War I than in all the Napoleonic Wars, and that was only the beginning of the wastage of men. No longer would there be great decisive battles after which armies would withdraw to bury the dead and regroup. Rather, there were constant battles draining countries of men and munitions and, in spite of major defeats of the Russians and Italians, armies remained intact. By 1918 on the Western Front, the lines of battle would have moved only a few miles from where they had been established in the fall of 1914. Two great alliances would strain all of their productive capacities to bring the maximum force to bear on the opponents' lines and the result would be stalemate. Total war, the mobilization of all the resources of a society for one end, would be the twentieth century's contribution to the art of war.

How did Europe arrive at the position where no compromise settlement was possible, particularly since at the beginning only Alsace-Lorraine appeared as a difficult issue? The nations began with classic Just War techniques: they declared war, set out their grievances, and proclaimed the necessity of defense. The Germans struck first, invading neutral Belgium, hoping to route the French left. Unfortunately for Germany's reputation, she was one of several guarantors of Belgian neutrality, and the invasion was a violation of treaties and international law. The Germans assumed that the Belgians, with whom they had no quarrel, would allow their armies to pass through. After all, Belgium's army was no match for German forces and fighting to the death in a doomed cause would be irrational, even against Just War theory that did not authorize a fight against overwhelming odds. German theologians found scriptural precedent based upon Moses' demands on Sihon to allow a right of transit to get at an opponent. (The Hebrews made war on Sihon who refused them.)

The Germans' miscalculation of the strength of Belgian nationalism and of the British reaction to the invasion was a major blunder. When the Belgian army resisted and disrupted the schedule to overwhelm France, the Germans reacted furiously. If there were snipers in towns already conquered, the German military took out reprisals upon civilians. Following one of Clausewitz's dictums, the Germans employed terror as a method of conquest. They shot civilians and burned cities - including the university library at Louvain - in their rapid march to France. If Britain had been tempted to stay neutral (as she had done in 1870), German actions over Belgium provided the moral cover for intervention. Britain may have made the decision to intervene based upon her alliances and balance of power considerations, but her public defense was the sacredness of treaties, the rights of small countries, and the "rape of Belgium." England allegedly fought for her ideals; Belgium and France warred for survival. The harshness of German tactics, described by journalists of neutral countries, provided the foundation for later false descriptions of the Germans as Huns prepared to mutilate women and butcher children. German conduct in the initial phases of the war provided a legalistic rationale for France and Britain (and, after April 1917, the United States) to conclude that a Central Powers' victory would undermine the rule of law in world conduct.

After overrunning Belgium, the German armies plunged into France and seemingly had an open road to Paris. The French high command frittered away men and resources in futile attempts to seize Alsace-Lorraine and strike into

Germany, but a weakening of the German right flank (to send troops off to fight the Russians) allowed the French to counterattack in the battle of the Marne and drive the Germans back, although Germany continued to control about one-third of France throughout the war. Then in an effort to over-flank their opponents, both sides extended their lines north and south from the coast to Switzerland.

The overwhelming casualties caused by heavy artillery and enfilading fire from machine guns prompted soldiers to dig trenches. The Allies and the Central Powers for the next four years tried to solve a simple problem: railroads could bring a practically inexhaustible supply of men and ammunition to a destination a few miles short of the front lines. Then artillery made forward movement for motor vehicles too dangerous. So at night, men and horses carried supplies to the front. The front was composed of a series of trenches running in zigzag lines with the no man's land in between (a distance sometimes as short as 300 yards) strung with barbed wire, and mines and pocketed with craters caused by constant shelling. Snipers crawling back and forth in craters in no man's land would shoot anyone who showed himself. Even during times of minor activity, the shelling caused the Allies 8000 casualties per day.

The only way to advance was by frontal attack; surprise was impossible because of the quantities of ammunition and supplies and men needed for a direct assault. For example, at the battle of the Somme, the English fired 1,000,000 rounds of ammunition, most of it during an intensive bombardment of several weeks before the onslaught across the no man's land. Even so, the barbed wire remained intact, and the German machine-gun operators had time to leave their concrete enclosed dugouts after the artillery barrage ceased before the soldiers could leave their trenches and advance. In the first day's attack, 15,000 British were killed; during that one summer's campaign, 145,000 British died with 500,000 wounded, with no gain.[11] When Germans tried to advance, the results

---

[11]Gwyn Dyer, *On War* (1985), 79-82; Paul Fussell, *The Great War And Modern Memory* (1975), 13. The statistics: 110,000 attack the first day; 60,000 killed or wounded; 20,000 dead between

were suicidal. And in this war even defenders suffered heavy casualties. During the battle of Verdun, the French and Germans each experienced about 400,000 casualties.

Normally men at the front had adequate food and medical care (at least on the western front), but life in the trenches was hell. Soldiers lived with northern European weather - occasionally warm, more often rain, cold, snow - in mud. They shared trenches with rats and lice and with a constant smell of excrement or decaying bodies. Their daily ration of whiskey or rum was supposed to overcome the revulsion of almost certain death if an attack was imminent. The constant thunder of artillery (which was loud enough to be heard in England) and the knowledge that death could come at any moment created such stress that shell shock became a common medical condition. In World War I, guns finally caught up with germs, and more men died in battle than from disease.

Soldiers learned to live believing that they would escape the trenches only by death or a serious wound, because they thought the war would go on forever. They did not hate their opponents, who were also having a miserable existence, and did not identify with the noble causes for which the war was allegedly being fought. Their loyalty was to their buddies, whom they did not wish to let down.[12] Those on the front lines gained a profound skepticism about politicians, generals, newspapermen, and preachers, whom they saw as incompetent, ignorant, and foolish.

The people at home remained generally ignorant of what life was like on the front. First, the censors would not have allowed accurate descriptions of trench warfare in the press or in letters home. Then the soldiers who went home on furlough found themselves unable to communicate an adequate sense of existence in the trenches. Literature was still suffused with Victorian

---

the lines. John Keegan, *Face of Battle,* Part II (1976), focuses on the experiences of men fighting on the Somme. Ferguson, 293-295.

[12]Robert Graves, *Goodbye to All That,* though written long after the war and fictionalized in part, contains much valuable information from the soldiers' perspective. Ferguson, chs. 10, 12.

sentimentality and moral uplift.[13] Not until after World War II would the canons of polite discourse dissipate enough to allow a realistic depiction of life at the front.

IV. Justice in the Conduct of War

Just War theory required restraint in the conduct of war. The peace movement and the Hague Conferences had attempted to humanize war by outlawing certain practices, but military advisers normally had sufficient influence to create loopholes. Some of the prohibitions held in spite of the conditions of total war. For example, neither side used dum-dum bullets (the soft encasing of which widened a wound), although both accused the other of violations. Neither side engaged in wanton destruction of civilians. Neutral and small nations at the Hague Conferences had not been able to persuade powerful countries of a generous list of rights of civilians in occupied countries. Military men expected civilians to obey and to make no trouble. There was no right to resist by speech, sabotage, or guerrilla warfare. The Central Powers' early victories meant that substantial numbers of Belgians, French, Russians, and Serbs spent the war under foreign control. Some 60,000 Belgians had to do forced labor in Germany.

Under grounds of "necessity," the belligerents violated many restraints, not all of which had been embodied in treaties. For example, gas warfare had been outlawed, but the Germans introduced it on the western front in 1915, and the Allies responded with their own gas attacks. Soon armies from both sides had gas masks as standard equipment. The first Hague Conference had attempted to outlaw bombs dropped from dirigibles. The second Conference weakened this prohibition, and it had never been extended to airplanes. Still, all the traditional Just War theories forbade the indiscriminate bombing of cities, which were populated by civilians. The Germans inaugurated dropping bombs on Paris and London, though with no significant impact on the war. The Allies, of course, reciprocated, even though President Wilson forbade U.S. bombing of cities.

---

[13]Fussell, 21-28.

The official policies of both sides required medical care for wounded enemies, adequate provisions for prisoners of war, and not targeting hospitals. The occasional shelling of a hospital and the camouflaging of guns under tents with the Red Cross insignia did occur, however. The International Red Cross visited prisoner of war camps. The press accused opponents of killing wounded prisoners of war, and there certainly were instances of atrocities, but men at the front thought there was little moral distinction between how the two sides dealt with prisoners.

After the initial stages of the war with armies on the western front settled into fixed positions, there were relatively few direct civilian casualties considering the immensity of the fighting. At the front, no structure within artillery range survived. As armies advanced and retreated, they destroyed trees, poisoned wells, and spared nothing that might benefit the enemy. The French government moved civilians from the immediate war zone. After the first months of war, the lack of civilian casualties did not come as a result of vigorous restrictions enforced by governments, but because of the confined and static nature of trench warfare. Even after major Allied defeats on the Russian and Italian fronts, armies moved so slowly that civilians could escape the direct war zone.

The genocide of Armenian Christians began shortly after the Ottoman Empire entered the war on the side of the Central Powers. Relations between the Armenians inhabiting central Anatolia and the Turkish authorities had long been strained, even before Sultan Abdulhamid II in the 1890s had allowed up to 200,000 Christians to be killed. Russia had followed similar policies in purging Chechyna of Muslims. Russia and the Ottomans utilized religion as a way of mobilizing their populations and remained suspicious of Muslims and Christians in their respective realms. In 1914 Russia called on the Armenians to revolt and a few did. Though easily put down, the revolt became the pretext for the young Turkish military officers who now controlled the government to begin a purge by forced migration or mass murder. Historians estimate that up to one million Armenians died.

Religion was a factor but not the primary cause of the new Ottoman policy. Previously, the Ottoman Empire. though ruled by Muslims, had been multi-ethnic and religiously pluralistic. Now in an attempt to reinvigorate the Empire, the Young Turks emphasized Turkish nationalism and Islam as unifying factors, and Armenian Christians remained distinct. Still, unlike the Holocaust, the genocide was not racial. Adults would be killed or die from disease or starvation in migration, and men might be used for forced labor and women as concubines. However, children – boys till age 10 and girls until 14 – were often adopted by Muslim families and forced to convert.

In spite of Ottoman attempts to keep the policy secret and official denials, news of the atrocities became public – partially through reports of missionaries and the American ambassador. Religious leaders in America and Germany denounced the mass murders, but the Wilson administration, anxious to preserve neutrality, and the German government, in order not to weaken an ally, did nothing. According to international law, how a government treated a minority was a domestic matter. The British promised trials of the perpetrators, but after the war only two men were tried and convicted.

The possibility of using total war as a cover for extermination of a minority was remembered by Adolph Hitler who said in 1939, "Who today still speaks of the massacre of the Armenians."[14] The Turkish government still has not acknowledged the genocide.

The Allies' blockade of foodstuffs and German submarine warfare occasioned a vigorous public debate over international law, morality, and the conduct of war and placed the Allies and Central Powers on opposite sides as each ignored traditional restraints against weapons that weakened the enemy.

---

[14]Samantha Powers, *"A Problem from Hell": America and the Age of Genocide* (2002). 23; Ronald G. Suny, "Religion, Ethnicity and Nationalism: Armenians, Turks and the End of the Ottoman Empire," and Ara Sarafin, "Absorption of Armenian Women and Children into Muslim Households as a Structure Component of the Armenian Genocide," in *In God's Name: Genocide and Religion in the Twentieth Century*, ed. Omer Bartov and Phyllis Mack (2001), 23-61, 209-221.

Often the moral revulsion against the weapon was clearer than international law. As a follow-up to the Hague Conferences to deal with maritime matters, the London Conference of 1909, under pressure from neutral trading nations, adopted a liberal policy on non-belligerent trade in war and specified that foodstuffs should not be considered contraband. Delegates from Great Britain accepted the Declaration, yet later more cautious policies determined British reaction, and Parliament by 1914 had not ratified the London Declaration. So after war began, the British proclaimed a blockade of Central Powers. Traditionally, a blockade required ships outside each enemy port, but submarines made this stipulation impossible to implement. Britain also forbade all non-belligerent shipping to neutral countries of goods that could be later transported to Central Powers, whether or not the goods were directly related to the war. The Germans protested that stopping food shipments was a violation of permissible practices in warfare because aimed to harm civilians, particularly women and children. The Germans accused England of attempting to starve the Belgians; the British response, at first, was that Germany had invaded Belgium and, thereby, accepted responsibility to feed the population. In time neutral pressure prompted the Allies to allow Americans to send supplies into Belgium, but the total blockade of the Central Powers continued. Germany and Austria by 1917 experienced serious shortages of food and an excess of 800,000 civilian deaths over peacetime rates.[15] The United States made only private complaints against the British food blockade.

The German response to the Allied blockade developed as the war turned into a struggle of attrition. The Germans in early 1915 sought to prevent any ship from going to Britain or France by declaring the seas around them a forbidden zone. Because the English fleet controlled the high seas and the Germans had no plans for their battleships, they remained in port for virtually the entire war. So the Germans also were in violation of the international law requirement for

---

[15]Dyer, 83.

blockade that ships be posted near ports.   Instead, Germany relied upon submarines.

Submarines posed major issues for international law. Traditionally, a navy ship warned a merchant vessel that it was going to be sunk and took the crew and passengers on board. Because submarines had little protective armor and were lightly armed, the British equipped merchant ships with guns that could sink any surfaced submarine. A surfaced submarine was extremely vulnerable (an Allied ship radioing for help to pick up passengers could be overheard by nearby destroyers) and was too small to pick up survivors. So the Germans adopted the policy of sinking ships without warning, including passenger liners. Few disputed Germany's right to sink Allied freighters carrying military goods or food. The issue was passenger ships, whether under British or neutral flags. So the moral dilemma concerned the rights of civilians under conditions of total war. Under pressure from the United States, Germany pledged that it would refrain from sinking neutral passenger ships. When Germany repudiated that pledge in early 1917, the submarine issue became the major cause for the United States' intervention in the war. So America's ostensible reason for entering the war was a defense of neutral rights under international law: in short, justice in the conduct of war.

Just War theories required a declaration of the faults that lead to war and a clear statement of concessions that could lead to the peace. Proportionality required that the harm done would not be greater than the resulting good. Underlying the theories was a presumption that wars should not be fought with a ferocity that undermined compromise. In World War I, the Allies and Central Powers did not accept this limitation. The fighting took place on Russian, French, and later Italian soil, and these countries suffered the most direct damage. For the Allies to make a peace without requiring the so-called aggressor nations to pay damages would be defeat. The French also had to regain Alsace-Lorraine and to restore Serbia and Rumania, overrun by Austria, to independence.

The Germans viewed these minimum Allied conditions for peace as a price of defeat. For they were now in control of much new land, and Pan-Germans claimed more. Germany's initial successes in the western and eastern fronts also allowed an expansion of territorial aims. Since Belgium had resisted and been conquered, Belgium and a buffer area of western France could now be added to the German Empire. After the Bolshevik revolution in Russia in 1917, the Communist government sought peace with Germany. In the treaty of Brest-Litovsk, Germany dictated an extremely harsh treaty and seized the area now known as the Baltic States. The severity of the treaty disillusioned any in the Allied governments who thought that a German victory would lead to equitable arrangements.

Even had the governments been interested in compromise rather than victory, their tactics used at home to mobilize the population for total war made a compromise solution unlikely. Proclaiming themselves as innocent victims of foreign conspiracies, the governments wrapped themselves in nationalist and religious rhetoric as innocent victims. The religious communities echoed the politician's claims.

V. Churches Respond to Total War

Beset with a war that they had neither wanted nor understood, the churches sought some perspective by which to interpret events for themselves and their congregations. Except for pacifist denominations, there was no dissent from government policies. However, differences of emphasis among and even within churches occurred, with those most committed to a universal Church faithful to apostolic traditions being less jingoistic. The papacy was caught in a delicate situation, with the faithful on both sides expecting vindication of their perspective. The Roman Church dealt with moral responsibility in a contradictory way. Within each nation the hierarchy on its own strongly supported the war efforts, yet remained cognizant that the Church's welfare was not the same as any nation's. Pope Benedict XV called the war a "mournful spectacle" creating "sorrow and distress" and pleaded for "other ways and means by which violated rights can be rectified."[16]

The Pope avoided any endorsement of the war or judgment of the different parties and made clear his desire to see peace restored. The strict neutrality of Rome tempered to some degree national Catholic chauvinism. The papacy devoted its efforts to encouraging charity for Belgians and quiet diplomacy. In early 1917 the papacy publicly offered as a concrete basis for the restoration of peace the status quo ante bellum that required German and Austrian evacuation of conquered territories and no reparations. The people and leaders of the Central Powers rejected the papacy's plan and called it pro-Allied. The Allies, including the United States, which had earlier sought a mediated peace, also showed little interest in the papal initiative.

The leaders of the German Evangelical Church, the Church of England, and various dissenting congregations were not constrained by obedience to a trans-national institution, although all professed adherence to the ideal of an invisible Church transcending all borders. The strongest supporters of the pre-war peace movement in England had been clergy of dissenting churches. The dissenters now became some of the most chauvinistic supporters of the war effort. (The Quakers spent the war trying to protect the civil liberties of COs, administering to enemy aliens caught in Britain at the beginning of the war, and planning for a post-war peace.) Those Protestants termed "high church," who were devoted to a catholic unity, and those termed "modernists" or "liberals," previously most active in ecumenical activities, tempered their rhetoric for national causes. Particularly at the beginning of the war, the liberals and high churchmen recognized that the war would not last forever, and eventually contacts would need to be resumed. The check on patriotism could come from an Augustinian view of the sinfulness of all human activities or a Modernist insight stressing the brotherhood of all mankind.

[16]*Papal Encyclicals* (1903-1939), ed., Claudia Ihm (1981), "Ad Beatissimi Apostolorum," 143-144; Robert Graham, *Vatican Diplomacy: A Study of Church and State on the International Plane* (1959), 305-317.

Whichever the perspective, earlier loyalties to ecumenical conferences or to cooperative endeavors on the mission field now took second place to support of the war effort. Even so, some church periodicals ignored moral issues posed by the war, concentrating upon pastoral concerns.[17]

The Protestant clergy on both sides sought, at a minimum, to portray the struggle as a Just War and in some instances a holy war. In general the British and German clergy were not well versed in Just War theory, and their rhetoric makes it difficult to conclude whether they thought the war was a necessary evil or a holy crusade. A few leaders insisted that Christians had an obligation not to hate the enemy. The British might detest what the Germans stood for but should not blame individuals. As the war dragged on, the popular press and influential clergymen lost the balance between hating causes and individuals. The Bishop of London pronounced the cause of the Allies holy and seemed to promise that those who were killed, no matter what their previous conduct, would go to heaven.

English rectors could participate in the vilification of Germany because few knew much about German culture, and they relied on religious leaders, politicians, and journalists who also had no profound knowledge. The British clergy rallied to the defense of innocent and heroic Belgium, forgetting how recently they had condemned King Leopold's conduct in the Belgium Congo. Selectively focusing on German writers who glorified war and the state, British intellectuals portrayed Germany as a country in which worship of the military had run amuck. From Luther to Frederick the Great to Clausewitz and the recent military theorist General von Berhardi, the Germans had allegedly separated morality from war. The result was a realm in which *realpolitik* or *machtpolitik* dominated foreign policy. The amorality interpretation was joined to a conspiracy thesis. Germany's early successes came because she had secretly planned and then begun the war.[18]

---

[17]Charles Bailey, "British Protestant Theologians in the First World War: Germanophobia Unleashed," *Harvard Theological Review,* 77 (1984), 195-221. Marrin, 75, 83-85.

[18] Marrin, 90-109; Hoover, 36-37.

In early 1915 Germany in an offensive employed gas for the first time, sank the British passenger ship Lusitania (that also secretly carried munitions), and bombed London from zeppelin dirigibles. Each of these the British presented as an atrocity. Shortly thereafter a commission, chaired by a distinguished British intellectual, Lord James Bryce, documented a series of German atrocities. The report presented persuasive evidence of widespread German abuses and had an enormous influence in Britain and America. (Not until after the war was the Bryce report discredited, its accuracy so flawed that historians have labeled it one of the war's atrocities.) Germany's firing the first shot, invading Belgium, killing civilians, using submarines, bombing from airships, and firing gas canisters, executing a nurse who had helped downed British flyers escape - all these contributed to an image of barbaric Huns who had repudiated the best in Western civilization. So a mere territorial compensation should not end the war. Instead, the military cancer and absolutism at the heart of German life must be ended. Love of family, ethics, and God were at stake.

Because censorship restrictions meant the people on each side could read only their nation's account of events and there was still trust in the honesty of governments and bishops, the peoples' outrage at the supposed behavior of the enemy is understandable. After 1915 the British bishops, journalists, and politicians preached hate.

German theologians accused the English of perfidy. They asked how the British, who had built an empire by stamping on the rights of small countries, could now be so hypocritical on Belgium? They claimed that the laws of war allowed extraordinary acts in time of necessity, including a right of transit and preemptive strikes against a nation preparing to attack. The unnatural alliance between autocratic Russia and republican France and their combining against Germany was an international conspiracy. The Germans ignored the inconvenient fact that "necessity" here allowed their invasion of three countries. No German theologian criticized his own country's actions, although a few did blame the general international situation and the arms races as causes of the war. Ninety-three prominent German ministers signed a report publicizing Allied atrocities on the battlefield and off, a report that served to alienate English religious leaders who had evidence that some of the claims were inaccurate. The German churches were particularly indignant at the alleged mistreatment of their missionaries in Africa.[19]

The main German ire focused on Great Britain. The dynasties and peoples of the two countries were linked. Both nations were Protestant and industrial powers with governments far more alike than either was to autocratic Russia or democratic France. The Germans saw the British as betraying ties of kin and culture. They should be standing together against the irreligion and irresponsible individualism typified by the French and the Slavic tyranny and barbarism of Russia. The French desire for revenge was understandable, but not the British actions. After the Allies used non-white members of their empires in their armies, the Germans accused the Allies of undermining racial purity. The Germans portrayed the English as greedy merchants, jealous of German prosperity and determined to dominate the world at all costs.

The Germans proclaimed that culture was at stake. French liberty was libertinism; Russia, with neither liberty nor true culture, and its hordes, was a Mongol state attempting to subvert western European civilization. English liberty was petty bourgeoisie. Only German liberty was Christian because it was a disciplined ordered existence that accepted neither tyranny nor anarchy. The Germans saw themselves as a unique *Volk* whose cultural attainments excelled those of all other nations. They saw the German Reich as the culmination of history, a state destined to dominate central Europe.

Germany and Britain saw themselves as Protestant nations with Catholic minorities. Protestants traditionally distinguished themselves from Catholics by downplaying church customs and exalting the authority of the *Bible* in all issues of faith and morals. The New Testament's commandments to love enemies and forget grievances and become peacemakers were too important to be ignored.

---

[19]Bailey. "Got mit uns," 55-56; A. J. Hoover, *God, Germany, and Great Britain* (1989), 53-59, 203.

How then did the churches justify supporting the war? The conservative theologians who disliked Modernist scholarship's placing the scriptures in historical context could rely upon a tradition of biblical exegesis justifying war going back to Augustine. Like Augustine, they cited as precedents the Hebrew wars, and insisted that Jesus had accepted the legitimacy of the soldier's occupation, and quoted Paul on obedience to the state. War proved no more of a problem for the German and British Protestants pioneering literary and historical exegesis who insisted that the scriptures be interpreted as a product of a specific time and place. These theologians claimed that Jesus had given no political advice. His teaching was oriented towards an eschatological vision, and the Sermon on the Mount provided an interim ethic for his followers in the church. There was no incompatibility between loving one's enemy and seeking to reform his evil through war. Both theological liberals and conservatives insisted that the New Testament assumed the inevitability of war in this imperfect world. Not until the millennium dawned would mankind be free of the scourge of war. In the meantime the New Testament required obedience to the governing authorities, and they now required support of the war.

Religious liberals had stressed the immanence of God in creation, identifying the highest human values and accomplishments with the will of God. For example, a father's love was analogous to the love of God. The great beauty in a Michelangelo painting or Bach chorale pointed the way to the creator. So did the ordered liberty of existence within a state. The values of western civilization - freedom, morality, and harmony - showed the presence of God in culture. Under the pressure of war, the God of Western culture stopped being a fatherly bourgeois and became a harsh warrior. So German, British, and American Protestant nationalists all insisted that their culture was worth fighting and dying for because it reflected the values of God.

As the casualties mounted, making sense of the carnage was more difficult. Superficial explanations linking the lack of victory to not going to church on Sunday or to the materialism of the people back home lost credibility. The only public languages for interpreting war and pain were chivalry, Victorian sentimentality, the *Bible,* and liturgies like the *Book of Common Prayer.* Picturing the dying soldier calling for his mother or stressing his heroic exploits as a modern day Achilles or Sir Galahad caricatured the impersonality, even irrelevance, of the carnage to ending the war. The clergy linked the sacrifice of Jesus on the cross to the sufferings of the soldiers and the mourning of their families. The English used flowers, red roses or the red poppies of Flanders, to illustrate the fragility and loveliness of youth. Red was a poignant reminder of the blood shed for the nation, and also a memorial to the blood of Jesus shed for sin.[20]

The language church leaders used to interpret the war was not precise. A few leaders insisted that Christians had an obligation not to hate the enemy. The British might detest and fight against what the Germans stood for, but should not blame individuals. The popular press and influential clergymen often lost the balance between hating causes and hating individuals. They went beyond insisting that the war was "just" according to the traditional categories of self-defense against aggression and called it "holy." The excesses of the clergy in identifying God's church with the aims of the war would contribute to the discrediting of organized religion in the post-war period. For if organized religion could not provide a detached Christian perspective on contemporary events, would not preach love and forgiveness, then the church was part of the wretched system that caused the war.

Initially, churchmen viewed that war as having a positive impact, with class-consciousness and political disputes disappearing in a wave of patriotism. Those who had worried about the pervasiveness of materialism and frivolity in the youth felt encouraged by the new spirit of national dedication. The churches, worried about their loss of influence among socialists and workers, hoped that the war would bring a revival of religion. To the disappointment of the clergy of all nations, there was no religious revival among the soldiers. Soldiers who would

---

[20]Paul Fussell, *Great War And Modern Memory,* 243-53.

partake of the sacraments before major battles would visit brothels on leave. Some saw the providence of God in the occasional preservation of crosses and altars in ruined churches and took confidence in a widely circulated but false story of a visitation of the angel of Mons.[21] Front-line troops accepted any belief system that might bring security. So soldiers might pray, carry a rabbit's foot, and insist that an impersonal luck or fate would preserve them. There was too much randomness to survival, and the best preservative was to be behind the lines or, at least, in the trenches rather than going over the top into no man's land. Infantrymen had no illusions that goodness and God were on their side and would carry them to victory and keep them safe. As the war dragged on, those at the front lines assumed that their only escape would be a disabling wound or death. And while the soldiers read and composed sentimental poems about beautiful ennobling deaths, they saw buddies maimed or killed, heard the wounded scream for help in no man's land while they were dying in agony, and witnessed too many nameless corpses and decomposing bodies to affirm that "God's in his heaven, all's right with the world."

Protestant churches saw their responsibility as providing moral perspective or standards for judging contemporary society. After Germany's initial success, a Pan-German movement sought to greatly enlarge her borders. Several prominent German theologians argued that expansionism would change the war from a defensive struggle to an aggressive one. They cautioned that a war for territorial aggrandizement was not a Christian Just War. When irrefutable evidence came that the Turks were carrying out massacres on Armenian Christians, German theologians denounced these actions by their allies. In Britain, after Germany engaged in bombing raids, there was a cry for reprisals. Leaders of the Church of England denounced any use of reprisals. A few theologians in Germany and England who had established close professional and personal links before the war attempted to continue a correspondence, though there could be no

---

[21]Ibid., 115-16.

discussion of issues growing out of the war. The Bishop of Upsalla, Sweden, a neutral country, tried to keep contacts with both sides in the efforts to preserve the ecumenical movement.

The churches saw their main task, the same in war and peace, as ministering to the people. Chaplains held services at the front and gave the sacrament before major battles. Priests buried the dead and comforted the bereaved, insisting that the sacrifices of lives in a Just War were acceptable to the God of battles. In the meantime the church began considering how to prevent another war from occurring. For committed Christians, whether pacifists or holy warriors, an essential activity was planning for the peace in order to prevent another Great War.

VI. The United States

The outbreak, extent and duration of war surprised the people of the United States. President Woodrow Wilson advised Americans to preserve "neutrality in thought and action." Many Americans thought Europeans had gone mad in the summer of 1914 and approved of the traditional foreign policy of non-involvement in European affairs. Initially, stories of suffering Belgians and of German atrocities brought sympathy for the Allies. The traditional empathy of Eastern upper classes for England balanced Irish-American and German-American hostility to the British Empire. In 1916 the Americans denounced Britain for harshly suppressing the Easter Rebellion in Ireland and attempting to blacklist American firms trading with the Central Powers.

Although the Wilson administration wished to preserve freedom to trade and travel, it acquiesced in the Allies' embargo of trade, even of foodstuffs, with neutral European states. Because of the Allied blockade, trade with the Central Powers declined while that with the Allies increased dramatically and eventually the U.S. approved bankers' making major loans to the Allies. Britain handled American concerns about neutral rights with some adroitness and, within the Wilson administration, high officials supported Allied war objectives. The administration's most consistent neutralist, Secretary of State William Jennings

Bryan, an evangelical and pacifist committed to arbitration, resigned in 1915 over what he saw as too strong a statement of Americans' right to travel on British passenger ships in the German-proclaimed war zone.

The issue that eventually led America into the war was submarine warfare against neutral shipping and passenger boats, whether British or American. The Germans originally claimed the right to strike at any ship approaching the war zone. The Wilson administration demanded the right to trade and sought to exempt all passenger ships from being sunk. In 1915 after the sinking of the Lusitania, the Germans acquiesced and, henceforth, did not sink passenger ships, even when flying the British flag. In early 1917, believing that a total embargo of shipping to the British coupled with a major offensive would bring victory, the Germans announced unrestricted submarine warfare. The German general staff prepared to risk American intervention in the war in a gamble for quick victory.

The evolution of American thinking about the war can be shown in the public utterances of Wilson. Wilson, a devout Presbyterian who had a Ph.D. in political science, had long favored strengthening international law and supported the aims of the peace movement. Originally interested in mediation, Wilson in 1914 and 1915 established contacts with both sides. In early 1916 he outlined a possible settlement with Germany giving up Alsace-Lorraine and restoring Belgium and Serbia and gaining compensation in colonial areas and trade. Although neither side showed much interest in Wilson's peace, they sought to portray their opponent as the obstacle. In late 1916 in response to an earlier German request that he undertake mediation, Wilson proposed that each side state its war aims as a preliminary to a peace conference. The Germans now refused and the Allies' conditions contained no grounds for negotiation. The response from both belligerents showed that each believed a military victory was still possible. Wilson in January 1917 called for the post-war creation of an international body with the responsibility for preserving the peace and asked for "a peace without victory."[22]

Private American citizens, the most prominent of whom was Henry Ford, sought to create the conditions for peace by sending a peace ship to Europe. Jane Addams and other prominent women, including some citizens from the belligerent powers, attempted to meet with government officials in Europe to suggest ways for peace. Wilson and the private citizens hoped that a neutral party could facilitate negotiations; they did not attempt to use pressure and did not threaten American intervention.

Unlike the European peace movement in 1914, the American peace advocates had ample warning that Wilson's policies might lead to war. They protested the British embargo on food to Europe, suggested that Americans should stay off the passenger ships of belligerent nations, and opposed loans to the Allies. When Wilson said the U.S. was "too proud to fight," they approved, but lobbied vigorously against his plans to expand the navy and to arm merchant ships. Supported by midwestern Progressives who favored domestic reform and isolationism, the peace movement had considerable Congressional clout. In 1916 Wilson won a close re-election bid emphasizing neutrality and preparedness by utilizing the slogan "he kept us out of war."

As 1917 began, the peace movement weakened after the defection of many conservative businessmen who had earlier favored international law and mediation and now supported a stronger navy and larger army in case America entered the war. The impact of economic factors and particularly the influence of bankers and big business on American policies is still debated, but clearly an Allied defeat would jeopardize American loans and trade. Even Wilson worried that basing a right for American trade with a belligerent on international law allowed Germany to determine if peace with the U.S. would continue. Important members of

---

[22]Arthur Link, *Wilson the Diplomatist: A Look at his Major Foreign Policies* (1957); the historiographical controversies are discussed in Jerald Combs, *American Diplomatic History: Two Centuries of Interpretations* (1983), Part 4.

Wilson's administration favored U.S. intervention on strategic grounds: a German victory might threaten America. As relations between America and Germany deteriorated, the peace movement publicized concrete steps to keep America out of the war and proposed them to Wilson. They included an embargo on trade and travel to warring nations, but there was little public response. Although there had been a strong religious component to the American peace movement before 1918, America's churches, whether evangelical or liberal, showed more interest in the domestic reforms associated with Progressivism than in foreign policy.

In February 1917, Germany resumed unrestricted submarine warfare. When in April 1917 the U.S. declared war, Wilson denounced German submarine attacks as "warfare against mankind" and declared that an Allied victory would "make the world safe for democracy." Unlike Italy, America was not bribed by secret treaty to enter the war. Nor did Wilson use the power of America to force the Allies to repudiate their secret treaties. The U.S. did not claim to have entered the war to preserve the balance of power, strategic necessity, or for economic or territorial advantage, but to create a lasting peace. America fought to end war, to make the world safe for democracy, and refused compromise with an evil regime. When in early 1918 the Pope called for a peace on the basis of the status quo ante bellum, Wilson was not interested, for he had come to believe that German militarism and autocracy needed obliteration. Peace now required victory.

American Churches in the Great War

Due to the separation of church and state, American churches had traditionally been able to offer a moral critique of U.S. norms. In World War I the clergy chose not to exercise that freedom. Virtually all clergymen insisted that America's participation was justified. At its onset, the Federal Council of Churches rejected the notion of a crusade, affirmed ties to Christians in all lands, even with "those from whom for the time we are estranged," demanded that America live up to its high ideals, and pledged to serve the soldiers and society.[23]

---

[23]John F. Piper, Jr. *The American Churches in World War I* (1985), 16.

The official tone of moderate support remained the predominant tone of some denominations and some prominent advocates of the Social Gospel, like Walter Rauschenbusch. Professor Melvin Endy has questioned the conventional stereotype of a unified Protestant response of patriotic chauvinism in support of war.[24] Instead, he argues, churches' responses corresponded to their earlier theological stances on the relation of Christianity to culture; Quakers and Mennonites, for example, continued pacifism. By contrast, Roman Catholics, relying upon Just War theories, saw the struggle as a defense of family and society. Lutherans, many of whom had relatives in Germany, supported the war but remained skeptical of the war or any other human means of transforming society. The southern fundamentalists who looked forward to the imminent return of Christ did not see a corrupt America as creating a brave new world. Those most susceptible to Wilsonian rhetoric were the churches in the Federal Council of Churches - Methodists, Presbyterians, Episcopalians, and Northern Baptists - who as supporters of the Social Gospel already approved of President Wilson's emphasis upon international law and restraint in war. They saw altruistic America's democracy as the best form of government.

During the war, the predominant message from clergy became that the conflict was a kind of holy war. Liberal, evangelical, and fundamentalists vied in jingoism, and the government-sponsored Committee on Public Information took the lead in denouncing German society and culture. Newspapers vilified pacifist Jane Addams, the government jailed the socialist Eugene Debs, and business and government together destroyed the leftist union Industrial Workers of the World. The only public clerical debate was whether the war was a justified war, a necessary evil, or a holy struggle ordained by God. Could a Christian legitimately hate the Germans; would Jesus, as a Yale Divinity School teacher claimed, tell a soldier to bayonet or shoot a German who stuck his head above the trench? Government censorship laws and the militant patriotism of newspapers and

---

[24]William Hutchinson, *The Modernist Impulse in American Protestantism* (1986), ch.7. Melvin Endy, lecture delivered at Swarthmore College, ca. 1994.

publishers stopped those clergymen who opposed the hate literature from disseminating their views.[25]

Ecumenical agencies, like the YMCA, broke ties with Germany and sought to administer to the needs of soldiers. Protestants in the Federal Council of Churches formed a war agency to coordinate church ministry in military bases and overseas. America's Roman Catholic bishops created a commission to coordinate their war work at home and abroad. Wilson militarized the American Red Cross and entrusted it with responsibility for a large variety of relief activities for soldiers and civilians in France.

In America, as in Europe, hatred for the Germans was more extreme at home than at the front. Opponents of the war - whether socialists, religious pacifists, or isolationists - were labeled as subversive. German-Americans had to act circumspectly. Anything that reminded people of Germany had to be avoided -- Beethoven, German language, historical criticism of the *Bible*; even sauerkraut was renamed "victory cabbage." Beer, a traditional German drink, fell into disfavor because the grain used could be better sent overseas to feed the Allies. Prohibition, supported earlier as a movement to Christianize American society, now became a way to force conformity to American ideals. Whether liberal or evangelical, Protestant or Roman Catholic, the American churches spoke with one voice in favor of the war and against Germany.

The Americans had little patience with dissenters because her young men fought for high ideals: international law, the rights of small nations, democracy, and free trade. After the Bolshevik revolution in Russia, the communist government published the text of secret treaties in which the Allied nations promised each other extensive territorial gains. In response, Wilson's Fourteen Points speech outlined the U.S. version of a just peace. It would restore Belgium, Poland, and Alsace-Lorraine, allow self-determination to the ethnic minorities in the Austro-Hungarian empire, give colonies some role in determining their status,

---

[25]Ray H. Abrams, *Preachers Present Arms* (1933), 51, 54, 67-70.

reduce trade barriers, allow disarmament, and create a league of nations. Wilson's international vision merged American republican values with goals of the peace movement and Christian Just War theory. Eighteen months after America entered the war, Germany asked for an armistice on the basis of Wilson's Fourteen Points. At the peace conference at Versailles, Wilsonian internationalism would confront the other Allied nations who after four years of struggle wanted the spoils of winning a "just" war.

VII. Creating a Peace

The victorious Allied nations wanted the fruits of victory and to avoid another war. Humanitarians were outraged that, after the armistice, when the Central Powers were prostrate and their populations severely malnourished, the Allies continued the embargo on food. Those Americans active in the pre-war peace movement began planning for the post-war world in 1917. Their hopes for a generous peace rested on Wilson, who was not interested in vengeance. The U.S.' direct war fatalities amounted to fewer than 50,000 and she emerged from the war a major world power to which the Allies were deeply in debt. By contrast, Great Britain and France had casualties numbering in the millions, enormous debts, and a substantial chunk of France lay devastated. France, Italy, and Britain wanted Germany punished with a severe treaty such as Germany had imposed on France in 1870. They also wanted a weakened Germany that would not threaten them and a U.S. commitment to collective security. Pope Benedict's plea for charity, the burying of animosities, and forgiveness encountered politicians and people who wanted compensation for their sacrifices.[26]

At the end of the war, as in the beginning, religious leaders had little influence. At the Versailles negotiations, the political leaders ignored the suggestions of the peace advocates. The treaty was punitive: Germany had to accept sole responsibility for starting the war. She lost colonies overseas, and, in addition to Alsace-Lorraine, lands on her eastern and western borders. Her army

---

[26]*Papal Encyclicals* (1903-1939), "Quod Iam Div," December 1, 1918; "Paterno Div," November 24, 1919; "Pacem Dei Manus Pulcherrimum," May 23, 1920, 169-175.

and navy were dismantled and she was forced to pay reparations. She was not admitted to the League of Nations. Austria-Hungary had disintegrated at the end of the war and was now replaced by the small independent nations of Austria and Hungary, a re-creation of Poland, and the new nations of Czechoslovakia and Yugoslavia. The League of Nations combined elements of a world organization for the settlement of disputes and prevention of war with a collective security agreement of the Allies to keep Germany subjugated.

The end of the war and the Versailles Treaty brought no peace. The battles between communists and their opponents in the USSR cost more lives than Russia lost in the war. The new Union of Soviet Socialist Republics was more unpredictable and dangerous to liberal democracies than the Tsar. The German Empire was now the weak Weimar Republic, but the Germans regarded the treaty as harsh and unfair. Ethnic conflict divided the new states in the Balkans, and Poland and Russia fought a war over the location of the eastern boundary. France remained terrified of Germany and ready to occupy territory if provisions of the treaty remained unmet.

The churches had not gained by the war. They were blamed for preaching hate, exaggerating atrocities, and raising false expectations. In Britain, the Bishop of London apologized for his rhetoric. In America the Fundamentalist/Modernist and Catholic/Protestant animosities eroded the churches' moral authority and ability to shape society. In Germany the Evangelical Churches disliked the Weimar Republic and longed for the restoration of imperial authority, which had guaranteed their privileged position in society. In France, Britain, Austria, Germany, and even the United States citizens looked at the world of the 1920s and concluded that they preferred the order, stability, and civilization of the pre-war world. The U.S. would wage no more crusades to make the world safe for democracy.

Leaders and people agreed that there should be no more war. Unfortunately, they were not sure how to ensure this. Was the best policy a collective security arrangement by the victorious allies? How important was the new League of Nations, particularly without American participation? Should efforts be made to conciliate the two pariah states, Germany and the Soviet Union, and then bring them into the family of nations? Had arbitration and international law failed or had they not really been tried? Or was the best way to peace to follow Tolstoy's advice by ignoring governments altogether and creating a people who would never fight?

The myth grew that following the end of fighting came an immediate reaction against the war. In actuality, American soldiers came home exhilarated by victory and having seen Europe. The British soldiers also felt vindicated by victory. About ten years later in the late 1920s soldiers writing about their experiences spread cynicism about the war. By then it was apparent that the "war to end wars" resulted in bitter fruit. Now many in the United States and Europe gave up trying to build peace, disillusioned with everything except personal gratification. They are now known as the "lost generation."

XV.

Searching for Peace, Finding War
1920-39

The prominent French novelist and pacifist Roman Rolland reacted scathingly to news of the contents of the Treaty of Versailles: "Sad peace! Ridiculous intermission between two massacres of people. But who thinks of tomorrow."[1] Rolland was right in his prognostication of a new war growing out of unsolved issues from the last war, but wrong to see Versailles as written by those who ignored the future. Everybody in 1919 wanted no more war and feared that there might be a second Great War, but diplomats in Paris had no more certainty than their critics about how to prevent it. This first section will examine the various methods advocated during the 1920s to keep the peace, most of which grew out of diagnoses of what had gone wrong before 1914, and compare the peace movements' and the churches' attitudes to international affairs in America, Britain, France, and Germany.

The effects of the Depression, Japan's invasion of Manchuria in 1929, and Hitler's ascension to power in 1933, which brought major challenges to those working for peace, will be the themes in the second section. The pessimism of the 1930s replaced the optimism of the 1920s as churches encountered totalitarian states hostile to Christianity and willing to glorify war even while professing a desire for peace. Situated in the middle of a fascist state, the papacy sought to protect the Church's autonomy by negotiating a modus vivendi with Germany and Italy and then dealing with the Spanish Civil War. In Japan, a new religion, termed State Shinto, rationalized a quest for empire and promoted war with China.

---

[1]Quoted in "Interwar Pacifism and the Problem of Peace" in *Peace Movements and Political Cultures,* ed. Charles Chatfield and Peter Van den Dungen (1998), 46.

For those interested in peace, the only encouraging events seemed to come from India, where Gandhi's campaign of nonviolence seemed to show an alternative to war. After 1938, internationalists, Just War advocates, and pacifists had to decide whether to emphasize keeping their countries at peace or risking war in pursuit of freedom, issues emphasized in the debate in America between pacifists and Reinhold Niebuhr's Christian realism.

During the 1920s Christians who approached peace issues from religious perspectives worked, often in tandem, with academics practicing the new discipline of international relations, and against politicians who vacillated between disarmament and arms build-up as methods of preserving the balance of power. There were often no clear distinctions between religious and political solutions for what atheist and theist saw as the moral issues posed by the carnage of war. Socialists saw peace coming from a new equitable and, therefore, more moral economic system. Christians agreed that there was a relationship between wealth and war, but divided between progressives, who wanted to humanize capitalism with welfare legislation, and conservatives, who saw peace as a by-product of trade and opposed state intervention on economic matters. In France and Germany, ongoing tensions among Catholics, Protestants, and Socialists on religious and economic issues made achieving unified actions for peace difficult to achieve.

In Great Britain and America, liberal Protestants affirmed that there could be no ultimate divergence between the conclusions of the natural and social sciences and the teachings of Jesus Christ. Jesus was the supreme peacemaker, the example for all, but he left the tools of how to achieve peace in the hands of reasonable women and men. Because humans were basically good, a polity based upon Christian love would foster peace.

Whether Christian, Socialist, utilitarian, or humanitarian, peace advocates arrived at the same conclusion: war was qualitatively and quantitatively the worst form of violence and could never be the best option.[2] Even the majority of the population among the Allies who wrapped themselves in patriotism and justified the Great War as morally necessary disliked the tawdriness of the results and strove to avoid a repeat performance. Even so, with only a twenty-year break between wars, to observers then and now, seemingly incoherent events rushed toward inexorable tragedy.

Part I. Peacemaking and the Quest for Security

I. The Versailles Settlement

The new international order set up at Versailles left out two temporarily weakened but potentially strongest continental European states: Germany and the Soviet Union. They were not invited to join the League of Nations, though both later became members, and the Allies invaded Russia in what proved to be a futile effort to replace the communist regime. The Allies proved they did not believe reconciliation to be the way to peace by placing sole war guilt on the Central Powers, levying stiff reparations, transferring German colonies to the victors, enforcing disarmament and demilitarization of the Rhineland, and continuing the trade embargo, even on food, for months after the armistice until the German parliament ratified the Versailles Treaty.[3] Churches in the Allied countries agreed with politicians that Germany should be punished by admitting guilt and paying the total cost of war.

The French who had been invaded twice by Germany since 1870 wanted a drastically weakened opponent and a strong alliance with Britain and America, but obtained neither. For the French, multilateral guarantees through the League were no substitute for military power, and they spent the next years first being tough on Germany, then seeking reconciliation, and finally building their military, trying to strengthen the League, and seeking alliances to contain Hitler. Italy received

---

[2]Martin Ceadel, *Pacifism in Britain 1914-1945* (1980), 11-16, 49-51, 62, 69.
[3]Henry Kissinger, *Diplomacy* (1994), ch. 9, stresses that Versailles was neither tough enough to permanently weaken Germany nor containing sufficient conciliatory features to re-establish a concert of powers. *Diplomacy* is an excellent introduction from a "realist" perspective to the security dilemmas facing Europe.

fewer spoils of war than promised, and its unhappiness and economic problems allowed the Fascists and Mussolini to come to power in 1922. Britain wished to preserve its traditional freedom of action in Europe, not to be closely tied to any European nation, including France, whose alleged ambitions it distrusted.

Newly republican Weimar Germany, not invaded but economically devastated and labeled an outlaw state, could be expected to try to redress what its people and many intellectuals in the Allied nations viewed as the unfairness of the Versailles system. German nationalists diverted attention from their provocative actions in the summer of 1914 and later poor strategy in the war while they blamed defeat upon allegedly disloyal peoples, chiefly Socialists and Jews, and current troubles on the Versailles Treaty. Still, under the Socialists, liberal democrats, and Catholic center parties in France and Weimar, there was a healthy ferment of ideas, widespread war weariness, and a willingness in 1925 to sign the multilateral non-aggression Locarno Pact guaranteeing the boundaries of Europe.

Russia had also been left out of the Versailles settlement and forced to recognize the independence of the Baltic republics, Finland, and Poland. Unlike most socialists who had endorsed their countries' war efforts, Lenin consistently had opposed communist participation. The new Soviet Union labeled the war a product of the imperialist capitalist system and saw a violent struggle and conquest by the proletariat as necessary to bring true peace. Having been beaten by Germany, forced to sign a harsh treaty giving up one-third of its territory, enduring a bloody civil struggle, and finally another defeat in which it was forced to surrender land in the Ukraine to the new Polish state, a very weak Russia wanted war with no nation. International communism, now committed to the survival of the Soviet Union and following its dictates on foreign policy, proclaimed the necessity of peace. Still, Lenin and his successor Stalin proclaimed world revolution as the goal, not cooperation with capitalist colonist powers who created the League.

The Allies sought to reshape central Europe into states based upon peoples' self-determination, a task made possible because the Austro-Hungarian Empire had disintegrated by 1919. But because ethnic divisions overlapped, virtually all the new, weak states had ethnic minorities. Czechoslovakia, for example, contained Czechs and Slovaks, but also a German minority. Yugoslavia had Slovenes, Croats, Serbs, Hungarians, and Bosnian Muslims. Poland now included the former German province of Silesia and surrounded the Danzig free city of Germans. Poland ended with two powerful dissatisfied states on its eastern and western borders. Virtually all these new states as well as Austria and Hungary succumbed to authoritarian regimes and experienced severe economic difficulties even before the Great Depression.

The Versailles Treaty, by legitimating ethnicity as a basis for statehood, contributed to instability in Europe and inadvertently fostered anti-imperial sentiment in colonies. For many minority and subject peoples, ethnic self-determination had now received international justification as a permissible cause for war. If, as many believed, imperial rivalries and ethnic hatred in the Balkans had caused the last war, the Versailles solution would not bring stability or peace.

America did not trust the imperial aims and secret treaties of its European allies and, as enunciated by Wilson, sought to transform relations among states by open diplomacy, freedom of the seas, and free trade. Wilson proclaimed that cooperation of the great powers in the new League of Nations and the force of public opinion against war would keep the peace. He reasoned that the Versailles Treaty, though imperfect, was the best that could be obtained and would have been harsher except for his efforts.

Peace organizations emerged as harsh critics of the Versailles Treaty. The newly formed Women's International League for Peace and Freedom (WILPF) was one of many organizations that during the war began planning for the peace. WILPF members denounced the treaty as violating "the principles upon which a just and lasting peace can be secured."[4] French socialists concurred in this negative evaluation of the treaty. The economist John Maynard Keynes saw the consequences of reparations and break-up of the Austro-Hungarian Empire as leading to economic disasters. Western European intellectuals realized the war had unleashed abiding hatreds rather than inaugurating a new world of democracy.

The British and American Friends Service Committees, as they administered relief in France, Germany, Poland, Austria, and Russia, witnessed the peoples' views of their former enemies and discovered that the war had made peacemaking more difficult. Relief workers hoped that feeding the hungry and helping reconstruction of ruined villages would ease the tensions, but had no illusions about the depth of animosities. For religious and secular groups in England and America, service to war victims became a way of building peace. In order to feed the children of central Europe, the American Relief Administration, a semi-official agency, raised millions to transport the surplus food grown by American farmers. The leaders of British and American peace organizations were not veterans disillusioned with their experience of fighting, but men and women who had opposed the war and had refused to fight.[5] Peacemakers relied on a widespread revulsion against war and prognostications that the next one would be worse because airplanes would carry the battle to cities. Newly formed multinational peace organizations like the feminist WILPF and the Fellowship of Reconciliation did not initially rally to support the League of Nations because they feared its ability to wage collective war and saw it as a victor's club.

For those seeking to prevent a future war, a first requisite was understanding what had caused the Great War. Just War theory and propaganda during the war blamed individuals (the Kaisar or Tsar) or entire peoples (the Huns, perfidious Albian). In hindsight and with vision unclouded by wartime

---

[4]Jo Vellacott, "Transnationalism in the Early Women's International League of Peace and Freedom," in *Pacifist Impulse in Historical Perspective* (1996); John Maynard Keynes, *Economic Consequences of the Peace* (1920).
[5]J. W. Frost, "'Our Deeds Carry Our Message,' The Early History of the American Friends Service Committee," *Quaker History* (1992), 27-39.

hysteria, diplomats and politicians realized that the war could not be blamed on the moral failures of an individual or nation rather than systemic flaws, but it was discouraging even to list potential culprits: autocracy, capitalism, colonialism, racism, false propaganda, the arms race, economic inequality, and rigid alliance systems.

Peacemakers claimed that the war proved that an exorbitant nationalism was an enormously destructive force, but there was a fine line between legitimate patriotism and chauvinism. Somehow a means of education had to be found to instill a chastened nationalism providing a populace with a sense of belonging and security without instilling the unquestioned obedience that allowed rulers to raise the mass armies that brought death to millions. Still, optimists saw promise because democracies triumphed in the war and destroyed three autocracies, replacing two of them with parliamentary republics, while the third was an experiment to build an egalitarian non-capitalist society.

II. Reforming the International System: The League of Nations,

The World Court, Disarmament

President Wilson's solution to keeping the peace was the League of Nations and collective security. Even those who thought the League flawed hoped it could be reformed. The French government was skeptical of the League's utility, but the socialist opposition strongly supported it. Elsewhere support for the League became a way of showing that the moral purposes of the war had been fulfilled, and Wilson was compared to Moses bringing new commandments to international politics. The Church of England and dissenting churches in Great Britain strongly endorsed and continued to support the League as a Christian reform of international relations.

In America, where debate on isolationism was most intense, the Federal Council of Churches and major Northern and Southern Protestant denominations including the Methodists, Baptists, and Presbyterians, announced public support for the League. Those who had been most active in the pre-war Social Gospel continued to advocate American participation in the international system and remained constant supporters of the League until the mid-30s. They saw in the League not just a concert of powers of the Allies prepared to use military force, but an agency for international cooperation capable of using economic sanctions and other forms of nonviolent pressure to restrain an aggressor state. Few proponents of the League reasoned that America's role in the League might require military action.

Self-proclaimed pacifists dominated the Federal Council of Churches, perhaps a majority of the clergy of the Methodists (the largest Protestant denomination), the faculties of major seminaries, and leading interdenominational periodicals like the *Christian Century*, though just what pacifism meant in addition to opposition to war was not spelled out clearly. Polls taken by religious publications showed pervasive clerical support for pacifism, but it is unclear to what extent the laity agreed.[6]

Protestant Fundamentalists, concentrated before 1940 in the South, disapproved of what they saw as secular political wisdom about war and peace, being more concerned with discerning the signs of the dawning apocalyptic war between the forces of Christ and anti-Christ. Yet the Southern Baptists, the largest Fundamentalist denomination, endorsed American participation in the League and the World Court. Before the war, leading evangelicals espoused temperance, pacifism, and women's rights. However, during the 1920s the strong identification of leading Modernist seminaries and ministers with pacifism made evangelicals suspicious of all religiously inspired social reform, although both groups continued to cooperate on prohibition. Protestants continued to speak out on moral-political issues, but the Modernist versus Fundamentalist controversy, which took place within and among denominations, consumed their energies and weakened their authority to influence national legislation.

Roman Catholics, the largest American denomination, had actively supported America's participation in the war, but remained wary of political

---

[6]Robert Miller, *American Protestantism and Social Issues 1919-1939* (1958).

controversy. Catholic bishops, worried about the resurgence of nativism exemplified by the Ku Klux Klan, concentrated upon defending the Church's predominantly immigrant population and demonstrating its commitment to American values by opposing socialism and communism. The bishops took no public positions on the League and issued no public pronouncements on the debate over America's role in world affairs between 1924 and 1936.[7] Major Catholic periodicals read by priests concentrated upon spirituality and individual morality and devoted little attention to issues of war and peace. As early as 1870, a pope had wondered about the applicability of Just War theories to modern warfare, but officially the Church's opposition to pacifism remained unchanged. Dorothy Day's small pacifist and radical Catholic Workers Movement, centered in New York City, was tolerated but officially ignored.[8] Since the League of Nations allowed self-defense but opposed aggressive war, Catholic Church support was compatible with Just War precepts.

In spite of strong public support from virtually all churches, the Senate rejected the Versailles Treaty, because neither Wilson nor the Republicans would transcend partisan politics in order to compromise. The American isolationists who wanted no part of European affairs remained a small but vocal minority. Even after the Republican triumph in the election of 1920, many church spokesmen and leaders from both parties sought for some form of American participation in the League.

Seeing the near impossibility of ever obtaining two-thirds of the Senate to ratify League membership, the internationalists then sought to gain American participation in the World Court. Conservatives who in the pre-war period had supported arbitration treaties and the Hague conferences now saw the court as a

---

[7]Esther McCarthy, "The Catholic Periodical Press and Issues of War and Peace: 1914-1946," (Ph.D. diss., Stanford University, 1957), 153-8, 180.
[8]Dorothy Day, *The Long Loneliness: The Autobiography of Dorothy Day* (1952); Mel Piehl, *Breaking Bread: The Catholic Worker and the Origins of Catholic Radicalism in America* (1982); Anne Klejment and Nancy Roberts, *The Influence of the Dorothy Day and the Catholic Worker Movement* (1996).

non-political way to solve interstate disputes and a method of strengthening international law. Others saw Court membership as a first step in persuading the United States to exercise an international responsibility commensurate with its economic dominance. In actuality, the Court was a very tame organization and had little power for good or ill in international affairs, so the issue was really symbolic. In spite of a campaign endorsed by every president, both political parties, women's groups, pacifists, internationalists, and spokesman for all major Protestant churches, the Senate refused to ratify American participation throughout the 1920s.[9]

If increased armaments created tensions and led to war, then reducing the size of the military should foster good relations. Revisionist historians of the 1920s dealing with the causes of World War I placed much blame upon the arms race. Versailles had imposed disarmament upon Germany. The Harding administration, seeking through arms control to undercut agitation for American membership in the League, proposed a meeting of the victors: Britain, France, Italy, Japan, and the United States. The Washington Conference of 1922 resulted in a series of treaties scrapping ships, creating a ten year "holiday" in which no capital ships were to be built, establishing ratios for the size of navies, restricting submarine warfare, guaranteeing China's territorial integrity and restoring its authority over customs and former German-held territories, and providing for four-power consultation in the event of "aggressive actions" in the Pacific.

The American churches through public announcements, sermons, and articles in periodicals mobilized their parishioners to support the Washington Conference. Nearly fourteen million signed a petition supporting disarmament.[10] With overwhelming support in America for what was seen as a positive step for peace, the Senate ratified all the treaties. The Washington Conference appeared to be a great triumph for the post-war peace movement. It was followed by successful negotiations creating conventions on submarine warfare, treatment of

[9]Charles Chatfield, *For Peace and Justice: Pacifism in America 1914-1941* (1971) 108-122.
[10]Robert Miller, *American Protestantism and Social Issues* (1958), 329.

prisoners of war, and air warfare. Other conferences strove to settle major unresolved issues such as limits on the number of submarines and, most importantly, land armies.

Euphoria soon ended, as it became difficult to obtain meaningful treaties. France and Italy boycotted a 1927 naval disarmament conference at Geneva and there were no conventions; a 1930 conference resulted in agreements with Britain, the U.S., and Japan with some readjustment of naval ratios. A 1932 conference in which President Herbert Hoover, whose initial fame had come as an organizer of relief for Belgium in World War I, asked first for the abolition of all offensive weapons and, after that was defeated, a 30% reduction, broke up after two years with no accomplishments. The new Roosevelt administration centered its activities on domestic problems arising from the Depression. Governments now abandoned arms control and disarmament as ways of keeping the peace. The churches in Britain and America refused to give up so easily and continued until the late 1930s to advocate arms control and oppose appropriations for new ships and guns.

For peace advocates, the Kellogg-Briand Pact outlawing aggressive war, signed by sixty-two nations, compensated for the failure of the 1927 Geneva Conference. (Germany signed; Russia, not invited, did not.) There were two sources of the convention: an attempt by France's foreign minister Aristide Briand to use an outlawing of war as a way of enticing America into a joint-security pact. The second source was the popular peace movement that had publicized the fact that international law restricted how a nation could wage war but had never stipulated that war itself was a crime. If all nations could be persuaded to renounce war as an instrument of policy, then insecurity would diminish and peace would be fostered. America's Secretary of State Frank Kellogg, who disdained the peace advocates, transformed Briand's bilateral initiative into a multilateral pact, to great popular acclaim. In an additional protocol, fifty-two nations agreed to submit any dispute likely to lead to war to the Court of International Justice. There was, however, no enforcement mechanism, and careful students of politics noted that the Pact was accompanied by America's occupation of Nicaragua and its largest ever peacetime appropriation for naval vessels.

The Kellogg-Briand Pact shows the strengths and weaknesses of the peace movements of the 1920s. The critics of traditional power politics could influence the major powers but controlled the foreign policy of no nation. And they could not agree among themselves on what was the most efficacious method of influencing military and foreign policies that traditionally had been and continued to be the preserve of a small elite of white males who thought they alone understood statecraft. The peace movement of the 1920s sought to solve the problems that caused World War I. If the pre-war regimes, that had been basically satisfied with the world order, had still been in power in the 1930s, the reforms might have succeeded. Unfortunately for peace, three powerful and dissatisfied states sought to achieve hegemony.

III. A Plethora of Pacifisms

With virtually everyone claiming to be advancing the cause of peace, there was considerable ambiguity in terminology and confusion on the meaning of pacifism among the general public and among those who claimed to be pacifists. A pacifist could be a person who worked for peace through the League of Nations, or one who hated war, or who believed all wars were wrong but self-defense could be necessary and justified, or who refused to fight but who would be a medic for the military, or who would do alternative service outside the military, or a person who would neither fight nor do alternative service.[11]

Absolute or Integral Pacifists were those who believed that all war was morally wrong and who proclaimed their unwillingness to fight on any occasion. The men in the new War Resisters League took a pledge that they would never in any circumstance wage war because of the absurdity of distinctions as to offensive and defensive war. Religion, normally, was the motivating factor for absolute

---

[11]Ceadal, 4-22.

pacifists. For the Jehovah's Witnesses, all governments were corrupt, and believers would salute no flag or take no pledge of allegiance. They, like many traditional Anabaptist Churches, did not see their pacifism as a political doctrine.

Liberal Protestants claimed to base their pacifism on an imitation of Jesus and the early Church. C. J. Cadoux of Oxford University published *Early Christian Attitudes to War* in 1919 showing that the passages in the New Testament advocating war had been misinterpreted and that Jesus in the Sermon on the Mount and in his conflicts with Jewish religious authorities had practiced nonviolent resistance. In addition, Cadoux found no evidence of early Christians' practicing war. The lesson was clear: modern Christians should return to their religion's roots and not serve in any military. Christianity had for centuries insisted that priests should not shed blood. New in liberal pacifism was the assumption that Jesus in the Sermon on the Mount gave political advice that was binding upon all members of society. The absolute pacifists who disdained political relevance remained a minority in the peace movement dominated by pacifists who saw Christianity as a moral and pragmatic way to harmony.

Pacifism appeared attractive to many Christians because they associated it with nonviolence. Previously, pacifism had been associated with nonresistance or being passive. Gandhi's mobilization of India's people in a nonviolent struggle offered an attractive alternative to war, but even well-informed peace advocates knew little about its philosophy, prospects for long-term success, or general applicability.[12] Richard Gregg became enthralled with Gandhi and in 1925 made a four-year pilgrimage to India to study his methods. Gregg's *Power of Non-Violence* (1934) provided a psychological explanation why nonviolent resistance, involving moral purity and a willingness to undergo suffering, would change opponents. Advocates of Gregg's methods of catching an opponent off-balance (a

---

[12]C. Seshacari, *Gandhi and the American Scene* (1969). Scott Bennett, *"Pacifism not Passivism:" The War Resisters League and Radical Pacifism, Nonviolent Direct Action and the Americanization of Gandhi 1915-1963* (1998); Charles Chatfield, ed. *The Americanization of Gandhi: Images of the Mahatma* (1976).

kind of moral "jujitsu") ransacked history to find examples of nonviolent successes against businesses opposed to unions and against repressive governments. By providing a moral way to bring social change and defeat armies, Gregg created a textbook to teach the technique of nonviolent action in a manner appealing to religious, humanitarian, and utilitarian pacifists.

Members of the organizations created to support the League of Nations and responsible international actions claimed to be and were referred to as pacifists. They agreed that war was morally wrong and socially unproductive and worked to prevent it, but allowed self-defense. They accepted the need for a police force to keep domestic order and a small unthreatening army. Unwilling to fight in an aggressive or foreign war, they would defend the homeland if invasion threatened.

Some Marxists in Britain, France, and Germany claimed to be pacifists because they would not fight in an international war, but they would not eschew violence in the more basic class war against the capitalists. Violence here would serve as a prelude to creating a peaceful order. The French Socialists had a dual tradition. They had rallied to support the flag in 1914 and were proud of their contributions to the war, but these Marxists also saw the war as a result of the capitalist-colonialist system and were resolved to support collective security and reconciliation with Germany. The working class would no longer be cannon fodder for conservatives.[13]

Some who claimed to be pacifists subscribed to Just War theories. Adherents to Just War theory - including most Roman Catholics, Anglicans. and Lutherans - said that defensive war, while regrettable, as a last resort was not immoral and the citizen's obligation was to obey legitimate authority. The official Catholic position had long been that there was no right for conscientious objection to a war duly declared by a legitimate government. Although remaining within the

---

[13]Norman Ingram, *The Politics of Dissent: Pacifism in France 1919-1939* (1991), 133, 146-7, stresses the class differences in the French anti-war movement between the bourgeoisie and the Marxists over the necessity for internal revolution.

Just War framework, after 1919 significant numbers of Anglican priests engaged for the first time in a critique of their government's economic and foreign policies. A 1924 conference of all English Protestant denominations declared that "war, although fundamentally incompatible with the Christian gospel, might be necessary at that particular stage of man's ethical evolution."[14]

In the 1920s peace was a popular and "necessary reform" and, with no war appearing imminent, churches made idealistic pronouncements about war being contrary to the way of Jesus and the spirit of Christianity and the need for love of neighbor as the foundation for a peaceful world. One historian characterizing the movement for peace in the American churches as a "crusade," claimed that it would take a "volume to cite the anti-war statements coming from Protestant church sources" between 1919-1929.[15] The laity would nod in agreement because there was no cost to being peaceful. Modernist clergy asserted that human nature was basically good, and humans could construct a world order in which force was no longer an option. All nations would ultimately come to see that war was foolishness, destructive to all concerned, and that real self-interest was compatible with a harmony of pursuits. Pacifist optimism had a tinge of desperation - because failure was unthinkable.

Beginning in the late nineteenth century, British Christian socialists proclaimed that restraining capitalism would end imperialist rivalries, unite workers, end poverty, and create a more humane economic system. A pro-Marxist Socialist Party before the war backed England's naval build-up, but there was a strong pacifist strain in the Labour Party, whose leader in Parliament, Ramsay MacDonald, denounced World War I in 1914 as immoral. During the war, many bourgeois peace advocates from Dissenting churches left the Liberal Party and became an important constituent of the Labour Party. MacDonald, a supporter of the League and disarmament, became Prime Minister in 1924 and again in 1929. The Marxists in Britain's small Socialist Party varied their peace

---

[14]John Oliver, *The Church and the Social Order* (1968), 70.
[15]Charles DeBenedetti, *Peace Reform in America* (1980), 108; Miller, 331.

advocacy depending upon Soviet policy, but socialists in the Labour Party in the 1920s stood for reform of the international order, reduction in armaments, and conciliation among nations. Unlike the continent where Marxist socialists were anti-religious, the Labour Party in England enjoyed the support of many clerics who desired some form of guild socialism or new economic policy to end widespread unemployment.

In Canada and America, pacifists supported an increase of state involvement in the economy in favor of the poor. Norman Thomas (1884-1968) - seminary graduate, secretary of the League of Reconciliation, and founder of the American Civil Liberties Union - became a pacifist during the Great War and preached a non-Marxist socialism owing much to the Social Gospel.[16] The crash of 1929 and the Depression seemed to show the deep flaws in capitalism and prompted Protestant clergy to demand social reform. The radicalism of the peace movement attracted progressive clergyman and academics, but frightened businessmen and conservatives, who denounced the reformers as communists.

After American women gained the right to vote in 1919, the suffragettes needed a new issue and focused on peace as way to unite feminists and traditional women. In America peace reform had been an integral part of the Women's Christian Temperance Union, social work movement, and evangelical and liberal religion. Because women constituted the majority of church attenders, clergy and women could easily work together for peace; both, after all, saw themselves as custodians for morality and believed that war was evil. Peace reformers could appeal to maternal instinct; mothers did not raise sons to be cannon fodder.[17]

Radical and conservative women agreed that war depended on female activity. During the Great War, females worked in the factories and field, encouraged their husbands and sons to enlist, nursed the wounded, and staffed government bureaus. Soldiers fought to protect their homes. After the war,

---

[16]W.A. Swanberg, *Norman Thomas: The Last Idealist* (1976).
[17]Harriet Alonzo, *Peace as a Women's Issue: A History of the U.S. Movement for World Peace and Women's Rights* (1992)

women lost their jobs to returned soldiers, mourned the dead, and cared for the unemployed, shell-shocked, or wounded. Women reformers advocated taking foreign policy out of an entirely male realm because war was women's business. Women peace advocates saw themselves as having a unique power to end war because they raised children and could educate them to abolish such folly. The visibility of female leaders and their organizations in the peace movement stands out because there were few other political-moral issues on which women agreed.

Drawing upon their success in creating new attitudes that led to legislating suffrage and prohibition, peace advocates stressed the power of education. If a primary cause of war was a learned ideology of nationalism, then educating people in internationalism could be efficacious. History and political science books should spend less time studying the glories of war and instead show its cost, while demonstrating that progress and prosperity came from peace. Women and men peace advocates employed tactics utilized during the campaigns for suffrage: petitions, parades, fairs, conventions, speeches, pledges, essay and poster contests in schools and churches.

Assessing the impact of the education campaign is difficult. Absolute pacifists remained a small minority. Great Britain and the U.S. had the most important peace constituencies within the churches and in major political parties. The anti-war constituency in Britain had for over a century been based in dissenting churches that now allied themselves with new peace organizations. On occasion, the peace movement could obtain thousands of signatures in favor of disarmament and could influence politicians. However, the men who controlled all nations' foreign policies remained distrustful of alleged sentimental enthusiasts. In 1925 the Archbishop of Canterbury labeled pacifism a heresy. Historian Martin Ceadel concluded: "Before 1928, [in Britain] it needed some courage to renounce war from a public platform, and no church with the exception of the Society of Friends had expressed any strong sense of devotion." [18]

---

[18]Ceadel, 67.

Ironically, the peace movement became stronger in Great Britain after 1929 as economic conditions worsened and Germany appeared unstable. The tenth anniversary of the end of the war brought a torrent of anti-war literature, most memorably Robert Graves, *Good-bye to All That* (1929) and Erich Maria Remarque, *Im Westen nichts Neues* (*All Quiet on the Western Front*, 1929), and Ernest Hemingway, *The Sun Also Rises* (1926) and *A Farewell to Arms* (1929). These books looked at the war from the standpoint of the men in the trenches. By 1930 the Church of England became deeply involved in the peace movement. As one moved to the left from Tory, to Liberal, to Labour, the peace constituency became stronger. Even within the Tory Party, after the mid-20s there was little interest in building weapons and considerable sentiment that Germany was entitled to adjustments in the restrictions placed upon her by the Versailles Treaty to keep peace.

The French called the British and American peace movement too "Quakerish." By this they meant these two nations, separated from the continent by water and not fearing invasion, had the luxury of adopting a religious and moralistic tone and of relying upon the power of public opinion to keep peace. By contrast the French saw themselves as rational and juridical, emphasizing the necessity of positive international law in which war would be forbidden and nations obliged to enforce the new international order.[19]

The Association de la Paix par le Droit (APD), the primary French postwar peace organization, claimed to have been Wilsonian long before the President, and did not change its emphasis throughout the 20s and 30s. Pacifism here did not mean absolute refusal of violence, but collective action through the League of Nations. Initially the APD opposed any individual right of conscientious objection, but later after COs were imprisoned for violating France's two-year compulsory military service obligation, the organization praised their moral stance but insisted that such actions were politically useless. Initially, the

---

[19]Ingram, 38, 108-9, 259, 293-98.

APD supported the Versailles' Treaty because the Germans bore responsibility for the war and should pay stiff reparations. No reconciliation would be possible for many years. After the Ruhr occupation in 1923, pacifist organizations sought to establish friendly contact with Germans and welcomed the Locarno and Kellogg-Briand treaties.[20]

The French peace movement remained splintered. Parties of the left denounced the APD as ignorant of the class revolution, and the right considered it unpatriotic and defeatist. Women in the French section of WILPF worked for social reform, supported pacifism, and advocated conscientious objection. Eschewing direct political action, the Protestant minister Andre Trocmé based his absolute pacifism on religious obedience; the Swiss Pierre Ceresole sought to build good will through international service projects in which youth of many nations participated. Ceresole initiated the modern youth work camp movement, a forerunner of the later Peace Corps. [21]

Germany had the smallest peace movement of all the major European powers. Those who had supported peace during the war sought to begin again afterwards by participating in the WILPF and the Fellowship of Reconciliation and by seeking German membership in the League. Pacifists remained a tiny minority with little support in the state-supported Roman Catholic and Evangelical Churches. They worked with bourgeois liberals in the German Democratic Party and with socialists in the Social Democrats. Foreign minister Gustav Stresemann (1923-1929) sought membership in the League and reconciliation with Russia and France, but also advocated redrawing Germany's border with Poland. Historians still debate whether Stresemann, who preferred the monarchy to a republic, sought to create a new European concert of powers whose balance would keep the peace, or if he was a conservative nationalist whose anti-leftist policies' support of repression paved the way for the Nazis.

---

[20]Ingram, 48-50; Michel Bilis, *Socialistes and Pacifistes 1933-1939: Ou L'Impossible Dilemme des Socialistes* (n.d.).

However, in the late 1920s Weimar courts convicted pacifists of disloyalty; neither the Right nor the Left approved of pacifists.

IV. The Churches and the Fall of the Weimar Republic

The Evangelical Church in Germany did not like the Weimar Republic and would have welcomed the restoration of the Emperor.   Before the war, the established Protestant churches dominated what they saw as a moral Christian culture and enjoyed the patronage of the Kaiser.   The only gain for them in Weimar was the right to criticize the government, but the state continued financial support for clergy and religious schools.   The clergy labeled as immoral the Versailles Treaty's placing exclusive responsibility for causing the war on the Central Powers, opposed reparations, and wanted border rectification, particularly in Poland.   They felt little loyalty to a government dominated by a pro-Catholic Center Party and by anticlerical socialists, with the Jewish Walter Rathaneu as the first foreign minister.   The economic distress occasioned by the rapid inflation of the mark after the French occupation of the Ruhr in 1923, a series of coalition governments, and then the brief respite before the Depression showed the instability of the Republic.

For many Germans, weaknesses in the democratic center meant that the future would be dominated by extremists of the right or the left.   The churches feared the extreme anti-religious tone of the rapidly rising Communist Party.   The Soviet Union showed that the communists would use the power of the state against any church. German Protestants also disliked the violence, anti-Semitism, and German folk-religious themes of the National Socialist Democratic Party (Nazis), but they preferred Hitler, who promised religious freedom and would not actively support the Weimar democracy.   Hitler and the Nazis might be crude in technique and thought, but allowing them political power would reintroduce a conservative influence to government.   In the 1932 presidential election, 75% of

---

[21]Brief biographies of Pierre Ceresole (1879-1945) and Andre Trocmé (1901-1977) are in *Biographical Dictionary of Modern Peace Leaders*, ed. Howard Johnson (1958), 150-51, 959-61.

Hitler's support came from Protestants and 60% came from those who were not just nominal but active church members.[22] After Hitler came to power and unleashed anti-Semitic propaganda, instituted Aryan laws, arrested communists, destroyed trade unions, drove out liberal professors and pacifists, the Protestant churches kept silent, officially being neutral.

The Catholic Church had no great love for the Prussian monarchy, which always favored the Protestants, and found the Weimar government more receptive to working out formal concordats for regularizing relations between church and state. However, because of socialist opposition, the Center Party could not gain a treaty. The Catholic Center Party had an important role in government and exercised a moderating influence. Even so, the Catholic Cardinal of Munich publicly voiced his support for the monarchy. Although the faction-ridden center party campaigned against Hitler in 1932, the Party voted for the enabling act giving Hitler dictatorial powers.[23] Catholic bishops seemingly endorsed Hitler by lifting the ban on Catholic membership in the National Socialist Party and expressed approval of cooperation with the new regime. Pius XI, pope from 1922 to 1939, had been in Poland at the time of its war with the Soviet Union and had an abiding fear of communism. If the choice came down to the right or left, Hitler at least was a Catholic who promised full freedom of religion and would end the communist threat.

Immediately after his ascension to power, Hitler pulled Germany out from the League, denounced the restrictions of the Versailles Treaty as unjust, persecuted actual and potential foes of the regime, and began creating a totalitarian system in which the state sought control of all organizations, including the churches. In private Hitler railed against Christianity and sought to replace it with a religion based upon old Germanic gods like Wotan and Thor, but publicly he

---

[22]J. R. C. Wright, *"Above Parties:" The Political Attitudes of the German Protestant Church 1918-1933* (1974), 106.

[23]Ellen L. Evans, *The German Center Party 1870-1933: A Study in Political Catholicism* (1981); Ernest C. Helmreich, *The German Churches Under Hitler: Background, Struggle, and Epilogue* (1979).

continued to boast of religious freedom and of the support the government gave to churches. Even at the height of his power, Hitler preferred to keep a low profile in religious affairs, encouraging lesser ranking officials or the Party to attack or harass the church. Still, Nazi propagandists denigrated a transnational agency that worshipped a Jew and exalted peace as unGermanic.

At first Hitler supported the rabidly nationalistic "German Christians," a group constituting one-third of the Evangelical Church. "German Christians" announced that the Gospel was the "highest eternal good" and German nationality the "highest temporal good."[24] Under a program of "Positive Christianity," the German church must free itself from the Old Testament and "Jewish money morality" and restore a "heroic image of Jesus." With support from the "German Christians" within the Evangelical Church, the Nazis could neutralize any potential opposition from the Protestants who would spend much energy just defending their autonomy.[25]

Hitler's attempts at unifying and instituting state control of Protestant churches through his handpicked Reichsbishop failed and occasioned a backlash from the newly organized Confessing churches. The Confessing Church, composed of the major Protestant denominations, cooperated in drawing up the Barmen Confession of Faith in 1934 that denounced totalitarianism and the attempt to adapt Christian doctrine to Nazi beliefs. The Confessing Church became almost a separate dissenting church within the Evangelical Church in defiance of the Reichsbishop. By 1939, Hitler lost interest in controlling the churches, seeing this as a battle not worth the risk.

Protestant churches managed to maintain limited autonomy even after a 1937 anti-church campaign prompted 396,000 Protestants (and 108,000

---

[24]*The Encyclopedia of the Third Reich*, ed. Christian Lenter and Friedemann Bedurfig (1991), I, 327.
[25]Ernest Helmreich, *The German Churches under Hitler: Background, Struggle and Epilogue* (1979), 286-87. Hitler planned to abolish all Christian churches in Germany after victory in World War II, Gerhard Weinburg, *A World at Arms: A Global History of World War II* (1994), 477-79.

Catholics) to withdraw membership. The state restricted religious education, controlled the funding of churches, required permission for public meetings, and harassed ministers, with a few being arrested - the most notable being Martin Neimöller, who was acquitted in a trial, and then spent eight years in a concentration camp as "the Fuhrer's personal prisoner."[26] Neimöller had been a decorated submarine captain in World War I and a supporter of the Nazis in the 1920s, but he became an open critic and refused an offer to remain free if he would be silent. In 1939 Protestant bishops' public protests forced suspension (but not cancellation) when Hitler ordered a policy of euthanasia for epileptics and those with birth defects. The Confessing Churches protested against Hitler's racism, but there was a long tradition of anti-Jewish feeling in the Evangelical Church, and most Protestants kept quiet about the anti-Semitic laws. They took more initiative in protecting the 19,716 Jews who had converted to Christianity than the 233,646 who had not.

Protestant churches pursued a delicate policy, seeking to preserve their pastoral mission in a hostile environment, not wishing to cause members to have to choose between church and state, and seeking to preserve their ability to minister to all, even Nazi Party members. Pastors prayed for peace but, whatever their private opinion, they took no public position on the morality of the approaching war.

V. The Papacy and the Dictators: Italy and Germany

Pius XI, a former librarian who dedicated his pontificate to creating peace, believed that treaties (concordats) would protect the Church. So he sought to regularize relations with many states, even those of whose policies he disapproved. For example, though a staunch anti-communist, he tried unsuccessfully to negotiate a treaty with Stalin. Mussolini came to power in 1922 with the support of many Italian Catholics who saw him as bringing order to the state and ending the threat from the Bolsheviks. Mussolini had no sympathy for

---

[26]Ibid., 293.

religion, and early in his career uttered many anti-clerical statements, but he soon realized he needed a settlement with the Church. Pius also recognized that Mussolini had firm control of the state, the Church could not dislodge him, and a policy of opposition to all Italian governments followed since 1870 weakened papal influence. In 1929 Pius and Mussolini negotiated a concordat assuring the autonomy of the Vatican and the Church's ability to minister and educate youth, but ending support for the pro-Catholic political party. The Vatican became a state within Italy with the Pope agreeing not to interfere in Italian politics and foreign policy.[27]

Mussolini thought he could manage the Church; the Pope hoped to control Mussolini; both failed and their relationship throughout the 1930s remained rocky because the Fascists reneged on the agreements. Pius kept silent on Mussolini's conquest of Ethiopia and intervention in the Spanish Civil War, but the Italian church hierarchy acclaimed both actions, leading foreign observers to believe that the Church approved of Fascism. Church opposition helped forestall Mussolini's attempt to transform Italy into a totalitarian state like Germany. By 1937 the papacy opposed the Steel Pact between the two dictators, supported Austrian independence against Hitler's *Anschluss*, and worked to find a negotiated solution to the issues that caused World War II.

Pius had been negotiating concordats with Weimar, and he continued the policy with the Nazis, giving Hitler in 1933 his first major diplomatic success. Pius thought his treaty, granting virtually all the religious goals the Catholic Center Party had sought since the 1870s, preserved the Church's independence and ability to educate children. To gain this, he sacrificed the anti-Nazi Catholic Center Party and its check on Hitler. The Nazis soon violated the terms of the concordant by requiring Hitler Youth to belong to no other organization, seeking to dissuade children from attending and then having the state take over Catholic schools, forbidding public processions, removing crucifixes from schools and

---

[27]John Pollard, *The Vatican and Italian Fascism 1919-1932: A Study in Conflict* (1985); D. A. Binchy, *Church and State in Fascist Italy* (1941).

vandalizing those along roads, having the press charge that priests and nuns had committed 7000 moral offenses, and staging "Priest Trials" in 1937 over alleged currency smuggling by religious communities.

The Nazis' attempt to drive a wedge between people and parish failed. Neither Catholics nor Protestants informed against their ministers. Yet when Father Joseph Spieker of Cologne in 1931 spoke out openly against the Nazis and was arrested by the Gestapo, Church authorities in Rome and Germany rather than protesting treated him as an embarrassment. Until the war, the Gestapo might call a priest in for questioning, but few were sent to concentration camps.[28] Catholic bishops' protests to authorities sometimes brought redress. Some bishops kept silent, others like Bishop Rankowski approved of some Nazi policies; a few, most notably Bishop Von Galen in Münster, issued pastoral letters and preached against the regime's violations of the concordant and its idolatry of Hitler. Mostly Catholic clerics silently prayed: "We will fulfill our patriotic duty to Germany. Beyond this, O Lord, deliver us from the Nazi regime."[29]

In 1937 Pope Pius issued an encyclical condemning communism, and the German bishops promised Church support in the battle against bolshevism. Shortly thereafter, the Pope had an encyclical, smuggled by personal carriers, read in churches throughout Germany on a Sunday. The surprised and furious Nazis heard themselves condemned for worship of the state, paganism, and racism.[30] The Pope did not speak for the whole Church; the papacy opposed *Anschluss* with Austria; yet Cardinal Innitzer of Vienna welcomed *Anschluss* in 1938 and urged a yes vote on union with Germany. Like the Protestants, Catholics attempted to protect Jews who had converted but were mostly silent about Jewish persecution. By 1939 the Catholic and Protestant churches remained the

[28] Eric Johnson, *Nazi Terror: The Gestapo, Jews, and Ordinary Germans* (1999), 196-212, 226-27.
[29] Anthony Rhodes, *The Vatican in the Age of the Dictators* (1973), 294-96.

only institution in Germany not directly under Fascist control, but both survived by acquiescence, without direct challenge to the regime. Pius made clear the Church's opposition to Fascist militarism, but he had little influence over Mussolini and none over Hitler.

VI. The Spanish Civil War

The Spanish Civil War (1936-1939), often seen as a prelude to World War II, was also a battle over religion. Spain in the 1930s was a polarized country with parties of monarchists, conservative Catholics, Fascists, anti-clerical liberals, socialists, a trade union movement dominated by anarchists, and a small communist movement. The political parties bitterly disagreed on the best form of government, the necessity of economic reforms, including redistribution of land to end the disparity between rich and poor, and whether church and state should be separated. Since the mid-nineteenth century when the state seized Church lands, the government paid the salaries of clergy and the Church controlled education and the content of moral legislation. The Vatican consulted with government officials before appointing bishops and cardinals. Spain officially remained an overwhelmingly Catholic country, with the Church, supported by peasants, landowners, and monarch, working to preserve a traditional society against the forces of modernity. The Spanish Church, more conservative than the Vatican, opposed the Republic and wished a return to the monarchy.[31] Yet Spain was also a country with 50% of the population illiterate, a large landless class of agricultural laborers, and an anti-clerical working class whose poverty the Depression accentuated.

After the fall of the monarchy in 1931, the Republic, first dominated by liberals and socialists, passed a series of anti-clerical laws stripping the Church of its monopoly over education, dissolving the religious order of Jesuits, and ending

---

[30]Helmreich, 279; "Mit Brennender Sorge," March 14, 1937 in *The Papal Encyclicals 1903-1939*, ed. Claudia Ihm (1981), 534-35. The main Nazi attack on Roman Catholicism took place between 1935-37; then Hitler called off the campaign because it was not succeeding.
[31]Frances Lannon, "The Church's Crusade Against the Republic," in *Revolution and War in Spain 1931-1939*, ed. Paul Preston (1984), 14-34.

salaries for clerics. A reaction in the next election brought a conservative government that, after brutally suppressing strikes, lost power in 1936 to a left-wing Popular Front government that banned the rightist Falange Party (whose leader was assassinated), but could not stop anti-clerical violence and church burnings or 60,000 landless peasants from seizing 3000 farms.

General Francisco Franco, a conservative monarchist, led an army revolt that rapidly occupied the southern half of the country, but its march on Madrid stalled. The Republic slowly mobilized its forces, checked Franco's Nationalist Party, and the resulting stalemate lasted for three years, with 500,000 killed, only half of them in battle, and nearly two million refugees.

Because it was such a powerful institution in Spain, the Church's attitude can serve as a test of the impact of Just War theories. The Nationalist army, supported by the land and factory owners and conservative bourgeoisie, claimed that the war was a "holy crusade in God's name" against godless communism, and sought to enlist the Church's active support. But the rebellion was also against a legitimate government, and the Catholic Church normally opposed rebellion - allowing it only as a last resort when there was a general uprising against a usurping tyrant. The Vatican, in keeping with its policy of negotiating concordats, had been attempting to reach a settlement with the Republican government, much to the disgust of the local hierarchy. The Spanish bishops strongly supported Franco, a backing that intensified as anarchists during early stages of the rebellion killed nearly 6,832 priests and nuns and 13 bishops and burned or desecrated Catholic churches. The struggle became, as Cardinal Goma proclaimed, "a war of love or hatred of religion."[32] The Church now mobilized its

---

[32] Luis Aguirre Prado, *The Church and the Spanish War* (1965), 22, 38-42 The Spanish bishops' declaration accused the Republic of being a revolution which was "most cruel," "inhuman," "barbarous," against "the law of nations," "anti-Spanish," and "above all anti-Christian." The Nationalists, by contrast, supported morality and the Church and chanted the slogan "Long live Spain; Long Live Christ the King."

followers for the right wing cause in this "holiest war in all history" fought against communist atheists. This was not only a Just War; it was a new crusade.[33]

Just War theory also had a doctrine of proportionality and just means. Violence against the Church had never been sanctioned by the Republican government, being mostly carried on by anarchists who had refused to join the Popular Front because they distrusted all governments. By contrast, Franco and the Nationalists used terror as a systematic policy, having prisoners of war and political opponents shot without benefit of trial. His reign of white terror continued throughout and even after the end of the war. He regarded even pre-war peaceful democratic opponents of right-wing power as dangerous. In addition, the Nationalists used airplanes obtained from Germany and Italy for bombing of civilians, both in little towns like Guernica and major concentrations of population including Madrid and Barcelona. The Nationalists engaged in the first sustained bombing of civilians, a policy allowing Germany and Italy to see how the airplane could best be used as an effective instrument of war.

If the Spanish bishops had applied the Just War standards of proportionality and right conduct in war, Franco and the Nationalists should have been publicly condemned. Instead, the bishops ignored inconvenient parts of Just War doctrine and focused on Republican atrocities, of which there were many, and the danger of communism. There was no Church statement on Italian and German intervention in a civil war, but Stalin's support for the Republicans brought condemnation.

The Spanish Civil War posed difficult issues for Catholics in France, Britain, and America, as well as for European democracies. Catholics in America and Great Britain tended to support Franco, because of the Republican attacks on the Church. A Gallup poll in America showed that 83% of Protestants favored

---

[33]W.J. Callalhan estimates 4,184 secular priests, 2,365 clergy from religious orders, and 283 nuns killed, "Catholicism," in *Historical Dictionary of Modern Spain* (1990), 136-39; José Sanchez, *The Spanish Civil War as a Religious Tragedy* (1987), 9-10, stresses that most killings took place during the six months at the beginning of the war when the government essentially lost control.

the Republic; 64% of Catholics supported the Nationalists.[34] The editorial staff of *Commonweal*, a leading lay Catholic journal, was divided and so added a forum page for each side to state its preference. Official Catholic support of the Nationalists meant that the working class would not identify with the Republican cause. Intellectuals including Ernest Hemingway and George Orwell, who were newspaper correspondents, supported the Republic, and 40,000 foreigners - mostly socialists from America, Britain, and France - came to fight for the Republic and democracy in the Abraham Lincoln Brigade.

In France, in response to Nationalist claims backed by conservative Catholics that the war was a crusade against irreligion, the distinguished neo-Thomist philosopher Jacques Maritain argued that the war was not a crusade, not even a Just War, because both sides had committed deplorable acts, and the Spanish Church had corrupted religion by identifying with political power. The atrocities of the right were worse than those of the left. Now the choice, Maritain argued, was between two bad choices, and democracy was better than fascist totalitarianism.[35] However, French Catholic and conservative support of the Nationalists made the Popular Front government of socialist Leon Blum unwilling to intervene, particularly without the support of Great Britain.

In 1936 the democracies proposed non-intervention, a policy agreed to and immediately violated by Hitler and Mussolini. Britain and America placed an embargo on all military supplies, a policy approved by the churches and peace movement, which looked the other way when the Fascist countries intervened. France also acquiesced and would not even allow arms to be sold to the Republic, even though a triumph of Franco meant that it was encircled by three Fascist countries. It did accept refugees, some of whom later enlisted in the French army to fight Hitler.

Stalin supported the Republic by selling arms, but its accepting of his support also increased communist influence in Spain. Russian communists

[34]McCarthy, 164.
[35]Sanchez, 150-56

brought order to the Loyalist army, but their opposition to and violence against anarchists and Trotskyite communists weakened the Republic. After Munich, Stalin changed his policy from supporting Popular Front opposition to Hitler to conciliation, and so he curtailed shipments and undermined the Republic. Franco's triumph brought a conservative dictatorship resting upon military force and a restoration of the Catholic Church's privileged position in society, but he ignored the Vatican's plea for mercy to defeated opponents.

PART II

Nonviolence and Militarism: Nationalism in India and Japan

Religious leaders who seek a political transformation of society usually end by supporting coercion either through picking up the sword themselves or providing a rationale for their disciples to use violence. Gandhi is a unique figure because he took India's religious traditions that had long been used to legitimate warfare and brought to prominence a subordinate theme of nonviolence (*ahimsa*). His success in mobilizing public opinion against British rule demonstrated that a religiously motivated campaign of nonviolent resistance could be a dynamic political force.

The contrast is with Japan, where government officials utilized the religious traditions of Shinto, previously centered on ancestral reverence and agricultural fertility, and consciously adapted them to loyalty to the Emperor, the state, and the military. Japan created a unique form of nationalism, whose ostensible similarity to fascism camouflaged basic differences. Unlike India where an individual symbolized the change by drawing upon the religious feeling of the masses, in Japan an elite of government officials and military officers who controlled the schools gradually overcame opposing traditions of Buddhism and western democracy. So the focus of these two sections is on the conscious adaptation of religious traditions for political purposes in India and Japan.

I. Gandhi and Nonviolence

Mohandas Gandhi (1869-1948), educated in India in schools that ignored traditional Indian learning and in law school in London, experienced the brunt of racial oppression backed by legislation when he lived in South Africa from 1893-1914. Here he learned how to mobilize the small Indian minority into nonviolent resistance and developed the religious and political perspectives that he would utilize in a long struggle against Great Britain for Indian self-government.

Gandhi drew upon many religions - Hinduism, Jainism, Buddhism, Christianity - and many thinkers - Thoreau, Emerson, and Tolstoy - in his search for God or Truth. Nonviolence became his method because there could be no one conceptualization of Truth or way to God. All religions sought to experience *atman*, or universal soul that made all humanity one. For Gandhi, Krishna, the Buddha, the Hebrew prophets, Jesus Christ, and Muhammad sought a nonviolent religious and social transformation. Even within Hinduism's tolerance of eclecticism, Gandhi's breadth was unusual. He sought inward truth through structured meditation, but claimed no visions or ecstasy.[36] In essence, his religion was moral action as described in one section of the *Bhagavadgita,* which he made the essence of Hinduism and all religion: "A man of disciplined mind, who moves among the objects of sense, with the senses under control and free from attachment and aversion, he attains purity of spirit. And in that purity of spirit there is produced for him an end of all sorrow: the intelligence of such a man of pure spirit is soon established [in the peace of the self.]"[37]

For Gandhi, God was Truth and Truth was God, so means and ends were convertible, in fact, the same. Pure truth could never come from impure methods. Under the right conditions, all persons could obtain a realization of *atman* and the purpose of the *satyagraha* (*satya*=being or truth and *graha*=struggle or "Soul Force") was to emancipate humanity individually and collectively - to make them

---

[36]Geoffrey Ashe, *Gandhi* (1968), 97 is an excellent biography. Dalton, 17, 33
[37]*Bhagavadgita,* 126-27; Jorden's essay in *Modern Indian Interpreters of the Bhagavadgita,* ed. Robert Minor (1986), 93-94.

aware of *atman.* So for Gandhi the religious and the political, the individual and the collective struggle were the same. He saw himself as a religious reformer forced by necessity to emphasize societal goals. His aim was not victory or conquest, but Truth. This meant that both sides would learn Truth during the *satyagraha* and the campaign would end not by compromise or consensus but when both sides willingly came to the same conclusion, occupied the same space.[38]

Gandhi's *satyagraha* warrior resembles the soldier of the *Bhagavadgita;* she or he is detached, accepting a duty for struggle while indifferent to outward success or failure. There was no room for self-interest or cowardice. If forced to choose bad alternatives, Gandhi preferred violence to cowardice and hated passive acceptance of injustice. His peaceful warrior is courageous, prepared to die because the ultimate weapon in a *satyagraha* is self-sacrifice. *Ahimsa,* nonviolence, is crucial; there could be no coercion at any stage. So the warrior lived an ascetic, celibate simple life. He was a vegetarian, self-reliant, and a totally dedicated warrior for God. When questioned that this was a "feminine" ethic, Gandhi agreed and insisted that feminine qualities, not masculine violence, kept society together and allowed civilization. Any society ruled solely by war and power politics would end with everybody dead. The passive nonresistance of Western pacifists was the tactic of the weak. By contrast, *satyagraha* was for the strong.

Being a nonviolent soldier required discipline, training, and education, and Gandhi sought to educate the Indian population so that they could maintain their rights by nonviolent actions. His was a religious vision that encompassed politics, and his hold on the Indian people came from the congruence of his lifestyle with his ideals. His source for authority in his re-interpretation of Hinduism and his campaigns came not from scholarship or intellectual acumen but from his constant

---

[38]In addition to M. K. Gandhi, *Satyagraha,* reprinted (1958), see William Borman, *Gandhi and Nonviolence* (1986) and Mark Juergensmeyer, *Fighting With Gandhi* (1984), for perceptive analyses of *satyagraha*

efforts to live the precepts of the *Bhagavidgita*. Even his British opponents learned to admire him, even if they hated having to deal with him. Soon after his return from South Africa to India, the Nobel laureate poet Rabindrath Tagore called him *Mahatma*, "Great Soul," a label Gandhi disliked, but the masses revered him as a holy man, even a reincarnation of Krishna.

Upon his return to India in 1914, Gandhi found 300,000,000 people ruled by 100,000 British. The English had a monopoly on military power, and British rule, concluded Gandhi, was founded on force, preserved by immoral methods, and destructive of the people's welfare. Gandhi saw his task as teaching the Indians not to fear, awakening them to the knowledge that all government depends upon the consent of the masses. If the people withdraw that consent, the government will collapse. His ultimate goal was self-government through emancipating Indians from fear without causing them to hate the imperialist or making the British afraid. India's destiny, her mission, was to convince the world that violence and coercion did not lay at the heart of politics. Gandhi created an irresistible nationalist movement by repudiating chauvinism and power politics.

Satyagraha, Gandhi insisted, worked only if the cause was moral and the people were nonviolent, but tactics varied according to the evil to be changed. Each campaign involved study of issues, attempts to negotiate with the British government, announcing methods and goals methods and goals. All was to be done openly, and Gandhi informed the British and the public of his immediate and long-term aims, tactics, and timing. Gandhi wrote extensively for newspapers, and his activities gained coverage by journalists in India and later by the British and foreign press. Campaigns often began with civil disobedience; that is, Gandhi as the leader of the Congress Party would select one oppressive law and his followers would disobey it. If threatened, arrested, or beaten, they would use no violence and accept their imprisonment. Sacrifice, after all, was the way to Truth.

The Salt March to the sea in 1930, Gandhi's most famous campaign, was against a government monopoly and tax on salt. Gandhi began the march with a select small group trained in nonviolence and was joined by thousands who walked with him to salt flats at the ocean and then broke the law by picking up the raw salt. The issue to him was clear: the British had no right to own sea salt, to force some of the poorest people on earth to pay a tax equal to several weeks wages for a necessity of life. When large numbers of Indians refused to pay, the government's ability to enforce the tax collapsed.[39]

When unarmed men and women attempted to enter a government-owned salt depot, the police beat the unarmed men and women severely with metal tipped staves in full view of an American journalist whose account carried by the world's press embarrassed the British government. In one month over 60,000 were jailed, including Gandhi. But the violence always came from the opponent. In 1922 a campaign against an unjust land tax appeared on the verge of success when the Indians began using violence. Gandhi called off the protest and accepted defeat. By so doing he demonstrated that his quest for Truth was uppermost. In the negotiations after his campaigns, at no time did Gandhi gain everything he desired and sometimes accepted far less than other Indian leaders thought attainable. But by successfully defying the British raj, he promoted Indian self-respect and nationalism and finally made Britain realize that self-government was inevitable.

Satyagraha often involved non-cooperation campaigns. The Congress Party used general strikes; Indians boycotted elections and refused to serve in advisory councils; students withdrew from government schools; eminent citizens returned government honors and medals; and lawyers refused to practice in British courts. The Congress created an alternative government from within. All these measures demonstrated that Britain could not rule India without the consent of the people.

The external battle against England was accompanied by an internal struggle to make India ready for self-rule. Economic subordination to British factories could be ended by a boycott of foreign goods and by each individual's

---

[39] Ashe, 284-97.

spinning cotton. So even in the Salt March, Gandhi and his followers spun for three hours each day. Gandhi, who had dressed like an English gentleman in London and South Africa, now wore a loincloth of homespun cotton. He argued that simplicity in life would end India's capitulation to factory machinery.

Hinduism's great sin, announced Gandhi, was a caste system that made millions untouchable. Opposing Hindu scriptures that created different moralities depending on caste and required separation of castes for purity, Gandhi invited untouchables to his commune (*ashram*) and welcomed their participation in his campaigns. He used a *satyagraha* against a semi-autonomous Indian state that denied untouchables the right to enter a temple or even walk on a road outside it. He welcomed women into his campaigns, and sought to end child marriage.

India was an area of many religions, and the British had ruled by allowing faith communities much self-regulation, but also by fostering animosities and then insisting that distrust among Hindus and Muslims made independence impossible. For Gandhi, India's unity required a subordination of religious differences so that she could set an example of religious toleration. So he sought to include both groups within the Congress Party and Muslims initially participated in the nonviolent struggles, but distrust developed in spite of his efforts to build a community of interests. In part, this was because Gandhi was seen as a Hindu holy man and the Congress used Hindu themes. Muslims feared being subordinated in a Hindu land and so sought separate enclaves where they could rule. Gandhi thought theology unimportant; his religion was moral purity, but many Muslims and Hindus disagreed and wanted their religion to be a dominant influence in an independent India.[40]

After World War II, Britain determined to grant independence to separate Muslim Pakistan and an ostensibly secular Indian state. In 1947 religious-ethnic baiting by extremists on both sides, conflicts over borders in Kashmir and elsewhere, and mass migrations resulted in riots, murders, and massacres. Gandhi,

---

[40] Dennis Dalton, *Mahatma Gandhi: Nonviolent Power in Action* (1993), 75-76,141-49.

now an old man with no official position, moved into one of the most violent areas in Bombay and, inviting a prominent Muslim politician to join him, began a fast for peace. Self-sacrifice might end the bloodshed. Realizing that Gandhi was near death, the two sides in Bombay pledged peace. A few weeks later, still weakened, he fasted in Delhi, again ending the violence. His assassination a short time later in January 1948 by a Hindu who thought Gandhi too sympathetic to Muslims shows that his interpretation of the *Bhagavadgita* had not gained universal assent.

Gandhi insisted that a *satyagraha* was the method to solve all disputes at all levels. Earlier in South Africa, Gandhi admired Great Britain. In India he recognized that dealing with the British who, however arrogant and cruel, had a parliamentary system and a free press was better than dealing with Nazi Germany, or imperialist Japan. He supported Britain in the Boer and both World Wars as the lesser evil. Still, when questioned as to what he would advise if Hitler invaded India, Gandhi said that thousands of Indians would be willing to lay down their lives in order to convert the troops.[41] For Gandhi, as for Arjuna in the *Bhagavadgita*, Truth not life was the supreme value. The new Indian government, led by the Congress Party and Prime Minister Jawaharlal Nehru, admired Gandhi but did not follow his methods. India in later years would waver between advocacy of nonviolence in the Cold War and creating an army that would fight against China and Pakistan.

II. State Shinto in Japan

Japan like India fused traditional religious ideas and nationalism in a search for political autonomy. But while Gandhi transformed Hindu beliefs into nonviolent social protest, Japan created a cult of State Shinto that legitimated the quest for empire and military glory. These two nations provide contrasting examples of impact of western nationalism on issues of war and peace, a difference related more to the desires and status of leaders than to earlier religious customs. The section will examine the origins of State Shinto, then discuss its

---

[41]During the war when Japan threatened India, Gandhi and the Congress Party opposed the Fascists but remained dissatisfied with Britain's policy. Ashe, 340-41, 344-50.

beliefs, and finally evaluate its role in the Japanese attack on China which eventually led to war with the United States. Although State Shinto facilitated the mobilization of the people, allowed the making of war, and influenced the manner of fighting, the military elite's decisions to go to war first against China and then against Great Britain and the United States derived from power politics and the desire for autarky.

Japan, unlike India, was never a colony of a European nation. The defeat of China in the Opium War in 1842 and the visit of American warships under Commodore Matthew Perry in 1853 prompted the Japanese to reconsider their two hundred fifty-year policy of attempting to maintain isolation from the West. Fearing that the decentralized authority of the Tokugawa Shogunate left them vulnerable to imperialism, an oligarchy of Japanese leaders in 1868 restored the authority of the Meiji Emperor as a means of creating a more powerful centralized government. Importing advisers from the West and sending students to study in Europe and America, the Meiji government sought to incorporate into Japanese society only the useful parts of Western civilization: constitutions, business, science and military weapons.

III. Traditional and State Shinto

Japanese officials sought to create an ideology that would preserve traditional values and at the same time create unity in a country undergoing rapid social and economic change. The result was State Shinto, a new amalgam of several old customs: rituals in the Emperor's household, village ancestor and spirit (*Kami*) worship, and the communal ceremonies of major shrines. Before 1870 the Japanese would not have linked these inchoate activities as part of a religious system termed "Shinto;" in fact, even the notion of a religion as an individual belief separate from communal norms was new. So State Shintoism was a product of nationalism, an attempt to bind the people to the government through the symbol of the Emperor.

Under the Shoguns before 1868, Buddhism enjoyed state patronage and prestige, and its monks provided the ethical teachings and pastoral functions associated with religion. The Confucian ethic of filial obedience and duty to authority blended into Buddhist teachings; similarly, folk ancestor and worship at numerous shrines was incorporated into but kept subordinate to Buddhism. Rites performed at village shrines sought purification or material blessings (crops, children) but there were no Shinto ethics or theology or priests who conducted weddings and funerals. Under the Meiji Emperor, officials attacked Buddhism and Confucianism as foreign imports destructive to the state. The Confucian ethic of filial obedience and duty was preserved when divorced from its Chinese origin and relabeled as essentially Japanese.

Now the government promoted Shintoism as an authentic expression of the Japanese way of life by sending evangelists and building shrines. State Shintoism's contents consisted of honoring the Emperor, paying taxes, sending children to school, and furnishing sons for the army. Even so, before 1900 State Shintoism was more a theoretical construct than practical piety, with the peasants unwilling to forsake Buddhism or village rituals.

Realizing that a frontal attack upon Buddhism might cause unrest, the government from 1890 until the end of World War II insisted that State Shintoism was a form of civic obligation and inculcation of virtue and not a religion. All schools, private as well as public, taught State Shintoism as part of the Japanese culture. Citizens must engage in its rites and there could be no criticism of its basic tenets. Unlike traditional Shintoism which was unstructured, diverse, and difficult to define, State Shintoism was unified because created, supported, and controlled by the government. There would be no sermons or creative reinterpretation of the traditions by priests.

Local shrine rites and new worship movements and practices, which were often anti-foreign, the government renamed Sect Shintoism. Sect Shintoism was a "religion" like Buddhism and Christianity, and these were of little official concern to the state so long as their teachings did not conflict with State Shinto. The new constitution of 1882 guaranteed all these religions freedom of practice with no government financial support.[42] The constitution was one way of reassuring Christian missionaries that there would be no persecution, and also demonstrated to the West that Japan accepted modern theories of government. Sect Shinto, Christianity, and Buddhism would remain free until the late 1930s when the government brought all under its control.

War was a second method of gaining Western respect. Defeating China (1895) and Russia (1905), conquering Korea and Formosa, and creating a sphere of influence in China demonstrated Japan's power. Great Britain signified that Japan was a member of the family of nations by signing an alliance in 1902. Military prowess and foreign influence increased State Shinto's popularity at home. Until the 1930s State Shinto had to compete with democracy, communism, and socialism, particularly in urban areas, but then the state sought to stamp out foreign political and economic ideologies.

IV. The Emperor and the Cult of the War Dead

State Shinto consisted of two linked basic tenets: loyalty to the Emperor and homage to the War Dead. Using as a primary source an ancient Nihongi chronicle written down in the eighth century, State Shinto traced the lineage of the present Emperor back 2500 years to the first historical king of Japan (Jimmu Tenno 660-585 B.C.E.) and then through various gods to the female Sun God (Amaterasu-Omi).[43] The present Emperor derived his status from lineage, and the form of government had been instituted by the Sun God and was, therefore, divine. Article I of the Constitution stated "The Empire of Japan shall be reigned over and governed by a line of Emperors unbroken for ages eternal." and Article III declared "The Emperor is sacred and inviolable." One scholar terms the Japanese

---

[42]Helen Hardacre, *Shinto and the State* (1989), 116.
[43]D. C. Holtom, *The National Faith of Japan: A Study in Modern Shinto* (1938, reprinted 1965), 77

government an "immanent theocracy" because the Emperor and the Sun God had "one and the same will."[44] Whether the present Emperor was a God or only an intermediary to the *Kami* was unclear; certainly he received homage and reverence from all, and his exalted status approached that of *Kami*. The government created official shrines only for past emperors who were worshipped as *Kami*. In theory the Emperor did not just symbolize the state; he was the state, and to question the Emperor's status or the authority of the state was to deny a divine order created by the Sun God. An 1890 prescript of education required that all children be taught about the divine lineage of the Emperor; each school had a small shrine with a picture of the Emperor and a copy of the decree that was to be read daily. A similar prescript for the military linked the army to the Emperor and announced that an honorable death in battle was the supreme sacrifice. The Meiji Emperor proclaimed that in the old days every man was a soldier and "for the Future I wish the army to consist of the whole nation."[45] The Sun God conferred a unique exalted status on the Emperor and also on the entire Japanese people and their islands, the land of gods.

During the 1930s State Shintoists asserted that Japan had a divine obligation to bestow the blessings of a superior government and civilization upon surrounding peoples, "to expand sovereignty and righteousness over ever-widening territories." The Nihongi chronicles prophesied that the "whole World [would be] under one Roof," even though it did not specify whether this ideal existence of peace was to be attained by war or example.[46] Even if a war was required to fulfill the Japanese destiny, the end result would be the emancipation of Asian peoples from western imperialist tyranny and the creation of a new order of peace and prosperity. Any war sanctioned by the Emperor would, by definition, be not only just but holy. "Japan was the incarnation of morality and

[44]Joseph Kitagawa, *Religion in Japanese History* (1966), 212; D.C. Holtom, *Modern Japan and Shinto Nationalism: A Study of Present-Day Trends in Japanese Religion* (1947), 55.
[45]Quoted in Meirion and Susie Harries, *Soldiers of the Sun: The Rise and Fall of the Imperial Japanese Army* (1991), 40; Helen Hardacre, *Shinto and the State 1868-1988* (1989), 123.
[46]Holtom, *Modern Japan and Shinto Nationalism (1938)*, 20.

justice; by definition its wars were just and it could never commit aggression."[47] The army was a visible manifestation of the Emperor's will, symbolized during the 1930s by Hirohito's public appearances in military uniform.

The shrine of the war dead reinforced State Shinto's cult of the Emperor. Before 1860 shrines for those killed in war provided a home for the restless spirits of the dead. This was transformed after the Meiji restoration into a cult where the souls of those killed in battle fighting for the Emperor became national deities or *Kami*. The state created the Yasukuni shrine at Tokyo as the place for dead warriors to be entombed. These *Kami* warriors supported and fought in advance of Japanese armies in the Emperor's wars. The Emperor on ceremonial occasions worshipped at the Tokyo shrine, informed the *Kami* there of significant events in the life of the nation (i.e., war, peace, victories, and birth of a prince), and asked for blessings. The Tokyo shrine for the dead became a popular place of pilgrimage visited by millions of school children because it symbolized the linkage between the Emperor, the army, and the nation in past and present. As such, in the early twentieth century the newly created cult of the war dead contributed to the glorification of the military and self-sacrifice in war. Dying for the Emperor was a victory. Soldiers entering into battles in the later stages of World War II in which they were virtually certain to die told each other that they would meet again at Yasukuni.[48]

V. Buddhism and Japanese Militarism

Before the Meiji restoration, Buddhism had been almost a state-sponsored religion with virtually the entire population considered as adherents. Now the reformers labeled Buddhism an alien import, and the government closed 40,000 temples and laicized monks, of whom 80,000 became the teachers of the Shinto-inspired Doctrinal Instruction. The response of leaders of all the major Japanese

---

[47]Herbert Bix, *Hirohito and the Making of Modern Japan* (2000), 326.
[48]Harries, 30; Haruoko Cook and Theodore Cook, *Japan at War: An Oral History* (1992), 324, 355.

Buddhist sects was to create a "New Buddhism" that would overcome its foreign origin by inculcating obedience to the Emperor and support of the government. Wars with China and Russia provided the opportunity for Buddhists to prove their worth. All the major sects provided chaplains for the military and rationalized the conquest of Formosa, Korea, and enclaves in China. Japan's conquests served to promote true Buddhist practice, and missionaries would aid in promoting civilization and rooting out corrupt religious emphases that had brought weakness to China. Allegedly, Japan's soldiers conquered China and Russia because their Buddhism instilled obedience and self-sacrifice, a willingness to die for a greater cause. The merit of Japanese soldiers and citizenry gained through Buddhist practice prompted the gods to give victory.

After 1912 until the end of World War II, no Buddhist sect would publicly oppose the government's military, domestic, or foreign policy in an organized way. Religious dissenters would be silenced either by the sectarian leaders or the government. Now Buddhist scholars proclaimed that Japan's wars were just in cause and conduct, expressions of compassion for the conquered peoples who needed their lives improved. Heavy casualties in Japan's army could be endured because fighting to the death was a way to repay a debt of gratitude to the Emperor and the Buddha. The Japanese army ought to be composed of *bodhisattvas* prepared to die to rescue the "Mongolian race" from Caucasian imperialism.[49]

As Japan prepared for war during the 1930s, Zen Buddhist scholars emphasized the compatibility between Zen and *bushido* (way of the warriors) as the embodiment of the spirit of Japan. Both required a belief in "emptiness," accepted self-sacrifice, emphasized a plain and frugal lifestyle, required self-reliance and activism, stressed the "here and now" rather than an afterlife, and

---

[49]Brian Victoria, *Zen at War* (1997), 30, 54. It should be noted that Christian churches in Japan, which had also been attacked as foreign, became equally supportive of the government and imperialism.

brought a life of active service to the Emperor and the empire.[50]   Buddhism guaranteed that all Japan's wars were "just" and killing within them was carried out by an army motivated by sympathy and compassion as a means to a blessed future.   As D. T. Suzuki wrote in a statement that reflected official policy: the sword killed and not the person who wielded it.

> The pillar of the Spirit of Japan is to be found in Bushido. Although Bushido employs the sword, its essence is not to kill people, but rather to use the sword that gives life to people. Using the spirit of this sword we wish to contribute to world peace. [51]

Schoolboys and soldiers learned the advantages of meditation as a way of instilling a samurai spirit.   A soldier's basic training included Zen meditation. *Bushido* became a goal not just for the military but for all Japanese citizens who must live austerely in a spirit of self-sacrifice and total obedience in order to serve the Emperor. In pre-war Japan any incompatibility between Buddhist practice and loyalty to the Emperor disappeared.   Imperial Way Buddhism rested upon the syllogism that the Emperor and the state were one, Buddhism and the state were one, and so Buddhism and the Emperor were one.   So Japan's war with America became a holy war and Avalokiteshvara, the *bodhisattva* of compassion, became a warrior with the rank of shogun.[52] Buddhism like Shintoism before and during the war became a way to build morale by ignoring Japan's very real industrial weaknesses and the poverty of much of the population and by insisting that the Yamoto spirit would bring victory.

---

[50]Ibid., 105.
[51]D. T. Suzuki, 145; the quotation is from the celebration of the Tripartite Pact, Victoria, 112.

VI. Shinto and Buddhism as a Cause of War

During World War II American propaganda blamed the war upon a Japanese fanaticism fed by a religious ideology. Today it is not easy to assess the importance of State Shinto in the creation of Japanese imperialism and fascism. The Emperor was a symbol of unity, but his prestige did not translate into direct political power, and the army did not always obey him and the Prime Minister. An oligarchy of well-educated men dependent upon an elected parliament or diet governed Japan. In theory the cabinet set all policy, but the army and navy even under the Meiji Emperor had become essentially self-governing, and right-wing military officers who played a major role in foreign policy, fomenting wars with China, assassinating political opponents, and attempting *coups d'état*. Actions of European states in creating empires in Southeast Asia and spheres of influence in China had more influence on Japan's early colonial conquests than the teachings of State Shinto. At this time the cult remained defensive, a sign of the government's weakness and insecurity against Britain, France, and Russia. The government built Shinto shrines in colonial possessions as a way of gaining loyalty of the subjects, but in all periods economics, not religion, determined the treatment of colonies. The policy followed in conquered lands of exploiting all for the benefit of Japan belied the slogan used against western imperialism , "Asia for Asians".

During the 1920s, State Shinto flourished at the same time that Japan supported collective security and the League of Nations. Debates in the cabinet on military policy centered around balance of power and the need for autarky if Japan were to become a major military power. Germany's defeat in World War I made the Japanese realize how vulnerable they were to a long war because the islands lacked essential raw materials - coal, steel, and oil. The desire for economic self-sufficiency, not emperor worship, drove Japan's expansion into Manchuria in 1929 and then into war with China in 1937.[53] The intellectuals who created

[52]Victoria, 142.
[53]Michael Barnhart, *Japan Prepares for Total War: The Search for Economic Security 1919-1941* (1987).

Japanese fascism cited European more often than Shinto sources. Yet unlike Nazis who used naked force against opponents, the Japanese Peace Laws, used to suppress criticism, rested upon communalism and a desire for order. Dissenters could be imprisoned for a time, but they were not executed and were instead re-educated or converted into supporters of Japan's unique destiny.[54] Conservative politicians who wanted to preserve the traditional moral order viewed with alarm the dominance of the army and navy in starting war first with China and then with the United States. The Emperor Hirohito's sole contribution to his cabinet's debate over war with the United States was to read aloud a poem about peace, but he did not disapprove of the final decision. Recently historians have documented that Hirohito knew and helped make crucial decisions before and during the war. The Japanese in the immediate aftermath suppressed information so that the Emperor would not be tried as a war criminal.[55]

State Shintoism's glorification of militarism and unquestioned obedience made it easier for Japanese leaders to lead the people to war. First person accounts show that belief in the Emperor's divine status reinforced the unquestioned obedience of civilians and draftees to the political-military system. The cult pervaded army life, but of course those who questioned the divinity of the Emperor did not dare to say so. State Shinto also imposed no ethic on correct practices in beginning or waging war or on the treatment of civilians or captured enemy soldiers. The ancient *bushido* or samurai ethos that allowed catching an enemy off guard could be adapted into justifying the surprise attack as occurred against Russia, China, Great Britain and the United States. The government officially repudiated the Laws of War in treating POW's in China, and used

[54]Richard Mitchell, *Thought Control in Prewar Japan* (1976), 183-193. William Miles Fletcher III, *The Search for a New Order: Intellectuals and Fascism in Prewar Japan* (1982), 5-6.
[55]Herbert Bix, *Hirohito and the Making of Modern Japan* (2000), 223, 329, 359, 398, 412, 419-24; Peter Wetzler, *Hirohito and War: Imperial Traditions and Military Decision Making in Pre-War Japan* (1998), stresses the complexity of decision-making and the difficulty of applying western concepts of monarchy to Japan; John Dower, *Japan and War and Peace* (1993), 337-349.

biological and chemical weapons there. The doctrine of Japanese racial superiority contributed to the contempt with which the military treated subject peoples.

By supporting unconditional obedience, State Shinto helped to steel the civilian population of Japan to bear severe deprivations even before 1941. Particularly in rural areas, the entire community encouraged young men to join the army or to submit to conscription. Shintoism served to maintain soldiers' morale and willingness to face a death in battle rather than the dishonor of surrender even in the face of overwhelming odds and defeat. So State Shinto made the Japanese army and navy a more effective fighting force.

The leaders' sense of Japan's destiny, their sense of the "Yamato (Japan) Spirit," that "true combat is army multiplied by fighting spirit,"[56] allowed them to overlook material weaknesses in their position. Yamato Spirit influenced military officers to believe that surprise attack, offensive capability and the alleged innate superiority of the Japanese troops outweighed having sufficient oil, planes, tanks, and guns to defeat an enemy. State Shinto also fostered the generals' and admirals' disregard for the human cost of their tactics for the Japanese and the enemy's soldiers and civilians. By making surrender unthinkable, the alliance of nationalism and State Shinto prolonged the war unnecessarily long after the Japanese high command knew defeat was inevitable. Even so, the power politics of fascist-admiring army leaders, not religion, caused Japan's involvement in World War II.

PART III

Peace or Freedom: The Pacifist Dilemma

After Hitler's rise to power, pacifists were less concerned with reform of the international order and more devoted to keeping their countries out of war, no matter what the price. In France, a new movement of *Integral* pacifists repudiated

---

[56] Cook, 210. Bix, *Hirohito and the Making of Modern Japan);* Wetzler, *Hirohito and War: Imperial Traditions and Military Decision Making in Pre War Japan.*

the conservative, internationalist, and Just War approach of the 1920s. The Integralists insisted that they would never fight in any war. They viewed World War I as the greatest of all evils, which should never be repeated. Germany was shamefully treated at Versailles, and Hitler, about whose regime they had no illusions, had legitimate grievances that needed to be addressed.

British intellectuals and governments used guilt over Versailles, a recognition of need for border rectification, and hope that meeting Germany's wants would lead to a more moderate policy in order to rationalize appeasement of Hitler's demands. Churchmen insisted that Just War theory allowed for conciliation of legitimate grievances to avoid war. Germany had lost colonies and had become, like Italy, a have-not nation. Mussolini's conquest of Abyssinia (Ethiopia) was like Britain's colonial conquests a generation before. Not much attention was paid to the Ethiopians, who some pacifists suggested should practice nonviolence.

French and British socialists sought to strengthen international sanctions, to keep Mussolini from joining Hitler, even at the price of allowing Italy's conquest of Ethiopia, and to avoid war at all costs. Because they believed that war was the greatest possible moral evil, that good results could not come from war, and that arms races caused wars, European politicians, leftists, and churchmen relied on Hitler's claims that he wanted peace and would be satisfied with just one more demand. The Nazi regime was odious, but then so was the Soviet Union, and one nation did not have the right to interfere with another's domestic policies. Countries had to do business with existing leaders, because the alternative was unthinkable. Those who might have been tempted to advocate preparedness faced indictments from two histories showing the too-ready support and chauvinism of the churches and intellectuals in World War I: Ray Abrams' *Preachers Present Arms* (1933) and Julien Benda's *Trahison des Clercs* (1927).

The American Federal Council of Churches' 1934 program for peace included abolition of aggressive weapons, no new naval construction, non-aggression pacts, and arms embargoes against aggressive nations. The pacifist

Catholic Worker and the liberal Protestant *Christian Century* agreed with this platform, arguing that modern warfare made traditional Just War doctrines obsolete. In 1936 clerical and lay delegates of a general conference of the Methodist Episcopal Church declared that they did not "endorse, support or propose to participate in war." When the Northern and Southern Methodists reunited in 1939, the church denounced war as "utterly destructive," "our greatest collective social sin and a denial of Christ's ideals," but it also condemned totalitarianism. Southern Presbyterians in 1936 denounced the arms race, advocated "true neutrality," and urged members to advocate peace to the government. Presbyterians had a long debate whether a war of defense could be justified. The Southern Baptists voted for resolutions condemning war and warmongering.[57]

Supported by pacifists in America, isolationists backed by the Roosevelt administration passed neutrality laws in 1935, 1936, and 1937 designed to prevent the sale of arms to anyone, if a state of war existed. (Roosevelt, arguing that neither Japan nor China had declared war, rationalized sending arms to China on that basis.) A large coalition of peace groups organized the Emergency Peace Campaign in 1937, circulated petitions supporting strict neutrality and non-involvement in any future European war, rejoiced when thousands of college students took the Oxford pledge not to fight for "king and country" in any future war, and advocated the Ludlow constitutional amendment which required a popular referendum on any decision to declare war. (A Gallup poll showed that 73% of the country supported the amendment.) Well aware of what Hitler stood for, pacifists worked with Jewish organizations and on their own, pressuring and even defying the U.S. State Department, to aid German and Austrian Jews. The small pacifist organizations in Britain and France found that their efforts to prevent war were supported by extreme right-wingers who sympathized with

---

[57] McCarthy, 169; Herman Will, *A Will for Peace: Peace Action in the United Methodist Church: A History* (1984), 54-55; Ewing, 8. Richard Nutt, *Toward Peacemaking: Presbyterians in the South and National Security* (1994), 22-23; Edward Queen, 59.

Nazi Germany. Hitler concluded that the reluctance of the liberal democracies to fight meant that he could pursue his expansionist plans with impunity.

Events of 1935-40 clarified that there were major differences between internationalists who advocated collective security and, if need be, self-defense, and "pacifists" who refused to support war of any kind and who defended their position as a moral and religious vision rather than as a pragmatic guide to creating a peaceful world. Europe's plunge towards war dealt a severe blow to religious, humanitarian, and utilitarian pacifists who trumpeted the power of love and good will and the fundamental decency of all people. The change in atmosphere was typified by two ecumenical conferences: one at Stockholm in 1925 and another at Oxford in 1937. At Stockholm the delegates optimistically talked about the power of love and building the Kingdom of God. At Oxford delegates from forty countries and virtually all churches, except the Roman Catholics (who declined to come) recognized the diversity of responses, with some Christians advocating pacifism, others reluctantly accepting war under the mandate of international law, and others willingly obeying the state if they could not determine that conflict was obviously evil. The conference voiced sympathy for their absent brethren suffering in the Soviet Union and Germany, and called for efforts to end racism and promote religious liberty. Reinhold Niebuhr's influence showed in the declaration that the Church was a vehicle for "grace and love," while the state's sphere was "the power of constraint, legal and physical."[58]

Reinhold Niebuhr (1892-1971), an American, led the theological attack upon pacifist sympathies of the liberal Protestants and created the movement termed "Christian Realism" that would define the Protestant debate on the churches and war from the late 1930s until the end of the Cold War. As a young pastor of the German Reformed Church, Niebuhr supported American participation in World War I, but as a theological liberal in the postwar reaction he became a pacifist and board member of the Fellowship of Reconciliation. His

---

[58]Oliver, 7.

experience as a minister in a church in Detroit supporting unionization against Henry Ford made him a socialist, but he also soon learned the dangers of communist infiltration of peace organizations. Appointed a professor at Union Theological Seminary in New York in 1928, Niebuhr pioneered the field of Applied Christianity or Christian Social Ethics. In the late 1920s, Niebuhr began criticizing Modernist theologians and liberal pacifists not over international war, but over the necessity of violence to break the hold of capitalist classes. Niebuhr added an awareness of evil to the liberals' quest to bring Christianity into harmony with modern thought by making biblical insights relevant to politics.

Niebuhr, like the liberals, applied historical-critical standards to the *Bible*, seeing doctrines like original sin through Adam's fall not as literal events but as expressing through myth the fundamentally flawed nature of humans. The prophets condemned the tendency of nations to magnify their virtues into idolatry. The incarnation and resurrection illustrated the eventual triumph of God's truth, but Niebuhr, like Augustine, saw the perfection of the City of God as beyond this life. Recognizing that pure love uncorrupted by selfishness was unattainable, he sought an ethic that was "realistic about power, committed to justice, sensitive to traditional loyalties, and humbly aware of its own temptation to self-righteousness."[59]

In *Moral Man and Immoral Society* (1932) Niebuhr argued that the moral attainments of an individual and state differed. A person could operate by love and self-sacrifice, but a state could not risk annihilation, and its highest moral achievement was a rough justice. Coercion by a state was not immoral, but a necessary and inevitable ingredient that could not be eschewed in favor of a sentimental Christian love. The goal of a Christian realism was to utilize power, but to use as little violence as possible in obtaining justice.

Niebuhr charged pacifists with distorting Christianity by ignoring the paradoxical nature of man as a creature of sin as well as goodness. All human

---

[59]Richard Fox, *Reinhold Niebuhr: A Biography* (1987), 170.

activities, he insisted, are tainted by the human will to pride, an unwillingness to accept limits. The pacifists, claimed Niebuhr, naïvely thought that Christian love could overcome sin and could create the Kingdom of God on earth. This heresy derived from political ideology, not the gospel, which had a more pessimistic understanding of the possibility of human goodness. (Communism was also guilty of overvaluing human merit.) So even genuine human accomplishments were inevitably tainted by pride. God's grace was not just an enabling power to overcome sin, as Modernists assumed, but was a redemptive and forgiving action.

Niebuhr insisted that an individual Christian might imitate the self-sacrificing love of Christ, but such love could not serve as a guide to political action. Jesus was an eschatological prophet calling people to repent, not a political theorist or advocate of nonviolence. There was nothing holy or moral about nonviolent resistance; it was just another method of coercion and one with limited efficacy when opposing a totalitarian regime. Christian realism valued pacifism as a model of sacrificial love (but not as political advice), valued Just War theory for upholding a universal moral order (though natural law theories tended to sanctify the status quo), and valued realpolitik for recognizing the need for power (but it ignored the moral element in humans and society). None, however, provided a sufficient guide to politics. Niebuhr advocated combining the best of all three, but accepted the inevitability of getting dirty hands in politics while working for but never obtaining justice.[60]

By 1935 Niebuhr became the spokesman for those who believed Nazism must be opposed by political power, even military force if necessary. War was a scourge, but not stopping totalitarianism was worse, a betrayal of Christian responsibility for those in need. From his position at Union Seminary, a frequent preacher on college campuses, prolific writer for leading magazines and as a contributor to a new magazine *Christianity and Crisis*, Niebuhr helped change the debate on foreign policy within the churches and the nation by seeking repeal of

---

[60]*Reinhold Niebuhr on Politics*, ed. Harry Davis and Robert Good (1960) chs. 6, 7, 13, 14, 20, 21. Donald Meyer, *The Protestant Search For Political Realism, 1919-1941* (1961).

neutrality legislation, support for military preparedness, and aid for the European democracies and China. To Americans who found political pacifism lacking, Christian Realism offered a chastened liberalism that seemed politically relevant to a world of totalitarian menace.

Critics charged that Niebuhr's paradoxical world gave no role in human history to the salvic role of Jesus or the Church. Did not mythologizing Adam, the incarnation, and the resurrection distort Christian theology as much as the optimism of liberal pacifists? Was history just a series of events with no progress, and was the only hope for redemption in the next world? Christian pacifists insisted that Niebuhr's realism was unduly pessimistic; humanists wondered whether adding Christianity to his analysis of politics really clarified the nature of moral action more than pragmatism or utilitarianism. A. J. Muste - socialist, pacifist, and labor organizer - accused Niebuhr of denying the possibility of religious experience to transform an individual. G. H. C. MacGregor's *The New Testament Basis of Pacifism* (1936) saw Niebuhr as more indebted to Luther and Augustine's view of the state than the New Testament.[61] Christian Realism undermined political pacifists far more than it weakened religious absolutists.

In 1938 British Prime Minister Neville Chamberlain flew to Munich to meet Hitler's latest demand, the incorporation of Sudetenland into Germany by dismembering Czechoslovakia. Hitler proclaimed that now he was satisfied and peace would be preserved. In England, the Archbishop of Canterbury compared Chamberlain with Jesus Christ as a great peacemaker, a judgment echoed by pacifists, Just War theorists, politicians, and leading newspapers. Niebuhr was outraged, arguing along with Churchill that appeasement only strengthened Hitler and would make the coming war more difficult. Just in case, Britain, France, and the United States began arming. Shortly thereafter, Germany occupied the rest of Czechoslovakia (Hitler's first conquest of non-Germans) and signed a non-aggression pact with the Soviet Union. No longer could the democracies assume

---

[61] *Essays of A. J. Muste*, ed. by Nat Hentoff (1967) delineates the controversies between Niebuhr and pacifists in chapters XVI - XVII.

that righting the wrongs of Versailles would appease Hitler and bring peace. Eleven months after Munich, Hitler invaded Poland in August 1939, and Britain and France declared war.

XVI.
World War II: The Apotheosis of Barbarity

In sheer brutality, World War II exceeded any previous conflict. Before ending, it caused the deaths of twice as many soldiers as were killed in World War I, and at least twice as many civilian fatalities as soldiers. Estimates of total deaths range from 30 to 50 million, an enormous disparity that results from the impossibility of knowing how many millions died in China and the Soviet Union. Eventually all but six independent nations were at war, and at least three of the neutral states - Spain, Switzerland, and Sweden - profited greatly by selling supplies to belligerents. In essence there were two linked but separate conflicts - a German war for hegemony in Europe and a Japanese struggle for dominance in East Asia. In spite of their contrasting racisms, Japan and Germany were allies. They joined for convenience against their common enemies of France, Britain, and later the United States and Soviet Union (even though Japan and Russia maintained an uneasy non-aggression pact until 1945). Hitler, who disdained "Orientals," disliked Japan's initial victories over white European Aryans, and Japan exalted its own racial purity.[1] Only Germany practiced genocide.

Unlike World War I with its static trench lines, World War II was fought over much of the globe. The geographic scope of the land war resulting from the increased mobility of armies meant that civilians could not escape the path of destruction. To make matters worse for non-combatants, the Japanese army in northern China and the German army on the Eastern front deliberately targeted civilians, and the scorched-earth policy followed by Germans and Russians as they advanced and retreated left millions to starve.

Added to the primary weapons of World War I - artillery, machine guns, battleships, and submarines - were motorized divisions of tanks and armored guns, aircraft carriers, radar-equipped bombers and fighter planes, flamethrowers and bazookas, and two atomic bombs. This war required the total mobilization of nations to supply the one billion people who served in armed forces whose battles consumed prodigious quantities of planes, guns, and ammunition. Russia produced over 100,000 planes, an equal number of tanks, and 175,000 artillery pieces, two-thirds of which were destroyed in the war. Germany built 189,000 military aircraft; the U.S., 325,000. The Allies made 4.7 million machine guns; the Axis and Japan one million. Hitler's *blitzkreig* (lightning-war) victories in Poland and France used the speed of a tank attack supported by fighter planes and followed up by motorized infantry. By the end of the war the Allies, having produced three million military trucks and lorries, were more mobile than Germany; the Axis and Japan built 595,000.[2]

Religious institutions played a minor role in the conflict. Allied leaders and politicians did not consult with church leaders on major policy issues, including the decision to drop the atomic bomb. Religion will be our primary focus only in the sections on U.S. intervention, the churches' response to the fighting, and the Vatican's response to the Holocaust. A strong moral condemnation of the acts of Germany and Japan based upon Just War theories and international law accompanied the marginalization of organized religion in Europe and America. Religion's impact on the war came through this moral debate that is our main focus.

This chapter will consider a few selected aspects of the war in which, at the time or later, religious institutions and ethical evaluations played a role: the Eastern front, the debate in America's churches over U.S. policy and their interpretation of the war, the treatment of conscientious objectors, the Holocaust, the role of the Vatican, the Japanese-American war, and finally saturation bombing in Europe and Japan and the dropping of the atomic bomb. The diversity of

---

[1]John Dower, *War Without Mercy: Race and Power in the Pacific War* (1986), 378.
[2]Gwen Dyer, *War* (1985), 89; John Ellis, *World War II: A Statistical Survey* (1993), 277-78; "Remembering World War II," *Washington Post*, July 26, 1995, H3, H7.

topics reflects the enormous impact of the war. The events described in this chapter require us to ask whether the religious traditions of justice in the conduct of war could be applied in any meaningful sense to modern, industrialized total war.

I. The Eastern Front

In 1939 Hitler professed his desire for peace as the best option, but only if he could fulfill his aims by other nations' policies of appeasement. Nazi and Fascist propaganda glorified armed might and welcomed war as the ultimate test of a people's will to power. Few doubted that this war was to repel Nazi aggression because no one outside of the Axis took seriously Germany's propaganda about its defensive reaction to Poland's instigating the war just five days after a German-Soviet pact. Hitler and Stalin divided Poland, and Russia gained a free hand in the Baltic States and Finland. The German invasion and conquest of Poland in September 1939 took only eight weeks and cost 245,000 casualties from both sides, but the total number of Polish deaths would be over six million, about half Christians and half Jews, and 90% of these deaths would not be in war.

Hitler saw Poles, Russians, and other Slavs as *Untermenschen* (subhuman), and on August 22, 1939 he authorized killing "without pity or mercy all men, women, and children of Polish descent or language. Only in this way can we obtain the living space we need." The American ambassador reported that German strategy was "to terrorize the civilian population and to reduce the number of child bearing Poles irrespective of category."[3]

Ultimately, the Germans in an attempt to make Poland an intellectual desert would kill 45% of the physicians and 40% of the professors. Overall about 18% of Roman Catholic clergy (1,811) died, but in the area of Poland seen as an integral part of the Reich, roughly following the pre-World War I Curzon line, nearly 40% of Catholic clergy were killed. Here a priest who preached or heard confession in Polish could be executed. The SS troops and Einsatzgruppen

---

[3] Richard Lukas, *Forgotten Holocaust: The Poles Under German Occupation 1939-1944* (1986), 2-4.

(special killing squads) carried out the most brutal acts, shooting children or unarmed civilians, but the Wehrmacht also participated in the atrocities. The argument made after the war that the special forces and not the army committed the atrocities is untrue. The Nazi leaders learned in Poland that the army would resist no order, no matter how cruel; such knowledge allowed the Nazi leaders to plan strategy in the Russian campaign and later the "Final Solution" for the Jews.

Poland also served as a test for the German policy of reprisals against those who resisted occupation. Polish resistance remained strong, with only about 8,000 collaborators out of a population of more than 20 million; enough Poles fled the country so that ultimately more Poles than French fought in the Allied armies. In Poland guerrilla fighters, so called "francs-tireurs" whose status in international law had never been formalized, attacked isolated Nazi soldiers and assassinated officials, killing 150,000 Germans during the war. In response the Germans began a practice of reprisals, with the official policy requiring killing ten Poles for every German, but in actuality sometimes increasing the number to 100 to one.[4] Reprisals were also used in the Balkans. When a Czech assassinated Reinhard Heydrich, head of the security police, in 1942 the Germans destroyed the village of Lidice. Against the advice of the British who saw no reason to risk civilian lives, partisans who wore no military insignia in Poland and Yugoslavia continued to attack Germans, because to stop would appear to acquiesce to German rule.

Hitler instructed his officers to observe the laws of war regarding civilians on the Western but not on the Eastern Front.[5] French partisans remained quiescent after the fall of France until 1944 when they saw a chance to aid the Allies preparing to invade. When the Germans shot as bandits eighty captured

---

[4]Ibid., 9, 13, 14, 35, 87, 93. The systematic killing of Polish Jews did not begin until thirty months after the invasion, but then was carried out with industrialized efficiency. For a brief discussion of the controversies over Polish anti-Semitism and the tendency of Poles to focus on their nation's survival and to ignore or in some instances to betray the Jews, see Michael Marrus, *The Holocaust in History* (1987), 96-99. "Soul Searching at Another Polish Massacre Site," *New York Times*, April 19, 2001, A3 on the killing of Jews by Poles in August, 1941.

Free French partisans wearing insignia, the French executed eighty German prisoners of war as a reprisal. This action had the desired effects, and the Germans began treating French partisans as POWs.[6]

There were atrocities in the West but they occurred on a smaller scale and less often as a matter of policy than in the East. The difference can be illustrated by the survival rates of prisoners of war; the western Allies had a mortality rate in German POW camps (that were visited by the Red Cross) of 4%; of the 3.5 million Soviet prisoners taken in 1941 when Germany was winning the war at least 2 million died by February, 1942, a rate of 60%.[7] Such a mortality rate, substantially higher than in Soviet or Japanese camps where there was often insufficient food, was not caused by unplanned shortages or a breakdown of order.

The Nazi leaders deliberately embarked upon a campaign of starvation and brutalization of Soviet prisoners of war. The German army systematically stripped eastern Russia of food, which was used for the Germany army or shipped to the Reich, a policy designed to starve Russian civilians. An Italian officer on the Eastern Front described the German treatment of a large group of Soviet POWs. Saying that intellectuals would have better jobs, the police asked for all those who could read to hold up their hands. These they shot.[8] German troops labeled Soviet partisans operating behind the lines bandits and in response to attacks executed large numbers of hostages (mostly old men, women and children) and obliterated whole villages. And the troops made little effort to insure that the village had any responsibility for or could have restrained partisan attacks. The systematic cruelty of the Germans alienated Ukrainians and Russian

---

[5]On the stockpiling of chemical and biological weapons and the reasons they were not used, see Gerhard Weinberg, *A World at Arms: a Global History of World War II* (1984), 558-60, 691.

[6]Michael Walzer, *Just and Unjust Wars: A Moral Argument with Historical Illustrations* (1977), 208-09. The issues of the responses of various subjected populations to the Nazis should be seen in the context of the German use of reprisals against families or whole communities.

[7]Theo Schulte, *The German Army and Nazi Policies in Occupied Russia* (1989), 181, 203; Omer Bartov, *The Eastern Front 1941-1945: German Troops and the Barbarisation of Warfare* (1986), 27, 29.

[8]Curzio Malaparte, *Kaputt* (1946); Bartov, 4.

Orthodox Christians who had no loyalty to Stalin and might have been enlisted for the German cause.

In Russia, as in Poland, the regular army in cooperation with the Einsatzgruppen and SS troops carried out the violations of the rules of war and of anything like civilized behavior. After a few officers protested that the slaughter increased the animosity of other Russians, the Germans eased the policy of extermination of POWs and peasants in 1942. No one, including chaplains accompanying the army, raised humanitarian objections. Historians ponder how the Wehrmacht, traditionally so dedicated to professionalism and honor, could have acted so cruelly. One answer is that the army officers and their men, most of whom came of age under the Nazis, accepted the racist ideology of Hitler, who insisted that the enemy was not a soldier, but an animal. Nazi newspapers and films, the only source of information for soldiers on the Eastern Front, portrayed the Soviet Union as dominated by Bolsheviks and Jews who should be exterminated. After the elimination of Communist Party members and intellectuals, Russian Slavs, a barbarous "Asiatic horde," were to become a subject people to provide labor for the German masters. Conditions in Russia brutalized German officers and conscripts who were fighting far from home in a savage war. They endured bombardments for long periods with no relief and little prospect for surviving and gained information only from Nazi propaganda tirades against "Judeo-Bolshevik culture."[9]

There was no respite for Soviet citizens from their own government; at the beginning of the war, Stalin unleashed a purge of German-speaking Ukrainians and alleged opponents of his regime during which Beria's secret police killed additional millions.

The Eastern Front bore the brunt of the fighting from 1941 until 1945, and even after D-Day, the Germans had 179 divisions in the East as compared with 62

---

[9] Bartov, 64-66, 104. Doris Bergen, "Between God and Hitler: German Military Chaplains and the Crimes of the Third Reich," in Omer Bartov and Phyllis Mack, eds. in *In God's Name: Genocide and Religion in the Twentieth Century* (2001), 123-38.

in France.[10] The battles in the East were constant, savage, and merciless on both sides, with a major siege of 950 days at Leningrad and another at Stalingrad, and civilian starvation in both. The Soviets took their revenge on German prisoners of war after Stalingrad and on civilians as their armies pushed toward Berlin in 1945.

II. America's Churches Debate Intervention

Hitler's and Stalin's carving up of Poland in 1939 disgusted Americans. Catholics saw Poland taken over by "atheistic hordes" and likened it to a new Calvary, but showed no inclination to intervene. *America*, a Catholic journal, polled its readers and students at 182 Catholic colleges and found that 97% of students and 95% of readers opposed U.S. intervention and 35% of students and 62% of readers would be COs. These figures showing the impact of the peace movement upon lay Catholics are extraordinarily high because, except for the small Catholic Worker movement, the Church officially endorsed Just War doctrines, disapproved of COs, and took no position on the war. In essence, American Catholics shared the views of other Americans. A Gallup poll found 93% of Americans opposed intervention. As late as April 1941, 81% favored staying out of the war, and at no time before Pearl Harbor on December 7, 1941 did a majority of Americans tell pollsters that they favored going to war.[11]

Peace sentiment remained dominant among religious groups so long as the issue remained focused on Christianity against war. Virtually all Protestant churches insisted that war was unchristian, and against the love exemplified by Jesus. War was also an irrational response to economic and political issues and, as World War I proved, created more problems than it solved. There was no reason to assume that a second victory by Britain and France would be better than their

---

[10]Ellis, 178, 184. The Americans concluded that a soldier could be in combat no more than 88 days without serious battle fatigue or shell shock. One can barely imagine the cost on both German and Soviet soldiers for the months of combat on the Eastern Front. John Appel, "My Brush with History," *American Heritage* (Oct 1999), 28. The sieges of Soviet cities took more civilian lives than the saturation bombing campaigns.

[11]The Gallup Poll, *Public Opinion 1935-1941* (1972), I, Jan. 12, 1939; Sept. 23, 1939; October 5, 1939; May 4, 1941, 222-223, 243, 279, 300; McCarthy, 184-185, 194. The polls show a shift in favoring more aid to Britain and consistently high negative ratings of Germany. By Oct. 5, 70% said it was more important for Germany to be defeated than to keep out of the war.

earlier triumph. No one approved of Hitler, but initially prominent pacifists, like Harry Emerson Fosdick of New York's Riverside Church, insisted that the moral differences between Germany and colonial powers like Britain, France, and Italy were not so significant as to require America's involvement in an immoral war. World War I exposed the frailties of American democracy; a second war might so increase intolerance and militarism that U.S. freedoms would evaporate. Like the Pope, the American churches sought for a negotiated settlement and believed that the U.S. would have more influence as a non-belligerent. Nonintervention became the position of the Protestant churches and the political isolationists who advocated leaving European problems to the warring parties.

The fall of France in the summer of 1940 and Battle of Britain shifted the nature of the debate. Now for many Americans the issue was not war or peace, but war or the triumph of Nazi Germany. Internationalists concluded that staying out of the war was no longer an option. There would be a stark future for American democracy in a world dominated by Germany and Japan. Policy issues would be decided upon national security rather than theological grounds, but theology still determined how religious leaders defined the national interest. Protestants who in the mid-30s called themselves pacifists because for pragmatic reasons they supported the League of Nations, international reform, and disarmament now had to decide whether war or totalitarianism was the greater moral evil.

Critics charged that the pacifist belief that all the warring powers in Europe were equally guilty was intellectually irresponsible, imposing an impossible personal standard of moral purity on nations. Britain's democracy and empire were not the moral equivalent of Hitler's dictatorship and aggressive war. All now agreed that whatever the faults of the Versailles Treaty and the moral failures of Britain and the U.S., these conditions paled in contrast with Nazi evil.

Beginning in October 1939 and gathering momentum up until December 1941, the Protestant churches debated whether Augustine and Niebuhr were right that Christian love could involve intervention to protect one's neighbors threatened by tyranny. Was isolation as a means of preserving freedom in America a Christian response to events in Asia and Europe or was it an abdication of Christian duty to work and perhaps even risk war for a suffering neighbor? The political debate was not over America's direct involvement in the war - only a few organizations and no churches publicly advocated this - but on support for President Roosevelt's policies of aid to China and Britain, an economic embargo on Japan, building America's military might, and peacetime conscription. Would becoming "the arsenal of democracy" involve America in war or preserve America from war by preventing Britain and China from being conquered?

For the churches, politics was less important than first principles: was the gospel compatible with war? In the 30s the answer from virtually all Protestants was no. Seeking to avoid the mistakes of World War I, churches warned against government propaganda, false atrocity stories, and military aid to the Allies. The *Christian Century*, devoted to liberal theology and social reform, decried the falling away of inconsistent pacifists and opposed Roosevelt's lend-lease policy of furnishing destroyers to the British. Its editor accused Roosevelt of camouflaging his desire to involve America in war (which was true) and of aiming at becoming a dictator (which was ridiculous).

Within the Catholic Church, the divisions were essentially the same as among Protestants. The editor of the Jesuit periodical *America* was an isolationist and very distrustful of Roosevelt. More sympathetic to the President's positions on rearmament and aid to allies were the liberal *Commonweal* and the most influential Catholic organization on foreign policy issues, the National Catholic Welfare Council. Representing the pacifist minority, the *Catholic Worker* opposed American intervention and rearmament.

Although they had made statements against war in the 1930s, Southern Baptists and Southern Presbyterians in 1940 endorsed the legitimacy of defensive or Just Wars and by 1941 the Baptists declared, "We hold it were better to be dead than to live in a world dominated by the ideals of modern dictators."[12] In the South, politically conservative evangelicals and fundamentalists who had long opposed Modernist theology and Social Gospel reform now linked the peace movement with both and accused it of being unpatriotic, a betrayal of church and country.

The Northern branches of Presbyterians, Baptists, and Congregationalists engaged in an agonizing debate over the legitimacy of defensive war. In 1940 Presbyterians, unable to agree on a common policy, recognized that "good and honest men differ violently upon what is the right and Christian thing to do," and Congregationalists printed the arguments of those who accepted the necessity of defensive war and others who insisted upon strict pacifism as a Christian imperative. Although in 1940 it defeated a resolution about approving defensive war and affirmed that the Methodist Church "will not officially endorse, support, or participate in war," the Methodist General Conference statement restricted its applicability to the church as a church (i.e., not as a guide to politics) and claimed no "attempt to bind the conscience of its individual members."[13] Still the Methodist Youth Fellowship, a commission on social affairs, and the leading Methodist periodical continued to issue strong anti-war statements. A poll in late 1941 shows the limited influence of the churches on war. Asking whether the clergy should even be discussing the war (not taking a position for or against intervention), 59% of Catholics and 54% of Protestants said, No.[14]

III. American Churches in the War

The Japanese attack on Pearl Harbor and Hitler's decision to declare war on the U.S. ended the debate, and polls indicated that 96% of Americans supported going to war. All the churches supported the government and sought to do their duty, but they resisted any attempt to make the struggle into a holy

---

[12]Gerald Sittser, *A Cautious Patriotism: The American Churches and the Second World War* (1977), 48.
[13]William Orser, "The Social Attitudes of the Protestant Churches During the Second World War," Ph.D. diss., University of New Mexico (1969). 94-95.
[14]The Gallup Poll, *Public Opinion 1935-1941*, I, 308.

cause. The Methodist bishops in 1942 professed "unreserved support for the war" even though war is "un-Christlike." The churches sought to minister to their boys in the service, but there would be no identification of America's aims with those of the church. In 1944 the Northern Baptist Convention first approved and then deleted a declaration that "God has a stake in this war," and its final statement was carefully worded: "We do not pray for man's mere triumph over his brother man . . . We will not bless war, but we will not withhold our blessing from our sons who fight and from our country's cause." The Methodist General Conference in 1944 expressed "its moral force against tyranny, aggression, persecution, and all the forms of political dictatorship and totalitarianism" and commended "our cause" to God. Those wanting the Methodists to approve the use of force and to pray for victory amended this declaration that they said had been written by pacifists, to say, "God himself has a stake in the struggle." The lay delegates approved overwhelmingly (233-133), but the ministers split evenly (170-169).[15]

Although all denominations and most ministers supported the war effort, there were prominent pacifists - bishops in the Episcopal and Methodist churches, theologians and church historians including Georgia Harkness and Kenneth Scott Lattourette and Roland Bainton, and famous radio preachers who served in large metropolitan churches like Ralph Sockman, Ernest Freemont Tittle, and Harry Emerson Fosdick. Denominational declarations reflected a continuing debate on Christianity and war, although pacifism was largely confined to the clergy. The Protestant churches found a method of maintaining unity by focusing on planning for the peace.

A recent study of the responses of the American churches to World War II is entitled "Cautious Patriotism." That is, the churches supported the war effort as a defense of democracy. Democracy guaranteed the freedom of religion and totalitarianism threatened religion, and so World War II was a necessary but not a

---

[15]E. Keith Ewing, *The Pacifist Movement in the Methodist Church during World War II*, 1982, 128; Osner, 129-132.

holy war. One exception was New York's Archbishop Francis Spellman who described the Japanese attack: "With fire and brimstone came December 7 ... America's throat was clutched, her back was stabbed, her brain was stunned; but her great heart still throbbed ... America began the fight to save her life." More typical was a November 1942 official statement by the Catholic bishops supporting as a "positive duty" waging this war in "defense of life and right."[16] As in World War I, Catholic periodicals published statistics to show that Catholic boys contributed to the war effort. Since for America the war was defensive and the nation had passed a law mandating conscription, there was no right to be a Catholic conscientious objector.

The churches saw in the war the opportunity to evangelize and to show their patriotism. They furnished 10,000 chaplains, staffed canteens for soldiers, and provided additional services to the vastly increased populations in cities with major defense industries. Church members grew victory gardens, bought war bonds, and sought to support families whose sons served in the army. In sermons and tracts, preachers insisted that freedom was worth fighting and dying for. But the churches resisted a campaign of hate by distinguishing between German leaders and the people, and attempted, with little success because they knew less, to do the same for the Japanese.

When the American government decided to resettle 110,000 Japanese living in California, the churches provided an undertow of reservations at first that, within a year, became a formal denunciation by leading religious periodicals and the Federal Council of Churches. A war fought for civil rights should not result in the denial of liberties at home. Spokesmen contrasted the treatment of Japanese Americans in Hawaii, where there was no internment, with the inhumane

[16]Gerald Sittser, *A Cautious Patriotism: The American Churches and the Second World War*; Lawrence Wittner, *Rebels Against War: The American Peace Movement 1941-1960* (1969), 36; National Conference of Catholic Bishops, *In the Name of Peace: Collective Statements of the US Catholic Bishops on War and Peace, 1919-1980* (1983). 7-8

conditions in California. At the same time, many California churches took the initiative in trying to make the resettlement process humane.

The churches, Northern and Southern, denounced anti-Semitism and Nazi racism and complained about the hypocrisy in the rigid discrimination practiced in the Armed Forces. How, they asked, could the U.S. denounce German racism while practicing racism at home? Racism was a sin, but, of course, the churches, North and South, remained segregated.

The careful rhetoric of the church on war stemmed from four sources: memories of World War I and its aftermath, a tradition of attempts at peacemaking in the 1920s and 30s, an ecumenical movement in America seeking to preserve a relationship with churches in Germany, and a recognition that the churches would need to play a vital role in rebuilding relationships in Europe if a peace were to be preserved. The restrained nature of the churches' pronouncements on the war brought hostile editorials in two national magazines, *Fortune* and *Time*, which accused religious leaders of not supporting the country. The restrained nature of church rhetoric stands out when contrasted with the jingoism and racism exhibited by the national press. Churches made few comments on America's conduct of the war or the weapons used, but did regularly pray for the men in service. An analysis of Catholic writing found little use of Just War concepts on any subject and a total absence of evaluating American conduct in the waging of the war. American Catholic periodicals designed for instructing priests in pastoral matters generally managed to ignore the war. Religious periodicals worried about the effect of the war on religious life of men and women, and some chaplains refused to issue the ration cards for whiskey or to instruct the men in the use of contraceptives. In general, the chaplains had a good press, the most famous incident occurring when the ship Dorchester was torpedoed. After helping the men get into lifeboats, four chaplains (Protestant, Catholic, and Jewish) gave up their lifejackets to four sailors and, while linking arms and praying, perished as the boat sank.

IV. The Pacifist Minority

Britain and the U.S. were the only belligerent countries that recognized a right of conscientious objection. In Britain there were 60,000 COs, four times as many as in World War I. Conscripted pacifists, virtually all of whom accepted alternative service as a way of proving their humanitarian motivation, did not experience the former kind of official harassment and only 3% ended in prison as against 30% in 1914-1918.[17] Peace organizations continued to publish newsletters and maintained a core of membership. British pacifists divided between those who withdrew from open opposition to the state because their emphasis was religious and sectarian and others who were secular, aggressive, and willing to confront the government. The individualism of most pacifists meant that they were not easily organized for any collective action.

American pacifism went from being a mass movement in the 1930s to being an isolated minority in World War II. Initially, the membership of all major peace organizations shrank drastically, though by the end of the war the religiously based Fellowship of Reconciliation had more than recouped. America had fewer COs than England, 43,000 out of 10 million drafted, but a slightly larger percentage (.42% vs. .14%) than in WWI.[18] Most conscientious objectors came from pacifist churches like the Brethren, Mennonites, and Quakers, with a small number of Jews, Catholics, and liberal Protestants, and even fewer political radicals including socialists and anarchists. There were almost no racial minorities and working class men and women among COs; most non-Amish pacifists were middle class and college educated.[19]

Even before the war, the three self-described Historic Peace Churches (Quakers, Brethren, and Mennonites) supported by major mainline denominations sought to work out an arrangement with the U.S. government over the rights of conscientious objectors. They sought unsuccessfully to expand the definition of

---

[17]Ceadel, 302.
[18]Wittner, 41.

pacifism so that those who were not members of the Peace Churches or whose pacifism was secular could qualify. The Federal Council of Churches sought to ensure the civil rights of COs throughout the war. The Peace Churches sought opportunities for young men to work overseas doing social welfare as they had done in World War I. Believing that COs must not receive special privileges because they might be draft dodgers, Roosevelt insisted in vesting overall authority in Selective Service. Congress barred any overseas work and authorized the creation of Civilian Public Service Camps that would be paid for and supervised by pacifist churches. Although the COs worked full time, they received no pay and no benefits, and voluntary contributions paid their expenses. The government located the 133 camps in isolated areas so that the general public, which proved to be hostile to pacifists, would not be contaminated by anti-war feelings. The COs wanted to do work of national importance, but the government confined their duties to conservation work, caring for patients in mental hospitals, and - with their consent - conducted medical experiments in which they experienced semi-starvation, extreme heat and thirst, and were infected with malaria, typhus, and pneumonia. They received no compensation from the government in case of permanent injury or even recognition of their service.

Neither Selective Service, the peace churches, nor the men were happy with the arrangements. The War Department thought the men were coddled and should be better disciplined; the peace churches chafed at having to operate under the military; the men, particularly those with wives and children, disliked providing free labor to the government and thought much of the work a waste of time. Some staged non-cooperation revolts or left the camps to become absolutists, even though it meant jail. More pacifists in the Second than in the First World War (6086 vs. 450) spent time in prison.

---

[19]Jehovah's Witnesses were also pacifists (although they do not use this term), but they refused to accept the government's right to force them to join CPS camps.

V. The Holocaust

Hitler in *Mein Kampf* (1924) had proclaimed a "Jewish problem," and persecution of the Jews commenced with the founding of the Third Reich. Emigration reduced the Jewish population in Germany by more than half so that in 1939 there were around 250,000 remaining, a negligible percentage of the population. So, in spite of the reluctance of nations to receive German Jews before 1939, the numbers seeking asylum were few as compared with earlier European migrations. The conquest of Poland and eastern Russia, which together had over 4 million Jews, allowed Hitler to decide in 1942 to exterminate all Jews.[20]

In one sense the Final Solution is a separate topic from the ethics of war, for the torture and murder "took place independent of military operations."[21] To build and operate 10,005 concentration camps in Germany (there were 4 in 1936) and occupied territories and to engage in the roundup of Jews took thousands of men away from direct war efforts. Building railways to the camps and using fuel and rolling stock to transport Jews also hampered moving war supplies. Killing millions when Germany desperately needed labor for factories, farms, and army was militarily stupid. The Final Solution represented the triumph of racist ideology over military strategy.

The Holocaust should be discussed in a book on religion and war because it was instituted in 1942 in the midst of the war, made possible by conquests, and could not have occurred without the increased totalitarian control during the war. In essence, one of Hitler's war aims became the elimination of all Jews. The Holocaust could be implemented because the German people and churches had not protested against persecution of the socialists, communists, liberal democrats and Jews before the war. By 1942, the SS and Wehrmacht had already been so

---

[20]Arno Mayer, *Why Did the Heavens Not Darken?: The "Final Solution" in History* (1988), 128, 160, 208, 212, 216-17. Even though no direct order from Hitler for the extermination of the Jews has been found, evidence is overwhelming that the initiative came from him. An excellent introduction to the different theories of the Holocaust - locating responsibility in German history, the nature of fascism, or totalitarian governments - is in Saul Friedlander, "From Anti-Semitism to Extermination," in *Unanswered Questions: Nazi Germany and the Genocide of the Jews*, ed. Francois Furet (1989), 3-32.

barbarized by the German way of fighting on the Eastern Front that they could be relied upon to carry out mass executions. Originally the SS and army shot Jews. Seeking to relieve the psychological burden on the soldiers and the SS, the Nazis built gas chambers and crematoriums, essentially factories for death.

Hitler's anti-Semitism found receptive hearers because Germany had a flourishing tradition of religious bigotry. Anti-Semitism has such a long history within Christianity that it can almost be considered as integral to the religion, or at least a constantly recurring heresy. Passages in the New Testament like "His [Jesus'] blood be on us and on our children" (Matthew 27:25) were often interpreted as defining Jews as Christ-killers. Scholars have found a plethora of anti-Semitic statements made by high-ranking German Catholics and Protestants in the years before and after 1933. But there were theological limits upon Christian anti-Semitism because Jesus and his disciples were Jews, and the *Bible* declared that all people were of one blood. Also, the liturgy made all persons sinners who were in a sense responsible for Christ's death, and everyone needed forgiveness and grace. So churches outside of Germany during the 1930s regularly denounced Hitler's anti-Semitism.

Hitler detested Christianity's Jewish origins, opposed its emphasis on love and peace, and sought to substitute a religion of the German Volk. Hitler's anti-Jewish hatred derived from his extreme nationalism which sought to make all Germans alike and the nineteenth-century pseudo-science of classifying races, but his labeling of the Jews as evil found a sympathetic response from many within the churches. Prominent biblical scholars distinguished between early Judaism whose teachings Jesus echoed, and contemporary Jews who as bearers of an evil modern secularism needed to be purged. In 1939 a newly formed institute for Jewish research sought to prove Jesus was an Aryan. At least one-third of the Evangelical Church openly supported the Nazis. The Confessing Church's opposition to Hitler did not extend to a denunciation of his anti-Jewish policies.

---

[21]Daniel Goldhagen, *Hitler's Willing Executioners* (1996), 22.

The same limitation characterized Catholic Bishop Von Galen's opposition to the Nazis.[22] While the papacy before the war condemned racism, neither German Protestant nor Catholic clergy and laity even before the war sought to mobilize opinion against Jewish persecution. German wives of Jewish husbands openly and successfully protested outside Gestapo headquarters in Berlin and gained the releases of their incarcerated men, and Catholic and Protestant bishops stopped a program authorized by Hitler for killing mentally defective persons. German Christians mounted no similar demonstration against persecution of Jews, although outside denominations like the Friends found a few Germans willing to accept the risk of openly aiding Jews.[23]

The Final Solution was authorized in the middle of the war and carried through secretly by the military, police, secret police (SS), and Einsatzgruppen working together in a brutal campaign against the Jews. Historians remain divided about the degree of knowledge of and support for the Final Solution. On one extreme, Daniel Goldhagen found so much evidence of calm acceptance of the systematic and unnecessary brutality that he concluded that the German people as a whole accepted the Nazi view that Jews were by nature evil, unredeemable, and deserving elimination. By contrast, most historians conclude that before World War I German anti-Semitism was less than in France and Austria, had little political support, and was not a major factor in the rise of Nazism. They cite examples from the Von Klemperer diaries of many who opposed the persecution and stress the secrecy of the decision for the Final Solution.[24]

---

[22]Robert Erikson, "Genocide, Religion, and Gerhard Kittel: Protestant Theologians Face the Third Reich;" Susanna Heschel, "When Jesus was an Aryan: The Protestant Church and Antisemitic Propaganda;" Beth Griech-Polelle, "A Pure Conscience is Good Enough: Bishop Von Galen and Resistance to Nazism," in *In God's Name: Religion and Genocide in the Twentieth Century*, 62-138.

[23]Hans Schmidt, *Quakers and Nazis: Inner Light and Outer Darkness* (1997), shows that the small community of Friends openly sympathized with the Jews and aided many to emigrate, actions tolerated by the Nazis. For a successful protest against Hitler by Gentile women married to Jewish husbands in 1943, see Nathan Stoltzfus, *Resistance of the Heart: Intermarriage and the Rosenstrasse Protest in Nazi Germany* (1996).

[24]Victor Klemperer, *I Will Bear Witness: A Diary of the Nazi Years 1933-1941*, tr. Martin Chalmers (1998); Mayer, 46, 73-77; Eric Johnson, *Nazi Terror: The Gestapo, Jews, and Ordinary Germans* (1999); Marrus, 34-47 draws the distinction between "intentionalists" who see

When accounts of mass executions initially reached the Allies, many citizens who remembered the untrue atrocity stories of World War I failed to give credence. By November 1942 the Allies presented persuasive evidence of the Final Solution and threatened to hold German leaders accountable. The Church of England, American Catholic bishops, and the Federal Council of Churches publicly condemned the Holocaust.[25] However, until 1945 the U.S. emphasized Japanese atrocities far more than German acts. So most people in the Allied nations learned only at the end of the war about the extent of the Final Solution in which Germans murdered six million people only because they were Jewish.

Pictures of Auschwitz and Buchenwald and the testimony at the Nuremberg trials provided legitimacy to Allied conduct in World War II and meant that there would be no backlash, even when the peace turned out to be flawed. People concluded that the Nazis were even worse than as portrayed in wartime propaganda and that the war was justified, in Eisenhower's phrase a "Crusade in Europe." It should be remembered, however, that no nation entered the war because of German anti-Semitism, that nations reluctantly admitted Jewish refugees during the Great Depression, that in 1939 the Allies did not foresee the Final Solution, and that there was little they could do for the Jews after 1939 except to win the war.[26] However, no satisfactory reason has ever been given for the Allies' failure in 1945 to bomb railroads leading to the concentration camps. For the Jews who escaped or survived, the Holocaust provided a moral justification for creating the state of Israel.

Hitler intending the Final Solution from the beginning and "functionalists" who see a very uneven policy. See also the *Encyclopedia of the Holocaust*, ed. Israel Gutman (1990) for articles on all phases of the persecution of the Jews. Samantha Power, *"A Problem from Hell": America and the Age of Genocide* (2002), 27-29, 33-36.

[25]The bishops of the Church of England consistently condemned Nazi persecution of the Jews and others beginning almost as soon as Hitler came to power. During the war, bishops within the House of Lords publicized Nazi atrocities, joined with other denominations in public declarations, and attempted to pressure the government to provide relief and asylum to refugees. A. M. Chandler, "The Church of England and Nazi Germany 1933-1945," Ph.D. diss., Cambridge University (1990), 93-4, 124, 206, 210, 224.

[26]By 1938, 250,000 of the Jews of Germany and 100,000 from Austria had emigrated; 100,000 came to the U.S.; 63,000 to Argentina; 52,000 to the UK, and 33,000 to Palestine. *Oxford Companion to World War II (1995)*, 364-71.

VI. The Papacy in the War

Eugenio Pacelli, a deeply spiritual man and also a shrewd diplomat who as papal Secretary of State had negotiated with Mussolini and Hitler, became Pope as Pius XII in 1939. In 1939 and early 1940, Pius sought to avoid war as the greatest of moral evils, even if peace meant appeasing Germany. When the Nazis invaded Poland, Pius did not condemn the action though he expressed concern for the sufferings of the Poles, perhaps because he wished to be in a position to mediate a peace. In June 1940 after the Nazi invasion of their lands, he also expressed sympathy to the rulers of Holland, Belgium, and Luxembourg, but again did not denounce the aggression, nor did he at any later date condemn the Nazi or communist atrocities by name. Still, the papal letter of sympathy to occupied countries that was printed in the Vatican's newspaper infuriated Italy's Fascists, who mobbed his car when Pius attended a church in Rome, and caused Mussolini to grumble that the Vatican was the chronic appendicitis of Italy.[27]

Pius XII's ability to influence events was limited. The Lateran Treaty denied the papacy the right to speak out on Italian politics. Behind the scenes Pius worked to keep Mussolini from declaring war, but his counsel was ignored, a clear illustration of the limits of Church power. The Vatican was a semi-state surrounded by an unsympathetic belligerent who could at any time harass by cutting off water or ordering troops to occupy the buildings, knowing there would be no armed resistance. Pius XI had condemned Nazism and communism in 1937, and that declaration had changed little and brought increased persecution of Roman Catholics.[28] Pius XII, far less outspoken than his predecessor, would not make verbal pronouncements that would bring suffering. The Church's pastoral mission must be fulfilled, he felt, no matter what the internal political arrangements of a country.

---

[27]Owen Chadwick, *Britain and the Vatican during the Second World War* (1986), 107.
[28]Pius XI had prepared a denunciation of Nazis' persecution of Jews in secret, but died before he could publish it. See George Passelecq and Bernard Suchecky, *The Hidden Encyclical of Pius XI* (1997).

In World War I, the British allowed the Americans to send food to starving Belgians. In World War II Pius failed to persuade the British to allow food aid to be sent to occupied Greece in 1940 to prevent massive starvation. According to the laws of war, feeding a conquered country was the duty of the occupier, Germany. Germany, which was invading Russia, ignored the Greeks. Germans and British treated Greek civilians as expendable pawns. The American government followed the British policy and refused Herbert Hoover's and the churches' desire to send food to occupied countries, similar to what had been done for Belgium in World War I. Only the pacifist *Catholic Worker* supported sending food also to Axis countries.

In contrast to the Pope's careful silence, cardinals and bishops in Italy, Germany, France, England, and later America spoke out in support of their respective countries' war aims. For example, when Germany invaded Russia, the Catholic military bishop wrote the armed forces: "Be confident in your mission! Then victory will be yours, a victory that will allow Europe to breathe again ... Many European states know that the war against Russia is a European *crusade*." Over 1000 Protestant and Catholic chaplains preached an anti-Bolshevik gospel to the troops.

Hitler and German bishops sought to obtain public papal blessing for their crusade against godless communism. Although many in the Vatican desired the destruction of godless Marxist-socialism, the Pope had far too much knowledge of Hitler to see him as a champion of Christendom. Officially, he kept silent. Unofficially, his view of the invasion was "to set a thief to catch a thief," and he would have preferred to see both Hitler and Stalin weakened so that the democracies would prevail. A triumph of either dictator would be a disaster for the Church. Of course, the Vatican never publicly admitted to such a realpolitik strategy.[29]

---

[29]Quoted in Stehle, 206-11.

After Italy experienced defeats in 1944, opponents of Mussolini sought to enlist the Pope's aid. Careful not to jeopardize official neutrality, the papacy facilitated communications between Italian military leaders, King Victor Emmanuel, and the Allies. After the King dismissed Mussolini in 1944 and the new government sought to surrender to the Allies, the Germans seized control of Italy.

The Pope opposed the Allies' demand for unconditional surrender as likely to prolong the war. He also sought unsuccessfully to have Rome declared an open city so that it would not be bombed. Pius' public condemnation of the saturation bombing of cities and of unconditional surrender can be seen as a response to his knowledge of Italian conditions as well as a reiteration of Just War protection of civilians.

The Vatican knew about Nazi execution of Jews, though not of its extent, by late fall, 1942 and was pressed by the Allies and American Catholic bishops to condemn Germany's actions. Pius, in his Christmas message, addressed the issues of this war caused "by a social order which hid its mortal weakness and its unbridled lust for power." The outbreak of war brought "a sad succession of acts at variance with the human and Christian sense. International agreements to make war less inhuman by confining it to the combatants, to regulate the procedure of occupation and imprisonment of the conquered remained in various places a dead letter." The Pope called for a re-founding of society upon the law of God that brought peace and justice as a tribute for those exiled from their homelands, those sacrificed in battle, the thousands of non-combatants killed by aerial-warfare, and "the hundreds of thousands of persons who, without any fault on their part, sometimes only because of their nationality or race, have been consigned to death or to a slow decline."[30]

The Christmas message was the Pope's strongest comment on the nature of the war and the Holocaust. Notice that he never mentioned the Jews, Poles, or

---

[30]*Major Addresses of Pope Pius XII, Christmas Messages*, ed. Vincent Yzermans (1961), II, 64.

Russians by name or mentioned that the Nazis committed the atrocities. He later told the secretary to the American ambassador that he had not specified the Nazis because then he would have had to list the Bolsheviks as well. The Pope had softened initial reports of two million Jewish executions to hundreds of thousands because he did not believe all the atrocity reports, and he did not mention Judaism as a cause of persecution.

Because Pius used his normal language of diplomatic circumlocution plus the vagueness of pastoral exhortation, those not attuned to the intricacies of papal language missed the allusion, but the Vatican thought the condemnation "candid and forceful." German security analyzed the speech as "one long attack on everything we stand for . . . He is *virtually* accusing the German people of injustice towards the Jews."[31] Pius disappointed the Catholic priests, nuns, and bishops who had provided the Holy See with evidence on the death camps and who were working to aid the Jews. The Pope's failure on this and on any future occasion to condemn forcefully the Nazi policy on the Jews meant that the Catholics seeking guidance from the Holy See did not receive an authoritative announcement. If Pius XII had spoken out with the moral clarity of his predecessor, Catholics in France, Poland, and Germany could have mobilized the resources of the Church to save Jews. No one argues that Pius could have stopped the Holocaust, but his public silence provided no guidance to those who wished to rescue Jews and allowed those in the hierarchy and lay Catholics who wished to claim ignorance to avoid taking action.[32]

Lutheran Martin Niemöller, who spent the war in a concentration camp, apologized after the war for German Protestants' failure to oppose the Holocaust; Pope John Paul II, whose Polish seminary teachers were also killed by the Nazis, apologized in 1998 and again in 2000 for the long tradition of Christian anti-

---

[31]Chadwick, 214-19. Also entry "Pius XII", *Encyclopedia of the Holocaust,*. ed. Israel Gutman (1990), I: 1135-1139.
[32]Michael Phayer, *The Catholic Church and the Holocaust, 1930-1954* (2000), 80-118, 132. Phayer's treatment of the role of the papacy in The Holocaust is more balanced than John

Semitism and for the silence of the Catholic Christians during the Holocaust.[33] Even after the war, the Church did not change its policy on Jews; only after John XXIII brought pressure did the bishops in Vatican II repudiate the traditional policy of believing that Jews should be converted. The Church now declared the legitimacy of Judaism as a religion and the Jews as still the children of God.[34]

If Pius' words were too discrete, Catholic actions against the Holocaust saved many. The Italians, the Papacy, and even Mussolini's government opposed and stalled the German request to hand over Jews in Italy and Croatia. Archbishop Stepinac in Croatia and Bishop Preysing in Berlin denounced the Holocaust. Women Catholics, particularly nuns, including Margareta Sommer in Berlin, and Matylda Getter and Margil Slachta in Hungary, successfully rescued Jews; Gertrud Luckner was sent to a concentration camp for her efforts. Apologists for the Pope point to over 10,000 Italian Jews saved by the Church's opening monasteries, churches and other buildings to Jews and providing baptismal certificates. The Vatican warned the leader of Slovakia, the priest-collaborator Joseph Tiso, that Jews were being killed. Church action in Turkey and Hungary saved Jews, but the papacy never rebuked its pro-Fascist nuncio in Berlin and neither warned nor publicly protested when the Germans arrested Jews in Rome. The few Catholic leaders in occupied Europe who spoke out must be balanced against the silence of most churchmen.[35] Moreover, just as the Pope failed in his attempt to stop the Jewish, Polish, and Russian holocausts, so he also

Cornwell's, *Hitler's Pope* (1999) and David Kertzer, *The Popes Against the Jews: The Vatican's Role in the Rise of Modern Anti-Semitism* (2002).

[33]John Paul II apologized for individual Catholics, but did not implicate the Church as doing wrong. Gary Wills, "Vatican Regrets," *New York Review of Books* (May 25, 2000), 19-20.

[34]Michael Phayer, chs. 8 and 9, shows how the papacy and bishops worked against war crimes trials and aided the escape of some perpetrators of the Holocaust. Phayer sees Pius as too legalistic, too much the diplomat, concerned to rebuild Germany as a bulwark against communism, and anxious to preserve the Church's concordat with Germany.

[35]Chadwick, 214-19. In France, opposition to Vichy and efforts to save Jews came from Calvinist Protestants. Robert Zaretsky, *Nimes at War: Religion, Politics and Public Opinion in the Gard, 1938-1944* (1995), 10-11, 27-30, 113-124. Philip Hallie's *Lest Innocent Blood be Shed: The Story of the Village of Le Chambon, and How Goodness Happened There* (1979) is the story of French Protestants in mountain villages who took in Jewish children to save them from the Holocaust. See also *Églises et Chrétiens in Deuxieme Guerre Mondiale*, ed. Xavier de Montclos, et al (1982).

could not prevail upon the Allies to refrain from the saturation bombing of cities.[36]

VII. The American Perspective

The American people as a whole never experienced the costs of modern mechanized war. As compared with the millions of deaths of other belligerents, the U.S. lost 321,999, with 800,000 wounded or missing, and ten percent of the 124,000 POWs died. By contrast 2.5 million men of the Japanese Imperial Army died, but only 600,000 in combat, with the rest killed by illness, starvation, and accidents. For the U.S., after initial defeats in the Pacific, by mid-1943 the tide of war had turned and eventual victory seemed likely. War disrupted daily life and families had to learn to live with the possibility that their young men would not return. In spite of rationing, Americans lived better during the war than in the Depression.

In popular mythology World War II remains the "Good War" in which the U.S. conquered the forces of evil. The memoirs of the fighting men who landed at Anzio, Normandy, Okinawa and then fought across France or in the jungles of the Philippines or New Guinea are likely to use the "Good War" in an ironic sense. Their writings convey anguish and disgust at the anarchy on the battlefield, fear at the seeming randomness of survival or death, exaltation at victory, revulsion at having to kill. Enlisted men and conscripts disdained officers whom they saw as uncaring and incompetent. Killing was bad enough when the enemy was impersonal, but soldiers felt guilt when they saw the bodies of German or Japanese young men.[37] A survey done at the end of the war by Colonial S. L. A.

---

[36]The policies of Pius XII seem very similar to those of the International Committee of the Red Cross. The ICRC had early knowledge of the Holocaust, but at first relied on the German Red Cross, which meant that no action was taken. The ICRC did not wish to jeopardize its ability to visit POW camps and the status of internal political prisoners was ill defined. Although the ICRC undertook actions to aid Jews, particularly in satellite nations, there was no public denunciation of the Holocaust. See "International Red Cross," *Encyclopedia of the Holocaust* (1990), 1228-1233.

[37]Samuel Hynes, *A Soldier's Tale: Bearing Witness to Modern War* (1997) summarizes the contrast in soldiers' narratives in WW I, WW II, and Vietnam. Studs Terkel, *"The Good War:" An Oral History of World War II* (1984); John Keegan, *The Face of Battle* (1976) tries to capture the experience of battle. Paul Fussell, *Wartime Understanding and Behavior in the Second World War* (1989) shows how dehumanizing battle actually was and contrasts the corrosive impact of the

Marshall, a distinguished military analyst, concluded that only 15% of American riflemen fired their weapons when in battle. An overwhelming majority of front-line soldiers never discharged their guns in anger, even when under attack.[38] At home the war was portrayed as an ideological struggle of peace-loving democracy against aggressive totalitarianism, but in battle loyalty to one's buddies became the primary motivation for soldiers to fight. In Europe the Western front may have been better than the Eastern, but to those baptized in modern industrialized fighting, war was still a living hell. Still, if the memoirs are soldiers are to be believed, the experience of being in combat became the climax, a defining experience of their lives, and they continued to relish their participation in war.[39]

VIII. The Pacific Theater: White Demons vs. the Yellow Peril

Long before Pearl Harbor, Japan received a bad press in America for the way it waged war. Because of the reports of missionaries, Americans had long sentimentalized the Chinese, and after 1937 denounced the Japanese invasion of China. The press focused on the "rape of Nanking" in which the Japanese soldiers, for six weeks after the fall of the city, killed, tortured, or raped an estimated 200,000 - behavior repeated on a lesser scale in other Chinese cities. Against territory in the north of China controlled by Mao Tse Tung's communists, the Japanese created the "three all" policy: "kill all, burn all, destroy all," after which the population fell from 44 to 25 million.[40] Japanese newspapers also reported contests in which army officers competed to see who could behead

---

war with the sanitized images in the mass media. Most memoirs of the war are written by officers; one of the best is Paul Fussell, *Doing Battle: The Making of a Skeptic* (1996); the foot soldier's experience is vividly captured in Harry Pagliaro, *Naked Heart: Soldier's Journey to the Front* (1996). A sociological perspective based on World War II is J. Glenn Gray, *The Warriors: Reflections on Men in Battle* (1959). The psychological cost of war is discussed in Norman Brill and Gilbert Beebe, *A Follow-up Study of War Neuroses* (1955).
[38]Gwynne Dyer, *War* (1985), 118. Marshall's research methods have been questioned, but there is impressionistic data supporting his conclusions. The American military changed its methods of training soldiers to shoot, to make the action more a mechanical reflex, and in Vietnam there was little reluctance to fire rifles.
[39]Hynes, 173.
[40]John Dower, *War Without Mercy: Race and Power in the Pacific War* (1986), 43; Bix, 333-6, 360,-367. One estimate is 2.7 Chinese civilians killed in battles in northern China.

the most Chinese POWs and printed pictures of previously mutilated, hanging British POWs.

The Japanese troops thought that surrender was dishonorable and they looked down upon British and American prisoners as cowards who had surrendered rather than fight to the bitter end or commit suicide. Their contempt for whites' weakness showed in the inadequate provisions provided by imperial authorities for POWs and in the guards' constant brutality. In spite of official manuals ordering Japanese soldiers to treat POWs well, 27% of Japan's prisoners did not survive the war; the cause was not genocide but mistreatment and lack of food and medical attention. Not until after the war did Americans discover medical experiments on POWs and only recently learned of the abuse of women from Korea, China, and Indonesia, who were forced to become prostitutes for Japanese soldiers.

The surprise attack on Pearl Harbor and early defeats created an intense hatred of Japan. Because diplomats were negotiating in Washington in December 1941, the Americans concluded that the Japanese were inherently treacherous.[41] In the months after America's defeat in the Philippines, the Bataan death march of American POWs further fueled hatred of the Japanese. In 1942 the Americans staged the so-called Doolittle air raid, the first attempt to bomb the Japanese mainland. The raid had little military but enormous psychological significance for Americans and the Japanese. The Japanese captured eight flyers. Using a law passed after the raid that made bombing civilians a capital offense, the eight were sentenced to death and three were executed, behavior termed by President Roosevelt as "barbarous," and "uncivilized" - language expressing how Americans had come to see the Japanese.[42] American newspapers published the diary in which a Japanese soldier in New Guinea described how he decapitated a captured American flyer.

---

[41]There is an historical controversy over whether failure to notify Americans was due to conscious decision or a result of mistakes, but clearly it was to be a surprise attack.
[42]Ibid., 49

American racist fears of a "yellow peril" contributed to the belief that the "Japs" were sub-human, vermin who should be exterminated. Americans distinguished between good Germans and the Nazis, but all "Japs" seemed to be the same.[43] Cartoonists caricatured "Japs" as little people, nearsighted and bucktoothed. Movies showed them as exalting in cruelty, not valuing life, and portrayed Japanese mothers as lacking feeling for their children. National character studies published by sociologists and psychologists described Japan as a nation of little people, conformists (a herd mentality) with a well-deserved inferiority complex, a perpetually immature people characterized by emotional instability. Having denigrated Japan's military prowess before the war, Americans ascribed its early successes to the almost superhuman fighting qualities of the soldiers. America's military men saw the Japanese as primitive, savage-like and concluded that their duty was, in the words of Admiral "Bull" Halsey, to "Kill 'Japs,' Kill 'Japs,' Kill more 'Japs.' "[44]

Interested in avenging Pearl Harbor, the Americans did not wish to take prisoners. At the beginning of the war there were incidents when the Japanese put up a white flag and then shot Americans or booby-trapped the bodies of the dead. Stories of such behavior circulated widely. The result was that Americans who did not wish to take prisoners did not take many. At Tarawa the Marine battle cry was "Kill the Jap bastards! Take no prisoners." Whether because they preferred to commit suicide or engage in a futile last *bonzai* charge into certain death, at Tarawa only one hundred were captured out of 4,700 defenders.[45] The Japanese labeled the 41st Division "The Butchers" because they disliked capturing prisoners.

The killing of the helpless by U.S. forces was no secret. *Time Magazine* in March 1943 ran a story about how American fighter pilots shot "Jap survivors" in lifeboats. Sailors and marines also killed Japanese flyers parachuting from shot-

---

[43]Hynes, 162-64, 171.
[44]Dower, 55.
[45]Haruko Cook and Theodore Cook, *Japan at War: An Oral History* (1992), 265.

down airplanes, even though Americans had earlier condemned the Japanese for similar behavior. Americans at home as well as on the front openly discussed the need to exterminate "Japs," and of course the Japanese publicized such language to their troops to show the character of the enemy.

The Japanese high command insisted that surrendering was dishonorable and dying fulfilled the Yamato spirit. The strategy pursued by the Imperial Forces during later stages of the war needlessly sacrificed Japanese soldiers in to-the-death defenses. Soldiers in the Imperial Armies hated to surrender, having been told of the duty of *gyokusai* (crushing the jewels) in order not to dishonor one's family and serve the emperor. Those few Japanese who surrendered almost always did so as individuals; officers rarely led their men to capitulate. A survey after the war found that 83% of Japanese soldiers believed that if they surrendered, the Americans would torture and kill them.

Like the Americans, the Japanese ransacked history and newspaper accounts to construct a selective portrait of their enemy, with each side emphasizing the worst features of the other. So the Japanese used their tradition of beliefs about "white peril" to picture the Americans as imperialists, racists, and economic exploiters who discriminated against the Japanese in California and exploited all non-whites. "In the course of the war in Asia, racism, dehumanization, technological change, and exterminationist policies became interlocked in unprecedented ways."[46]

The ferocity of the Japanese defenders amazed the Americans. On islands in the Pacific, soldiers continued to fight to the death when hope for victory was gone. In eastern New Guinea, out of 170,000 troops, 160,000 died.[47] Starving Japanese soldiers in the Philippines and Okinawa saved one last grenade for suicide; at Okinawa, as instructed by the military, fathers killed their wives and children rather than surrender. The alternative to killing oneself was to begin a

---

[46]Dower, 66-71, 93.
[47]Cook, 276. The Japanese film *Fire in the Plains* is a gripping account of the starving soldiers in the Philippines.

suicidal attack upon American positions. At the end of the war at the battle of Okinawa, the Japanese high command created what the Americans called *kamikaze* pilots. These young men, many of whom had interrupted their university studies, served the emperor by committing suicide through becoming human bombs, crashing their airplanes or torpedoes into American ships. The old Just War attitude that treated surrender as a legitimate action to save lives when further defense was futile (that happened on the Western Front) succumbed to *bushido*, an ancient *samurai* doctrine of dying while fighting. (*Bushido* had also required treating one's enemy with respect, however.) The tenacity of the Japanese defenders and what seemed a cavalier attitude towards death influenced the Americans to seek new weapons that might end the war without a costly invasion of the main islands.

IX. Saturation Bombing: Europe and Japan

From the scattered bombing of cities, factories, and military installations during World War I, advocates of air power in Italy, Great Britain and the United States drew the lesson that in the next war bombing would be decisive. Air power allegedly provided a solution to the enormous military casualties caused by trench warfare because planes could leap over the front lines. In the future, mass bombings could disrupt the industrial production necessary for total war, but, above all, theorists declared, bombing of urban areas would provide a weapon that could break the morale of civilians. The British, in particular, did not wish to fight another land war in Europe and so devoted considerable resources to making sure their island had sufficient air power, concentrating upon bombers, of which they alone produced as many as the Axis powers.

Because many believed that there was no effective defense against bombing, the peace movement in the 20s and 30s trumpeted the dangers of bombing civilians as an added reason to avoid war. Due to the widespread revulsion at the prospect of bombing civilians, diplomats in negotiations at The Hague sought to outlaw the practice but could arrive at no convention acceptable to the military and enforceable in wartime. So the assumption prevailed that in the next total war, air bombardments would occur.

In actuality the claims for the decisiveness of air power in a future war rested more upon optimistic prophecy than reality. The Italians and Germans tried out the bombing of civilians in the Spanish Civil War in attacking Guernica and Madrid; the Japanese bombed Shanghai and other Chinese cities. (American opponents of the Japanese invasion of China in 1937 stressed the horrors of bombing of civilians.) Yet in none of these cases was bombing a crucial factor in defeating the enemy. Consequently, Hitler designed his air force to provide support for massed, mechanized armored divisions of tanks and promised the German people that his effective air defenses would preclude the bombing of his cities.

When World War II began in September 1939, the Luftwaffe engaged in prolonged bombing of Warsaw, Poland and, during the invasion of Western Europe in the summer of 1940, bombed the Dutch city of Rotterdam, in spite of its being declared an open or undefended city. (We know now that this bombing was unauthorized and took place because of a breakdown in German communications.)[48] Nazi fighter planes fired on civilians fleeing the advancing German armies as well. So Hitler's wish to outlaw bombing of cities met with general skepticism. The fall of France in the summer of 1940 and British evacuation of troops at Dunkirk left the Nazis no opposition on the continent and meant that the only weapon the British could use for striking Germany proper was the air force. Initially, Britain's primary purpose in bombing was not to defeat the Nazis but to strengthen British morale.

The British quickly learned that bombing was not a panacea. Their attempts to bomb German naval vessels and shipyards often failed. Bombers needed reasonably clear skies before they could find their destination; even if the target was located, it was difficult to hit when harassed by enemy fighter planes

---

[48]Charles Messinger, *"Bomber" Harris and the Strategic Bombing Offensive 1939-1945* (1984), 36.

552

and the flak from ground artillery that became more deadly the lower to the ground the planes flew. Because casualty rates from day bombing remained unacceptably high, night raids appeared to be the only solution, but the darkness that helped planes survive made hitting the target more difficult. As late as 1943, after better training, experienced crews (those who survived the appalling casualty rates), improvements in the range and carrying capability of planes, and new bomb-sighting equipment, a majority of bombs dropped still fell outside a five-mile radius of the target.

During the Battle of Britain after the fall of France, the Luftwaffe initially attacked radar installations and airfields, but Hitler soon decided that the way to conquer was to engage in blitz bombing of London and industrial cities like Coventry as a way of disrupting the British economy and destroying morale. Initially just stemming the onslaught of German bombers occupied the Royal Air Force. The fighter pilots' contribution to the defense of Britain has become legendary: in Churchill's words "never was so much owed to so few." Pilots and airplanes seemed to recapture the romanticism and glamour formerly reserved for horse cavalry. Because Britain would devote 7% of its total wartime expenditures to air power, advocates of air power needed to prove their value to winning the war.[49]

Having seen the German blitz, British civilian and neutral (i.e., U.S.) opposition to the bombing of German cities evaporated, and, after prodding from Churchill, Britain's bomber command focused on what was termed area bombing. That is, in spite of the British experience that the blitz strengthened their own people's will to resist, the government concluded that in a totalitarian state like Germany morale was brittle, and bombing of civilians would cause support for the regime to evaporate.

During the first years of the war, there was little public controversy about British bombing policy; striking Germany directly served to boost the morale of

---

[49]Ibid., 214; Paul Fussell, *Wartime,* 13-22 cites Allied losses of 20,000 bombers and 110,000 men and the failure of bombing to help troops because of inaccuracy.

civilians having to endure hardships with little hope for imminent victory. Under conditions of total war, the British government accepted as a matter of policy that male and female workers, whether or not directly involved in war-related industries, and children became acceptable targets of war.

Because they could not hit synthetic oil factories and transportation centers (targets advocated by the army and navy), British bomber command decided that Germany could be defeated by massive attacks upon cities.[50] From 1939 until 1943 only two such attacks, on Cologne and Hamburg, were successful and they were costly in numbers of airplanes and pilots lost. Because precision in aim remained an unattainable goal, the aim became to create a firestorm that would burn all the structures in a wide area.

Until late summer of 1944, saturation bombing of German cities remained a rare occurrence because the risks were great and resources were needed elsewhere. Churchill made clear that there should be no bombing of French civilians in cities because the Allies needed the assistance of the Free French, but, under American pressure, the policy was changed to accept civilian deaths in Normandy as a byproduct of bombing to destroy rail links. The Americans continued to insist that area bombing was not preferred strategy. What was needed was precision bombing of oil fields, airplane factories, and later V-1 rocket installations. (Because of their imprecise targeting mechanisms, Germans designed and used V-1 and V-2 rocket systems to attack large targets, normally cities.)

The main contribution of Allied air power before the fall of 1944 was to achieve air supremacy by eliminating German fighter planes, and the Allies succeeded because America could build more fighter aircraft and send them into battle more quickly than the Nazis. (The Allies produced 633,000 military aircraft; Germany and Italy 200,000.)[51] Soon Nazi air losses outstripped production capacity, and German technical breakthroughs in rocket technology

---

[50]Ibid., 193, 195, 209; Max Hastings, *Bomber Command: The Myths and Reality of the Strategic Bombing Offensive* (1979), 277, 324, 334.
[51]Ellis, 278.

and jet engines came too late to make a significant impact. By the fall of 1944 with Germany hard-pressed on Eastern, Western, and Italian Fronts and with Allied dominance of airspace, Germany had no effective defenses against area bombing of cities.

Arthur Harris, commander of the British bomber force, determined to show that air power alone through saturation bombing could win the war. Although the Americans continued to proclaim that they were doing precision bombing, they joined the British in attempting to break German morale through the saturation bombing of its cities. Rather than bomb oil refineries (which had earlier proven effective and it is now believed would have shortened the war by several months) or railroad lines or support ground troops (with a medium error of three miles, bombs were still very imprecise) or even rail links to concentration camps, the Allies began a systematic day and night bombing of Germany cities in an effort to curtail industrial production and break civilian morale by making them homeless. The object in each case was, through combining of incendiaries and high-explosives bombs, to create hundreds of little fires that could coalesce into a conflagration which would consume the center of the city.[52]

Few attacks were successful in creating a firestorm, but at Hamburg in November 1943 and Dresden in February 1945 the emergence of a firestorm with winds of tornado strength and temperatures of 1000 degrees centigrade sucked the oxygen away and left inhabitants in bomb shelters to suffocate. By the end of the war, there were no German cities left to firebomb. Of the estimated 2 million German civilian deaths, air power resulted in 593,000 deaths with 2 million made homeless. On the Western and Eastern Front, far more civilians died because they could not escape the path of the armies.[53]

---

[52]Between October 1944 and May 1945, the distribution of allied bombing was 53% on large cities, 14% oil, 15% railways, and 13% on enemy troops. In these attacks 181 women and children died for every 100 men; 15% died in the blast, 15% were incinerated, and 70% from suffocation. Anthony Verrier, *The Bomber Offensive* (1969), 299; Hastings, 325, 352.
[53]More civilian casualties resulted from the sieges of Soviet cities than all the bombings of German cities. Adam Roberts, "Land Warfare 1899-1946," *Laws of War: Constraints on Warfare in the Western World,* ed. Michael Howard, et al. (1994), 132.

In Britain, pacifist Vera Brittain published a strong attack upon saturation bombing during the war (in World War I, censorship would have made such a publication a crime), and John Bell, the Bishop of Chichester, and a few members of Parliament attacked the practice in the Houses of Commons and Lords.[54] The population in rural areas who had escaped the blitz was more favorable to the bombing than people in industrial areas like London who knew what being bombed was like.

Initially saturation bombing did not cause much controversy in the United States, partially because the government insisted that it was doing precision bombing of military targets. After Brittain's pamphlet was republished in the United States with a preface signed by twenty-eight important clergy, vociferous condemnation of her ideas came from the American press and political leaders like Franklin and Eleanor Roosevelt, who also had no first-hand experience of being bombed.[55] Such controversy did not deter either the Protestant *Christian Century* or Catholic *America* and *Commonweal* from endorsing Brittain's critique of saturation bombing.

The bombing of Dresden became the most controversial example of saturation bombing, because it occurred when many believed that total defeat of Germany was imminent. Dresden was a charming historic city with no heavy industry and crowded with refugees and prisoners of war. Its ancient structures, many of wood and built close together, would burn easily, but civil defense had been neglected because Dresden had no military significance. Churchill had instructed bomber command to hit Eastern cities as a way of showing support to the Russian armies, now only seventy miles east of Dresden.

For once, everything worked to perfection for the Allies. Successful decoy raids meant there was no effective air defense, the skies cleared, and initially two waves of 1400 British bombers at night dropped high explosives and 650,000

---

[54]Andrew Chandler, "The Church of England and Obliteration Bombing of Germany in the Second World War," *English Historical Review* (1993), 920-946; Paul Berry and Mark Bostridge, *Vera Brittain, A Life* (1995), 436-442. The British pamphlet was titled *Seed of Chaos* (1944).

incendiaries and the next day - although after the conflagration little was standing and clouds and smoke covered most of the city - a force of 1350 American planes bombed. The firestorm could be seen for two hundred miles. Just to make sure nothing escaped, the Americans bombed the rubble again the next day.

Dresden was described two days later as "the ghost of the city." Kurt Vonnegut, Jr., an American prisoner of war in Dresden, described bringing the dead out from basements: "They were loaded onto wagons and taken to parks, large, open areas in the city . . . The Germans got funeral pyres going, burning the bodies to keep them from stinking and from spreading disease. 130,000 corpses were hidden underground."[56] A friend who served on one of the American bombers told me that Dresden was at the time just routine: we reported, received our orders, flew over Germany, bombed, and left. His moral revulsion about the effects of saturation bombing occurred only after the war ended when he was driving through Germany and saw the results of bombing a militarily insignificant village, hit only because it was a visible target and Berlin was fogged in. At the time, civilians did not know and crews could not see the results because airplanes, for security reasons, left the scene as soon as they released the bombs.

The Associated Press, quoting an official news brief, described Dresden as exemplifying a new practice of "deliberate terror bombing of German population centers," an accurate description of the policy's intent. The resulting outcry in the press in Britain and America forced a change of policy, ostensibly done because the Allies would have to take responsibility for housing Germany's population after the war. The moral debate on Dresden and by implication saturation bombing in Europe has continued ever since. The British after many years in 1992 dedicated a statute to Bomber Harris, the primary advocate of the policy.[57]

---

[55]Vera Brittain, "Massacre by Bombing," *Fellowship* (March, 1944), 50-64; Sittser, 218-19.
[56]Quoted in Richard Rhodes, *Making of the Atomic Bomb* (1986), 593; Max Hastings, 339-342; David Irving, *The Destruction of Dresden* (1963), 11, 15.
[57]*New York Times*, Jan. 6, 1992; Irving, 233-243; Messinger, 186-187, 191. The debate focuses not only upon the civilian casualties, but also whether the air forces by focusing on area bombing actually played a lesser role in the victory and unnecessarily jeopardized the lives of crews. Out of every 100 men on the planes, 60 would be killed, 12 would become POWs, and only 24 survive

When the Queen Mother, who dedicated the monument, visited Dresden soon after, she was booed.

After the war, the Allies commissioned a survey of the effects of the bombing. The survey concluded, that in spite of the area bombing, industrial production did not significantly decline until the last months of the war and that morale did not break even after most Germans admitted the inevitability of defeat. Even had civilians wished to surrender, there was no way for German people to change governments or to influence Hitler. The unconditional surrender doctrine of the Allies, first announced in 1943, served to stiffen the general will to resist and weakened the influence of those who sought a negotiated end. The European theater seemed to show that air power alone, even when used against civilians, was not an effective weapon for victory. For our purposes, the Allies' bombing strategy is important as indicating how the course of the war changed moral standards.

With the defeat of Nazi Germany, the Americans turned their attention to Japan. The Army Air Corps in the Pacific Theatre sought to bomb Japan into defeat, to avoid a costly invasion, and to save the lives of American soldiers. The lives of Japanese civilians, like those of Germans, were the responsibility of their own government. A secondary benefit would be to convince the public of the overwhelming importance of a strong air force.

Even before the war, Americans recognized that the close-packed wooden houses in Japanese cities could be burned. Secretary of War Henry Stimson who objected to bombing cities was informed that the Japanese put lathes in homes and deliberately built houses close to factories. The official position was clear: because the Japanese government mobilized civilians and had widely dispersed manufacturing capacity, "the entire population of Japan is a proper military target."[58]

---

unharmed. It is a myth that Harris did not receive recognition after the war because the British government wanted to divorce itself from the bomber attacks.
[58]Rhodes, 596.

The Japanese mounted strong resistance and fought to the death against American amphibious forces in Okinawa and Iwo Jima. At Okinawa the Americans lost more than 12,000 and the Japanese more than 100,000; the landing on Iwo Jima was the bloodiest day in Marine Corps history with 7000 killed. Showing an awesome ability to resist to the end, only 1000 of the 23,000 Japanese defenders survived. The American strategy was to seize these islands so that fighters and bombers would be within range of the Japanese home islands. The person charged with developing an efficient use of bombers was General Curtis LeMay. LeMay sought an appropriate strategy for the air corps to justify the heavy casualties in taking the islands and found it in area bombing of cities. He sought to establish that air power was the decisive weapon for modern war.

The policy proved its effectiveness on March 9, 1945, with the firebombing of Tokyo, with 87.4% of the target area containing domestic residences. The strategy of using high explosives and gelled gasoline bombs, plus a stiff wind, created a firestorm devastating 15.8 square miles of the city with 100,000 deaths, 1 million injuries, 41,000 serious. The conflagration created temperatures so high that water boiled in shallow canals in the area. *Time* called the raid "a dream come true." In the next ten days, Americans burned 32 square miles out of Japan's four largest cities and killed at least 150,000.[59] By the end of 1945 Americans had dropped 104,000 tons of bombs on 66 urban areas; by contrast, 14,150 tons were dropped on aircraft factories and 10,000 tons on oil refineries. As if Tokyo had not suffered enough, on the night of August 14 (before Japan's surrender was officially announced the next day but when military commanders already knew it), General Henry Arnold, one of the planners of the firebombing strategy, succeeded in staging a raid of 1000 planes on the capital city to mark "as big a finale as possible."[60] Before August, airplanes bombed all major

---

[59]Sittser, 216; Rhodes, 600; different smaller casualty figures are in the *U. S. Strategic Bombing Survey, Summary Report* (1946), 17, 20. Robert Newman, *Truman and the Hiroshima Cult* (1995) claims that the bombing survey was distorted because of the influence of Paul Nitze. Newman's book is a defense of Truman's decision to drop the bomb.
[60]Dower, 301.

Japanese cities except the four reserved as targets for America's new secret weapon.

Unlike Dresden, there was no outpouring of moral condemnation because the Japanese had attacked Pearl Harbor (a military target) and Americans dreaded the casualties in a landing and conquest of mainland Japan. We now know that Japan's leaders had recognized that the war was lost before LeMay began his saturation bombing. Yet the U.S. Strategic Bombing Survey concluded that the bombing did affect civilian and military morale and accelerated the end of the war.[61]

The two commanders primarily responsible for the policy of bombing cities - Britain's Arthur Harris, after Dresden, and America's Curtis LeMay, in the immediate postwar period - defended their actions using similar language:

> Attacks on cities ... are strategically justified in so far as they tend to shorten the war and so preserve the lives of Allied soldiers ... I do not personally regard the whole of the remaining cities of Germany as worth the bones of one British Grenadier . . . (Arthur Harris).

> Killing Japanese didn't bother me very much at that time. It was getting the war over that bothered me. I suppose if I had lost the war, I would have been tried as a war criminal . . . But all war is immoral, and if you let that bother you, you're not a good soldier."[62] (Curtis LeMay)

X. The Atomic Bomb

By 1939 scientists in many countries had participated in the new discoveries of atomic energy and knew the potential for making a bomb. After the first splitting of heavy atoms occurred in Germany in 1938, fear of the Nazi research efforts prompted Leo Szilard, an Hungarian immigrant and scientist, to persuade pacifist Albert Einstein to write President Roosevelt about the potential dangers posed by a new weapon of tremendous energy. The result was the

---

[61] *U.S. Strategic Bombing Survey, Japan's Struggle to Surrender* (1946), 9-11.
[62] Quoted in *"Bomber" Harris*, 189; Richard Rhodes, *Dark Sun: The Making of the Hydrogen Bomb* (1995), 21-22.

initiation in early 1942 of the secret Manhattan project, a massive government expenditure on a scientific project that cost two billion dollars and involved 200,000 people. Urgency came because the scientists thought they were in a race against the Nazis who were known to have an atomic bomb project; the target would be in Germany. After conquering enormous scientific and technological obstacles, the first atomic explosion, named Trinity (Oppenheimer picked the name and no one seems to have considered its religious significance inappropriate) occurred in the New Mexico desert on July 16, 1945.

Scientists, particularly those at the Chicago lab, including Szilard, realized that the bomb would not be ready in time to use against Germany and sought to debate whether the atomic bomb should be used against Japan, a country believed to lack the industrial capacity to make an atomic weapon. Strict military secrecy meant that the debate occurred among only a few, and there is no evidence that President Truman knew of the controversy. General Eisenhower expressed his opposition to Secretary of War Stimson and later to Truman, arguing that dropping the bomb was not "necessary" and "I hated to see our country be the first to use such a weapon."[63] Scientist Enrico Fermi's approach to Churchill brought no result; Szilard had no better luck with Truman or James Byrnes, soon to be Secretary of State. The Interim Committee, a group of high-level politicians and scientists reporting directly to Stimson and the President, rejected as impractical the Chicago scientists' suggestions for a warning, or a test demonstration, or for international control of the bomb. The Committee reasoned that the bomb might not work, or the Japanese might ignore the test, and the Americans would have given up the element of surprise.

The President recorded in his diary the necessity of using the bomb on a military target, the aim also of the Interim Committee and Stimson. In actuality, the targets specified were all "large urban areas of more than three miles diameter,"

---

[63]Rhodes, *Making of the Atomic Bomb*, 142, 648, 688. Martin Sherwin, *A World Destroyed: The Atomic Bomb and the Grand Alliance* (1977), 194 ff, 302-308.

cities whose population had not been bombed so that the effects of the weapon could be assessed. [64]

The Soviet Union officially learned of the existence of the bomb after the Trinity test that had been speeded up to occur while Truman met with Churchill and Stalin in Potsdam after the surrender of Germany. At Potsdam, the Allies also reiterated their demand for unconditional surrender and promised a democratic Japan. James Byrnes, a member of the Interim Committee, envisaged the atomic bomb as a lever to use against the Soviet Union, whose policies in Poland worried the Americans and British.

The U.S. dropped a uranium core bomb without warning on the industrial city of Hiroshima on August 6, 1945; three days later a plutonium bomb exploded above Nagasaki. Downtown Hiroshima and Nagasaki disappeared. Casualty figures from the two bombs are still debated, but a recent estimate is 64,000 dead in the first and 39,000 from the second, or around one fourth of the total population of each city. The firebombing of Tokyo killed more than either atomic bomb. Of those who survived radiation blasts for more than a year, long-term cancer deaths are 2.5% higher than normal.[65] On August 11, the Soviet Union declared war on Japan. The surrender came August 14 after American assurances that the fate of the Emperor would be determined by the Japanese people.

Initially, the Allied nations greeted the dropping of the bomb with euphoria. Churchill called the event "a miracle of deliverance," and Truman announced "the greatest day in human history" and publicly promised a reign of terror on Japanese cities.[66] Polls after the war showed overwhelming approval in Britain and America. The scientists who had worked on the Manhattan project became national heroes, but those who questioned the necessity of dropping the bomb also began the moral debate on the use of atomic weapons.

---

[64]Rhodes, 626-27, 631.
[65]"A Fallout over Numbers," *Washington Post*, Aug. 5, 1995, A16.
[66]Alonzo Hamby, *Life of Harry S. Truman* (1995), 335.

Controversy grew after people saw graphic images of the destruction and learned the human cost, particularly as described in John Hersey's *Hiroshima*, first appearing in the *New Yorker* magazine, published separately in 1946, and soon translated into many languages. The fusion of moral and strategic issues in that debate shows that ideals originated in religion centuries earlier continued to command support, either because of or in spite of the events in World War II.

Here is a summary of the issues in this continuing debate:

1. Was the use of the atomic bomb just a continuation of a policy of saturation bombing of cities begun in Germany and used against Japan? If so, a debate focusing on the dropping of the atomic bomb has too narrow a focus, because the moral issue is area bombing of civilians. For many proponents, the bomb provided only a spectacular and more efficient form of mass destruction. Its main impact was surprise, but overall it was not more useful than area bombing. Radiation, which later became a major concern, concerned only a few at the time.

2. Was a test demonstration possible? What if the bomb didn't work or Japan was not impressed? If Japan saw a test bomb and decided not to surrender, America would have given up surprise, the shock value of its new weapon, and wasted one of only two completed weapons. Was the Interim Committee's decision not to have a test because of the risks prudential?

3. Were the targets appropriate? Could civilians have been spared? Should some warning have been given? Would Japan bring American POWs to the site after a warning? Did the racism that permeated Americans' views of the Japanese make it easier to drop the bomb on civilians? If the D-Day landings had failed, would the Allies have used the bomb on German cities without a far-reaching moral debate?

4. Truman insisted that the bomb saved lives. Was he right? Did the dropping of the bomb ultimately save lives, both those of American and Japanese soldiers and civilians who would have been killed if the saturation bombing

continued and if an invasion had occurred? Should Truman have considered only American soldiers' lives and not Japanese civilians? At the time and after, military estimates of casualties from an invasion varied greatly.

5. Could a continuation of the saturation bombing and interdiction of all trade bring about a surrender of Japan without an invasion? Would the human cost, particularly on women and children, of essentially starving Japan into submission have been greater than human costs of using the atomic bombs? In spite of the deprivations of its people, Japan had substantial reserves of food and an undefeated army of two million men. Its military leaders hoped that America might accept a negotiated settlement whereby Japan could keep Korea and Formosa if the initial landing were repelled.

6. Was Japan already on the verge of surrender? Did the U.S. government know this because it had long before broken the Japanese cipher codes? At the time, opponents of unconditional surrender insisted that this doctrine would only prolong the war. Americans even after the bomb allowed the Japanese to determine the fate of the Emperor. If the U.S. had said so earlier, then, some historians believe, the fighting could have ended earlier. Advocates for the bombing insist that in the secret cables, Japan rebuked its peace-seeking ambassador to Russia, sought to keep earlier conquests, and the government never sought to communicate with America. Peace advocates in Japan had to be circumspect because militarists assassinated leaders seeking peace before the war. Even after the decision to surrender, army officers attempted a coup the night before Emperor Hirohito was to broadcast the news. Proponents of the bombing insist that it was not America's responsibility to initiate negotiations with Japan, but Japan's duty to its own people and soldiers to seek negotiations with the Allies.

7. What was the attitude of the Japanese leadership? A cabinet determined to seek peace controlled the government, but even after two atomic bombs, the leaders remained divided, and only the Emperor's intervention brought a decision

to surrender. In interrogations after the war, Japan's high commanders told Americans that the bombs were justified because they provided a face-saving way to surrender.[67]

8. Was not dropping a bomb a realistic political possibility, granting the expenditures in creating it, the weakness of a new President dedicated to carrying on Roosevelt's legacy, and the demand of the American public to save soldiers' lives and totally defeat the enemy? Was there such a momentum built up by 1945 that it was a virtual certainty that the bomb would have been used, first on Germany had it not surrendered, and then on Japan?

9. To what extent was the real target of the bomb not Japan but the emergent enemy in the Soviet Union? Dropping the bomb would make Soviet participation in an occupation of Japan unnecessary and would remind Stalin that the democracies had a monopoly on a secret weapon, which could be used against him. There is strong evidence that the American government saw the bomb as strengthening its position against Russia, but most historians still believe the primary target was Japan.

10. Was three days too short an interval between dropping the first and second atomic bombs? Would Japan need longer to digest the news and make so momentous a political decision as to surrender?

11. Was the Japanese attack on Pearl Harbor the moral equivalent of dropping the atomic bombs? When President George Bush Sr. was asked whether the U.S. should apologize for Hiroshima, he responded that the Japanese should first apologize for Pearl Harbor. What were the long-term effects of dropping the bomb on America's view of its conduct and Japan's view of the war? Did dropping of the atomic bombs taint an already-assured American victory over Japan?

Those debating the necessity of dropping the two atomic bombs blend assessments of the morality of total war, individuals' and nations' past actions,

---

[67]Information provided by Prof. James Field of Swarthmore College who conducted some of these interrogations.

and future hypothetical events. Many of these issues like the number of casualties from invasion or attitudes of the Japanese military are "what if" and cannot be settled even after careful weighing of conflicting historical evidence. How in retrospect can scholars understand and assess the motivation of powerful men who may not have wished to leave too much information and who with advantages of selective memories later reinterpreted their actions? Today we have both more knowledge and less understanding than the participants in the events. Critics and partisans seek evidence in hindsight for politicians and scientists exercising the kind of objectivity in weighing evidence difficult to obtain in peacetime and unlikely to occur after years of total war. The debate still rages because, without military necessity and the imperative to save lives, the acts were atrocities; even with them, the acts violated the traditional prohibition against killing civilians.[68]

The controversy on Hiroshima exemplifies how people in the mid-twentieth century debate issues of morality in war: religious values are rarely directly invoked, even when the concepts arise from Just War traditions. Churches are only one of many foci for discussion, and theologians claim no more expertise and have less influence than journalists, historians, ethicists, professional soldiers, and politicians in setting the terms of ethical discourse. Moral judgments intermix tradition, context and utility: that is, just cause, the nature of the war, military necessity, and success or failure establish the parameters for evaluating the action. Moreover, the wartime reaction to Dresden and postwar controversy over saturation and atomic bombings echoes Aquinas' requirement of purity in motives in assessing the mindset of the actors and, because revenge and racism are immoral motives, of Suarez's demand for a dispassionate consideration of

---

[68]Kai Bird and Lawrence Lifeschultz, eds., *Hiroshima's Shadow* (1998), 317-409. Robert Newman, *Truman and the Hiroshima Cult* (1995), defends Truman's decision as costing fewer lives than an invasion. Robert Maddox, *Weapons for Victory: The Hiroshima Decision Fifty Years After* (1995),argues that Japan was not going to surrender without an invasion.

alternative strategies and the protection of the innocent. People still oppose a war without limits.

In retrospect we can see that the continuing debate over the strategy and morality of the atomic bombings paled before the impact of the visual images of Hiroshima and the stories of the hell experienced by survivors. Hiroshima and Nagasaki created a threshold of horror that the peace advocates within and outside of churches would use to make a moral case against another use of nuclear weapons on any kind of a target. From 1945 until today, all governments proclaimed their abhorrence of atomic war. The unimaginable tragedy of a nuclear war made conventional war seem tame, perhaps lowered the moral boundaries so it could remain a viable option and a perennial activity. Because World War II was a return to barbarity, in the postwar period churches, academics, and military strategists debated morality in war with an intensity driven by desperation.

XI. The Aftermath: Churches Condemn Total War

In 1942 Pius XII announced that the new weapons of mass destruction and the prevalent total war mentality had created a condition in which all war was immoral, even if the cause was just. As the war continued, Pius realized that the defeated nations would be so prostrated that he cautioned the victors not to expect reparations. In order to prevent World War III, the winners would need to create a new international order that would apply brakes to excessive nationalism and limit state sovereignty.

In America, the Federal Council of Christian Churches, composed of the most important non-fundamentalist Protestant denominations, echoed sentiments similar to those of the Pope about the immorality of total war and advocated policies that would not repeat the mistakes of the Versailles Treaty. As early as 1942, the Federal Council and many individual denominations established commissions to plan for the peace. General agreement in the sentiments of the

Federal Council came from major denominations like the Roman Catholics, Methodists, Presbyterians, and Northern and Southern Baptists.[69]

American church leaders advised that a wise settlement must provide a mechanism by which Germany, Italy, and Japan would be re-educated and weaned from racism and militarism. Moreover, the Allies' treatment of the defeated should not be so harsh as to lay a foundation for another war, because these temporarily weakened states must eventually be re-integrated into the family of nations. Before signing any peace treaty, there should be an interval to allow the hatreds of war to cool. The Federal Council advocated a reformed international economic order with lower tariff barriers and equality of access to resources, aid to help Europe rebuild, and less exploitation of poorer areas. Echoing an American heritage of anti-colonialism, the churches insisted that the U.S. was not fighting to restore to Britain and France their imperial possessions in Asia and Africa. Racism must be repudiated not only in fascist countries but in the democracies as well.[70]

The churches insisted that the key to building a peaceful world would be creating a new international organization that would have the authority and power to end conflicts. Repudiating balance-of-power diplomacy and spheres of influence divided among Great Powers, the Federal Council envisaged the United Nations as a forum for large and small countries to settle disputes peacefully according to international norms. Nations should grant the World Court authority to compel obedience to the precepts of international law. In 1944 the Federal Council and the American Catholic bishops criticized the proposed charter of the UN for placing no restrictions on state sovereignty and opposed the Great Powers' veto within and control of the Security Council.[71]

---

[69]*Christian Century* (March 25, 1942), 393; Esther McCarthy, 217-221
[70]William Orser, "Social Attitudes of the Protestant Churches During the Second World War," (Ph.D. diss., University of New Mexico, 1969), 140, 153, 168, 182-85, 191-201.
[71]Esther McCarthy, "Catholic Periodical Press and Issues of War and Peace, 1914-1946,"(Ph.D. diss., Stanford, 1977), 233-39.

XII. Picking up the Pieces or Creating a Brave New World:
The UN and Nuremberg

Perceptive commentators saw the UN as it emerged after the San Francisco Conference of 1945 as a compromise between political realism and idealism, with the Security Council based upon traditional collective security enforced by the Allies' economic and military power, and with effectiveness in preserving peace dependent upon their continued cooperation. The General Assembly embodied the internationalist vision of the equality of all nations but had little legislative power and would need to rely upon public opinion or the Security Council for enforcement. The League of Nations' agencies for humanitarian concerns had been successful. The UN created similar agencies (UNRRA, UNICEF, WHO, WLO, UNESCO) dealing with refugees, children, health, labor, education and cultural issues and a Trusteeship Council for the supervision of colonial possessions.

In spite of their disappointments in the limited political powers of the UN, the churches mobilized their congregations to work against a return to American isolationism. The churches welcomed the UN as a mechanism to foster cooperation among nations and a vehicle to end war. Whatever its weaknesses (and enthusiastic supporters tended to oversell its potential), the UN offered hope to an impoverished world that it might be possible to break the endless cycle of ever-more-destructive violence. Most American churches approved of accepting international responsibility as a promoter of what was now called the "American way of life": human rights, democracy, capitalism, and individualism. With bipartisan support, in 1945 the Senate approved the U.S.' joining the UN by a vote of 89 to 2.

The Charter of the UN and the Declaration of Human Rights (1948) established norms for international conduct endorsed by the founding states (no defeated states were admitted until the 1950s) and all later members, which by the 1960s included the newly free states in Asia and Africa. The charter drew selectively upon traditional Just War theory by outlawing aggressive war (which, however, was not defined) and threats of war, recognizing all states' right of self-defense (also not defined), suggesting that all conflicts between two nations be referred to the UN, and allocating to the Security Council the right to intervene against threats to the peace. The international system of sovereign states that emerged after the Peace of Westphalia in 1648 was explicitly affirmed, with the UN claiming no jurisdiction over the internal affairs of a state.

In addition, the 1948 Declaration of Human Rights, passed unanimously, proclaimed the inherent rights of "life, liberty, and security of person." Every person should have trial by jury, religious freedom, equal pay for equal work, the right to join a trade union, free education, and an adequate standard of living. The Declaration was less a reflection of existing practices than a goad to action. Since nations insisted that treatment of their citizens was an internal affair, the UN charter made enforcement of human rights impossible. Even in 1948 communist and western nations interpreted differently the meaning of these inherent rights and pointed out the flaws in their opponents' records.

Over the years, member states have created additional conventions dealing with economic and social rights, declaring the rights of children and women, and outlawing genocide. New organizations like Amnesty International and Human Rights Watch and even the UN monitoring agencies have concluded that observance on many of these conventions remains spotty.

Because the UN's Declaration of Human Rights did not contain any intellectual justification of the origin of inherent rights, members are free to use natural law, the law of peoples, divine revelation, various forms of moral reasoning or even to see the rights as purely convention based - that is, as arbitrary and as having authority only by virtue of the UN's declaration.[72] The content of the norms reflected the predominant role of the U.S. and its supporters during the

---

[72]Seyom Brown, *Human Rights in World Politics* (2000), and Geoffrey Robertson, *Crimes Against Humanity: The Struggle for Global Justice* (1999), assess the roles of human rights in recent history.

early years of the organization, a condition that would change during the 1970s as Third World nations became a majority.

XIII. Creating Peace Through Law

After the war, the Allies created two forums to increase the power of international law: a reformed World Court and the Nuremberg trials. The old International Court at The Hague continued under a new charter as the World Court to serve as a place for states to adjudicate disputes. The Court still had no power to initiate cases on its own and compliance with its decisions would be voluntary. In practice states would utilize the court only if they thought the matter in dispute was relatively unimportant or that supporting the rule of law was more valuable than the issues to be decided. The hopes of peace advocates that a world court would play a major role in reducing tensions remain unfulfilled.[73]

The Allies hoped that punishing the leaders of Germany and Japan who had allegedly plotted aggressive war during the 1930s would restrain leaders in the future. During the war, the Allies insisted that the leaders of Nazi Germany and Japan would be punished for their crimes. Churchill and, according to Gallup polls, a majority of Americans initially favored summary executions. Instead, the victorious Allies established a judicial tribunal, which met at Nuremberg soon after the unconditional surrender and tried twenty-four leading Nazis for crimes against the peace (plotting and waging aggressive war), crimes against humanity (genocide, exterminations), and war crimes (violations of international law and the Geneva Conventions).

Critics charged that there was no legal basis for the Nuremberg tribunal. Although the Kellogg-Briand pact had outlawed aggressive war, before the Nuremberg trials, plotting and waging aggressive war had not been a crime, and international law applied only to states and not to individuals. Ohio's Senator Robert Taft, the Republican minority leader in the Senate and presidential

---

[73]Richard Falk, *Reviving the World Court* (1986).

aspirant, at considerable political risk denounced the Nuremberg trials as ex-post-facto justice. Taft applied the norms of American jurisprudence to the tribunal, but because the court was an international tribune the U.S. Supreme Court refused to accept appeals. Other critics saw as hypocritical the participation of the Soviets who had signed a treaty with Hitler in 1939 that partitioned Poland, had invaded Finland and the Baltic states, and had massacred at least 10,000 Polish prisoners of war at Katyn Forest in 1940. In addition, the Allies sitting in judgment had engaged in saturation bombing that before World War II had been universally considered as immoral but not codified as a war crime in international law. Nuremburg was, after all, a victor's justice made possible by the unconditional surrender of Germany and Japan, which meant that the Allies had access to all their documents.

An issue difficult for critics to solve was whether it would be better legal procedure to create a new tribunal or to try the Nazis by a jury of Germans under new German laws (clearly they could not be tried under Nazi law) or the statutes of invaded countries like Poland, whose new communist governments bore only a tangential relationship to the pre-1939 state. Proponents of the tribunal insisted that allowing the Nazi leadership to go unpunished would be irresponsible and send the wrong message to future leaders. After all, the horrendous nature of Nazi offenses was unprecedented and could be best dealt with only by an international court.

The Nuremberg judges insisted that individual Nazis and not the state committed the offenses and that, previously, individual soldiers had been held responsible for war crimes. In its decisions, the court rejected the defense that a person who claimed to be obeying orders was not responsible for his actions, even though at Nuremberg only the highest-ranking officials were tried. Twelve of the defendants received death sentences; four were acquitted; others received long prison sentences. Even those commentators who questioned the legality of the Nuremberg trials agreed that the Nazi leaders should not escape punishment and that the trials provided an incontrovertible record of atrocities that should preclude later revisionism.[74]

War crimes trials against Japanese military and civilian leaders in 1948 should be more controversial in retrospect than the Nuremberg proceedings, but have received far less attention. Critics point out the arbitrary standards used in selecting twenty-eight Japanese defendants (the Emperor was not indicted), biased judges (one had been a POW, another participated in the Bataan death march, a third did not understand the languages used), tainted evidence, lack of historical perspective in dealing with Japan's pre-1939 actions, and failure of judges to reach unanimity on the seven sentenced to death (six were convicted by 7 to 4 and one by 6 to 5 votes).[75]

German war crimes trials continued after the Occupation, are still held, and, in many ways, constantly force new generations to examine events of the war. The Japanese trials, which ended, have not served this function. The Allies hoped that at Tokyo and Nuremberg they had established clear standards that could be used for future international tribunals for making leaders accountable for waging aggressive war and committing crimes against humanity. Yet in spite of the hundreds of wars since 1945, the Nuremberg precedents have been officially utilized only recently, in establishing tribunals to deal with war crimes in Bosnia and Rwanda and, in spite of U.S. opposition, in creating a permanent war crimes court.

---

[74]A good introduction to the issue of war crimes and World War II is in Marshall Cohen et al., eds. *War and Moral Responsibility* (1974), 85-158. (1974), 85-158. A brief summary of the Nuremberg precedents is in Geoffrey Robertson, 203-242. See also Robert Woetzel, *The Nuremberg Trials in International Law* (1962); Telford Taylor, *The Anatomy of the Nuremberg Trials* (1992); and Richard Falk, et al., eds., *Crimes of War* (1971).
[75]"Far East War Crimes Trials" in *Oxford Companion to World War II*, ed.I. C. B. Dear and Foot (1995), 347-50.

XVII.
The Cold War - I:
Conventional Weapons and Wars

Now that the Cold War has ended, scholars are gaining access to the archives of major and minor powers and beginning the long process of gaining historical perspective. One phenomenon seems clear: compared with the extraordinary changes in intellectual, social, and economic life, there is a sameness in the way the Soviet Union and the United States viewed each other and in their overall military strategy from 1948 until 1990. Each saw his opponent as aggressive and, by building and maintaining arsenals of conventional and nuclear weapons and by the threat of war, sought to restrain unacceptable behavior. Both feared nuclear war or a large-scale conventional war, yet were willing to increase the risk of a major confrontation by using troops or arming their allies in secondary theaters (Korea, Vietnam, Afghanistan).

Each of the two world powers wanted peace on its own terms, believing that its form of government and economics should be the model for the entire world, and each made certain that the countries it occupied in 1945 conformed to its view of society. Both powers justified their policies of realpolitik by an ideology that shaped its view of the world. The places where the Red and the West's armies stopped became the border between what the West called free, i.e., democratic, capitalist, pro-U.S. countries, and the Peoples' Republics of pro-Soviet, communist, authoritarian states. The West stressed individualism, human rights, and economic opportunity, and thought Russian imperialism and communism inseparable; the Soviets stressed social and economic rights and equality of condition, but saw democracy as camouflage for capitalist exploitation of workers. Capitalist countries, by their very nature, Stalin believed, would seek to destroy communism. Communist totalitarian countries, by their very nature, the West concluded, would seek to destroy capitalism and democracy.

After the Soviets imposed communism on Eastern Europe in a brutal fashion (which reflected the way Stalin ruled), the West concluded that Russia intended to dominate all of Europe. (Documents in Russian archives have not as yet proved that Stalin sought this conquest.[1]) It soon became an article of faith in America, dominating foreign policy for years, that no country would willingly adopt communism. After 1948 there would be no fundamental debate on America's attitude to the Soviet Union for a generation.

The 1948 coup in Czechoslovakia served to justify the U.S. and British plan to create a West German state, inaugurate the Marshall Plan to rebuild Europe, and institute a military alliance termed the North Atlantic Treaty Organization (NATO). There would be no peace treaty between a united Germany and the Allies; instead, Europe would be divided into two hostile blocs. Berlin, isolated in the communist zone and divided between the two systems, became the flash point for a potential war. Soviet fears that the new German Republic (West Germany) would be re-armed, and its recognition of the contrast between life in the western zone of Berlin and in East Germany led, in 1948, to the Soviet blockade of the land routes to Berlin, countered by an airlift by the Allies. The communist states then the created the Warsaw Pact. The border between East and West Germany became the most heavily militarized area in the world.

The churches responded to the Cold War in two ways: one was abhorrence of the Soviet system and a belief that the West should oppose it. The other belief was that even with just cause, war should be avoided as a greater evil. Neither of these emphases was confined to the churches, and the lines between religious, moral, and secular wisdom were very blurry. This first chapter on the Christian

---

[1]Daniel Yergen, *Shattered Peace: The Origins of the Cold War* (1990), 22. Melvin Leffler, "Inside Enemy Archives," *Foreign Affairs* (1996), 122-26; a different perspective is in John Gaddis, *We Know Now: Rethinking Cold War History* (1997).

churches and the Cold War deals with conventional war. Part I focuses on Catholic and Protestant churches and peace organizations. Part II focuses on America's Cold War policies and two armed conflicts: Cuba and Korea. Part III deals with the war in Vietnam: the causes and conduct of the war, the peace movement, and the debate within the churches. Lurking behind the conventional wars during the entire fifty-year period was the threat of nuclear war that will be discussed in the second Cold War chapter.

I .The Churches Confront the Cold War

The Roman Catholic Cold War

Religious animosity was not a primary factor in creating the Cold War, but Soviet antipathy towards all organized religions and religious belief and self-proclaimed atheism complicated relationships with the West and fostered distrust. After the 1917 revolution, the Soviet Union became officially anti-religious, and Stalin's policies of closing churches and persecuting priests almost destroyed the institutional church in Russia, although many people still practiced Christianity. In World War II, the Orthodox Church's enthusiastic support for the war against Germany and the need to unify the Russian people brought restricted freedom for the Church but did not end official hostility. Under the Tsars, the Orthodox Church had always supported the government, so priests and patriarchs under Stalin seeking to preserve the Church could more easily accept its inability to criticize the Soviet government as a necessary price of existence.[2]

The Cold War between the papacy and the Soviet Union began in the 1920s and continued until 1955. The Soviet's grudging tolerance of Orthodox Christianity never extended to the Roman Catholics. Stalin would not allow bishops owing allegiance to a foreign agency and sought to destroy Uniate churches (with Orthodox ritual but with bishops appointed by and loyal to Rome) in the Soviet Union. Even after it became clear that the Nazis would be defeated,

---

[2]Philip Walters, "The Russian Orthodox Church," in *Eastern Christianity and Politics* (1988), I, 76-80; Jane Ellis, *The Russian Orthodox Church: A Contemporary History* (1986).

Pius XII, believing that there soon would be another war between the Russians and the democracies, did not seek a *modus vivendi* with Stalin. He encouraged belief in the appearances of the Virgin Mary to children at Fatima, Spain, in 1917 when she forecast the destruction of communism. The Church insisted that it could exist under any kind of regime that would respect its spiritual autonomy, but Pius concluded that communist states would not tolerate Christianity and must be opposed. Real peace could not come with a regime that denied fundamental human rights and the moral law, because that state was at war with its own people, i.e., a tyranny.[3]

Even when it became clear that communist governments would dominate Eastern Europe, Pius did not seek to create concordats such as the Church had previously negotiated with Hitler and Mussolini. Pius' silence during the war about the fascist regimes and the Holocaust would not be repeated in dealing with communist regimes in the postwar world. In Poland, to the dismay of the Vatican, Cardinal Wyszunski worked out an arrangement with the communist government allowing some degree of autonomy, church schools, and preserving seminaries to educate priests. In Hungary, Yugoslavia, Albania, and in Czechoslovakia after 1948 when there was a communist coup, the Catholic Church remained openly hostile. Yugoslavia under Tito tried and imprisoned the Catholic Archbishop Stepinac who during the war had acquiesced in forced conversions and oppressions of Serbians by Croatians sympathetic to the Nazis. Hungary's newly appointed Cardinal Mindszensky typified a defiant Church whose leaders expected to suffer imprisonment or worse rather than compromise. For Czechoslovakia, the papacy secretly appointed bishops, all of whom were soon arrested. The papacy condemned the Russian Orthodox Church that had reached

---

[3]Hansjokob Stehle, *Eastern Politics of the Vatican 1917-1979,* tr. Sandra Smith (1981), 161, 170-2, 232; Rhodes, *Church and the Dictators*; Owen Chadwick, *The Christian Church in the Cold War* (1992).

a compromise with the communist regime to ensure its survival, forgetting that only recently it had pursued a similar policy with fascist states.[4]

The Catholic Church also encountered in France and Italy strong anti-clerical communist parties whose prestige resulted from leading partisan activities against the Fascists. These parties' foreign policy seemed made in Moscow. In a strongly worded rebuke to those who sought social justice through communism, Pius in 1949 implied that belonging to the Catholic Church was incompatible with membership in or even voting for a communist party. In postwar Germany, Italy, and France the Church threw its influence behind center Christian Democratic parties to stem communist influence. Voters from their parties supported the creation of the North Atlantic Treaty Organization in 1948 as a military alliance to counter the Soviet threat. The papacy continued to deplore the creation of nuclear weapons, to advocate a new world order, and to voice support for peace among nations, but its strident opposition to the Soviet Union and support of Catholic center parties allowed Eastern European communists to see the Church as a political opponent and weakened its influence for peace. The Church in essence had become a warrior for the West, and its diminished though still potent influence in free and communist Europe was a clear answer to Stalin's jibe repeated at Yalta "how many divisions does the Pope have?"[5]

America's Churches React to the Soviet Union

The hierarchy of the American Catholic Church followed the papacy's lead in opposing communism. Unsure of their status in a Protestant- dominated country, Catholics had long sought to counter nativism by stressing patriotic support for democracy and religious liberty. Anti-communism provided another means for Catholics to demonstrate loyalty. First and second generation Catholic immigrants from the Baltic countries, Poland, Hungary, and Czechoslovakia took a

---

[4]Stehle, 248-79.
[5]Stalin quoted by Harry Truman, *New York Times*, September 14, 1948, 24. For comments as to the accuracy, see *Respectfully Quoted*, ed. Suzy Platt (1986), #165, and Oral History Interview with Wallace Graham, Truman Library, online; Stehle, 225, 276.

keen interest in affairs in their homelands. Many Catholics feared that a communist takeover in Italy might jeopardize the independence of the papacy.

Catholics in American labor unions and in the Democratic Party also espoused anti-communism. Even in the late nineteenth-century, Catholics played an influential role in American labor unions and sought to minimize the influence of socialists and communists. American unions concentrated upon "bread and butter" issues in seeking better working conditions and wages for members rather than stressing a class-consciousness. After World War II, American labor at home was politically liberal but the leaders and members remained deeply suspicious of the Soviet Union. The anti-communist crusade lead by Wisconsin's Catholic senator Joseph McCarthy received the support of New York's influential Cardinal Spellman, the Kennedy family of Massachusetts, and conservative Catholic periodicals (but not the more liberal *Commonweal*.)[6]

In World War II, the Protestant churches embraced a theory of government that stressed the compatibility of democracy and religion and the spiritual underpinnings of the "American way of life." In both World Wars Americans felt they had saved Western civilization from tyranny. Now Western Europe and Asia appeared threatened by a new form of totalitarianism and America once again would rise to the challenge. The struggle between the USSR and the U.S. involved not just rival economic systems, but freedom and tyranny, atheism and religion. So the churches found once again an important social role in rallying the forces of Christianity against evil. The tempered form of cautious patriotism that in World War II contrasted American democracy, human rights, and religious freedom with Nazi Germany now was extended to comparing the U.S. and USSR. Reinhold Niebuhr stressed the compatibility of Christianity with democracy, because Christianity upheld the dignity of individuals while insisting upon limits of power because all were sinners. Billy Graham rose to prominence preaching the necessity of evangelistic revivalism to counter materialism and labeled communism

---

[6]Weigel, *Tranquillitas Ordinis* (1987), 64, 69-71, shows that many Catholics opposed McCarthy, who received about the same support from Protestants and Catholics.

anti-Christian.[7] By contrast, the roots and leadership of the American peace movement remained in liberal Protestantism.

The Peace Movement

Religious and secular leaders of a vocal but small American peace movement argued that the Cold War was the responsibility of both sides, with each using similar irresponsible half-truths to vilify an opponent. Doves insisted that the differences between the two governments and economic systems, while imposing, did not justify putting the world at risk of nuclear war. Rather, the peoples of both nations wanted peace that could be facilitated by small steps like cultural exchanges and arms reductions. The clerical leadership of liberal Protestant churches sympathized with the goals and tactics of many peace organizations and could obtain limited media attention in critiques of American society and foreign policy, but had little power to mobilize the voting power of the main-line denominations. Complaints about American foreign policy infuriated the right wing evangelical opposition who supported a strong national defense, conservative economic policies, and anti-communism.[8]

The peace movement of the 1950s gained potential strength from new tactics and a new constituency, Afro-Americans. Learning from the sit-down strikes to unionize General Motors and Ford in the 1930s and Gandhi's successful nonviolent campaigns in India, pacifists like A. J. Muste, a former Congregational minister who served in several peace organizations, had learned the value of direct actions and demonstrations in gaining media attention and in mobilizing people for a cause.[9] Sailing a ship into an area designed for a nuclear test, scaling the fence of a missile base, and picketing the White House provided visible dissent from America's military policies.

---

[7]Richard Fox, *Reinhold Niebuhr* (1987), 228-33, 240, 244-45; Marshall Frady, *Billy Graham: A Parable of American Righteousness* (1979), 197-98, 200-01, 236-39; William Au, 17, 43-58.
[8]Lawrence Wittner, *Rebels Against War: The American Peace Movement, 1933-1960* (1969), chs. 7, 8.
[9]Lee Ann Robinson, *Abraham Went Out: A Biography of A. J. Muste* (1981).

Peace advocates in the 1930s had been predominately white middle-class Protestants, but even then they had criticized the evils of segregation. Future black civil rights leaders including Martin Luther King, Jr., Bayard Rustin, and James Foreman would, in the late fifties, use the lessons and contacts gained through their earlier involvement with the peace movement in the emergent civil rights movement. In the mid-1960s, King and the Southern Christian Leadership Conference advocated ending segregation and stopping the war in Vietnam. Many Jews and Christians who learned the effectiveness of public demonstrations in the Civil Rights movement applied the same tactics against the war in Vietnam. One study of involvement in anti-Vietnam War activities concluded that a previous civil rights role was a better predictor of anti-war work than church attendance or theological perspective.[10]

Beginning in 1948 the Soviets founded or supported a variety of pro-peace and disarmament organizations and conferences, and communist sympathizers sought to join and influence the policies of religious and secular Western peace groups. These communist members, who might or might not be members of the Party, confronted peace advocates with a dilemma they had first encountered in the 1930s. American communists seemed more concerned with defending the Soviet Union and attacking the United States than with making peace.

Liberal peace leaders feared that the communists would enlist the efforts of well-meaning citizens in front organizations or would try to take over older peace organizations. Should communists be purged from the organizations and how, in voluntary societies, could this be done without estranging those members who were often pro-socialism but not members of the Communist Party and genuinely committed to peace? And should Western peace organizations attend conferences and cooperate with Soviet-sponsored or front organizations? If the conferences

---

[10]Starr, "Religious Preference, Religiosity, and Opposition to War," *Sociological Analysis* (1975), 327; Tygart, "Social Movement Participation: Clergy and the Anti-Vietnam War Movement," *Sociological Analysis* (1973), 205. Jervis Anderson, Bayard Rustin: *Troubles I've Seen: A Biography* (1997).

were just to reinforce Soviet propaganda, perhaps then it would be best to stay away. On the other hand, peace groups sought interactions with Soviet peace groups, even if staffed by Party officials, because a continuing attempt to build personal relationships was one means of reducing tensions and avoiding war, and even tainted support for peace was better than vituperation. Should Western peace groups engage in constant criticism of both Americans and Soviets, holding them both responsible for the Cold War, or would such actions be counterproductive at home and in making contact with Soviet citizens?

The peace commissions of the mainline Protestant churches criticized both sides. In contrast, the American Friends Service Committee, which sought constant dialogue with Soviet communists, decided that it would not publicly criticize Russian behavior. But since the Service Committee members were Americans, they exercised their democratic right to denounce U.S. military policy. Such a stance brought public denunciation by zealous anti-communists in the U.S. who saw the Service Committee and other peace organizations as communists or following the communist line either because their members were naïve or duplicitous.[11] And the pro-communist label was applied to socially progressive organizations like the National Council of Churches that supported liberal politics in America and a conciliatory policy towards the Soviet Union abroad. With peace organizations, churches, labor unions, and social reformers seeking to distance themselves from charges of being soft on communism, there was little opposition to Cold War rhetoric. In 1948 the Truman administration found it could unify the country behind increased military spending and foreign aid when it publicly embraced anti-communism.

II. Cold War Politics: Crises and War

By the 1950s many Americans believed that they had won the war and then lost the peace through nefarious tactics of communists first in Eastern Europe and then in China. Political conservatives, moderates, and even many

---

[11] Guenter Lewy's accounts of Women's International League for Peace and Freedom and AFSC in *Peace and Revolution: The Moral Crisis of American Pacifism* (1998), Part 2: chs. 2-5.

liberals believed that Russia could not be trusted to keep its agreements because communism allowed any means if the ends would advance Soviet power. Communist subversion abroad could take place because of undercover agents in American organizations and government. A legitimate concern for security against communist spies became under the influence of Senator Joseph McCarthy in 1950, a hunt for "Reds" in labor unions, businesses, universities, the military, State Department, Hollywood, and the churches. Rightist opportunists found it politically easy to portray all critics of the U.S. foreign policy as pro-communist and those who supported regulation of business and social reform legislation as leading the country towards socialism. The creation of communist-front peace organizations made more difficult the peace movements' activities within and outside the churches.

The Soviet control of Eastern Europe, communist triumph in China, strong communist parties in France and Italy, and the Korean War convinced the leaders of both major political parties and most Americans that it was necessary to oppose communism by any means. Church leaders shared in the suspicion, fear and distrust of the Soviet Union. Yet the Cold War was also invigorating, allowing Americans to create a sense of the unity they had felt in World War II.[12] Opposing totalitarianism allowed Americans to reaffirm their destiny as a beacon and citadel of Christianity and democracy. Western Europeans might cringe at Americans' self-righteous blusterings, but they wanted a NATO alliance bringing U.S. troops to Europe and the protection of a nuclear umbrella.

Korea

The first military test of the Truman administration's policy of containing communism occurred in Korea. Japan had ruled Korea since 1905, but in 1945, Korea had been liberated and then arbitrarily divided between a communist North and U.S.-supported "free" South at the 38th parallel. The new regimes, both led by authoritarian leaders, reflected the desires of their patron countries. Each

---

[12]Robert Wuthnow, *The Restructuring of American Religion: Society and Faith Since World War II* (1988), ch. 3: 41, 52, 143.

Korean government wanted to unify the peninsula, and there were many incidents on the frontier. A year after the triumph of Mao Tse-Tung's communists in China, North Korea in 1950 launched a surprise military invasion, and Truman decided to commit American troops. Kim Il Song, dictator of North Korea, assumed that dissidents in South Korea would support the invasion and victory would come quickly. The UN denounced the invasion and the Security Council authorized resistance under the U.S. commander, a decision made possible because of Soviet absence in order to protest Red China's failure to obtain a seat on the Security Council. Americans assumed that Stalin and the Chinese had instigated the invasion as a part of a strategy of military expansion into weak nations in Asia and concluded that Korea was the place to stop communism. [13]

The Korean conflict became a bloody conventional war with an estimated over two million total casualties, mostly from Korean civilians and soldiers, and Chinese and American soldiers.[14] Widespread civilian casualties resulted from the armies' movements up and down the peninsula and the intensive American bombing. Initial communist victories drove the UN forces to a small enclave in the South, but a successful American counter attack pushed North Koreans back beyond the 38th parallel almost to the Yalu River border with China. Chinese intervention, American retreat, and an eventual two-year stalemate characterized the war. At first, the Americans sought only to bomb military targets, but by the end, in an attempt to break the impasse, they bombed cities, particularly in North Korea where by the end of the war eighteen of twenty-two major cities were at least half obliterated. But unlike World War II, there was criticism from the Allies and neutral nations like India over the destruction of civilians.[15]

---

[13] We now believe that although China and the USSR knew in advance, provided supplies and approved the invasion, the primary push for military unification came from North Korea. Stalin wanted to divert attention from Western Europe, weaken any chance of a rapprochement between China and the U.S., and strengthen his border. William Strueck, *The Korean War: An International History* (1995), 31-41 assesses Stalin's and Mao's motivations. Struck argues that the experience of China, USSR, and the U.S. in Korea served as a substitute for World War III.
[14] Conrad Crane, *American Airpower Strategy in Korea 1950-1953* (2000), 8, 126.
[15] Ibid., 46-47, 63, 75, 168.

At a news conference in 1950, Truman mused that the U.S. might use atomic bombs to bring victory, a suggestion that occasioned an enormous outcry in Europe and helped to stimulate the anti-nuclear movement. When, in 1951, General Douglas MacArthur, commander of American forces, publicly advocated widening the war to include bombing targets in China, Truman dismissed his commander, but he gained the military Chiefs of Staff's approval by agreeing to send the unassembled parts of six atomic bombs to Okinawa. Truman and the Pentagon, under pressure from European NATO members, kept Korea a limited war because the U.S.'s primary enemy was Russia, not China. Within the American military, there was a constant debate upon the advisability of using nuclear weapons. After privately threatening the use of nuclear weapons, the Eisenhower administration in 1953 obtained a truce dividing Korea again at the 38th parallel. (It is not certain whether China and North Korea knew of Eisenhower's plans.) For the first time in recent history, America had fought a war it did not win.

For the next twenty years, the U.S. and Red China would be bitter enemies, but both sides avoided fighting each other, even over Vietnam. After undergoing a series of authoritarian leaders until the 1990s, South Korea emerged as a capitalist, prosperous, and democratic state while North Korea under Kim Il Sung and his son remains a repressive, poor, but militarily powerful dictatorship. The border between North and South Korea continues to be one of the most heavily militarized areas in the world, and American troops are still stationed there.[16]

The debate in America over Korea was not on the advisability of intervention, but on whether to fight a limited war. Seeing North Korea as an

---

[16]A short history showing the relationship of the Cold War in Europe to the Korean conflict is Peter Lowe, *The Origins of the Korean War* 2nd ed. (1997). Bruce Cumings, *The Origins of the Korean War*, 2 vols, 1981, 1990, is a thorough account of the history of North and South Korea before and during the war.

invader and approving of collective security through the UN, the National Council of Churches, Roman Catholics, Southern Baptists and mainline Protestant denominations approved of standing up to communism. Still, there was dissent in religious periodicals; a survey of twenty-three Protestant, Catholic, and Jewish periodicals in 1950 showed that twelve were in favor of American policy, eight opposed, and three equivocal. As the war dragged on, three periodicals, *Christian Century, Presbyterian Life*, and *The Lutheran* switched their positions from supporting to opposing. Of the nine that remained pro, four were Roman Catholic, three Jewish, and two Protestant (one of which was Niebuhr's *Christianity and Crisis.*)[17] Church critics of America's policies in Korea opposed what they labeled as the undue influence of the military and anti-communism in American foreign policy and the threat of a Third World War.

Cold War Politics

American foreign policy after Korea rested upon a bipartisan consensus that no country would willingly adopt communism, but poor undeveloped nations remained susceptible to Russian or Chinese-backed subversive movements. The West must on all fronts - military, political, economic, and religious - counter an expansionist ideology. So the United States embraced and supported not only the democratic governments in Western Europe, but also regimes run by dictators - Franco in Spain, Duvalier in Haiti, Somosa in Nicaragua, Chiang Kai-shek in Taiwan, Mobuto in Kinshasa (Congo) - under the theory supposedly enunciated earlier by Roosevelt about Somosa: "He may be a son of a bitch, but at least he's our son of a bitch."[18]

Russia and the United States created secret spy agencies (NKVD, CIA) willing to use dirty tactics because of the nobility of democracy or communism

---

[17]Harold Osmer, "United States Religious Press Response to the Containment Policy During the Period of the Korean War," (Ph.D. diss., New York University, 1970), 156-161, 211-216; Dunn, "The Church and Cold War: Protestants and Conscription, 1940-1955," (Ph.D. diss., University of Missouri-Columbia, 1973), 121.

[18]*Cassell Dictionary of Insulting Quotations*, ed. Jonathan Green (1996), 255, which gives the date as 1938. The standard biographies of Roosevelt do not mention the quotation.

and each nation accurately declaimed against the unethical practices of its opponent. In order to protect communism and Russia's national security (the two seemed identical to rulers in the Kremlin), the USSR denied freedom and intervened to squash rebellions in Eastern Europe, attempted to subvert pro-Western governments, sponsored terrorist groups, supported guerrilla movements in colonial dependencies, and exported arms to client states.

The U.S. saw itself as more moral than the Soviet Union because it identified its interest with democracy, capitalism, and Christianity and was, except on Eastern Europe, a status quo power, interested in building up rather than subverting republican governments in the so-called Free World. Americans took pride in the Marshall Plan that helped restore the economies of non-communist European governments. U.S. foreign aid to the Third World or developing countries sought to help economic development, partially for moral reasons, but mainly because eradicating poverty and furthering democracy would lessen the appeal of communism. However, the U.S. overthrew popular governments in Iran and Guatemala, undermined a duly elected Marxist President in Chile, supported guerrilla movements against pro-communist regimes in Cuba, Angola, and Nicaragua, subsidized anti-communist political parties in Italy, Japan, and El Salvador, and exported arms to friendly authoritarian states.

The Great Powers exploited other nations in their ideological struggle. So when King Haile Selassie was pro-Western, the U.S. supported what was essentially a feudal regime in Ethiopia's struggle over the breakaway area of Eritrea, whose rebels were aided by Somalia. The USSR favored Somalia. After Selassie was overthrown and replaced by a Marxist government, the Russians aided Ethiopia and the U.S. supplied Somalia. (In the 1990s the heavily armed Somalis would use the Great Power-supplied weapons against each other.)

For all the moral pretenses of both sides, realpolitik was ascendant. So long as frightened American people accepted the premise that all communist governments were engaged in a life or death struggle with democracies, they willingly followed their leaders' exhortations that "we shall pay any price, bear any burden ... to assure the survival and success of liberty" because "extremism in the defense of liberty is no vice."[19] Only after the discrepancy between moral rhetoric and dirty tricks became public knowledge in Vietnam, Watergate, and Iran-gate did a substantial number of Americans grow increasingly cynical about Cold War rhetoric. However, until the demise of the Soviet Union, both political parties insisted that America should negotiate only from a position of military strength.

Disarmament Talks

At one level Russia and the U.S. fought the Cold War as a propaganda battle to convince public opinion of its own peace-loving nature and of the aggressive stance of the adversary. Both used disarmament proposals made in bilateral talks and in the UN as attempts to influence neutral nations and charged the adversary with being disingenuous, of using peace sentiment to put its opponent at a military disadvantage. Western peace groups and the National and World Councils of Churches sought, with little success, to make both sides tone down belligerent statements and to translate their peaceful rhetoric into workable policies.

After the death of Stalin, the U.S. and USSR engaged in negotiations that seemed promising in 1954 but never led to any disarmament. The Soviet government's official position was that nuclear arms should be outlawed and abandoned and that this could be done unilaterally and without inspection. The U.S. also officially wanted disarmament of nuclear and conventional weapons and saw nuclear war as a disaster, but it feared the Soviet preponderance in conventional forces in Europe. America insisted that its nuclear weapons served as the means of keeping the Soviets from invading or blackmailing Western Europe, a view publicly embraced by the governments of all the NATO countries. The Catholic and Protestant churches that advocated mutual disarmament faced

---

[19]John Kennedy, "Inaugural Address," quoted in Theodore Sorensen, Kennedy, 246. Barry Goldwater, "Acceptance speech at 1964 Republican Nominating Convention" in *Where I Stand* (1964), 16.

governments that openly supported their objectives, but whose policies undercut any possibility of achieving an agreement.

The worldviews of pro- and anti-Marxist peace groups had little impact on national policies. In Western Europe conservative or center-left coalitions supported NATO, and in countries with strong communist parties, like France and Italy, governments undercut radical leftist parties' electoral potential by extensive social welfare programs and by nationalizing key industries. Pro-Marxist political parties and intellectuals blamed the U.S. for economic oppression and for the arms race at the same time that they turned a blind eye to Soviet provocations. Their demand for unilateral disarmament while defending Soviet military interventions to put down popular movements in Eastern Europe weakened their influence. Marxists, who remained anti-Catholic and anti-clerical, could not build an alliance with those who opposed the West's military stance for religious reasons. America had a small leftist, non-communist socialist movement and a smaller Communist Party, but even being a socialist seemed suspect in the 1950s. Unlike Europe, there was no prominent left wing of dissenters in America, the closest being the liberalism of the Americans for Democratic Action.

The majority Democratic Party was dominated by Southerners including Texas Speaker of the House Sam Rayburn and Senate Majority Leader Lyndon Johnson, and Georgia's Richard Russell - who supported progressive social legislation (so long as ending segregation was not involved) and a strong military. Southern Congressmen like Mendel Rivers, chairman of the House Armed Service Committee, controlled legislation. Northern Senators like Massachusetts' John Kennedy, Henry "Scoop" Jackson of Washington, and Missouri's Stuart Symington (all of whom would run for president) were hawks. After the Soviets launched the Sputnik space satellite in 1957 that seemed to indicate Russian superiority in rocket technology, all of the above mentioned senators and the Democratic Party criticized the Eisenhower administration for insufficient defense spending and supported an extensive rearmament program including building a huge new ICBM force to make up for what the Department of Defense admitted in 1960 to be an imaginary "missile gap" with Russia. Militant anti-communism characterized dominant forces within the Democratic Party: organized labor, Southerners, ethnics, and Roman Catholics.

The minority Republican Party since the late 1940s had utilized anti-communism as a means to gather votes and was even more committed to a strong national defense. Richard Nixon, candidate for Vice President or President in five elections from 1952 through 1972, symbolized the Republicans' visceral anti-communism. No ambitious politician could be seen as being soft on communism, but, as Barry Goldwater learned in the 1964 presidential election, neither was it advantageous to be labeled as a warmonger willing to risk nuclear holocaust.

The Cuban Missile Crisis

Fidel Castro's 1959 revolution against a corrupt dictator in Cuba turned out to be the one of the rare communist successes in the Western Hemisphere. Castro led a popular movement enjoying the support of all classes. To the surprise of most Americans and Cubans, Castro created a politically autocratic and socially progressive Marxist regime that sought a close relationship with the Soviet Union. Castro's willingness to export his revolution irritated and frightened the U.S., which viewed all Latin America as ripe for communist revolution. Assuming that a communist regime could not be popular and believing the tales of those who fled Cuba, the CIA and the Joint Chiefs of Staff persuaded President Kennedy in 1961 to support an invasion by Cuban exiles at the Bay of Pigs that was supposed to result in a popular uprising. The invasion was a disaster. Castro's survival and flagrant defiance of America, in spite of the U.S.'s attempt to economically isolate and subvert his regime by invasion, assassination, and assorted dirty tricks of Operation Mongoose (coordinated by the Robert Kennedy, the Attorney General) redoubled America's resolve to counter communism elsewhere.[20] Having failed to draw the line in Cuba, the Kennedy administration sought a success in Southeast Asia.

Castro's knowledge of American plots and fear of another invasion provided his rationale for accepting the Russian proposal to install nuclear missiles to be aimed at America. Soviet Premier Nikita Khrushchev sought to counter the American advantages in ICBMs and military bases surrounding Russia by secretly sending nuclear missiles to Cuba. He may have wanted ultimately to trade Cuba for West Berlin. Even though President Kennedy had declared that the U.S. would not tolerate the placing of nuclear weapons in Cuba, Khrushchev gambled that he could present the U.S. with a *fait accompli*. His memoirs claimed that he hoped that making America as vulnerable as the USSR would ultimately lead to better relations.[21] Instead, a confrontation ensued in which the world was poised on the brink of nuclear war.

Believing (incorrectly) that there were not yet any nuclear missiles in Cuba, most of President Kennedy's advisers wanted a military strike on Cuba, perhaps followed by an invasion. Seeing an American surprise attack as analogous to Pearl Harbor and unconvinced that a "surgical" military strike would work, the U.S. declared a quarantine with the possibility of later military action.

Kennedy feared Russia might react to an American attack by retaliating at Turkey's newly installed (but already obsolete) Jupiter missiles; such an attack would then bring NATO's response and a possible war over Berlin that could easily become a nuclear holocaust. Had the U.S. bombed Cuba's missile bases, Soviet troops would have been killed, and there is a strong probability that others would have responded with tactical nuclear weapons. Instead, the Soviet ships carrying missiles observed the blockade and returned to Russia, and the missile bases were dismantled. These actions averted war, with the Americans openly

---

[20]Graham Allison and Philip Zelikow, *The Essence of Decision: Explaining the Cuban Missile Crisis* (2nd ed., 1999), 369. The director of the CIA, a conservative Roman Catholic, refused to support assassination attempts, declaring that he did not wish to risk excommunication.

pledging not to invade Cuba and secretly promising to withdraw obsolete Jupiter nuclear missiles from Turkey. For public consumption, the U.S. denied any quid pro quo and claimed a victory. Khrushchev soon fell from power, but Castro survived, and Kennedy gained enormous prestige. The churches thanked God that war had been averted, but only a few questioned the wisdom of policies that had brought the world to the brink of nuclear war. The Kennedy administration concluded that firm but graduated resistance to Soviet advances in Cuba and acquiescence in the new wall dividing East from West Berlin presented the way to stability.

III. The War in Vietnam

In the aftermath of the Bay of Pigs debacle, the Kennedy administration decided that communist aggression had to be stopped in Southeast Asia. Vietnam had been a French colony conquered by the Japanese but restored to France after World War II, in spite of the complaints of a communist nationalist leader Ho Chi Minh. A communist insurgency defeated the French at Dien Pien Phu, and an armistice in 1954 divided the country into a communist North and non-communist South and provided for elections to unify the country. Thousands of refugees moved from the North to the South, including cadres of communists who joined nationalists and communists in the South who felt betrayed by Geneva Conventions. The elections were never held, because the U.S. concluded that there could be no free ballots in the North, and Ho Chi Minh might win in the South. Instead, America supported Ngo Dinh Diem as Premier of South Vietnam. Diem, a patriot who had opposed the Japanese in World War II, was a non-communist, and a Roman Catholic (his brother was a bishop) who enjoyed the support of New York's Francis Cardinal Spellman. Coming to power with American support, Diem turned out to be an autocrat who sought to quell communist and non-communist opponents through force, with America providing

---

[21]James G. Blight and Philip Zelikow, eds., *On the Brink: Americans and Soviets Reexamine the Cuban Missile Crisis* 2nd ed. (1990) and James G. Blight et al., *Cuba on the Brink: Castro, the Missile Crisis, and the Soviet Collapse* (1993).

financial support for his army.[22] In 1959 North Vietnam decided to provide military aid to the rebels in the South.

America's coming to Diem's aid occasioned little public debate at first because Cuba, Berlin, and even Laos seemed equally significant. Aiding South Vietnam was popular; the media and administration portrayed South Vietnam as a small country trying to remain free against Northern Vietnamese aggression sparked by China and Russia. Americans assumed (incorrectly it later turned out) that North Vietnam was a Chinese-Russian pawn to help spread communism. If South Vietnam fell, then a domino effect would follow in which the rest of Southeast Asia - Laos, Cambodia, Thailand, Malaysia and then maybe India, Indonesia, and Japan - would be threatened. America saw the violence in South Vietnam as an invasion from the North, not a civil war. Kennedy authorized a small force of experts in guerrilla warfare, the Green Berets, to aid South Vietnam's army.

Diem's repressive policies, persecution of Buddhists, and the growing war alienated the Buddhist majority in South Vietnam that sought a negotiated end of the conflict. In 1963 a Buddhist monk, dousing himself with gasoline and then setting it afire, demonstrated to the world Buddhists' opposition to Diem and their willingness to accept martyrdom as a witness to the need for peace. Instead of war, Buddhists sought a compromise solution - a policy unacceptable to Diem, the U.S., or North Vietnam.[23] When Diem proved inept, cruel, and corrupt, and

---

[22]Stanley Karnow, *Vietnam: A History* (1983); a good introduction to the issues is David Levy, *The Debate Over Vietnam* (1991); for retrospective on the tenth anniversary, see special issues of *The New Republic* (April 29, 1985), 1-34 and Robert McNamara et al., *Argument Without End* (1999). Because McNamara's book is based upon several conferences between American and Vietnamese Communist leaders, it offers a balanced account of the perspectives of both sides on the causes of the war and why, in spite of the wishes of both sides for a negotiated solution, no peace was obtained. A critique of the McNamara thesis is Jonathan Mirsey, "The Never Ending War," *New York Review of Books* (May 25, 2000), 54-62 and "No Trumpets, No Drums," ibid., (September 21, 1995). A recent history of the conflict is Robert Schulzinger, *A Time for War: The United States and Vietnam* (1997).
[23]Thich Nhat Hanh, *Fragrant Palm Leaves: Journals 1962-1966* (1998), and *Love in Action: Nonviolent Social Change* (1993); both Washington and Hanoi wanted a neutral government but were unable to breach cultural barriers and stereotypes of each other. The North did not wish to war with the United States and were willing to have Diem included in a neutralist government that might eventually join with the North. They viewed the U.S. as intending to replace the

procrastinated reforms, he was overthrown and assassinated - with American foreknowledge and even complicity. For the remainder of the war, South Vietnam would be ruled by a series of generals with limited public appeal. The U.S. again sought, but now in what soon became a major war, to build a democratic nation.

For the leadership of North Vietnam, the war was a continuation of a struggle for liberation begun against the Japanese, then the French, and now continued against the Americans. Believing that endurance was the key to victory, the leaders and the people sought to outlast the Americans and accepted heavy losses in the South and prolonged bombing. Learning quickly that they could not prevail in a war of fixed positions, the North Vietnamese regular army and the Viet Cong sought to infiltrate American positions and neutralize the U.S. firepower by controlling villages. They would conduct a psychological war against the Americans by assassinating local officials and demonstrating control of the countryside.

Johnson, who became President after Kennedy's assassination in 1963, sought for a neutral government, but he and his advisers - none of whom knew much about Vietnamese history and culture - interpreted communist actions as requiring a strong American response. With virtually unanimous support in Congress and the media, the U.S. decided to stop communist expansion in Vietnam, and so Americans began sending more advisers. When North Vietnam allegedly attacked American destroyers in the Gulf of Tonkin, Johnson asked for and received congressional authorization (two Senators and no Congressmen voted "no") to use all force necessary to repel aggression, but there was never a declaration of war. There was no significant opposition from religious leaders and general support from the mass media. The President had already initiated the bombing of North Vietnam, and soon the military sought to send increased

---

French as colonial masters of Vietnam. Neither the Kennedy nor the Johnson administration wanted a war in an area whose strategic value other than as a domino was minimal. McNamara, *Argument Without End*, 127, 148, 157. Critics say that the U.S. was not interested in a compromise solution and viewed negotiations from a weak position as surrendering to communist aggression.

numbers of American troops, but Johnson, who feared jeopardizing his domestic program of reform, did not inform the public of the extent of American involvement.

The administration insisted that the war was primarily an invasion from the North, not a civil war, and that North Vietnamese communists sought to conquer a free independent country whose government was recognized by most other states. In the Presidential election of 1964, Johnson presented himself as a candidate of peace and conciliation against Barry Goldwater, who was portrayed as irresponsible for allegedly giving commanders in the field the right to use nuclear weapons. Even leftist radicals supported Johnson, who won by a landslide.

In 1965 the bombing continued, but so did the military gains of the Viet Cong, and the United States sought to increase pressure on the communists by sending more U.S. troops; eventually there were over 500,000. Since America would not weaken its forces in Europe and since the administration, for domestic political reasons, decided not to mobilize reserves, the new troops were either draftees or volunteers who expected to fight another "good war." The soldiers were young; the average age was nineteen (as compared with twenty-six in WW II). Unlike WW II, there was a class bias in who did and did not serve. The educated middle class males who were college students with good grades obtained deferments or joined the national reserve. Draftees, about ten percent blacks and an equal number from other minorities, like other soldiers normally spent one year in Vietnam. They were sent into an alien country and told to fight a guerrilla war against an enemy they knew little about and could rarely see. They had no way of distinguishing between friendly or neutral peasants and sympathizers or soldiers for the Viet Cong. In this war the child who accepted candy from a soldier might also drop a grenade into a jeep's gasoline tank.

The war had no front, and the success of a mission was not judged by area controlled, but by body count. America embarked upon a "search and destroy" strategy in which troops with massive support from air power and artillery would comb large areas in search of the elusive enemy. The success of a mission was judged by the number of those killed. In an attempt to isolate patriotic South Vietnamese from the communists, peasants were forced to resettle in so-called strategic hamlets, with the area they had come from being termed a "free fire" zone. All living in that area were presumed to be pro-communists and could be killed. Television news programs showed American troops destroying villages by bombing or setting fire to homes.

Guerrilla wars in the past - in Spain and Russia during the Napoleonic campaigns, in the Balkans and Eastern Front in World War II - had been vicious and characterized by lack of regard for the conventions of war. Vietnam was no exception. The Viet Cong (pro-Communist South Vietnamese guerrillas) and the North Vietnamese army blended into the civilians by not wearing uniforms on many occasions, used women and children as spies, engaged in terrorist assassination of civilians, executed POWs at the front and tortured them in prison, violated the neutrality of neighboring nations, and staged its major offensive at a time when South Vietnam had announced a truce for the Tet holidays (the North had in earlier years proclaimed a truce at Tet). Many American casualties came from booby traps and land mines, although not until 1997 did the public learn that most of the mines were U.S. made and had been pilfered or dug up and reset by the Cong.

In all previous twentieth-century American wars, the troops had come home heroes. In Vietnam even while the fighting went on, the troops learned of anti-war demonstrations at home and saw themselves vilified. Twenty months after it occurred, the public learned and saw pictures of the March, 1968 My Lai massacre in which a platoon of American soldiers slaughtered between one hundred fifty and five hundred unarmed old men, women and children. Critics were not surprised and insisted that the My Lai incident and its attempted cover-up was only a more gruesome exemplar of what often occurred. When only Lieutenant William Calley, Jr., was convicted (and Nixon soon pardoned him), questions centered on whether he was a scapegoat for the policies of leaders.[24] Proponents of the war insisted that My Lai was an isolated incident, explainable by a poor caliber of officers because most college students avoided service.

The traditional image of GI's as sacrificing for freedom, enduring hardships, and giving candy to children became mixed with a counter image of soldiers who compensated for their bewilderment in an impossible military setting by smoking pot, "fragging" officers, frequenting prostitutes, and killing civilians. In Vietnam, heroes were "John Waynes" who got killed. Duty meant surviving your one-year term and going home alive. The confused, ironic anti-heroic Vietnam G.I., an image created by journalists and soldiers' memoirs published during and after the war, was a literary and Hollywood-made convention, a product of what Samuel Hynes calls the war in the mind which reflected and distorted the actual war. It should be balanced with a contrasting image presented by a poll in *Current History* showing that 74% of veterans enjoyed the war and 66% were willing to serve again.[25]

The United States engaged in a massive bombing campaign on both North and South Vietnam, dropping more bombs than had been used in all of World War II, in an attempt to stop supplies coming from China to North Vietnam, and then along jungle trails to South Vietnam. When the guerrilla forces expanded their supply lines to Laos and Cambodia, the military bombed there too. The CIA and American military also ran secret operations in these neutral countries. Chemical bombs in which napalm penetrated the flesh and then continued to burn for some hours was only one of many anti-personnel weapons used. In an attempt to flush out or to find the Cong in jungle and mountains, airplanes sprayed "agent orange," a defoliant later linked to health problems of GIs. In operation Phoenix, American and South Vietnamese military intelligence identified communist infiltrators who were imprisoned, held under horrendous conditions, and sometimes tortured and executed.

---

[24]Seymour Hersh, *My Lai 4: A Report on the Massacre and Its Aftermath* (1970).
[25]Samuel Hynes, *A Soldiers Tale*, 222.

The U.S. also had to deal with peace activists in European and neutral states that portrayed a military colossus ten thousand miles removed trying to bomb a poor Third World Country into submission. The Protestant and Catholic churches in Western Europe, the World Council of Churches, and even churches in East Asia - all condemned American policies in Vietnam, asked for restraint in military policy, and advocated a negotiated peace. Pope Paul called for a negotiated peace and offered the Vatican as a site for peace talks.

The Home Front

Under the pressure of what would become America's longest war, with casualties mounting and victories leading to no exit strategy, the postwar consensus on American foreign policy evaporated. The administration's defense and critics' questions echoed the categories of Just War traditions because the concepts had penetrated Western thought. President Johnson insisted that there was just cause: an invasion from the North trying to impose a communist totalitarian system on the South, and that the U.S. response was limited and proportionate. The bombing was directed at military targets and not civilians in the North. Cautious targeting meant that there would be no war with Russia or China, in spite of the fact that both supplied arms to the North. The U.S. also insisted that it sought a negotiated peace, would accept a neutral South Vietnam, and would be willing to rebuild North and South Vietnam after the war. As a sign of its desire for negotiations, the U.S. at various times suspended the bombing of North Vietnam. Yet it was clear that this was a war of attrition in which the administration and military sought victory by increasing the cost in lives to North Vietnam and its sympathizers in the South.

Prominent Protestant advocates of Just War theory, like Princeton's Paul Ramsey, concluded that the U.S. sought to wage the war in accordance with Just War criteria, particularly considering the difficulties of waging a guerrilla war.[26]

---

[26]Paul Ramsey, *The Just War, Force, and Political Responsibility* (1968) and *War and/or Survival* (1968). Ramsay initially supported the war, but later became a critic after concluding that

Prominent journalists like Stewart Alsop and Max Ascoli, editor of the *Reporter* magazine, agreed with the President that America must pay the price of opposing communist expansion in South Vietnam.

Opponents also used Just War precepts, mixing these categories often with pragmatic judgments that the war was unwinnable or not worth the cost at home. Academics and military strategists, including Under Secretary of State George Ball and realist Hans Morgenthau at the University of Chicago, disputed Johnson's account of the war as just, limited, and proportionate. First, there were issues about just cause. With China and Russia at ideological war, was communism a monolithic force? Could Ho Chi Minh become like Yugoslavia's Tito and get along better with the West than the Soviets?[27] Was the war, as the administration claimed, primarily communist aggression from the North, or was it a popular revolution in the South? Had the Americans taken on the French role as an outside colonial power? Was the U.S. responsible for the failure of elections mandated by the Geneva Accords?

Soon questions emerged about the candor of the administration, termed the "credibility gap." It appeared that Johnson knew that the second Vietnamese attack on the destroyer Maddox in the Gulf of Tonkin, used to gain the Congressional resolution, was a radar malfunction, that bombing pauses had been linked with stipulations that the administration knew the North Vietnamese would not accept, that body counts were inflated, and that the so-called "free" South Vietnamese government was autocratic and corrupt. The publication of the *Pentagon Papers* (1971) showed that Johnson had run on a peace platform while secretly planning to escalate the war.

Reputable scholars provided an alternative view of the causes and conduct of the war to that enunciated by the administration, and teach-ins held at leading

---

proportionality had been violated. See also the discussion in James Smylie, "American Religious Bodies, Just War, and Vietnam;" *Sociological Analysis* (1975), 325-34.
[27]North Vietnam was dependent for military supplies on both Russia and China, but wanted to keep both at arms length and had feared a war with the U.S. because it would increase dependence on the feuding communist giants.

public and private universities and colleges spread skepticism. Secretary of State Dean Rusk and supporters of the administration correctly pointed out the evils committed by the communists in Vietnam and hastened to add that internal disunity weakened American troops and aided the enemy. Their case was weakened by the administration's overly optimistic reports on progress in winning the war, the so-called "light at the end of the tunnel." Still, a poll in December 1967 showed that 75% of Americans believed that anti-war demonstrations helped the communists and 70% saw such demonstrations as acts of disloyalty.[28]

Unlike World Wars I and II in which military censorship effectively screened negative comment on the war by either soldiers or journalists, Vietnam was fought in full view of television cameras and the nature of the war precluded effective control of reporters. Almost immediately reporters began to raise questions about the conduct of the war.[29] Guerrilla wars required the support of the population. Why was it so easy for the Cong to blend into an allegedly pro-American people? Why was the South Vietnamese army so ineffective a fighting force? Were forced resettlement, massed bombing, and the destruction of villages the way to win the hearts and minds of the population? Was the U.S. army deliberately targeting civilians and counting the innocent as part of the body count? Most importantly, should American boys be forced to wage a war for freedom for the strong-armed military leaders of South Vietnam? Was this the wrong war against the wrong enemy in the wrong place?

Americans addressed the issues of justice in the cause and conduct of war with a new sophistication. Since 1945 virtually all moral writings on war dealt with the issue of nuclear weapons as a means of containment. Primarily after 1965, philosophers, political scientists, historians, theologians, newspaper

---

[28]Hall, 67. Gallup Opinion Index, *Public Opinion and the Vietnam War 1964-1967* (Dec. 1967), contains the polls showing the evolution of American public opinion from 1954 until Dec. 11, 1967.
[29]Francis Fitzgerald, *Fire in the Lake: The Vietnamese and the Americans in Vietnam* (1972). Philip Caputo, *A Rumor of War* (1977) was one of a series of influential first person accounts of being a soldier; others include Michael Herr, *Dispatches* (1977) and Tim O'Brien, *Going after Cacciato* (1978), all published after the war.

editors, and television commentators debated the morality of conventional war, particularly the ambiguities of fighting guerrillas. Was it possible to fight an immoral enemy using guerrilla tactics under the restraints of international law and the Geneva Conventions? What was the relevance of the Nuremberg precedents about obeying unjust orders in an immoral war?

Members of the Old Left and traditional pacifist organizations had a new visibility, and the Senate Foreign Relations Committee conducted what amounted to seminars for educating the people upon the issues. A fissure emerged within the dominant Democratic Party, with prominent Senators like J. William Fulbright, Wayne Morse, and Robert Kennedy dissenting from the President. On campuses, in mainline churches, and in Congress for the first time since the War of 1812, significant opposition to the cause and conduct of a war occurred while the war was going on.

The Churches and the War

The American churches rediscovered the tradition of Just War theory and wondered whether pacifism was a viable option. Could one practice conscientious objection to Vietnam but not to all wars? Many Protestant and Catholic clergy said yes, but the laypersons said no. The stances of different denominations on the war paralleled their positions on nuclear weapons. The Southern Baptists as a denomination took no public stance, but a poll of five hundred of its ministers in 1965 showed overwhelming support for the war, with one-third demanding victory, even at the cost of World War III. The Church of God (Anderson, Indiana) like the Southern Baptists continued to support the war. The right wing Presbyterian Karl McIntyre's fundamentalist American Council of Churches that was militantly anti-communist provided vocal support for Presidents Johnson and Nixon and a demand for victory. Evangelist Billy Graham took no public position, but his close identification with and praise of President Nixon during the re-election campaign of 1972 amounted to an endorsement. White neo-evangelical Christians, particularly in the South, combined conservative politics, fervent patriotism, and support for the war, although there were a few evangelicals, like

Oregon's Republican Senator Mark Hatfield, who became vocal critics of the war. Many Pentecostals and fundamentalists declined to take any position on the war, either because they awaited the millennium or thought the church should proclaim the gospel and stay out of politics. At the beginning of 1968 (before the Tet offensive) nine Protestant mainline denominations' magazines ran a questionnaire. Out of a combined circulation of 3.6 million, only 34,000 readers responded, including 2000 clergy. The laity were considerably more hawkish than the ministers, with 60% of the laity favoring continuation of the bombing, while 57% of the clergy wanted a halt; over two-thirds of the clergy opposed and over half of the laity favored using "all military strength short of nuclear weapons to achieve victory in war." As *The Lutheran* commented, "Officially the churches may coo like a dove but the majority of their members are flying with the hawks."[30]

The Vicar General of the U.S. armed forces was New York's Francis Cardinal Spellman. Spellman, who called the war a "moral crusade," became such an outspoken supporter of the war, that the Vatican - in an unusual step - disassociated itself from his views. Pope Paul VI early called for and tried to arrange a negotiated settlement.[31] Boston's Richard Cardinal Cushing joined the anti-war Concerned Clergy Against the War. *Commonweal, The Catholic Reporter*, and *The Catholic Worker* became early opponents of the war; *America* supported the war. In 1966 the Catholic bishops insisted that U.S. presence in Vietnam could be morally justified; in 1967 the bishops advocated negotiation and in 1968 endorsed Johnson's decision to limit bombing of North Vietnam and to seek negotiations.[32] In 1968, distressed that the American bishops had taken no public position on the morality of the war, the *National Catholic Reporter* sent to all bishops a questionnaire for their views. Only six of the 225 answered. However, individual bishops, like Chicago's Archbishop Joseph Bernardin,

[30]Hall, 65-75. *Christian Century* (Sept. 4, 1968), 1096.
[31]"Cardinal Spellman's Holy War," *Christian Century* (Jan 11, 1967), 36. Peter Hebblethwaite, *Paul VI: The First Modern Pope* (1993), 459-60, 510-13.
[32]Harold Quinley, "The Protestant Clergy and the War in Vietnam," *Public Opinion Quarterly*, 34 (Spring 1970), 109.

denounced as indiscriminate the policy of mass bombing. Not until 1971, long after most Americans had concluded that the war was immoral, did the bishops publicly concur in this judgment.[33]

Polls did not confirm the popular image of overwhelming lay-Catholic support for the war. In a Gallup poll in November 1967, 31% of Protestants and 46% of Catholics approved of Johnson's handling of the war; 55% of Protestants and 41% of Catholics disapproved. The disapproval rating included doves and those who wanted more military force. Whenever Johnson escalated the war, his approval rating rose dramatically.[34] Ethnic Catholics from Eastern Europe had only 7% as doves in 1967; Western European American Catholics were 29%; Western European Protestants 17% and Jews 48%. By 1971 Catholics showed more war opposition than Protestants. Offered a choice of withdrawal or victory in Vietnam: Anglo-Saxon Protestants split 40/36%, with higher percentages of Irish Catholics - 62%, German Catholics - 46%, and Polish Catholics - 41% favoring withdrawal. As early as October 1969, a Gallup poll indicated that 55% of the general public identified themselves as dove and only 36% as hawk.[35]

Poll evidence needs to be weighed against other sources because the way the questions are phrased influences results. Still, polls seem to support the conclusion that while clerical opposition to the war was visible earlier, in general, church members shifted their positions on Vietnam as a part of a national trend. (Of course, a random poll of the American people would have over fifty percent respondents as church members.) Paradoxically, while polls after 1970 showed strong opposition to the war, the organized anti-war movement had less influence than before 1968.[36]

---

[33]"Bishops and Vietnam," *Commonweal*, April 15, 1966, 93. Gordon Zahn, "The Scandal of Silence," *Commonweal* 95 Oct. 22, 1979, 79-85.
[34]Gallup Poll, November, 1967, 2.
[35]Greeley, *The American Catholic: A Social Portrait*, 98-100; Gallup Polls, Nov. 1967, Oct. 1969, 2222.
[36]Charles De Benedetti and Charles Chatfield, *An American Ordeal: The Antiwar Movement of the Vietnam Era* (1990), 298, 310, 318.

A member of the pacifist Catholic Worker Movement and a Quaker became sacrificial martyrs by burning themselves to death as a war protest. Two Catholic priests, Daniel and Philip Berrigan, who defended these actions were reassigned to Brazil. They soon returned to lead a radical Catholic pacifist movement that legitimized itself by quoting statements from Pope John XXIII and Paul VI. Beginning by joining demonstrations and frustrated by a lack of influence on government policy, the Berrigans soon began practicing civil disobedience. From encouraging young men to burn their registration cards as a sign of defiance, the Berrigans broke into a draft board at Catonsville, Maryland and destroyed or defaced registration cards by pouring blood over them or burning them with napalm. When arrested and convicted, the Berrigans violated their bail, thereby repudiating Gandhi's philosophy of accepting imprisonment as a price for breaking an unjust law. Instead, they went underground in order to continue to demonstrate publicly against an unjust society. These actions split the Catholic anti-war movement over allowable protest tactics.[37]

Reflecting divided sentiments within the traditionally strong anti-communist American Catholic community, labor leaders like George Meany of the AFL-CIO and politicians like Richard Daley, Mayor of Chicago, continued support of the war while Senators Eugene McCarthy and Robert Kennedy led the opposition.

The leadership of mainline Protestant denominations after early support soon became critics of the war. The *Christian Century* and *Christianity and Crisis* of Niebuhr pronounced the war immoral because of indiscriminate attacks upon civilians. There was no democracy in South Vietnam, only a corrupt clique of generals. America's inordinate firepower threatened disproportionate harm for any good that might result. Its forces destroyed the South Vietnamese culture and countryside in a vain attempt to save it. The U.S.'s strategy of bombing free fire zones, search-and-destroy operations, and body count almost required atrocities.

---

[37]Au, *The Cross, The Flag, The Bomb*, 95-97; 147-58; *Catholic Peacemakers: A Documentary History*, II, Part 2.

Even though planes bombing the North aimed at military targets, imprecision in hitting the objectives in Hanoi and Haiphong Harbor led to many civilian casualties.[38]

Protestant critics of the war tended to be vague on how to end the war. Most wanted a negotiated settlement; some advocated unilateral withdrawal because a communist government would not be worse than the present war. Liberal Christian critics had no illusion about the goodness of the Viet Cong and North Vietnamese or that there was an easy way to withdraw that would protect those who supported the U.S., but a few radicals spoke out in favor of a communist victory and belittled the government's fears of a potential bloodbath.[39]

The public statements of the churches reflected the divisions among their members. The laity toned down statements critical of the war proposed by commissions of Presbyterians and Episcopalians. Methodist and United Church of Christ (Congregationalists) tended to be the most anti-war. The leaders of mainline denominations and Roman Catholics joined traditionally pacifist churches in providing counseling for young men who were uncertain as to whether they should obey the draft. Philadelphia Yearly Meeting of the Quakers decided to break the law by sending medical supplies to North Vietnam as a sign of protest against American policies and an affirmation of love for an enemy. Vietnam Christian Service (VNCS) from 1965 until 1975 sought to provide refugee relief, aid for reconstruction, the training of social workers and physical therapists. VNCS, supported by Church World Service, Mennonite Central Committee, and Lutheran World Relief, and its staff of two hundred Vietnamese and two hundred overseas staff sought to provide impartial aid as a form of Christian service to relieve suffering. The organization spent over ten million dollars.[40] Churches

---

[38]The New York Times correspondent Harrison Salisbury went to North Vietnam in 1967, and his stories from Hanoi reported widespread damage of civilians.

[39]Guenther Lewy, *Peace and Revolution: The Moral Crisis of American Pacifism* (1998), 30, 57-59, 102-05, 138. A critic of Lewy's book is *Peace Betrayed? Essays on Pacifism and Politics*, Michael Cromartie, ed. (1990); De Benedetti, 96.

[40]Midge Austin Meinertz, *Vietnam Christian Service: Witness in Anguish* (1976) 3, 10, 30.

identified with support for the war and with opponents provided funds and personnel for alleviating the human costs of the war in Vietnam. The pacifist churches and established peace organizations (WILPF, FOR, SANE) joined with new religious and secular organizations (Students for a Democratic Society and Veterans against the War) to lead mass demonstrations in Washington, in major cities, and on college campuses. Catholics, Protestants, Jews and atheists joined pacifists in demonstrations against what they saw as unjust actions. In 1967 Senator Eugene McCarthy decided to run against President Lyndon Johnson after he saw an anti-war demonstration of America's religious leaders at the Capitol.

Sociologists studying the effects of religion on dissent came to divergent conclusions. Clerical leadership in the anti-war movement had high visibility, as reflected in a new organization: Clergy and Laity Concerned about Vietnam, whose initial forty religious leaders included Jews, Roman Catholics, and mainline Protestants. A study of 1500 California ministers found that 80% discussed the war with their congregation and that those who identified themselves as religious conservatives strongly supported the war while those who were liberals opposed. Another study of college students at the University of Pennsylvania concluded that those who had no religious commitment were far more likely to oppose the war than Protestants and Catholics who attended church frequently.[41] Ministers who opposed the war publicly from their pulpits could expect to receive either strong support or opposition or both from their congregations. It is probably safest to conclude that churches shaped as well as reflected divisions within the country over the war. Because for many Americans the churches are the most important source for moral values, it is probable that the strong protests of clerical leaders made it easier for the laity to conclude that the war was morally wrong.

---

[41]Richard John Neuhaus, "The War, the Churches, and Civil Religion," Annals of the American Academy of Political and Social Science (1970), 129-32 Clarence Tygart, 202; Quinley, 45-50; James Smylie, "American Religious Bodies, Just War, and Vietnam," *A Journal of Church and State* 11 (1969), 383-408; Starr, "Religious Preference, Religiosity, and Opposition to War," *Sociological Analysis*, 323.

Americans within and outside the church addressed the issues of justice in the cause and conduct of the war with a new sophistication. Since 1945, virtually all moral debate on war focused on nuclear weapons as a means of containment. Beginning in the 1960s and continuing to the present, philosophers, political scientists, historians, theologians, newspaper editors, and television commentators debated the morality of fighting a guerrilla war making explicit use of Just War traditions. Like other Americans, the scholars came to no agreement on the morality of the war. Conservatives Norman Podhoretz and Guenter Lewy pronounced the war as just in cause and conduct as World War II. Roman Catholic William O'Brien from Georgetown University, like Princeton's Paul Ramsey, concluded that there was just cause but unjust conduct because of disproportionate damage. O'Brien defended the bombing as aimed at military targets, but worried that the use of non-lethal gas to flush the Cong out of tunnels eroded the general prohibition against using poison gas. Michael Walzer, a political scientist at Harvard, insisted that the war was unjust in cause and conduct, because the South Vietnamese people, by sheltering the guerrilla fighters, showed lack of support and the Americans could not distinguish between civilians and guerrillas. In such a situation, Walzer argued, there could be no legitimate outside intervention. Critics of Walzer insisted that under his criteria no nation could fight against a guerrilla movement willing to use immoral tactics to terrorize people.[42]

If America had won the war easily and quickly, the debate might still have occurred but would have remained minor league. Polls before the Tet offensive of January 1967 showed overwhelming support for the President. After Tet, however, support for the war dwindled steadily until by 1971 a majority of the people declared the war immoral. Initially most college students favored the war and changed views along with their parents. At no time did the American people

[42]Complete citations to books of Guenther Lewy, Norman Podheretz, William O'Brien, Paul Ramsey, and Robert Tucker are in bibliography. Michael Walzer, *Just and Unjust Wars: A Moral Argument with Historical Illustrations* (1977).

or Congress desire unilateral withdrawal. They wished a negotiated settlement, not a surrender.

Although a majority of Americans came to accept the anti-war message, they disliked the messenger. Anti-war demonstrations coincided with and were often joined by two other far-reaching challenges to the status quo; civil rights and women's liberation. Old Leftists, pacifist organizations, and liberal democrats who began the anti-war movement were overwhelmed by a counter-cultural movement of youth that soon divided into Yippies and the New Left. The Yippies embraced sexual revolution ("make love, not war") and drugs (LSD and marijuana) as methods of self-realization and engaged in a wide range of what they hoped was outrageous behavior mocking America traditions. Drug culture, communes, assorted mysticisms, sloppy dress, foul language, and sometimes violence characterized the "yippie" challenge to America. Obviously, tuned-out and spaced-out youth could not create an effective anti-war movement. Those flagrantly flaunting what many Americans saw as immoral personal behavior could not command respect in condemning national immorality. Although the counter-cultural movement involved a small minority, its image tarred the entire peace movement.

The New Left would have been more effective if its members had ceased internal vituperation and narrowed its focus. New Left radicals argued that American institution needed a revolution, and that the war was a symptom of a corrupt social structure. Some embraced the cause of North Vietnam and wanted an American defeat, a position they flaunted by burning the Stars and Stripes and carrying the North Vietnam flag. Many denounced as corrupt the government, business, and churches. Since the radical youth often were university students, they sought to transform higher education as an instrument for social change. Student radicals attacked as misleading and immoral the so-called impartiality and objectivity of traditional scholarship and staged sit-ins as methods of disrupting campus life. The New Left scorned pacifists who opposed violence, denounced churches for preaching bourgeois morality, ridiculed labor unions for selling out to capitalism, and even attacked the Old Left for insufficient militancy. Some extreme radicals bombed a chemistry building at the University of Wisconsin, and others robbed banks to raise funds for a revolution. Anti-communist blue collar workers and ethnic Americans whose native lands were in Eastern Europe, in a backlash against the New Left, Yippies, and the anti-war movement within the Democratic Party, became part of what Richard Nixon termed the "silent majority."[43]

After proclaiming a secret plan to end the war, Nixon became President in 1968 and sought what he termed an honorable peace enabling America to exit the war. Complaints about the injustice of the draft subsided when Nixon replaced the policy of deferments with a lottery. Nixon found that a policy of reducing American troops, turning over more responsibility to the South Vietnamese army, intensive bombing, and negotiations with the North would silence the opposition sufficiently so that America could continue the war four more years. The President's expansion of the war into Cambodia (accompanied by the Ohio National Guard's shooting of four students during anti-war protests at Kent State) called forth major demonstrations and disrupted college life, but opponents to the war were too disorganized to mount a serious challenge. Even after four more years of war when the anti-war forces captured the Democratic Party, Nixon was reelected in a landslide, losing only one state.

By 1972 the war in Vietnam was obsolete. Nixon signed a SALT treaty bringing détente with Moscow and went to China, and the U.S. capitalized on the Soviet-China split to become a secret supporter of China. North Vietnam had taken years of bombing and casualties without accepting defeat or the need to compromise. So the treaty between America and North Vietnam, that South Vietnam accepted most reluctantly, called for American withdrawal while leaving the North Vietnamese forces in the South. The North seems to have signed the agreement only as a method of speeding an American exit and repeatedly violated

---

[43]The best history of the anti-war movement is Charles deBenedetti and Charles Chatfield, *The Antiwar Movement of the Vietnam Era* (1990), 222-37.

its arrangements. Nixon had resigned in disgrace over Watergate before North Vietnam defeated the American-equipped and disintegrating South Vietnamese forces in a conventional battle and occupied Saigon in 1974. Neither President Ford nor Congress wished to resume the bombing campaign to stop the North Vietnamese offensive.

Those Vietnamese who had trusted American promises now had to face re-education by an intolerant and repressive regime. Cost of the war: Vietnamese in North and South, around two million dead; Americans 58,000, whose names are now on a new sacred place, the wall in Washington, D.C.[44] To the surprise of virtually everyone, another blood bath at the end of the war took place not in Vietnam but in Cambodia, whose American backed military junta was overthrown by the communist Khmer Rouge. Under Pol Pot, the Khmer Rouge sought to build a communist society by emptying the cities while killing, as actual or potential opponents, one million people. The North Vietnamese created a police state in the South while creating camps for re-educating their former opponents. Rivalry between North Vietnam and China over Cambodia resulted in a brief Chinese invasion in 1975. Even Dean Rusk concluded that American had over-estimated the importance of South Vietnam and under-estimated the determination of the North Vietnamese. Increasingly, Vietnam appeared to be a tragic sideshow. Meanwhile, elsewhere, the Cold War continued.

---

[44]Hynes, *A Soldiers' Tale*, 189. There is little controversy on the American figures, but estimates of Vietnamese deaths vary greatly.

XVIII.
The Cold War - II: Nuclear Weapons

Anxieties caused by the atomic bomb tinged the euphoria at the end of the war as the military, political scientists, religious leaders and the general public sought to understand the policy implications of this new weapon. Could it be made an instrument for peace or would it make war even worse? The evolution of military strategy, the intensity of the Cold War, and the changes in Roman Catholicism and Protestant Neo-evangelicalism influenced the responses as religious and secular leaders adjusted traditional norms to deal with a weapon that exemplified Clausewitz's first definition of war: an act of violence carried to its uttermost. This chapter recounts the initial response of the American government, the churches, and the peace movement to the atomic bomb, then the changes in military strategy from massive retaliation to mutual assured destruction (MAD), and the variety of church responses in the late 1950s and the 1980s. Special attention will be devoted to the evolution of Roman Catholic, Protestant, and Neo-evangelical responses over a fifty-year period as the churches attempted to create a moral stance that would counter the Soviet threat and preserve at least a cold peace. Christians during the Cold War first faced the issues posed by atomic weapons. Now after the demise of the Soviet Union the strategic and moral issues remain: should America continue to possess nuclear weapons and threaten nuclear annihilation?

I. Atomic Warfare: First Reactions

After World War II ended, the military carefully controlled news stories of Hiroshima and Nagasaki, and initial reports stressed that both cities were military targets and did not mention radiation. Initial Japanese reports of thousands of civilian casualties and of radiation sickness compared to poison gas were dismissed as propaganda. Establishing a pattern that would continue, American authorities downplayed the dangers of radiation in nuclear fallout.[1] For twenty years the public did not see for films of the two cities made immediately after the bombings by the Japanese and later by American soldiers. The military occupation forbade unauthorized visits to the sites by newspapermen, and for the next five years made sure that the Japanese did not raise the moral issues. Since the Japanese had already experienced the full impact atomic power and since the U.S. government provided scientific information in the Smythe report about the power of the explosions, the conclusion seems obvious that the American authorities feared that too-graphic accounts of the effects of atomic bombs on cities might raise moral questions that would impact future use. The Pentagon strategy worked, and from 1945 onwards an overwhelming majority of Americans approved of dropping the atomic bomb.[2]

Within a week, news about the two bombs shared headlines with the Japanese surrender and contributed to the belief that dropping the atomic bombs brought the end of the war without an invasion. The GIs who had been training for the invasion celebrated and defended Truman's decision for the rest of their lives. The official position, stated by Truman and later argued in an influential article by former Secretary of War Henry Stimson, was that the bomb had saved one million soldiers' lives and had brought surrender. There was no mention that earlier estimates of the cost of lives were much lower or that the Japanese had made overtures to the Soviets to arrange a surrender. The misgivings of Generals Eisenhower and MacArthur and of Admiral Leahy about the necessity of the bomb became public only much later. Truman later claimed not to have lost any sleep over his decisions and never expressed reservations about dropping the bombs. After Robert Oppenheimer, who had been the scientist in charge of making the bomb, visited him in 1946 and expressed agony about "blood" on the

[1] Robert Jay Lipton and Greg Mitchell, *Hiroshima in America: Fifty Years of Denial* (1995), Part 1. Margaret Henriksen, *Dr. Strangelove's America: Society and Culture in the Atomic Age* (1997), is a provocative interpretation of the impact of atomic weapons on American culture, but devotes only cursory attention to religion.

scientists' hands, the President instructed his advisers that he did not want to see that "crybaby again." Even so, when the Pentagon in 1946 presented a battle plan that envisaged dropping fifty atomic bombs on Russian cities in the event of war, Truman rejected it saying that he did not want a weapon directed at "women and children."[3]

Polls of Americans showed relief that only the U.S. had the bomb and belief that it would keep its monopoly for years, conclusions shared by Truman and the military but not by the atomic scientists. Peoples also felt a sense of foreboding, for in the next war the bombs might drop on America or Britain, and there was no way to guarantee that a single airplane or rocket might not reach London or New York.

A few dissenters appeared among the voices of approval. Immediately after Hiroshima, a commission of the Federal Council of Churches, including John Foster Dulles, denounced the atomic bombing as "reckless and irresponsible" and deserving of "unmitigated condemnation." In 1946 the Federal Council addressed the whole issue of nuclear weapons, insisting that the bombings of Hiroshima and Nagasaki were "irresponsible," "morally indefensible," and a "grievous sin," even if they shortened the war a small amount.[4] The Council recognized that the decision to use the bombs followed precedents of area and saturation bombing in Germany and Japan. Such actions, though done in response to great provocation, were still "disproportionate" and eroded the distinction between civilians and soldiers. Because the atomic bomb was by its very nature indiscriminate, the Council called on America to freeze the building of atomic bombs. Any nation that had the bomb would gain an immediate overwhelming advantage by first usage; so the Council called on the U.S. to renounce first-use. Even though the Federal Council did not

---

[2]Lawrence Wittner, *One World or None* (1993), 56.
[3]Richard Rhodes, *Dark Sun: The Making of the Hydrogen Bomb* (1995), 205.
[4]Wittner, 58; Report of the Commission on the Relation of the Church to War in the Light of the Christian Faith, Federal Council of Churches, *Atomic Warfare and the Christian Faith,"* 8, 11, 12.

explicitly invoke Just War concepts, its pronouncement clearly drew upon that tradition.

David Lawrence, publisher and columnist for *US News and World Report*, used international law in describing the atomic bombing as an atrocity that struck at the heart of The Hague and the Geneva Conventions. The British Council of Churches in 1946 refused to condemn the bombing because it did not have all the facts. The Pope in 1946 called the new weapons of war "infernal creations" requiring disarmament, but did not comment directly upon Hiroshima.[5]

Those atomic scientists who had earlier worked through approved channels to have a demonstration of the bomb or a warning to Japan now could discuss their misgivings openly. Some scientists had disapproved of the withholding of knowledge about the bomb from the Soviets as likely to lead to an arms race. Led by Leo Szilard and Enrico Fermi, ninety percent of the scientists who had worked on the creation of the bomb joined the newly created Federation of American Scientists, publishers of the *Bulletin of Atomic Scientists,* in order to advocate international control of atomic energy. The scientists saw the atomic bomb as a radically different kind of weapon, not just a larger bomb that would require a new political structure. (However, many of these scientists either continued to work for the government on atomic weapons or later would help develop the hydrogen bomb. Just as the atomic and hydrogen bombs came about because scientists approached the government, so scientists initiated most later weapons developments.)[6] American atomic scientists sought with some success to enlist European scientists in the cause of international control.

Truman and American government experts also pondered the case for international control. A government commission proposed and scientists supported a plan to grant to the UN control of atomic energy, but the military opposed giving away America's atomic secrets. So in 1946 when America

[5]*Proclaiming Justice and Peace: Papal Documents from Rerum Novarum through Centesimus Annus,* ed. Michael Walsh and Brian Davies (1991), 120.

presented its ideas of international control to the UN, the Baruch plan envisaged a U.S. monopoly on the creation and manufacture of atomic weapons, a condition the scientists knew would not be acceptable to Russia. At the same time the U.S. tested atomic bombs in the Pacific to improve their design and to see their effectiveness against ships, actions that sent conflicting signals about the U.S.'s intentions. Policymakers feared atomic war and at same time wished to brandish the atomic bomb as a trump card in dealing with the Soviet Union. Scientists, politicians, and the military in America and the Soviet Union wavered between seeing the atomic bomb as an effective weapon that did not change geopolitics, or defining the bomb as an unprecedented force that would revolutionize warfare and the balance of power. Although relying upon the power of the atomic bomb, America's military did not create a strategy for use and an efficient method of delivery until during the Cold War.

II. Peace Movements

Unhappy with the weak structures created for the United Nations and convinced that the atomic bomb and total war made the present international system obsolete, Norman Cousins, editor of the *Saturday Review of Literature,* and Robert Hutchins, president of the University of Chicago, spearheaded a movement for world federalism. Arguing that state sovereignty and international anarchy inevitably lead to war, the world federalists sought to draft a constitution for all nations that would reduce national forces to the size necessary for internal policing, entrust control over foreign policy decisions to a representative assembly, and create a small military force that, when added to the police forces of states, could control an outlaw nation. Because the world government would own all atomic weapons, they would never be used. In 1948, responding to a request from the Secretary of State, Louis Sohn and Grenville Clark drew up an elaborate system of weighed votes, proportional representation, and checks and balances for

---

[6] Fred Kaplan, *Wizards of Armageddon* (1983), contains a description of the scientists who create nuclear weapons.

a world government with limited powers.[7] To its proponents, a world government offered a moral way to control nuclear weapons. Of course, lasting peace would require substantial agreement among communist and Western and rich and poor states on objectives, and critics pointed out that if there was already a consensus, war was not likely. If there was not, the world government would need to use coercion, which not only would not solve existing problems but might also create more wars.

Fear of war and second thoughts, particularly in Europe, about the advisability of using the Hiroshima bomb made world federalism a popular alternative. According to polls, creating a world government of limited powers in 1946 appealed to 63% of Americans and gained substantial support from Britain, France, and the defeated nations of Europe - but not the Soviet Union, which saw the plan as a capitalist plot to end world revolution. Public endorsements came from many churches and organizations like Young Republicans and Young Democrats, American Veterans Committee, Junior Chamber of Commerce, United Auto Workers, and twenty state legislatures. There were 111 co-sponsors in the House and twenty-one in the Senate from both parties of a resolution to turn the UN into a world government. The people of Massachusetts and Connecticut in public referendums approved of world government by 9 to 1 and 11 to 1 majorities.[8] But no government pushed hard for world federalism, disliking limitations on sovereignty and seeing immense practical problems in instituting a system of government that drew heavily upon U.S. practices and ideals. World federalism appealed to peace advocates in churches and universities who disliked international anarchy and power politics and had long sought for a moral and legal basis of international affairs, and it also attracted those who feared that without fundamental reforms there would be an atomic war between the U.S. and USSR.

The peace movements after 1945 differed markedly from those of the prewar period. Among the victorious Allies, the organized peace movement

[7]Grenville Clark and Louis B. Sohn, *World Peace Through World Law* (1948).
[8]Wittner, *One World or None* I, 70-71.

declined rapidly, and there were very few who called themselves pacifist, a term that for a short time had a precise meaning of refusing to fight under any circumstance. The effects of World War II stimulated pacifist sentiments in Germany and Japan, now under military occupation, but their citizens had little influence on the international peace movement until the mid 1950s. In France, Britain, Canada, and the U.S., the press and politicians often blamed the 1920s disarmament treaties and activists for contributing to a military weakness facilitating Hitler's early victories. The French also accused pacifists of cooperating with Nazi occupiers rather than supporting the Resistance. The Roman Catholic Church and the Church of England reaffirmed their opposition to pacifism, and those who accepted Reinhold Niebuhr's Christian realism decried pacifism as utopian.

Within all churches and many secular groups opposition to war remained strong, but support for the UN or world federalism or control of nuclear weapons did not translate into support for traditional pacifist religious organizations like the Fellowship of Reconciliation and the Peace Churches or their secular counterparts. In late 40s and 50s, American and British college students did not pledge never to fight again in an offensive or defensive war. The Federal Council, atomic scientists, and world federalists came close to advocating what would later be called nuclear pacifism - that the use of atomic weapons would always be morally wrong - but they did not advocate unilateral nuclear disarmament or argue that nations should forego the creation, possession, and use of conventional weapons. Their dilemma was that the U.S. and USSR, even while paying lip service to reassure the public that they wanted peace, in practice did not favor dealing with the problem of nuclear or conventional war through some form of international control and/or disarmament. The alternatives then became unilateral disarmament (which most thought dangerous, even a cause of war in the Cold War context), or learning to live with the bomb and hoping that it would not be used, or managing to ignore the problem.

III. Atomic Strategies 1952-1980: From Massive Retaliation to MAD

John Foster Dulles, as a member of the Peace Commission of the National Council of Churches, criticized the bombing of Nagasaki, but later sought to enlist the World Council of Churches, an organization he had helped found, in the battle against materialistic, atheistic, and unethical communism. As Secretary of State (1953-59), Dulles called for the liberation of Eastern Europe, non-recognition of Communist China, and mutual assistance treaties with nations that might be susceptible to communist subversion. Dulles believed that the future of Western democratic civilization required the victory of the Free World over communist slave states and lectured India and other newly independent Third World nations that their neutrality was immoral. Believing that building a conventional force in Europe as large as the Soviet's would be prohibitively expensive, President Eisenhower placed America's reliance in nuclear weapons that offered "more bang for the buck."

America's announced strategy rested upon the threat of "massive retaliation." That is, if the Soviets or Chinese used force against Berlin, Formosa, or any major target within the American defense perimeter, the U.S. would counter with nuclear weapons in an all-out strike against the Soviet Union. As a strategy, massive retaliation could work only if the U.S. had clear military superiority in weapons and means of delivery, a condition that occurred during the early 1950s. Unlike the Soviet Union and in opposition to the World Council of Churches, the U.S. refused to take a no-first-strike pledge, arguing that such a declaration would only strengthen Russia's advantage in conventional forces in Europe. Massive retaliation was based on the assumption that the Russians intended expansion that could be prevented only by destruction that was greater than that inflicted by the Nazi invasion, i.e., one-third of the people and industrial capacity of the Soviet Union. Using nuclear weapons as the U.S.'s main deterrent meant that the primary target would be Soviet civilians in cities. Special deep bunkers built for the President, members of Congress, and the military high command meant that if there were a nuclear war, civilians would die but not their leaders.[9]

The U.S. was initially more explicit than the USSR in detailing its nuclear strategy, but in general the Soviet defense posture mirrored that of America. Recent documents from Russia indicate that their leaders knew of America's nuclear superiority and saw themselves as constantly playing catch-up. The Russians viewed America as militaristic, seeking to expand its influence into the Soviet sphere of Eastern Europe, and saw itself as behind the U.S. in economic strength and quality of weapons. Russia sought security in numerical dominance of forces for conventional war in Europe and parity in nuclear forces. The result of real ideological and social differences between communist states and the West was an arms race motivated by fear and ambition in which the weapons became ever more sophisticated and destructive.

The weapons created by the Americans and the Russians made the atomic bombs dropped on Japan look insignificant. As the U.S. perfected its A-bomb technology in the postwar period, the Soviets built and tested its own A-bomb in 1949. The U.S. then announced that it was going to build a super or H-bomb, even though the strategic necessity for such a weapon had not been formulated. As in the A-bomb decision, atomic scientists and the heads of the new weapons laboratories at Los Alamos and Livermore lobbied for the H-bomb. Both the U.S. and Soviets soon created H-bombs, some as large as 50 megatons (the Hiroshima and Nagasaki bombs were between 13-20 kilotons), and tests in the mid-1950s drenched the northern world, including their own populations, with radioactive fallout.

As both nations worked to build bigger and smaller, cleaner and dirtier bombs, they also sought better delivery systems. So they created and tested theater (short range) and then strategic (intercontinental) guided missiles. Spy

---

[9]Alexander L George and Richard Smoke, *Deterrence in American Foreign Policy: Theory and Practice* (1974), and George Questor, *Nuclear Diplomacy: The First Twenty Five Years* (1970), are standard accounts of the evolution of nuclear strategy written during the Cold War.

airplanes like the U-2, and then spy satellites in space, allowed precise information on location of ICBMs, and sophisticated guidance systems allowed targeting each other's missiles sites. Such information made land-based missiles vulnerable to a first strike, so first the U.S. and then the Soviets created nuclear submarines armed with missiles with atomic warheads. After the Soviets matched the U.S. in rocket technology and nuclear weapons, massive retaliation seemed an unwise strategy because an atomic exchange would result in the destruction of America as well as Russia.

During the Kennedy-Johnson administrations (1961-68), defense analysts found in the theory of "graduated response" a way to allow a limited nuclear strike that would warn an opponent to desist from undesirable behavior. H-bombs might be directed at counter-force targets (i.e., missiles, military bases) rather than civilians and, thereby, reduce casualties and keep the war limited. However, a small nuclear exchange could approach the threshold of an all-out nuclear attack, and theorists also found that it might be impossible to have a limited nuclear war because an opponent might conclude that advantage would lie in a massive response. Even if only military targets were struck, the resulting collateral damage to civilians and fallout might end with casualties in the millions. That would be better than the end of civilization, but was still beyond the realm of moral acceptability. A third problem in counter-force was that it multiplied targets, so more missiles were needed. When the enemy generals saw the increase in missiles, they concluded that this was a prelude to first-strike capacity; so, in response they built more missiles. The result was that the USSR and U.S. created enough warheads to bury each other dozens of times, even though the purpose of counter-force strategy was to reduce casualties. By the early 1980s, the two super powers had sufficient explosive power in their nuclear arsenals to equal three tons of TNT for every person on earth, or the USSR could destroy every American city with a population over 100,000 forty-seven times; the U.S. could do the same for every Soviet city over 100,000 fifty-five times.

During the Nixon-Ford administration (1969-76), the reigning strategic doctrine was Mutual Assured Destruction or MAD. With both sides having thousands of nuclear weapons and no adequate defense against missiles, the U.S. and the Soviets began arms control negotiations that resulted in the first SALT (Strategic Arms Limitation Treaty) that allowed only one limited defensive Anti-Ballistic Missile (ABM) system for each side and set limits on the number of rocket launchers (but not warheads). It soon became clear that highly complex arms control treaties gained by long negotiations in which each side's military had veto power was not disarmament, but a way for the militaries of each superpower to know what the other was doing. The SALT process channeled, but did not end, the arms build up and resulted in first the U.S.'s and then the Soviets' creating Multiple Independently Targeted Re-entry Vehicles (MIRVs) that could be launched from one missile. MIRVs allowed each missile to hit more targets, but having three separately targeted warheads (as in the Minuteman system) or ten warheads (as in missile X also called "peacemaker") offered a tempting target for a first-strike capacity because one MIRV missile could take out a large number of the enemy's delivery vehicles.

In general throughout the period from 1947 until 1990 the U.S. pioneered new weapon systems that the Soviets soon duplicated and compensated for by building great quantities of less sophisticated versions. The asymmetrical shape of armies (i.e., the U.S. had more submarines and the USSR more land-based heavy missiles) made achieving balanced reductions very difficult. Both countries with their allies created massive land armies, equipped with tactical nuclear weapons (i.e., yields smaller than the Hiroshima bomb) that could be used on short-range missiles or in cannon shells.

IV. The Churches and Nuclear Weapons

The complexities of the Cold War made Protestant churches in the democracies circumspect with regard to moral pronouncements on war, and they often confessed internal divisions. Their postures reflected differing traditions on their role in society, understanding of Scripture and theology, and divisions among denominations and within congregations and clergy. How should the Church combine its biblical prophetic heritage of judgment with its priestly function as healer and bringer of salvation? Was the Church's role as moral counselor to deal only with individuals or also to provide political advice? And if political advice was required, should the Church confine pronouncements to aims and guidelines or enter into the minutiae of political/military decisions? Should the Church's efforts center only on educating its own congregations, or should churches establish lobbies to influence the powerful in Washington?[10]

In Western Europe in the postwar period, the numbers of those attending church services declined rapidly, diminishing the clergy's influence in the wider society. This change allowed the churches more freedom to dissent from government policies, but meant that the Church's voice had less impact. In the United States, the opposite occurred with more people becoming church members, financially supporting the institutions, and attending services; of those questioned, 98% told pollsters they believed in God and over three quarters said that the *Bible* was the revealed will of God. Yet at the same time, Americans appeared more secular (i.e., not using religious values in economics, education, and leisure) and the Church, while still a potent force, no longer saw itself as the primary moral arbiter of society, having to share that role with disciplines like sociology, psychology, and political science, whose professionals wavered between viewing themselves as scientific and value-free investigators and claiming to be experts on social policy. The American traditions of pluralism and of separating institutional religion from the state emancipated the churches from direct government control, but restricted religious influences on politics. Still, Americans looked up to the churches for guidance on moral issues and welcomed a gospel of peace.

However, when the issue was defense policy, lay people and the mass media relied on government spokesmen in the Departments of State and Pentagon,

---

[10]Ralph Potter, "The Response of Certain American Christian Responses to the Nuclear Dilemma 1958-1963" (Ph.D. diss., Harvard, 1965), 269ff, 370, 417 is an excellent analysis of how theology and exegesis determined various Christian responses to nuclear weapons.

defense analysts in "think tanks," and professors of international relations and defense policy in the universities. These men, and almost all such experts were male, made their policy recommendations in terms of national interest, an elusive concept that might involve seeing morality and religion as politically useful.

Modern realist theory of international relations, presented by academics like University of Chicago's Hans Morganthau and Harvard's Henry Kissenger, who later became Secretary of State, concluded that the national interest determining how nations did and ought to behave was based on calculations of power. Morality in foreign policy was dangerous because its tendencies to universalism, zealotry, and utopianism led to a disregard for compromise and a simplified view of power. George Kennan, the author of containment, compared America's foreign policy to a lizard sleeping in a mud puddle on a hot day. The lizard stayed somnolent under provocation unless someone nearly cut off its tail with a knife. Then the lizard became so mad and reacted so violently that it thrashed around destroying everything.[11] The lesson was that idealistic democracies were a danger to everyone, including themselves. The realists argued that the national interest included morality and religion, but these had little impact on state behavior. Modern states could and should operate with rational calculations of the national interest.

Theologians and political philosophers who argued that moral and religious values were ultimately what mattered in the superpower rivalry encountered military-industrial-academic bureaucrats who, whatever their views of personal morality, in practice, assumed that legions of church members seeking religious and moral truth had little real power. To be sure, in democracies politicians realized the importance of appearing moral and/or going to church and insisted that the ultimate aim of their statecraft was to preserve internal peace in a just international order. However, they concluded, since dictatorships understood only power, the Soviet Union would not be constrained by justice or morality.

---

[11] George Kennan, *American Diplomacy 1900-1950* (1951), 60, 85-9.

624

Differing from politicians who used the church as a tool in governing and in creating support for their policies, religious leaders saw Christianity's role as proclaiming a gospel of peace to sinful men and idolatrous nations. Our task in the rest of this chapter will be to look at the patterns of dealing with nuclear weapons and the Cold War among various denominations and types of churches, discussing first two national churches, Russian Orthodox and the Church of England, then various American sectarian and fundamentalist groupings, and the mainline denominations represented in the National and World Council of Churches, and Roman Catholicism before and after Vatican II.

The Russian Orthodox

During the Cold War, the Russian Orthodox Church served the Soviet state and survived by becoming a defender of communist rule and a supporter of all Russian peace initiatives. The peace movement was the only place that the Soviets allowed the church any public role.[12] Russian church officials proclaimed the peaceful intentions of Soviet rule, and their presence at foreign gatherings served to counter Western views of communists as denying religious freedom. The church also defended the Soviet armed interventions in Hungary in 1956, Czechoslovakia in 1968, and Afghanistan in 1979, and condemned American intervention in Korea and other conflicts in which the USSR had a stake. When the Russian Orthodox Church became a member of the World Council of Churches in 1961, it gained a major forum for disseminating its views, but its representatives were also exposed to other religious perspectives. For example, the Russian Church was a member when the World Council condemned the Soviet invasion of Afghanistan. The World Council first debated Soviet treatment of religion in 1975; a Russian priest who brought the complaints of Soviet religious persecution to the West was sentenced to ten years imprisonment in 1979.[13] Because the

---

[12]Jane Ellis, *The Russian Orthodox Church: A Contemporary History* (1986), 273.
[13]Philip Walters, "The Russian Orthodox Church," in *Eastern Christian and Politics* (1988), 84. Alexander Webster, *The Price of Prophecy: Orthodox Churches on Peace, Freedom, and Security* (1993), 253-65.

Russian Church's teachings followed so closely the imperatives of Soviet foreign policy, all but the unsophisticated remained wary of its peace initiatives.

The Churches in the United Kingdom

The Church of England did not provide a sustained critique of nuclear weapons or Britain's defense posture before the 1980s. The Labour Party came to power in 1945 with substantial support from left-wing clergy within the Church of England who supported a social reform agenda of comprehensive schools, universal health insurance, nationalizing major industries, and an extensive welfare network. Bishops in the Church of England often sympathized with socialism and the "Red" Dean of Canterbury regularly supported Communist peace initiatives. However, in foreign policy, Britain - reflecting its status as a minor power - relied upon an alliance with the U.S., and affirmed the necessity of international control of nuclear weapons, but also began a secret program to acquire its own atomic bombs. By what appears to be a tacit collusion between Labour and Conservatives, no parliamentary debate on nuclear weapons occurred from 1946 until after 1952 when Britain exploded an atomic bomb; a hydrogen bomb came two years later.

The British Council of Churches in 1946 refused to condemn Allied use of the atomic bomb because they did not have full possession of the facts. Later the Council noted internal disagreements with some members saying that under no circumstances should a Christian approve the atomic bomb, which was a "weapon of wholesale massacre." However, in 1948 a commission of the Church of England labeled possession of nuclear weapons "necessary for self-preservation" and insisted that a government "responsible for the safety of the community ... is entitled to manufacture them and hold them in readiness." This remained the posture of the British Council of Churches during the Cold War, although the churches at times also advocated a no-first-use position, cessation of H-bomb tests, openness to talks with the USSR, and in 1963 queried whether Britain needed an independent deterrent. The British Council rejected nuclear pacifism and, while respectful of pacifism as an individual's option, it announced that

626

neither pacifism nor unilateral disarmament was an option for a state that maintained the peace through deterrence.[14]

The main English grass-roots peace initiative, the Campaign for Nuclear Disarmament, became a major force from 1957-62 being sparked by external events: the Hungarian revolt, Suez invasion, Sputnik, ICBMs, Polaris submarines, and the British development of an H-bomb. A second CND mass movement came in the 1980s brought about by the Reagan administration's militant rhetoric and desire to put cruise and Pershing missiles in Europe. The CND could mobilize 200,000 people to march from the British nuclear weapons research center at Aldermaston to Trafalgar Square. The early CND movement has been described as a secular moral crusade uniting pacifists, liberal-internationalists, and leftist-internationalists.[15] Most of the participants in the two CND campaigns were middle-class, with some support from trade unionists. Women and men joined in equal numbers. They united in opposition to nuclear weapons, but differed in goals, with some being nuclear pacifists who wanted to build up conventional forces, others advocating disarmament and leaving NATO. Many wished arms control agreements between the U.S. and USSR, with Britain mediating as a spokesman for a Third Way of neutral nations. There was also disagreement about the nature of CND: should it be a mass movement, a political-pressure group to change policy of the Labour Party, or a non-political think tank to influence both parties? Did civil disobedience help or hurt the campaign? The CND succeeded in making Britain's nuclear policy a matter of public debate and electoral significance.

CND literature portrayed nuclear disarmament as a religious and moral imperative, with about forty percent saying that religious convictions moved them to participate but only twenty-five percent being church members. Individual

---

[14]David Ormrod, "The Churches and the Nuclear Arms Race, 1945-85," in *Campaigns for Peace* 1987), 189-220.
[15]Frank Myers, "British Peace Politics: The Campaign for Nuclear Disarmament and the Committee of 100, 1957-1962," (Ph.D. diss., Columbia University, 1965), 114-15; Paul Byrne, *The Campaign for Nuclear Disarmament* (1988), 55, 65.

bishops spoke out against nuclear weapons, but the Church of England, though endorsing a test ban treaty, played a minor role in the CND. Christian pacifists in the Anglican Pacifist Fellowship, Fellowship Of Reconciliation, and Society of Friends cooperated with the CND in insisting that atomic warfare was incompatible with Just War theory and advocating nuclear pacifism and unilateral disarmament. In a related campaign beginning in 1982, women initiated a highly visible, long-term encampment at Greenham Common outside a military base to protest stationing cruise missiles there. The CND advocates gained a following in the left wing of the Labour Party seeking unilateral disarmament in nuclear weapons. In power, Labour and Conservative governments supported Britain's deterrent and allowed American bombers and missiles to be stationed there.[16]

American Neo-evangelical Protestants

In the postwar period, conservative Protestants who affirmed the inerrancy of Scriptures subscribed to a variety of postures about war. Fundamentalist churches originally concentrated in the American South would, by the 1950s, become a national phenomenon as Neo-evangelicals and, by the 1970s, emerged as a major force of around 40% of American Protestants. A political branch of the Neo-evangelicals, termed the Moral Majority, through spokesman Rev. Jerry Falwell, an independent Baptist minister, rallied those claiming to be converted or born again Christians against the liberal social policies of the National and World Council of Churches, the UN, and other federations as showing the power of Satan. Falwell claimed the "goal of communist Russia is world conquest" and the "United States' position of peace through strength represents human responsibility." But at the same time the government was supposed to negotiate for "sensible" arms controls and disarmament in the interests of peace.[17] Billy Graham, the most important revivalist from the late 1940s until the present, had been anti-communist but generally refrained from political endorsements,

---

[16]Richard Taylor, "The Marxist Left and the Peace Movement in Britain since 1945," and Josephine Eglin, "Women and Peace: from the Suffragists to the Greenham women" in *Campaigns for Peace* (1987), 100-31, 221-60.

628

although in the 1970s he made public pronouncements about the dangers from the arms race and endorsed a nuclear freeze. Television evangelists like Falwell and Pat Robertson joined Ron Reed of the Christian Coalition with a political agenda for moral conservatism (defined as pro-family, anti-abortion, anti-homosexuality), free enterprise, support for Israel, and increased military strength. President Ronald Reagan's speech in 1983 calling the Soviet Union "an evil empire" was made to a convention of conservative evangelicals who had been saying the same thing for years.

At the local level, fundamentalist churches were less interested in secular foreign-policy pronouncements than in the interpretation of the prophecies in Scripture concerning the end of time and apocalyptic warfare. Many Neo-evangelicals discovered in the *Bible* a description of all history as divided into a series of discrete ages or dispensations. All signs allegedly showed that of the five dispensations, four had already occurred, and verses in Daniel and Revelation proved that the eschaton was near. Even those seemingly disinterested in the intricacies of dispensationist exegesis, like President Reagan, thought that a correct understanding of the biblical prophecies provided a clear history of the future. The return of Christ would be preceded by a "time of troubles" (Daniel 12:1) with "wars and rumors of wars" (Mark 13:7) earthquakes, droughts, famine, and plague (which could be polio, cancer, or AIDS). The founding of Israel in 1948 signified the return of Jews to Jerusalem in preparation for their conversion to Christianity and rise to world power; so America must support Israel. Israel would be attacked by a great evil power from the North (Ezekiel 38:39), which was undoubtedly the USSR in alliance with Iran, Ethiopia, Libya, and East Germany. Soon would come the armies of the anti-Christ that at Armageddon would battle with forces of the returned Christ. As Revelation made clear, Jesus' victory was

[17] Jerry Falwell, *Nuclear War and the Second Coming of Christ* (1983), 2, 3, 4.

assured, after all God was on his side, and he would usher in a thousand years of peace before the final judgment and destruction of the world.[18]

Interpretations of the prophecy could vary over details. Falwell assured readers that even if Christ returned tomorrow, a final earth-destroying nuclear war could not come for at least 1007 years, seven years of Tribulation followed by the peaceful millennium. Others who read the *Bible* differently thought that the description of 2 Peter 3:10, "The heavens shall pass away with great noise, and the elements shall melt with fervent heat, the earth also and the works that are therein shall be burnt up" might apply to an imminent nuclear war and be a part of the tribulation. According to most fundamentalists, any nuclear war in the seven-year tribulation period would not affect the elect of God. True Christians would at the beginning of the troubles experience the rapture, a bodily ascension up to heaven to meet Christ. Only sinners would experience the turmoil of the return of anti-Christ and final battles. Although fundamentalist, Neo-evangelicals, and Pentecostals might differ in details about the final days, all agreed that the function of the church was to proclaim the biblical truth to the rest of the world in order to save as many as possible from hell-fire. God had predetermined all history, and Christians must be faithful by preparing for the end.

The impact of apocalyptic fundamentalism was shown by a survey made of Amarillo, Texas, in 1983, a city of 150,000, in the "Bible belt" of the Southwest, with 191 Protestant churches, ten Catholic churches, and one synagogue. Theologically and politically conservative Christians dominated the town. The Pantex factory that assembled or reconditioned all American nuclear weapons was in Amarillo, so about 1,500 nuclear warheads passed through the city annually. Pantex presented itself as a family and civic-minded corporation under a football inspired motto: "We believe that peaceful coexistence is best maintained by being Too Tough to Tackle!"

---

[18]Paul Boyer, *When Time Shall be No More: Prophecy and Belief in Modern America* (1992), 181-224, recounts the impact of millennial thought.

The Roman Catholic bishop of Amarillo in 1981 concluded that because of the inherent immorality of nuclear weapons, a conscientious Christian should not work in the Pantex factory. Only one man resigned from Pantex. A Department of Energy survey in 1982 found that people had no moral qualms about the work of Pantex. The population insisted that Amarillo remained a good place to raise children, even though many believed the factory made the city a prime target.

A sociologist who visited the area sought to find how the conservative Christians who dominated the community viewed nuclear weapons. The ex-military men who ran Pantex and the workers believed that "the minute we throw our weapons down, there won't be twenty-four hours till you'll be dead." The bomb kept the peace and would be needed until all the world was of the same ideology. In Amarillo, discussion of the millennium was a popular subject. Dispensationalism stifled moral concern about nuclear weapons, because these Christians who seemed to want the return of Christ and the end of the world believed that they would be taken up in the rapture. "If I were not a Christian, I would be frightened," was one response.[19] The war might be initiated by the Soviet Union, but the real target and those who would suffer would be unbelievers.

Dispensationalism's pessimistic vision was counterbalanced by Amarillo's business classes who saw a bright future. These men and the minister of the large Southern Baptist church in town, described as a moderate Southern Baptist, professed a militant anti-communism and saw a strong military as a defense against a godless philosophy. The Old and New Testaments, inerrant in every word, showed that God not only allowed but authorized war for His holy purposes. Humans did not need to understand the purposes of God, why He allowed regimes like the Soviet Union, for example, but they should remain confident in His control of history. True peace could come only when Jesus

---

[19] A. G. Mujtabai, *Blessed Assurance: At Home with the Bomb in Amarillo, Texas* (1986), 76, 133.

bestowed it. "To me, a Christian is worth - the freedom of religion is worth - the chances that we take of a nuclear holocaust."[20]   Clearly there would be no preaching against the arms race by the fundamentalist ministers in Amarillo.

Pentecostal denominations also flourished in Amarillo.   A Pentecostal minister invoked the nuclear arms race as a sign of wicked humanity leading to destruction, but his message was to repent and lead a Christian life, not to become politically involved to end the arms race. The minister's apolitical stance echoed the statements of the national leaders of the Assemblies of God that the church's role was to save souls, not to offer political advice.

Amarillo's mainline denominational ministers - Methodists, Presbyterians - accepted the necessity of deterrence and did not preach about nuclear weapons, though they favored mutual disarmament. There were few Jews in Amarillo, but the only rabbi in town who had opposed Christian prayers in school and nuclear weapons felt compelled to resign. His successor said that his ministry would be devoted to spiritual issues. That left only the Roman Catholic bishop and one black minister to oppose the arms race and claim that the possession of nuclear weapons was a moral evil.

Southern Baptists dominated not only Amarillo but most of the South and are now the largest Protestant denomination. Southern Baptist commissions issued statements on policy matters, but the national gatherings have no authority to bind any congregation because of local autonomy. Southern Baptists from 1945 through the 1960s supported the United Nations, sought mutual arms reductions, endorsed the Salt treaties, and opposed new weapons systems. In the 1980s, the Baptists, reflecting increased conservatism and a militant fundamentalism that opposed having "moderates" in leadership positions (like Amarillo's minister), emphasized the legitimacy of deterrence, more spending for and the necessity of a "strong national defense," along with "a responsible limitation of nuclear weapons."[21]   The denomination took no position on the

---

[20]Ibid., 84.
[21]Donald Davidson, *Nuclear Weapons and the American Churches* (1983), 160-162.

632

Vietnam war, did not endorse the nuclear freeze or unilateral initiatives, nor reject all use of nuclear weapons, and insisted that the Christian commitment to peacemaking should not jeopardize the security of an orderly society.

The fastest-growing denominations in America are those that are theologically conservative and evangelistic. The Evangelical Lutheran Synod and the Missouri Synod Lutheran Church espouse a two-sphere theory in which the church addresses spiritual but not political issues. By contrast, the Church of Jesus Christ of Latter Day Saints (Mormons), that had issued strong statements against nuclear weapons in 1945, now cooperates with the social and political agenda of the Moral Majority and its successor, the Christian Coalition.[22] Neo-evangelical churches also sponsor missions overseas that have resulted in rapidly growing churches in Africa, Latin America, Asia, and most recently in Eastern Europe and Russia. Although these religious movements promise their adherents a better life in this world or the next and demand strict moral standards, they tend to be apolitical and ignore nuclear weapons.[23]

The American Protestant Establishment

The denominations that composed the National Council of Churches had, since the early Republic, seen themselves as spokesmen for Protestants, a natural assumption since until the 1950s they comprised a majority of American church members. The Protestant establishment had long been accustomed to speaking on behalf of all churches about moral issues to a country that saw itself as a defender as well as an exemplar of Christianity. These churches in the postwar period relied on policy statements made by commissions and national gatherings and also made their wishes known through lobbies in Washington. They emerged at this time as persistent critics of American foreign policy and supporters of peace with justice, but their influence declined as a gap in ideas emerged between those sitting

---

[22]The Mormon Church strongly opposed the Reagan administration's proposal to build a railroad system for missile X in Utah in the 1980s. There was also a small Mormon peace movement.
[23]David Martin, *Does Christianity Cause War?* (1997), 177-87.

in pews and the leaders of churches, as conservative evangelicals increased, and as Roman Catholicism entered the national arena as a full equal.

The churches in the National Council stressed the necessity of being Christian peacemakers, downplayed the categories of Just War theory, and questioned the morality of any nuclear war. Throughout the 1950s the Council argued that Americans placed too much stress on military preparedness and should instead seek peaceful co-existence that would be strengthened by constant negotiations and personal relations. The Council consistently opposed major new weapons systems while emphasizing support of the United Nations. Members welcomed signs of détente, summit conferences, and proposals for disarmament.

The National Council churches opposed biblical literalism, ignored apocalyptic imagery, and presented a picture of Christ as the bringer of religious and political peace. They distinguished between the wars of the Hebrews and modern conditions, relying on verses in the New Testament advocating love of enemy, and the example of self-sacrificing love by Jesus. Christianity's core doctrine proclaimed that the power of God could overcome evil. Religious liberals and nuclear pacifists in the National Council insisted that new policies should allow the peoples in the USSR and U.S. to fulfill their desire for peace.

A second major influence on the Council was Niebuhr's Christian realism, with adherents among mainline churches and politicians as diverse as Adlai Stevenson and President Jimmy Carter. Niebuhr saw the Soviet Union and the U.S. as idolatrous countries, magnifying their own virtues while refusing to see the value in opposing systems. That both nations were willing to risk the world over political/economic systems was a sign of their apostasy, but the Christian realists also saw the necessity of military power in a sinful world and did not advocate unilateral disarmament. Niebuhr defended democracy as the best system of government largely because all the alternatives were worse.

Throughout the Cold War the mainline churches distinguished between communism as an ideology, which they opposed, and the Soviet Union as a state with which the U.S. needed to co-exist in peace. Unhappy with the expulsion of missionaries from Red China, the Council condemned the communists' conquest in China but also called on the American administration to recognize and seek a modus vivendi with the new order in East Asia. Because the Council feared the militarization of American life, it (along with Roman Catholics and Southern Baptists) opposed the Truman and Eisenhower administrations' attempt to institute universal military training for young men. With support from liberal Democrats and conservative Republicans, the House and Senate repeatedly defeated UMT. The churches did not oppose the Selective Service System (draft) instituted during the Korean War which remained a feature of American life until the end of the Vietnam War.

In 1950, after the Soviet Union exploded an atomic bomb, President Truman announced a program to build a hydrogen bomb. The National Council of Churches continued to advocate international control of nuclear weapons, warned against the irrational fear of communism caused by "sensationalism" (i.e., "red scares"), and affirmed the fundamental difference on "moral issues" between the West and communism over "the dignity and worth of man." However, a crucial section on whether to build the hydrogen bomb showed that the 1946 unconditional opposition to atomic weapons was now weakened:

> Some of us feel deeply that the hydrogen bomb does not present a new and different moral issue but sheds vivid light on the wickedness of war itself. Some of us oppose the construction of hydrogen bombs, which could be used only for the mass destruction of populations. Some of us, on the other hand, believing that our people and the other free societies should not be left without the means of defense through the threat of retaliation, support the attempt to construct the new weapon. All of us unite in the prayer that it may never be used.[24]

---

[24]Executive Committee of the Federal Council of Churches of Christ in America, *The Churches and the Hydrogen Bomb,"* (1950), 2.

Paul Ramsey, a Methodist ethicist at Princeton Theological Seminary, re-introduced into Protestant thought in the late 50s an emphasis upon Just War theories that had been neglected by liberals, pacifists, and Niebuhrian realists. Ramsey argued that massive retaliation went against two fundamental tenets of Just War theory: discrimination (the immunity of civilians) and proportionality (harm done must not be greater than resulting good). Restraint in waging war against civilians took priority, and an ethically just military strategy would not target them, even when using grounds of necessity. The primary issue was not the nature of the weapon, but of the target. Ramsey thought nuclear war and targeting civilians by conventional weapons were immoral, but he was not a pacifist and he worked within a deterrence framework. His concern was to limit the casualties, to establish "firebreaks" in case of a nuclear war and he advocated that weapons not be targeted against soft targets, i.e., cities or civilians. Critics charged, and Ramsey agreed that targeting weapons lowered the nuclear threshold, but he thought the increased risk worth the potential benefit in reducing deaths and pled for numerous options in using military force.[25]

Divisions in American Protestantism among pacifists, Niebuhrians, Just War proponents, deterrence advocates, and those who thought religion should provide spiritual nurture but ignore politics meant that the churches contributed little sustained opposition to nuclear weapons during the 1950s. Instead, the National Council and mainline Protestants wrestled with a series of moral/strategic questions: Was the primary danger from a totalitarian dictatorship that must be resisted whatever the cost? Or was the main threat war, because nuclear weapons made all previous rationalizations for war obsolete? Americans agreed that nuclear war would be a catastrophe beyond comprehension, but could not decide a safe way to escape from deterrence. The most detailed study of the 1960s anti-bomb movement concluded: "America's major religious groups did comparatively little

[25]Paul Ramsey, War and the Christian Conscience (1961), ch. 7; also The Limits of Nuclear War (1965). A summary of Ramsey's contributions and also the additional qualifications of James Johnson are in Davidson, 43-56.

to encourage it." A survey of demonstrators in 1962 found 51% had no religious preference, 20% liberal Protestants, 13.5% from other Protestant groups, and only .5% Catholics.[26]

Outside America, the role of churches varied according to country: there was strong church involvement in anti-nuclear campaigns in Holland, Ireland, and New Zealand, but very little in Australia and Italy. The World and National Council of Churches and the Neo-evangelicals consistently invoked the necessity of prayer and the power of God in history, but did not make clear how these religious insights related to its secular advice on foreign policy and military affairs.

Although there was a constant debate on the morality of nuclear weaponry in the peace commission of churches, the general public became involved only at certain times: in the late 40s, early 60s, and, most significantly, early 80s. The cycles coincided with times of intense confrontation between the two super powers; at other periods, Americans dismissed their worries and went about their business as usual, essentially unaffected except by what psychologist Robert Lifton believes was a kind of psychic numbness to the dangers posed by nuclear war.[27]

Nuclear War: The View from Rome

The ascension of Pope John XXIII in 1958, his encyclical "Pacem in Terris" (1963), and the declaration of Vatican Council II "Gaudium et Spes" (1965) marked a significant evolution in Catholic policy, a change that grew out of but also modified Pius XII's pronouncements. Although militantly anti-communist, Pius continued to grapple with the moral issues caused by total war. He condemned a pacifism advocating peace at any price as an "artificial expedient" and dishonorable, because it purchased a false peace and surrendered the prime duty of a state, which was to provide a just moral order for the people. As late as

---

[26]Wittner, *Resisting the Bomb 1954-1970* (1997), 259-60. Since polls showed steady opposition to the use of nuclear weapons and a majority of Americans in support of a test ban, and since a majority of Americans were church members, one could argue that the religious influence in the movement was indirect.
[27]Robert Lifton and Greg Mitchell, *Hiroshima in America* (1995), ch. 6.

1956, Pius reiterated that there was no right of conscientious objection in a Just War of self-defense engaged in by a freely elected government.

However, Pius also insisted as early as 1948 that because based in God, "the Christian will for peace is ... as strong as steel," a foundation stronger than utilitarian or "humanitarian sentiment" or even a revulsion against atrocities and injustice. A Christian would never wage war for "natural prestige or honor" or even for rights which "however legitimate, did not offset the risk of kindling a blaze." Soon Pius made explicit that the only legitimate ground for a permissible war was self-defense. And even self-defense had to be qualified by the doctrine of proportionality.

Pius condemned the materialism and militarism of East and West and denounced as naïve the belief that weapons brought peace. In 1951 the Pontiff labeled nuclear weapons as monstrously cruel but came to no conclusion on whether possessing them was "licit or illicit" and insisted that the issue of weapons could not be divorced from "the absence of that Christian order which is the true guarantee of peace." He called for the abolition or international control of ABC weapons - atomic, biological, and chemical - but refused to say that such weapons could not be used in self-defense in extreme conditions. If the use of these weapons caused "the pure and simple annihilation of all human life within the radius of action," they should never be permitted even as a last resort.[28] The West, however flawed by materialism and lack of spiritual commitment, contained some elements of a just society, so a cold peace built upon "infernal" weapons was permissible, but only if these weapons were not used. The Church's position implied that nuclear deterrence was morally permissible for the West, but only if it was lying about intent to use massive retaliation and never under any circumstances would use them as weapons of war.

John XXIII sought to open a dialogue with communist governments in Eastern Europe. His openness to relations with the Soviets did not mean that

---

[28] *Proclaiming Justice and Peace: Papal Documents from Rerum Novarum through Cenestimus Annus* (1991),122-23, 131.

either the Church or communists changed their negative views of each other. His successor, Paul VI, welcomed to the Vatican Tito of Yugoslavia, the Soviet foreign minister on several visits, and the head of the Soviet Presidium; even Gorbachev would visit Pope John Paul II. Pope John demonstrated his usefulness as a mediator during the Cuban missile crisis of 1962. Under John and Paul VI, the Church now sought partial agreements with communist governments allowing it to exercise the pastoral functions of worship, confession, and instruction. Church officials began negotiations with officials in the Soviet Union, Poland, East Germany, Hungary, and Czechoslovakia after which Rome could again appoint bishops and Catholics could worship freely. By 1978 at the inaugural papal mass of John Paul II, representatives attended from all the Soviet bloc governments except Rumania.

Pope John's encyclical "Pacem in Terris" did not repudiate, but also did not explicitly use Just War theory. Neither did it denounce communism. Unlike Pius, John seemed to say that ideology was less important than the common good and the need for a new world order. He seemed to undercut any use of atomic weapons by insisting, "It is hardly possible to imagine that in the atomic era war could be used as an instrument of justice." "In this age of ours, which prides itself on its atomic power, it is irrational to think that war is a proper way to obtain justice for violated rights."[29] John's pastoral epistle also emphasized a theme that would become a constant subject for his successors: social justice must be placed in a global context. The money spent on a foolish and immoral arms race could be better used to alleviate the growing disparity in wealth between rich and poor nations. The division between the West and communist nations was no more important than the North/South division between the industrial powers and the Third World.

"Gaudium et Spes" (1965), an official declaration of the Church's position on war by the bishops assembled at the Vatican Council II, contained several

---

[29]Ibid., 218.

innovations. Although the Church continued to assert the legitimacy of a war in carefully defined and limited self-defense, for the first time the bishops recognized the legitimacy of pacifism by expressing admiration "for all who forgo the use of violence to vindicate their rights and resort to those other means of defense which are available to weaker parties, provided it can be done without harm to the rights and duties of others and of the community."[30] Gandhi's *satyagraha* campaigns of nonviolent resistance had now received official approval. The Council also called for legal recognition of conscientious objectors, provided they did some form of community service. Note that there was no approval of subjectivism: traditionally, Just Wars had been permitted because those fighting always sought to preserve community norms; pacifism and CO status had to meet the same test of love of neighbor.

The Council condemned total war, weapons of "indiscriminate destruction of whole cities or vast areas," and the arms race ("one of the greatest curses on the human race"). It suggested that neither balance of power nor deterrence could lead to a genuine peace and called for an international outlawing of war and the establishment of an "acknowledged public authority" with the power to guarantee security for all.

The Council established the parameters for a revised Catholic position on war and nuclear weapons: deterrence with conventional and nuclear weapons was not immoral so long as it produced a kind of negative peace, but it was also not acceptable because it was based on mistrust and threat. The actual use of atomic weapons on any kind of a mass scale would be immoral. The present condition of deterrence coupled with an arms race was immoral, because the arms race undermined any stability from a balance of power obtained through deterrence and diverted resources from the needs of humanity. The bishops seemed to be saying that the present military impasse was unacceptable. What was needed was a form of disarmament. Before his death, Pius XII called for disarmament, a cessation of

---

[30]Ibid., 216.

nuclear testing, and a strengthened UN. John XXIII, Paul VI, and John Paul II continued these emphases by encouraging UN conferences on disarmament and praising the Limited Test Ban Treaty, Nonproliferation Treaty, and SALT treaties as steps in the right direction. Above all, the popes sought to encourage the building of trust between opponents as the best way to guarantee that the arsenals would not be used.

The reception of the Catholic Church's new emphases depended upon one's perspective. Nuclear pacifists and the Catholic Worker Movement rejoiced that they had been officially legitimized and saw the Vatican as recognizing that there was now within the Church a plurality of voices on war. Some even called "Pacem in Terris" a pacifist document. By contrast, conservatives complained that the new rhetoric used by the popes and council concentrated upon weapons and not the differences between communist and capitalist states. They labeled as unrealistic John XXIII's call for a new international order controlling nuclear weapons and disliked the downplaying of traditional Just War theories both by lack of emphasis and in the legitimacy given to pacifism and conscientious objection.[31]

V. Living with the Bomb

The fallout from the atomic tests conducted by the super powers was the issue that created a mass movement in the 1950s. Radiation from an American hydrogen bomb test in 1954 drenched the Lucky Dragon, a Japanese fishing boat. This sparked enormous anti-nuclear protest in Japan and Germany, the two countries most knowledgeable of the effects of saturation bombing, and other states close to test sites. Atomic scientists, led by Nobel laureate Linus Pauling, insisted that the effects of radioactive fallout from American and Soviet tests

---

[31]Contrasting interpretations of the Catholic tradition are in William Au, *The Cross, the Flag, and the Bomb: American Catholics Debate War and Peace (1985)*, 167-77, and George Weigel, *Tranquillitas Ordinis: The Present Failure and Future Promise of American Catholic Thought on War and Peace* (1987), 102-03, 160. Just War theorists who opposed the new teaching of the Church as naïve include Ramsey and as ignoring ideological division were Roman Catholic William O'Brien and Michael Novak.

placed a generation of children at risk. Endorsements for a test-ban treaty came from America's baby doctor, Benjamin Spock, and Nobel laureate and missionary doctor, Albert Schweitzer. The Committee for a Sane Nuclear Policy, the National and World Council of Churches, Adlai Stevenson in the 1956 presidential election, and Democratic members of Congress supported a test ban. Neutral nations and America's allies like Japan insisted that the rivalry between super powers jeopardized the health of everyone in the northern hemisphere. Yugoslavia's President Tito and India's Prime Minister Nehru, who invoked the spirit of Buddhism, used the UN as a forum for denouncing the immorality of a nuclear arms race that contaminated the atmosphere.[32] When tests showed the presence of radioactive Strontium 90 in cow's milk, America and the Soviet Union for a brief time in 1957-59 initiated unilateral and unverified test bans while engaging in complicated negotiations over how to prove that neither cheated by using underground tests. The Soviets first, followed shortly by the Americans, resumed above-ground tests as tensions mounted in 1959. An above-ground test ban came only after the Cuban missile crisis had frightened the leaders of both sides and was first of a series of what came to be called "confidence building steps." Accepted with reservations by the militaries of both major adversaries, ignored by China and France, the above-ground test ban had little impact on the continuing arms race.[33]

Crises over Berlin and Cuba and a massive arms buildup in the early 1960s sparked what could have become a major worldwide debate on nuclear weapons strategy and the dangers of accidental wars. Popular movies like *Dr. Strangelove, Seven Days in May, Failsafe,* and *On the Beach* tried to show that Mutual Assured Destruction was madness, risking the survival of the world by accident or irresponsible generals. A new emphasis on surviving a nuclear war led to

---

[32] Wittner, *Resisting the Bomb* (1997), 65-66.
[33] The British responded to public opinion; the Soviets viewed the treaty as a way to contain China; the Americans responded to public opinion and saw a way to channel the arms race. In the campaign for Senate ratification, the Kennedy administration tried to downplay the role of anti-nuclear activists. Wittner, 421-32.

designating large buildings, including churches, as potential bomb shelters. Civil defense increased fear, but the public refused to take such precautions seriously, and it was easy to show the impossibility of mass evacuation of New York and Chicago. Neither movies nor civil defense influenced the nation's strategy of building more missiles, hardening missiles sites, and deploying missile-bearing submarines. Deterrence still reigned supreme, with defense intellectuals employing computers with sophisticated variations using game theory or playing chicken to predict various scenarios of challenge, response, and results. Like game theory, Herman Kahn's influential *Thinking About the Unthinkable* (1962) analyzed many forms of nuclear war while subordinating moral considerations to the quest for power. For example, Kahn argued that if the U.S. had a nuclear weapon explode with the loss of the population of Mobile, Alabama and the President not know for certain whether accident or Soviet sabotage was involved, the U.S. would achieve strategic advantage by immediately detonating one nuclear weapon upon the Soviet Union as a response. Otherwise the uncertainly of a long investigation would preclude action, and, if an accident were proved, the resulting outcry would weaken U.S. military power.[34]

Vietnam upstaged the debate on nuclear weapons that could have occurred in the early 1960s. Now attention focused on the morality of a conventional war, a topic barely mentioned during the 1950s. When nuclear weapons again took center stage, the climate of debate had changed drastically. Pacifism during Vietnam had been radicalized with many anti-war activists engaging in civil disobedience and seeking to foment a revolution in the society. After Vatican II cooperation between Protestants and Catholics in ecumenical gatherings, academic conferences, and the civil rights movement meant that the debate would involve many varieties of Christians.

Seeking to understand how he could oppose Vietnam but favor Israel's wars, political scientist Michael Walzer untied Just War theories from their

---

[34]Herman Kahn, *Thinking About the Unthinkable* (1963), Games I and II, 167-75.

religious moorings and sought to anchor them in a universal sentiment of peoples as expressed in UN declarations, international law, and common morality. Walzer's primary concern was conventional war, but his section on nuclear war concluded that the massive use of atomic weapons would not be war at all but a massacre in which the level of destruction would overwhelm any political purposes.[35] Walzer's *Just and Unjust Wars* (1977) allowed political science professors to debate the conclusions of ancient theologians without invoking love, natural law, or using the word God. Philosophers also debated permissible actions in war, trying to ground the prohibitions of Just War theory on something more reasonable or acceptable in the classroom than religion. So students encountered defenses of civilian immunity based upon utilitarianism, or rule utilitarianism, or moral absolutism and questions about the ethical legitimacy of deterrence. It was generally believed that none of these theories permitted nuclear war.[36]

Scientists re-entered the nuclear debate after the volcano Mt. St. Helen's erupted and the ash and gases affected climate. Using computer models of the effects on the atmosphere of the soil blown into the air and the smoke and soot from fires from burning cities after an all-out nuclear exchange, influential scientists including Carl Sagan insisted that the result would be a Nuclear Winter, with such massive climate and environmental changes that civilization would end. Jonathan Schell, in his best-selling *Fate of the Earth* (1982), argued that for the first time in recorded history, humans, through the possibility of nuclear war, had placed at risk the future of their species. His book was an extended meditation upon the meaning of extinction.[37]

After Vietnam, debate on nuclear weapons had been muted because the U.S. and China eased relations, and the U.S. and USSR entered into a period of

---

[35]Michael Walzer, *Just and Unjust Wars* (1977), 269-283; Stanley Hoffman, *Duties Beyond Borders* (1981).
[36]For examples, Marshall Cohen et al., *War and Moral Responsibility (1974); Richard Wasserstrom*, ed., *War and Morality* (1970).
[37]Owen Greene, *Nuclear Winter: The Evidence and the Risks* (1985) Carl Sagan, *A Path where No Man Thought: Nuclear Winter and the End of the Arms Race* (1990), and Jonathan Schell, *Fate of the Earth* (1982).

détente in which they negotiated the SALT I and SALT II treaties.[38] Frequent summits, a cooling of rhetoric, and increased cultural contacts gave assurance of gradually improving relations. Yet the arms race continued, and super-power rivalries contributed to armed conflict in Angola, Mozambique, Ethiopia, Somalia, Nicaragua, and El Salvador. When in 1979 a pro-communist government in Afghanistan seemed in danger of falling, the Soviet Union invaded, the first expansion of its sphere by direct military force since World War II. The U.S. mobilized world opinion against the Russians, cancelled ratification of the SALT II Treaty and, prompted by conservative hawks and the Pentagon's claims that America was falling behind in the arms race, began a massive arms build up under President Carter that expanded under President Reagan. Candidate Reagan denounced SALT II as advantageous to the Russians and, as President during his first term, showed no interest in arms control talks. Reagan sought to counter alleged Soviet advances by sponsoring pro-America guerrilla forces in Africa, Central America, and Afghanistan. The administration pronounced a "Reagan Doctrine" authorizing the U.S. to support anti-communist guerrilla movements anywhere because 1. communism was an immoral doctrine, 2. no people would ever freely choose communist governments, 3. no communist regime would ever allow free elections and willingly surrender power, and 4. all pro-communist guerrilla movements had been fomented by the Soviet Union in efforts to expand its power.[39]

The Reagan administration endorsed deterrence, but defense analysts began discussing a decapitation strike on Moscow and winning a limited nuclear war. A U.S. and NATO decision to place new medium-range Pershing II missiles in Europe to counter new Soviet missiles occasioned massive anti-nuclear demonstrations in Germany, Britain, and the Benelux countries. The Green political movement in West Germany became a potent party on a platform of

---

[38]John Newhouse, *Cold Dawn* (1973) is an account of Salt I; Strobe Talbott, *Deadly Gambits* (1985) is on Salt II.

anti-nuclear weapons and pro-ecology. The Western European peace movements' advocates feared their countries would be the place where any limited nuclear war would be fought. In America, the evangelical right whose votes help propel Reagan into the White House echoed the President's themes of anti-communism, standing up against opponents whether in Iran or Nicaragua, and building a strong military. Tough rhetoric about the "evil empire" accompanied the military build-up as the Cold War threatened once again to become hot. (We know now that Reagan's rhetoric scared not only doves in the U.S. but the leaders of the USSR who became convinced that America was going to initiate a first strike in the fall of 1983.) The result was the most intense debate on the morality of nuclear weapons in America since 1945 and a political movement against the arms race termed the Freeze.

VI. The 1980s Debate on Nuclear Weapons

The Freeze proposed to end the nuclear arms race by stopping the testing, production, and deployment of new strategic weapons. Russia and the U.S. would agree to the Freeze that each would verify by national methods, i.e., satellites and seismic monitors with no on-site inspection required.[40] There was nothing new about the concept; the National Council Of Churches had suggested something similar in the 1950s. The Freeze was also rather tame, essentially trying to maintain the status quo as a method of rebuilding the confidence of both sides and restarting arms control negotiations. New weapons systems took many years to develop from idea, to funding, creating prototypes, then testing, building substantial numbers, and finally deploying. There was no easy way to guarantee stopping the early stages of weapon development, but testing and deployment of new missiles could be verified.

---

[39]Charles Krauthammer, "Morality and the Reagan Doctrine," *New Republic*, (Sept. 8, 1986), 17-24.
[40]Edward Kennedy and Mark Hatfield, *Freeze! How You Can Help Prevent Nuclear War* (1982); David Meyer, *A Winter of Discontent: The Nuclear Freeze and American Politics* (1990); *Peacemaking: The Believers' Calling,* The Peacemaking Project, Program Agency UPCUSA (1982)

The Freeze seemed a politically easy and morally attractive proposal to unite anyone worried about the course and cost of the arms race and seeking more stability: pacifists, nuclear pacifists, Just War advocates, arms control advocates, those wanting improved relations between Russia and the U.S., and opponents of the arms race. The Freeze received endorsements from many Catholics and Protestants (including and Mormons), liberal Democrats, a few state legislatures, and proved popular on campuses and in polls, but was opposed by the Reagan administration that instead deployed missile X, Trident submarines, and cruise missiles. When Reagan won a landslide victory against Mondale in 1984, it became clear that strong religious and moral opposition to nuclear weapons brought no political advantage. So the Freeze as a movement died.

The American Roman Catholic bishops initiated discussions on an official statement on war in 1981. Before the bishops had finished, they had published several draft documents, received extensive comments, made revisions, and published the final document in 1983. The Reagan administration criticized the drafts as ignoring the positive elements of deterrence. European bishops also feared insufficient attention was devoted to the danger from a totalitarian state. The American bishops reaffirmed papal teachings on the irrationality and immorality of using weapons of mass annihilation on civilians in cities. The central issue on nuclear weapons became: "May a nation threaten what it may never do? May it possess what it may never use?" An answer hinged on judging intent and consequences. Defense analysts emphasized intent: deterrence was to keep the peace. Nuclear pacifists said the intent was also to threaten a war, the consequences of which would be incalculable. The bishops allowed the possession of nuclear weapons only IF the intent was peaceful and only as an interim measure in a policy aimed at disarmament.[41] Hawks thought the bishops

---

[41]The background documents are printed in *In the Name of Peace: Collective Statements of the United States Catholic Bishops on War and Peace, 1919-1980* (1983), which contains an analysis of the Just War theory by J. Bryan Hehir. The essential documents on the 1983 declaration are in Philip Murnion, ed. *Catholics and Nuclear War: A Commentary on "The Challenge of Peace:" The US Catholic Bishops' Pastoral Letter on War and Peace* (1982); James

went too far; pacifists complained that the bishops had not made their moral teachings consistent. Either way, the bishops' letter contained a rebuke of U.S. policies.

In 1986 the bishops of the United Methodist Church went beyond the Catholic position, which they cited, in a document whose title showed their priorities: *In Defense of Creation*: "We say a clear and unconditioned No to nuclear war and to any use of nuclear weapons. We conclude that nuclear deterrence is a position that cannot receive the church's blessings."[42] The Methodist bishops endorsed additional arms reduction talks, a no-first-use declaration, non-proliferation, a moratorium on all nuclear tests, abandoning the Star Wars anti-missile system, and the ceasing of testing or deploying all new strategic weapons systems. Even threatening a moral evil was not a permissible act. Therefore nuclear deterrence was not moral, and even the possession of nuclear weapons was immoral.

Catholics, Methodists, and Presbyterians issued study guides to teach their congregations the history of the church's positions on war and the implications for nuclear strategy.[43] Direct effects from the careful statements of Catholics, Methodists, and Presbyterians are difficult to discover. Protestant church officials do not speak with the same authority as Catholic bishops, and after Vatican II, discordant voices appeared within the American Catholic Church. Many Protestants disapproved of their churches' position on war. In addition, the mainline churches' membership was falling, while that of the conservative evangelical Protestant churches who supported the Reagan policies increased. Polls did show, however, a decided shift in Catholic position on nuclear weapons. Such sentiment did not translate into votes against Reagan by devout Catholics,

---

Dougherty, *The Bishops and Nuclear Weapons* (1984); George Weigel, *Tranquillitas Ordinis: The Present Failure and Future Promise of American Catholic Thought on War and Peace* (1987).

[42] The United Methodist Council of Bishops, *In Defense of Creation: The Nuclear Crisis and a Just Peace* (1986), 91; an analysis and critique is in Paul Ramsey, *Speak Up for Just War or Pacifism* (1998).

[43] United Presbyterian Church, USA, *Peacemaking: The Believers' Calling* (1982).

because during the 1984 presidential campaign the bishops stressed opposition to abortion more than nuclear weapons.

Surprising virtually everyone, the Soviet Union under Mikhail Gorbachev not only announced but actually sought peace, ceased inflammatory rhetoric, and proved receptive to arms control first using bilateral and later unilateral initiatives. Reagan, who had always insisted he disliked nuclear weapons and would like to see them abolished, sponsored arms control initiatives in his second term; a process continued under his successor George Bush. Unilateral reductions in nuclear and conventional weapons begun by both sides eventually resulted in START treaties that for the first time included actual arms reductions. The Senate easily ratified these treaties.

Gorbachev's refusal to use troops to intervene in Poland in 1989 or to prop up the governments of the Peoples' Republics allowed the opening of borders, the freeing of Eastern Europe, and the reunification of Germany. Conventional arms limitation talks proceeded more slowly than the actual withdrawal of troops from Eastern Europe. The breakup of the Soviet Union and the worldwide decline of communism allowed a new era of good will between the U.S. and Russia. Of course, the debate continues as to whether the Soviet Union imploded because of internal weakness in the economy and government or from pressure applied by America's defense build-up. We still don't know if nuclear deterrence worked or whether there was ever a Soviet intention to take over Western Europe by military force. We await accurate historical assessment of the influence of the good will of peace groups and inter-cultural contacts, economic stagnation, personality and policies of Gorbachev, and the reaction of Reagan and Bush to changes in Russia in the breakup of the Soviet Union. The end of the Soviet Union did not mark the end of nuclear deterrence and the dangers of nuclear war.

Even if the START treaties and the 2002 agreement between Presidents Putin and Bush are fully implemented, the U.S. and Russia will each retain 1500 strategic nuclear weapons (and thousands more in storage) and neither has repudiated the doctrine of deterrence. Proliferation of nuclear weapons to many more countries is an ever-present danger to which has been added the risk of so-called rogue states' and terrorist groups' stealing bombs. The moral issues posed by deterrence through nuclear weapons are still present, but neither churches, politicians, nor the public in America or abroad seem greatly concerned. A recent proposal by several retired Secretaries of Defense and high ranking military officers (i.e., a former Supreme Commander of NATO) for America to abolish all nuclear weapons because they were not usable weapons and served no military purpose was discussed briefly on news shows and then forgotten.[44]

Still, it seems miraculous that nuclear weapons were never used during the forty years the two super powers glowered at each other while their surrogates spread their conflicts throughout the world. The persistent questioning of the morality of nuclear war by the churches and the peace movement contributed to the restraint shown by the leaders who, beginning with Truman, seemed to have grasped that A and H bombs should never be used as weapons of war.[45]

---

[44]Joseph Rotblat and Jack Steinberger, *A Nuclear-Weapon Free World: Desirable? Feasible?* (1995).

[45]In the first two of his projected three volume history *Struggle Against the Bomb* Lawrence Wittner argues that although the peace movement could not stop the arms race or deterrence, it established a moral threshold that made political leaders realize that nuclear weapons should never be used and made them aware of the dangers of proliferation. However, the Bush, Jr. administration has recently proposed developing new tactical nuclear weapons designed to penetrate deep in the earth and destroy enemy bunkers.

XIX.
Religion and War in the Creation of Israel

Since the 1930s, no region has had more instability and wars than Palestine. The Arab-Israeli conflicts illustrate that, at the end of the twentieth century, war could be caused by complex patterns of religious fervor, ethnic identification, historical consciousness, emergent nationalism, and competition for material resources (land, water). Zionism now appears not to be a unique phenomenon but a modern example of resurgent religious-ethnic-nationalisms whose adherents use selective history to claim a right to land or sovereignty. This chapter focuses on the background to the wars beginning in 1948 in order to understand how a religious myth, God's gift of the promised land to the Jews, remembered through centuries of exile, became fused with nationalism and climaxed in the birth of a new, ostensibly secular state with a biblically based civil religion. Our theme is to explain why, as a recent history argued, "once the Zionist movement came to Palestine with the intention of creating an independent state with a Jewish majority, war was inevitable."[1]

Zionism rested on two premises: a Jewish historical claim to a land dominated for 1300 years by Muslims and the belief that Jews could fulfill their potential and be safe from persecution only in a country they controlled. The Jews created Israel to be a land of peace, and yet the manner of its creation and its quest for safe borders resulted in displacing Arabs and guaranteed war. Understanding recent Arab-Israeli wars requires knowing the history of the Jews and their relations with the Palestinians. This chapter is a chronological account focusing on the conditions facing Jews in nineteenth-century Europe, religious and secular origins of Zionism, Jewish migration to Palestine, British policies beginning with the 1917 Balfour Declaration and ending with withdrawal in 1947,

---

[1]Tom Segev, *One Palestine, Complete: Jews and Arabs under the British Mandate* (1999), 490. British officials made similar claims beginning in the 1920s, see 147, 180, 432.

the origins of Palestinian nationalism, the impact of World War II and the Holocaust, and the war leading to founding a new nation surrounded by a hostile population and states.

Israel has fought five actual wars, beginning with the struggle for independence in 1948, invading Egypt in concert with the British and French in 1956, responding to a threatening coalition in 1967 with a surprise attack that ended with Israeli troops seizing the West Bank of Jordan, the Golan Heights from Syria, and the Sinai up to the Suez Canal from Egypt. In 1973 Egypt and Syria staged a surprise attack in which Israel eventually triumphed but at considerable cost. Israel's invasion of Lebanon in 1983 was the last official war. After 1967 Palestinian groups, seeing little results from the support of Arab states, became radicalized and initiated acts of terrorism (or freedom fighting, depending on your perspective) to which Israel responded with punitive reprisals, an incursion into Lebanon designed to destroy the Palestinian Liberation Organization, and the carving out of a security zone occupied by Israeli troops and extending some twenty miles into Lebanon that lasted seventeen years. Two Intifadas, that could be labeled unofficial wars six and seven, have occurred since; the first, in the 1980s, consisting of demonstrations by young Palestinians throwing rocks and, from 2000 to 2004, a second using suicide bombers. All of these wars, raids, and reprisals had one basic cause: Jews and Palestinians claim the right to rule the same land.

There is an enormous quantity of high-quality scholarship that also reflects the passionately held convictions of those drawn to study the Israeli-Palestinian disputes.[2] Our aim is not moral judgment for or against either side but historical understanding of the roles of religion in war and peace in a volatile area.

---

[2]The bibliography shows how dependent this chapter is on books written by Israelis, British, and Americans. Because of the sources, we know far more about the Jews and the British than about

I. The Origins of Zionism

The Jews endured in Palestine after Roman conquest in 74 C.E., even though they had no state and even in Palestine soon became a small minority in an area ruled first by Romans, then Byzantium, and finally Muslims. By the third century C.E., the Pharisees had re-fashioned Judaism without dependence upon temple worship in Jerusalem or dwelling in Israel, although much of the law continued to emphasize practices in the Holy Land. The new Judaism, drawing upon the past through rituals and the Hebrew *Bible* plus commentaries like the *Mishna*, evolved over the centuries into a unique and not easily defined phenomenon - a religion, way of life, ethnic group, and civilization - practiced by peoples calling themselves Jews.

By 1800 the largest concentration of Jews was in central and eastern Europe in the German principalities and Prussian, Austrian, and Russian Empires. There were Jews in Iran, Egypt, Ethiopia, the U.S. and Portugal. Most Jews lived in ghettos or isolated villages and in language, religious practices, and custom remained separate from their Christian or Muslim neighbors, yet there were also distinct German, Spanish, and Russian Jewish cultures. In Palestine a few Jewish settlements retained limited self-government under the Ottoman's policy of allowing religious minorities toleration but not full political rights.

Even though the traditional Seder prayer at the end of the Passover feast included the hope that the ceremony would be performed "next year in Jerusalem," few considered actually returning to a poor, semi-arid land in the Ottoman Empire. To Jews, the land of Israel remained a symbol of God's covenant with his chosen people, a link to the past and hope for deliverance from discrimination imposed primarily by Christian Europe. The devout prayed that the future would bring fulfillment of prophecies proclaiming that with the coming of the messiah there would be a gathering of all peoples to Jerusalem and the dawn

---

the Palestinians. I have relied on the research of Jewish revisionist historians, but in the footnotes have indicated continuing controversies.

of a golden age of God's rule. God's act would bring about the deliverance of the people of Israel living in the diaspora.

Jews living in isolated communities in Eastern Europe felt no urgency to reclaim the land of Israel and regarded as idolatrous the Zionist political reform movement to create a new Jewish state led largely by those who did not observe Judaism's laws and customs. However, a series of pogroms in Russia in the 1880s began a movement among observant Jews to consider Palestine as a refuge and a few even migrated to small existing farming communities, termed *Yishuv*, or to Jerusalem where they lived in peace with their Muslim neighbors under Ottoman rule. Western European Jews financed as philanthropic endeavors these small-scale settlements. The Russian colonization movement to Palestine was apolitical and did not envisage creating a Jewish state through influencing the great powers. Settlers who became discouraged and left Palestine were not accused of betraying Jewish destiny.

The "Zion" for most Eastern Jews was the United States. Of the two million Jewish immigrants between 1880-1914, 70% came to the United States, with an additional 150,000 to Great Britain. The U.S. by 1920 had 3.6 million Jews. By contrast, the Jewish population in Palestine in 1882 was 24,000 (about 5% of the population); by 1897 the number had risen to 50,000; by the end of World War I to 65,000 - around 10% of the population.[3]

II. Nationalism and Jewish Identity

After the French Revolution, Jews, particularly in Germany, sought to apply the standards of reason to Judaism and ended by jettisoning many parts of traditional law and custom that they saw as superstitious, useless observances. These practitioners of what was later labeled "Reform" re-defined Judaism so that it was not an all-encompassing way of life but a "religion" of morality designed to appeal to all peoples of the world. Rather than exulting in their status as a

---

[3]There were 512,000 Muslims and 61,000 Christians. Jehuda Reinharz, *Chaim Weizmann: The Making of a Zionist Leader* (1985), 16; Sykes, *Crossroads to Israel* (1973), 12. At the height of Jewish migration, only four out of every 1000 went to Israel. Segev, 225.

separate God-elected people, the Reformed rejoiced in the legal emancipation of Jews that began after the Napoleonic invasions. For example, Prussia repealed all discriminatory legislation in 1869. (Tsarist Russia, however, never changed its restrictive laws.) Reformed Jews saw no incompatibility with preserving their religious commitments while assimilating the culture of their native countries and paid little attention to Israel. Nationalism initially promoted assimilation. Introduced to most of Europe during the Napoleonic era, nationalism reigned by the 1850s, and Reformed Jews saw their identity as a religious minority living in a nation; they were first of all Germans or English or French. They welcomed the repeal of old laws restricting Jewish activities, sought full participation in the economic and cultural life of their nations, and looked forward to the end of anti-Semitism.[4] Assimilation was so attractive to many late nineteenth-century German Jews that conservatives who feared the destruction of Judaism hoped that escape from Europe to Palestine would preserve Jewish identity.

Before 1900 many assimilated Jews found that nationalism, instead of ending, had accentuated prejudice, particularly when combined with pseudo-scientific racism. Those asserting or attempting to create a unity of the German *Volk* or Pan-Slavic or Russian identity regarded the Jews as non-conforming members of society. Seemingly reputable scholars insisted that culture reflected a unity of blood, and Jewish blood would dilute the purity of the nation. For various peoples in the Balkans as well as for Italians, Germans, and Russians, because their distinctive forms of Christianity served as a symbol while reinforcing the beliefs in their unique identity, Judaism stood out as different from and a seeming rebuke to the national religion unifying a people. Nationalism provided a new rationale for an old prejudice originating in Christianity.

---

[4]Geoffrey Wheatcroft, *The Controversy of Zion: Jewish Nationalism, the Jewish State, and the Unresolved Jewish Dilemma* (1998) Part 1. This is a readable popular history of Jewish attitudes to Zionism from its inception to the present. Gideon Shimoni, *The Zionist Ideology* (1995), is a more scholarly account of the early history.

In Germany and later in Eastern Europe, young educated Jews embraced the dominant intellectual trends that for some meant adopting a hostile attitude to all religion, rejecting Judaism's rituals, and embracing socialism, anarchism, or democracy as a means to end repressive capitalism and rule by monarchy. When Russian or German authorities before World War I quelled attempts to create a new world based on socialism, these men who affirmed their identity as Jews but often were non-religious saw in Israel a place to create a more just society. David Ben-Gurion (1886-1963), the political leader of the Zionist movement in Palestine and first Prime Minister of Israel, exemplified the tradition of socialism, morality, and Zionism while remaining attached to Jewish spirituality. Originally a leader of a Jewish trade union movement, he hoped the socialism exemplified in the *kibbutz* settlements in Palestine would help to inaugurate a social transformation. Ben-Gurion saw God as an impersonal force and did not "believe in the existence of a spiritual, eternal, all-embracing superior being." Yet he saw the land of Israel as the land God gave to Jews, frequently quoted the Hebrew *Bible* to justify the linkage of the people and the land, and saw those who continued to live in diaspora as betraying Judaism.[5]

III. Herzl and Early Zionism

Theodor Herzl (1860-1904), an assimilated non-observant Austrian Jew, created modern Zionism. Herzl despaired of creating a tolerant European society after he encountered anti-Semitism in Austria and again in France during the Dreyfus affair in 1894. Herzl concluded that real assimilation and equal rights were impossible to create in Europe. Zionists argued that every state since the fall of Jerusalem had discriminated against Jews. Such oppression had distorted the character of the Jewish people, leading to negative traits like submissiveness. Only by creating a land in which Jews ruled could the distinctive genius of the Jewish people flourish.

---

[5]Quoted in Avraham Avi-haim, *Ben-Gurion: State Builder* (1974), 44. Shmuel Almog, "The Role of Religious Values in the Second Aliyah," and Anita Shapira, "The Religious Motifs of the Labour Movement," in *Zionism and Religion* (1998).

Political Zionism as it emerged in the 1890s can be viewed as a nationalist and imperialist form of Judaism, similar to other forms of European colonialism. Assimilated Jews did not escape the influence of the racism, myth, history, and religious consciousness sweeping over Europe. Political Zionism drew upon nationalism and racial and/or folk consciousness by portraying Jews as a distinct race (or blood) not allowed to blend into any European nation. Like other nationalists, Zionists asserted that Jews remained a distinct *Volk*/culture/race who needed a homeland in which to flourish. Herzl believed that the Jews would bring a superior culture to their new state and, by introducing just rule and modern business and industrial techniques, would raise the living standards of those around. Herzl and many assimilated secular Jewish Zionists had their own version of the "white man's burden." In one sense Herzl was not a Zionist, because he was willing for the Jewish homeland to be established in Argentina or Uganda, but the World Zionist Congresses he organized beginning in 1897 insisted on the primacy of Israel.[6]

The Reformers showed little understanding or sympathy for traditional Jewish life. According to them, given freedom and lack of persecution, Jews would throw off servility, greed, and cowardice - traits imposed upon them in the diaspora - and become a new race of sturdy pioneers. During the 1920s and 30s, Zionist propaganda insisted that living in the land of Israel would create a new kind of Jew: one no longer willing to accept discrimination and willing to fight for his or her rights. Zionists early manifested two contrasting tendencies with some stressing a slow peaceful occupation of Palestine and others insisting on the necessity of fighting for the land and displacing the Arab population. Both groups, like other Europeans, saw the Arabs as backward and devoted little thought to them.[7]

Herzl and his supporters soon discovered that most Jews opposed or ignored Zionism; many were not willing to emigrate anywhere, and even those

---

[6]Shmuel Almog, *Zionism and History: The Rise of a New Jewish Consciousness* (1987), ch. 4.
[7]Wheatcroft, 132, 163.

willing to move to Palestine might not be supporters of political independence. German Jews did not wish to jettison their economic opportunity and cultural heritage to go to Uganda or Argentina or Palestine. However, observant and oppressed Russian Jews retained an emotional tie to Israel and might be prepared to migrate. In Russia (which before W.W. I included part of modern Poland and the Baltic States), they encountered continuing anti-Semitism and pogroms beginning in 1883 that the Tsarist government and Orthodox Church tolerated and even encouraged. So Zionist propaganda reached villagers whose traditional Jewish life in Russia was already under siege and many prepared to emigrate. Even so, migration to Palestine had very limited appeal to Jews in Eastern Europe who flocked in large numbers to the United States between 1880 and 1924. It is likely that had the United States not choked off Jewish immigration in 1924 and had Hitler not come to power in 1933, there would have been no successful Zionist movement leading to the creation of the state of Israel.[8]

European Zionists like Herzl faced enormous difficulties in justifying a new state because Jews lacked the basic prerequisites for nationalism: a land, a language, and a common culture. Most Jews spoke Yiddish, and yet the language of the *Bible* was Hebrew, which often only the rabbis knew. So Zionists began a program to make Hebrew a popular, spoken language. Jews in the diaspora had assumed much of the culture of the lands where they resided. All identified themselves as Jews, but there were major differences in teachings and ritual among Sephardic, Ashkenazi, emergent Reform, Conservative, and Orthodox, on one hand, and the Hasidic. Religious animosity among proponents of varieties of Judaism as well as their distrust of secularist or atheist Marxist Jews complicated the process of creating a nationality out of diverse peoples. Some Orthodox Jews, for example, moved to Palestine as a religious duty but regarded political activity to create a Jewish state as an idolatrous attempt to usurp God's role in sending the messiah who would inaugurate a new Israel. In the U.S., Zionism had a very

---

[8]There was no move by the administrations of Franklin Roosevelt or Harry Truman to repeal the 1920s national origins legislation.

limited appealed to Jews. A few Conservative Jews early espoused Zionism, but Reform leaders opposed it, seeing their goal as blending into American civilization.[9] Many assimilated Jews viewed their homes as the nation in which they lived and denied that there was any Jewish nationality. In addition, Zionists disagreed on whether diaspora Jews had a duty just to support the creation of a state or must prepare to migrate to Palestine. Was the future of Judaism among all people of the diaspora and Palestine or only in a new Jewish state of Israel?

The Zionists also faced the daunting task of persuading the great powers of Europe to allow a Jewish state to be created in a poor land populated by Muslim Arabs. Politicians from Britain and France had a romantic image of the Jews based upon their appreciation of the *Bible* and Jewish contributions to culture, and yet they also on occasion expressed anti-Semitic sentiments. Herzl sought first to approach the Ottoman Sultan with a proposal for a semi-autonomous area in Palestine to which Jews could migrate. After all, he reasoned, other religious groups in the Ottoman Empire lived in essentially self-governing enclaves. The Ottoman Sultan refused, fearing the creation at some future date of a Jewish state.

The opportunity for the Zionists to gain Great Power support came in World War I when the Ottoman Empire entered on the side of the Germans. The British and French sought to mobilize the Arabs to oppose the Turks by promising them independence. At the same time the Allies entered into secret arrangements with the Russians to divide the Middle East. Chaim Weizmann, a noted scientist, Zionist, able diplomat, observant Jew, and migrant to England from Eastern Europe, persuaded the English foreign minister, Arthur Balfour, to write a letter promising British support to create a "national home" in Palestine for the Jews; the Declaration also guaranteed that "nothing shall be done which would prejudice the civil and religious rights of existing non-Jewish communities

---

[9]See Shmuel Almog, Jehuda Reinharz and Anita Shapira, eds., *Zionism and Religion,* in Part two, "Reform, "Conservative, and Orthodox Judaism: Zionism in the United States," and in Part three, "Orthodoxy, Liberalism, and Zionism in Western Europe."

in Palestine."[10] Few asked whether the two promises were contradictory. The Balfour Declaration, issued as a unilateral statement with no legal status, was incorporated into Great Britain's Mandate over Palestine at the end of the war.

IV. One Land and Two Peoples: Palestine 1917-1948

The Arabs, who in 1917 had over 90% of the people and land in Palestine, insisted that many centuries of occupation gave them full rights and neither Jewish religious beliefs nor ancient history created a just claim to land or sovereignty. So the Arabs demanded limits on immigration and refused to cooperate with the British in creating either a multinational state or partition of the land. For them, Zionism was an unacceptable form of European imperialism. Claiming that Jews and Arabs had once been brethren, they argued that now the Jews were simply Europeans seeking to buy land. A dawning Palestinian consciousness of themselves as a distinct nation, rather than as one of many peoples in the Ottoman Empire, is a post-World War I phenomenon.

The history of Zionism and Palestine from the Balfour Declaration until 1948 revolved around whether the promises made by the British to the Jews and Arabs could be made compatible. The British assumed that they could create a compromise so that the two groups could live together on one land. The British government's policies had three aims: to preserve its authority in Palestine as a strategic protection for the Suez Canal in nearby Egypt; to keep good relations with the Arabs to guarantee the supply of oil; and to create a homeland for Jews.[11] The Balfour Declaration promised the Jews a "national home," but, as Winston Churchill declared in 1922, not a state.

British officials in the Mandate territory of Palestine sought to keep the peace by restricting Jewish immigration and conciliating the Arabs. However, the

---

[10]Document printed in Don Peretz, ed., *The Arab-Israel Dispute* (1996), 235-238. Balfour did not consult Arab leaders and referred to Palestinians only as "existing non-Jewish communities."
[11]None of these aims appeared well thought out. Palestine complicated relations with Arabs because of the Jews; the area had no strategic value for Suez; and Britain did not favor creating a Jewish state. British policy appears muddled and ill thought out from the time of the Balfour Declaration until 1948. Segev, 4, 33, 137.

sympathy for Zionism among many civil servants meant that in practice, restraints on the Jews were not consistently applied.[12] Moreover, in Britain, the government and opposition parties, for domestic political advantages, made promises to Zionists that, once in power, they could not keep without irritating Arabs. So British policies seemed to Zionists to favor Arabs. Jews in Palestine saw these policies as a result of a conspiracy in high places caused by anti-Semitism or Arab influence. By the late 1930s in Palestine, Zionists' mistrust of Britain led them to view Britain as the enemy.

Most Zionists did not accept the British insistence that a "national home" was not a state, but there was considerable debate on the final status of Jews in Palestine. Chaim Weizmann sought a place for Jews to settle in which Arabs would be welcome, but in much private correspondence and in Zionist Congresses, he and other Jews insisted that the goal was for an independent state dominated by Jews in which Palestinian inhabitants could live with equal rights but in a subordinate position. Weizmann had access to officials in Britain and appeared moderate in his demands. Zionists who sought good relations with Palestinians did not stress an independent state and were even more vague on the borders of that state.

Another group associated with the Polish Jew Vladimir Jabotinsky (1880-1940), a minority in the 1920s but more influential in Palestine in the 1930s, advocated using force to drive out the Arabs to create a state populated only by Jews. The rhetoric of the Jabotinsky group drew upon themes of the Italian Fascists in asserting the morality of force. Israel's boundaries would include the lands God bestowed on a chosen people and should stretch from the Mediterranean to the Jordan River and beyond.

Arabs in Palestine who became aware of the discrepancy in Zionist intentions concluded that the extremists advocated what all the Jews believed. Arabs, like the Jews, had learned to distrust the promises of European nations.

---

[12]Segev, 5, 226, 335-37. The older view was that the British in Palestine during the Mandate consistently favored the Palestinians.

Muslims saw their kingdoms as subject to British, or French, or Italian power. Learning stories of secret Jewish manipulation from European anti-Semitic writings, they feared Zionists' political influence and financial ability to buy lands in Palestine.

In Palestine, a Jewish Zionist nationalism encountered a new Arab nationalism. At the end of World War I, Palestinian nationalism was a part of an emergent pan-Arab movement for a state composed of Syria, Iraq, Transjordan, and Palestine under the Hashemite Amir (King) Ibn Faisal. British and French imperial rivalries made such a large Arab state impossible, and the French in the 1920s used force to quell a major revolt against their rule in Syria. When Faisal lost the Syrian throne, the British installed him as King in Iraq and made his brother, Abdullah, King of Transjordan. Egypt, Syria, and Saudi Arabia opposed the expansionist aims of Amir Abdullah who sought to annex Palestine to Jordan. The British sought to control the emergent Arab nationalism by influencing the kings of the various semi-independent Middle Eastern states. Neither British nor Zionists took much cognizance of a Palestinian nationalism that was far less well expressed at the time.

Haj Amin Al-Hussaini first became a Palestinian national hero as an instigator of an anti-Jewish riot in 1920, a disturbance related to news of the Balfour Declaration, Jewish migration, and Zionist plans for the Middle East. Haj Amin was a Muslim cleric who, partially due to clan connections, became in 1921 the Mufti of Jerusalem, the primary religious leader in Palestine. The Mufti, though initially willing to cooperate with the British, made clear that he opposed Jewish migration to Palestine and an eventual Zionist state. Instead, Haj Amin supported a Palestinian state with the Arabs in control and the Jews as a tolerated but legally subordinate minority. He also opposed the expansionist aims of King Abdullah. Divisions among the Arab factions within Palestine, suspicion between Haj Amin and Abdullah, and rivalry between Egypt's monarch and the Hashemite rulers in Iraq and Jordan meant that there was no unified Arab leadership to counter the Zionists.

No Arab political leader could appear to be willing to compromise; rather, the Mufti and claimants to power utilized anti-Jewish sentiments to rally a population who, through long years of Ottoman misrule, had become accustomed to mistrusting any government. So when the British proposed various limited forms of self-government, the Palestinians, adhering to a policy of non-cooperation, said no, even though they would have dominated. They also opposed because the *Yishuv* Jews (the original groups of Jews living in Palestine) would have received too much authority. The *Yishuv* also said no, because any representative government based upon population would give the Arabs overwhelming control and thwart Zionist ambitions.

During the 1920s a few Zionist leaders, most notably Chaim Weizmann and David Ben-Gurion, saw the need to conciliate the Palestinians. Weizmann, who never wavered in his goal of a Zionist state, saw immigration and integration occurring over a long period of time.[13] In 1929 the Zionist World Congress repudiated the gradualism of Weizmann to demand unlimited immigration in order to create a Jewish state as soon as possible. The Congress also welcomed but did not endorse those advocating fighting to create an Israeli state. Zionists at the Congress claimed the right to rule not just the small settlements with a Jewish majority but a larger area including Jerusalem, although there was no agreement as to whether *Eretz Israel* (the land of Israel) would include only the coastal area, the east and west bank of the Jordan, or only the lands west of the Jordan River. In 1931 the *Yishuv* settlers constituted about 18% of the total population.[14]

The uneasy peace between Jews and Palestinians ended in 1929. News of the Zionist Congress complicated a dispute over the holy sites in Jerusalem, namely, the Western Wall (sacred to Jews as a remnant of Herod's temple) and the Al Aqsa Mosque or Dome of the Rock (sacred to Muslims as the place where Muhammad ascended into heaven and learned the correct prayers). After a rumor spread that Jews wished to seize the Dome of the Rock, Arab attacks killed 133

---

[13] Sykes, 22, 34, 95.
[14] Shabtai Teveth, *Ben-Gurion: The Burning Ground 1886-1948* (1987), 459.

Jews and wounded 339; British troops took three days to arrive and ended by killing 116 and wounding 232 Arabs.[15]

Following the riots, the *Yishuv* repudiated a policy of restraint in the face of provocation and created a defense force, the Haganah. Even former moderates like Weizmann and Ben-Gurion jettisoned any plans they had for unity with Palestinians. Both leaders, like other Zionists, essentially ignored the Palestinians. The Palestinians, led by the Mufti, had shown again their implacable hostility to increased Jewish settlement and Zionism. Zionists and Palestinians now focused only on their own demands and grievances, and each viewed the other and the British as well as enemies. Because Zionists and Palestinians saw themselves as victims in need of political power, they became more self-absorbed and extremist. There were no serious negotiations between them after 1935.[16]

Hitler came to power in 1933 but, even so, before 1935 the main increase of immigration came from Poland and not from Germany. All could see Hitler's extreme anti-Semitism, but his initial policies seemed designed to impoverish Germany's Jews and to force them to migrate. In a world caught in economic depression in which all nations had massive unemployment, German Jews who wished to migrate found few who would welcome them. Zionists insisted that the only legitimate home for the refugees was Palestine, so they were not unhappy with the cold shoulder given to Jewish refugees and encouraged illegal entry in addition to legal immigration to Palestine. By 1935 the Jewish settlers of Palestine had increased to 355,157, nearly 30% of the population, most of whom lived in the area around Tel Aviv.

The Arab response to the increased visibility of Jews was predictable. Demanding an end to both Jewish migration and any land sales to Jews while seeking independence, the Palestinians staged a general strike in 1936 that turned into a three-year revolt against the British and Jews. Both Arabs and Zionists

[15]Zvi Elpeleg, *The Grand Mufti: Haj Amin Al-Hussaini*, tr. David Harvey (1993), 16-24; Sykes, 109.

created military forces. Earlier violence against the *Yishuv* had been by rioters and mobs, but the Palestinians created terrorists groups, the Green Hand and Black Hand, whose targets could be Jews, British, or moderate Arabs. The Palestinians also created their own political parties/armed forces/guerrilla bands - the dividing lines between these was often indistinct. The Mufti's armed force was named Holy War, *al-Jihad al-Muqaddas*.

The Haganah, tolerated even though the British saw it as an illegal force, sought to protect Jewish settlements. There were also Jewish terrorist groups, the Stern Gang and the Irgun Zvai Leumi. The Stern Gang directed its bombs and assassinations against those who opposed Zionists aims - Muslims, British, and sometimes even Jews. The Irgun, which took its inspiration from Jabotinsky, whose leaders included two future prime ministers of Israel, Menachem Begin and Yitzhak Shamir, targeted the British and Muslim forces. Irgun sought to create a Zionist state by force. Additional terrorism resulted from political rivalry among the labor coalition led by Ben-Gurion and the Revisionists of Jabotinsky as to who was the more forceful advocate for a Jewish state.[17]

The British now had to deal with not only Palestinian but also Arab nationalism. By 1939 British troops had put down the revolt and disarmed the Arabs, but not ended terrorism. From 1929 until 1939 there were 10,000 incidents with 2000 killed, half of them Palestinians.[18] The strike and the Mufti's efforts to internationalize the conflict succeeded in mobilizing all surrounding Arab governments and their populations to espouse the cause of the Palestinians. The Mufti embarked upon an ambitious plan to restore the Dome of the Rock, and he succeeded in making Jerusalem again a center for Muslim pilgrimage. From now on there would be unified Arab agreement to protect the Palestinians and Jerusalem from what was seen as British and Jewish imperialism.

---

[16]Sykes, 122; Michael Cohen, "The Zionist Perspective," in William Louis and Robert Stookey, *End of the Palestine Mandate* (1986), 95.
[17]Segev, 472 ff, 483.

The British sent a commission to investigate. With hope for a bi-national state eroding, the commission proposed partition, a solution acceptable neither to Zionists nor Palestinians. Since partition would involve the forceful transfer of population into different zones, which the British were not willing to do, there was no meaningful prospect for partition. By the late 1930s, the British saw Palestine as a problem with no solution.

V. World War II

As war approached and Hitler spread his empire to Austria and Czechoslovakia, pressure on the British government and on European Jews increased. For the Jews, finding a refuge was now a matter of life and death, and there seemed no alternative to Palestine. The British seemed not to understand the desperation of the Jews, and their seeming bureaucratic stalling and moral myopia enraged Zionists. However, the British feared that increased migration to Israel would alienate the entire Arab world. With war imminent, Britain decided to conciliate the Palestinian Arabs in order to bring peace and in 1939 decided for the next five years to freeze the Jewish population at one-third (i.e., to stop immigration), to forbid land sales to Jews, and promised no national state would be created without Arab agreement. The Palestinians would receive self-government. The Arabs were satisfied.

Zionists within and outside of Palestine believed Britain had betrayed them because of Arab violence. Reservations by Orthodox over cooperating with secular Jews now evaporated as they, along with Reformed Jews from America, embraced Zionism as the cement to unite Jews of all persuasions. In Palestine, moderate and extremist Zionists now agreed that Britain was the enemy to creating an independent Israel. Terrorist tactics were permissible, but should not be used now because Jews could not afford to weaken Britain when Hitler was a worse enemy.

---

[18]Segev, 420-27, 367-71, argues that strong British measures against the Palestinians during the uprising contributed to their overall weakness. This would be important in the Jewish war for independence in 1948.

During the war, Palestine remained relatively quiet. Most Palestinians accepted that recently announced British policies served their interest. Jewish immigration slowed; the British offered Jewish refugees asylum on the island of Mauritius, a policy that disgusted the Zionists but served humanitarian purposes. The Mufti went to Iraq where he tried to foment an anti-Hashemite, pro-German revolution, a policy that meant that the King of Iraq would not support him after the war. Eventually the Mufti fled to Germany and tried to interest Hitler in the cause of Arab independence. His anti-Semitic and pro-Nazi radio broadcasts destroyed his ability to represent the Palestinian cause to the British after 1945, but did not jeopardize his popular standing.

David Ben-Gurion enunciated the Zionist wartime policy: support Britain in its war efforts and oppose British policy in Israel.[19] Jewish settlers in Palestine sought to create an independent Jewish army, but the British government resisted, sensing potential postwar dangers from such an army. Many Jews enlisted in Allied armies and the *Yishuv* in Israel produced war supplies and arms, thereby gaining skills that would help Zionists in the postwar conflicts.

During the war, leadership of the Zionist movement passed from the diplomatic and cautious but now elderly Chaim Weizmann to the activist David Ben-Gurion, a shift reflecting a policy change to a more militant program. The center of Zionist action shifted from cultivating Great Powers to political and military action in Palestine. Even before they knew of Hitler's "Final Solution," a Zionist conference in New York in 1942 spelled out the new policy aimed at creating a state of Israel after the war.[20] Zionists insisted that never again would Jews be dependent upon outsiders to defend their interests.

The nature and the extent of the Holocaust in which 90% of Europe's Jews died came as a shock to most people and created an immense amount of sympathy for the Jews. There was also a feeling of guilt that the democracies during the

---

[19]Teveth, 717, 721.

1930s had not taken stronger actions, even though most of the victims had been in lands occupied by the Nazis during the war when the Allies could do nothing. The American President Harry Truman felt that the Allies owed special consideration to the 100,000 Jewish displaced persons living in camps, but he made no move to admit them to the U.S. Zionists insisted that the only legitimate home for these people was in Palestine.

The Arabs dissented, pointing out that the Holocaust had taken place in Europe, and it was the home of these refugees. Palestinians argued that Europe and the United States with much more economic capacity and area were the logical homes for the European Jews. The Arabs should not have to pay for Axis policies. If there was to be a Jewish state, it should be in Germany.[21] The Zionists, who had better contacts in America and England and presented their case skillfully, won the propaganda battle by linking the Holocaust to the necessity of a Jewish state in a manner that utilized the sufferings of concentration camp survivors for political advantage.[22]

VI. Israel 1945-48

In 1946 a Joint American-British Commission after visiting Palestine and the refugee camps, recommended admitting 100,000 Jews to Palestine and creating a multinational state. The British thought the multinational state impossible to create and sought for a limited Jewish immigration of 1,500 a month, a number that horrified the Arabs and the Zionists thought too small. In 1947 the ship *Exodus* arrived at Palestine with a cargo of Jewish refugees. The British intercepted the ship and returned its human cargo to France, where they were refused admittance, and then to Germany to a refugee camp. The *Exodus* affair

---

[20]Text printed in Peretz, 253-54; Sykes, 236-40, 247. The official attitude is summarized as "to be anti-Zionist was to be anti-Semitic; to disapprove of Jewish territorial nationalism was to be a Nazi."

[21]Sykes, 292-93

[22]Segev, 49, argues that the foundation of the Jewish state and independence existed before 1942. "There is therefore no basis for the frequent assertion that the state was established as a result of the Holocaust." The traditional view is that events during the war and the attitudes of the Great Powers after were decisive. Another issue is whether Jewish refugees wanted to migrate to Israel, stay in Europe, or come to America.

was a public relations disaster and served to discredit British policies. The Soviets also encouraged Polish Jews to attempt to migrate, probably as a way to embarrass the British, and these actions increased the number of refugees to 250,000. The Haganah, openly defying British immigration restrictions, sought to smuggle 70,000 refugees to Palestine. The British intercepted most of those, who ended up in camps in Cyprus.[23]

Legal and illegal Jewish immigration to Palestine heightened animosities between Muslims and Jews with both sides arming and preparing for war. The Arabs felt that Britain had betrayed them by not continuing the prewar embargo on land sales and migration. Britain, greatly weakened by the war, could not enlist American military or economic support for halting migration and continuing the Mandate. The U.S. State Department understood the British dilemma and saw creating a Jewish state as leading to additional conflicts and war. President Truman, who had been impressed by discussions with Weizmann and wanted the support of Jewish voters, sympathized with the Zionists and he set policy. Truman decided that partition might be necessary.

In 1945, Zionists in Palestine sought to prove that the land was ungovernable by blowing up railroad bridges and other disruptive acts. A temporary alliance between the Haganah and Irgun resulted in several terrorist actions, including blowing up the British headquarters in the King David Hotel with ninety-four deaths. When the British executed two Jewish terrorists, Jewish forces captured two sergeants, executed them by hanging, and booby-trapped their bodies. The reprisal worked: the British executed no more Jewish soldiers. Between 1945 and 1948, Jewish terrorists killed 338 British.[24] The British public wished to be rid of Palestine. Concluding that maintaining their rule in Palestine was too costly at a time of turmoil in India and Egypt and with relations with the

---

[23]Michael J. Cohen, *Palestine and the Great Powers 1945-1948* (1982), 85.

[24]Eric Silver, *Begin: The Haunted Prophet* (1984), 83-95; by the end of 1946, Irgum and Stern had killed 373 people in Palestine, of whom 300 were civilians, Stykes, 307. Ben-Gurion after a brief period of endorsing terrorism saw such actions as hindering the Zionist cause and began again to work closely with the British.

Soviet Union deteriorating, the British announced that they would pull out and dumped the problem on the newly formed United Nations.

In 1947 the United Nations General Assembly recommended a partition by vote of 25 to 13 with 17 abstentions. There was to be an Arab section, and a Jewish section, with international control of Jerusalem. The partition was the only major vote on which all the Great Powers agreed in that UN session, and only last minute pressure applied by the United States on Latin American governments obtained the needed two-thirds majority. Anti-U.S. riots occurred in major Arab capitals.

The UN may have given permission, but it was already clear that war would determine the destiny as well as the boundaries of Palestine. The Zionists would have been hopelessly outnumbered and outgunned if the surrounding Arab states had cooperated, but rivalries among the Arab states and also among the Palestinians, plus inept leadership by Haj Amin al-Hussaini, hampered military preparations.[25] Amir Abdullah of Jordan carried on secret negotiations with the Jews aiming at incorporating the Arab sections of Palestine into his kingdom. He was opposed by the Mufti and some but not all Palestinians, who desired to create an independent state. As the British withdrew, chaos and virtual anarchy resulted. In the ensuing war Israel soon had more soldiers, better weapons, and clearer objectives.[26]

The Zionists in Israel utilizing the Haganah created an army, evolved the Jewish Agency overseeing the *Yishuv* into a government, and obtained arms from Czechoslovakia in spite of a UN sponsored embargo. President Truman without consulting the State Department extended de facto recognition a few minutes after the Israeli state was proclaimed in May 14, 1948.

The Israelis triumphed militarily, increasing by 40% and adding part of Jerusalem to the land allotted by the United Nations, which meant that there

[25]Walid Khalida, "The Arab Perspective" in William Louis and Robert Stookey, *End Of the Palestine Mandate*, 110-126.
[26]Ahron Bregman, *Israel's Wars: A History since 1947* (2000), 26.

might be a majority of Muslims in the new Israel. Amir Abdullah annexed the remainder of the West Bank and Old Jerusalem to the Kingdom of Jordan, but he was assassinated by Muslims who distrusted the Amir's secret dealings with the Israelis. Arab leaders including King Farouk of Egypt and King Hussein of Iraq would shortly be overthrown by national revolutions led by army officers alienated partially because of what they saw as inept policies that had not stopped the creation of a Jewish state.

Atrocities on both sides marked the war. The Arab radio stations publicized Israeli terrorist acts, most notably the massacre on April 8, 1948 of nearly 120 men, women, and children in the village of Deir Yassin, which had sought to remain neutral.[27] The Arabs in response attacked an Israeli convoy under Red Cross insignia on the way to a hospital and killed seventy-seven while a British garrison nearby did nothing.

Fearing additional atrocities, many Palestinians followed their leaders and sought to escape from the war zone to safety. The Jews did not publicize Arab atrocities to Jewish settlers, who followed the instructions of their leaders and remained in their homes. Initially, the Zionist political leaders were surprised by the depopulation of Arab sections, but most historians agree that the Israeli Army by mid-1948 adopted policies designed to force Palestinians into exile. When the truce was worked out in 1948, the Palestinian population of the lands within the new state of Israel had dropped from 600,000 or 700,000 people so that there were only about 167,000 Muslims left. Palestinians remaining in Israel would be living in a Jewish state. Exiles living in refugee camps in Gaza, Jordan, and Lebanon denied the legitimacy of the state of Israeli and sought to return to their lands.[28]

---

[27]The death toll is normally described as 250. A BBC documentary using Arab sources places the number of dead at less than 120. Eric Silver, "Arab witnesses admit exaggerating Deir Yassin massacre," *Jerusalem Reporter,* April 2, 1998, 6.

[28]Sykes, 350-356; Silver, 88-96; Benny Morris, *The Birth of the Palestinian Refugee Problem, 1949-1949* (1987); "Debate on the 1948 Exodus," in *Journal of Palestine Studies,* 21 (1991), 66-97.

The exodus of the Muslims meant that the Zionist state did not have to adopt policies designed to appeal to a large ethnic-religious minority. Jews settled the lands and occupied or destroyed villages left by the Muslims. Muslim depopulation made Israel a more unified country.

The United Nations, mediating the truce in 1948, sought to persuade Israel either to permit the Palestinians back into Israel or to grant them compensation. The Israelis did neither, insisting that allowing the Palestinians back into the land would compromise security, that those who fled showed that they were enemies to Jews, and that the Arab states should admit and take responsibility for them. Instead, the Palestinians settled in refugee camps surrounding the state of Israel. Unlike most other refugee populations, fifty years later they are still there and have become bitter foes of the Israelis. Neither Israel nor Arab governments are willing to accept responsibility for the Palestinians whose overcrowded settlements, lack of economic opportunity, and poverty have created despair leading to violence.

VII. Israeli-Arab Conflict

The new state of Israel proclaimed itself a secular democracy, but the heritage of Judaism and Zionism continues to play a major role. The symbols of ancient Israel are used to legitimate the existence of the state and to unify the diverse peoples into a nation in a way that links both religious and secular Jews with a common history. For example, new Israeli soldiers are taken to Masada, site of the last Jewish resistance to the Romans, and take the pledge, "never again" – an invocation of centuries of persecution and the Holocaust.

Israelis and their supporters in the diaspora debate the relationship of the biblical Promised Land to modern boundaries and the definition of a Jew. In 1950 the Israeli parliament passed the law of return which gave all Jews everywhere the right to migrate into Israel. Note that this is a pre-modern idea of citizenship, and rabbis still debate what makes a Jew. Before 1951 650,000 had migrated, most of whom were European refugees. Thousands of Jews who had lived in peace in many Arab countries now were at risk because of the uncompromising hostility of their nations to Israel. Since 1948 there has been an ingathering to Israel of Jews from all the Arab countries. Israel has welcomed 1,700,000 Jews from Europe, the United States, Ethiopia, and after the breakup of the Soviet Union from Russia.[29] Fewer have come from the U.S., U.K. and Western Europe. Those who migrate, particularly from the United States, are strong supporters of Zionist ideology and tend to be Ultra-Orthodox. By contrast, those from the former Soviet Union were non-observant and left for economic reasons. Israel's liberal immigration policy reaffirms the Zionist belief that Israel is the national homeland and the defender of all Jews. Its military strength is to guarantee that there will never again be a holocaust.

From 1948 until 1978, no Arab government recognized Israel or would trade with it. Diplomatic contacts, and there were many, took place in secret. Hostility to Israel rested upon popular pan-Arab, Muslim, anti-imperialist (particularly anti-American), and nationalist sentiments - a potent mixture which Arab governments could not ignore and could fan or use to divert attention from internal problems. However, recent revisionist historians have suggested that Israel's leaders were never really interested in peace with the Palestinians and after the state was established turned down several promising initiatives from Arab governments for peace.[30]

During the Cold War, the United States became the primary patron of Israel. Because Hitler's genocide destroyed most European Jews, there are now two primary centers of Jewish population, the United States and Israel. The American Jewish community became strong supporters of Israel and used its political muscle to influence U.S. government policy. American patronage and military and financial assistance allowed the Israelis to ignore the Palestinian

---

[29] A Zwergbaum, "Zionist Thought." in *New Enclyopedia of Zionism and Israel* (1994), 1476.
[30] Recent Jewish revisionist historians include Zeev Sternhell, *The Founding Myths of Israel: Nationalism, Socialism, and the Making of the Jewish State,* tr. David Maisel (1997), and Avi Shlaim, *The Iron Wall: Israel and the Arab World* (2000). Shlaim argues that Israel did not wish to acknowledge contacts with the Arab world until after it had obtained an expansion of borders. He shows how militants often undermined moderate policies and helped cause the 1954 and 1967

problem while creating a democratic, prosperous, and powerful state. The Soviet Union sought influence with neighboring Arab states, including Egypt, Syria, and Iraq.

Israel has fought three major wars with its neighbors in 1956, 1967, and 1973, invaded Lebanon in 1982, and has engaged in repeated reprisals in an attempt to stop terrorist actions by Palestinians. In the 1967 war Israel attacked after Egypt's President Nasser took actions that Israel had declared would be a causus belli, even though he knew his army was inferior. Egypt, joined by Syria and Jordan, was soundly defeated when the Israeli army seized the Golan Heights from Syria, the Sinai desert from Egypt, and the Old City of Jerusalem and the West Bank from Jordan.[31] As a price for a peace treaty and recognition from Egypt in the Camp David accords arranged by President Carter in 1978, Israel returned the Sinai. Since 1967 Israel has continued to rule the West Bank as occupied territory, annexed Jerusalem and the Golan Heights, and has created over two hundred settlements in the West Bank and suburbs around Jerusalem. Israel now claims 40% of the area of the West Bank.

The conquest of the West Bank changed the political debate in Israel. Before 1967 the Israelis saw themselves as a vulnerable state surrounded by powerful neighbors and saw criticism of the government as almost a betrayal. The Israeli government saw itself as creating a secular and democratic state and the lands it occupied on the coast did not include the heart of ancient Israel: the old city of Jerusalem, Judea, and Samaria. Jews could not pray on the Temple Mount. Consequently, the *Yishuv* and Ultra-Orthodox residents in Jerusalem had little concern with politics, believing instead that the true Israel would be restored only with the coming of the messiah. The conquests of 1967 transformed the relationship of the ultra-Orthodox to the Jewish state. Now the settlement of the occupied territories became a religious duty, an action that was necessary before

---

wars. Opposing the revisionists is Yoram Hazony, *The Jewish State: The Struggle for Israel's Soul* (2000).

the return of the messiah. Ultra-Orthodox rabbis became supporters of the Gush Emunium, a strongly nationalist organization of settlers who argued that all the West Bank should be included in Israel.

The Likud government under Menachem Begin in 1973 depended for its majority in the Knesset upon a variety of Ultra-Orthodox and Orthodox right-wing nationalists.[32] The Likud, openly sympathizing with the Orthodox desire to incorporate the West Bank into Israel, promoted settlements on the West Bank. These two hundred new settlements, often strategically located on high ground or surrounding Jerusalem, would provide additional security for Israel, but Ultra-Orthodox nationalist Jews would now be living in enclaves close to hostile Palestinians. The Israeli government provided financial incentives to move to the West Bank. The 400,000 Jewish settlers dwelling in the West Bank have become a potent political force in Israel.

The state of Israel now controlled the entire Temple Mount and could restrict access in times of emergency to the Muslim Dome of the Rock. A minority in Israel talked about dismantling the Dome of the Rock and recreating the ancient temple. Since neither Jews nor Palestinians trusted each other, the predictable mixture of rumor and fact brought an increase in incidents and terrorist acts on the Temple Mount committed by extremists from both sides. Since its founding, Israel has faced sporadic attacks from Palestinian fedayeen who see all settlers as enemies. These terrorists acts are designed to create insecurity. To counter infiltrators, Israel has consistently followed a policy of strong reprisals, resulting in more Palestinians being killed than Israelis.

Defeat in 1954 and again in 1967 radicalized the Palestinians, who would no longer trust their fate to neighboring Arab states. Instead, Yasser Arafat became the leader of the Palestinian Liberation Organization, an alliance of several secular groups dedicated to the destruction of Israel. The Palestinians who

---

[31]Bregman, 66-83 sees the 1967 war as caused in part by irresponsible actions by the Soviet Union and the United States.

comprise over 90% of the population of the West Bank have shown through popular demonstrations, two uprisings termed the Intifada, and terrorist acts that they do not wish to be a part of Israel.[33] The entire Arab and Muslim world supports their demand, though it debates whether the Palestinians should become an independent state or be linked to Jordan. Frequently since 1948 groups of Muslims have concluded that the Arab governments' actions against Israel are insufficiently militant. Often with the implicit sanction of their governments, religious groups like *Al Fata* or *Hezbollah* proclaimed their willingness to be martyred as a way to fulfill a *jihad.* Israel's military dominance, occupation of the West Bank and Gaza, and creation of a security zone in Lebanon did not diminish the frequency of these religiously motivated acts that were defended as continuing a war in which there were no innocents.

Zionists in Israel now faced a dilemma caused by their success. Should Israel seek to incorporate or rule the West Bank, knowing that granting the vote to Palestinians would compromise and probably end Jewish domination? However, denying the Palestinians equal rights in *Eretz Israel* would make Zionism another form of imperialism, undermine democracy, and jettison the religious and secular idealism that attracted settlers and caused diaspora Jews in the United States to support the new nation. What price must Jews and Palestinians pay to meet the security needs of Israel? The Likud political party and the small Orthodox parties associated with it refer to the West Bank as Judea and Samaria and see it as part of the biblical kingdom of Israel. For religious and security reasons they do not wish to curtail settlements or to allow a Muslim Palestinian state. Neither the UN nor the U.S. has recognized the West Bank as belonging to Israel.

---

[32] A major factor in the Likud's defeat of Labour was the inadequate preparations before the Egyptian and Syria attack on Israel in 1973.

[33] Edward Said, *The Politics of Dispossession: The Struggle for Palestinian Self-Determination, 1969-1994* (1995) 84-106. The book contains essays on the dilemmas of Palestinians living in Israel and the West Bank. Said is often a critic of the tactics of the Arab governments, Yasser Arafat and the Palestine Liberation Organization, and Israel.

The dilemmas faced by the Palestinians and their Arab allies are no less acute. Israel's military and political might and backing by the United States guarantees its long-term survival. What is the best strategy for the Arabs to follow which would allow their strength in population and natural resources to influence Israel and its patron the United States: military confrontation, terrorist acts, or negotiations over the West Bank, hoping to persuade the Israelis of the advantages in easing the grievances of the Palestinians? The Arab states must convince a fearful Israeli public and a resentful Palestinian people that their long-term welfare lays in an agreement. At the same time, the Palestinians must decide upon the kinds of government they wish to establish on the West Bank, whether authoritarian or democratic. Yasser Arafat, who has led the PLO since its founding and was the primary negotiator for the Palestinians, is now an old man whose health has visibly deteriorated and whose control of the factions within and outside the PLO is uncertain. Whether he or anyone else can create an economically viable state on the West Bank is debatable.

For observant and secular Jews in Israel and also in the diaspora there is a religious-historic-nationalist rationale for identifying with and holding on to the land of Israel. Also, for the Palestinians and Arab and non-Arab Muslims throughout the world there is a religious-historic-nationalist motivation for a *jihad* against an expansionist Zionist state occupying lands seized by conquest. The religious fervor and persecution experienced by Muslims and Jews have compounded the sense of self-righteousness and legitimate grievances dividing Israelis and Palestinians. Whether religious and political leaders in the Arab and Jewish world will mobilize the tolerance and hope for peace intrinsic to both Judaism and Islam is uncertain. The Middle East remains a potent rebuke to those analysts who argued that religious-ethnic differences would decline in significance under the influence of nationalism, industrialism, and modernization.

XX.
Islam and Modern War: Iran and Iraq

Islamic peoples' encounter with modern European war has reflected their isolation from two developments in the West associated with the 1648 Treaty of Westphalia: the first was the recognition of the autonomy of the state as sovereign over its inhabitants within well-defined borders, as primary focus for dealing in international affairs, and as the only legitimate actor to make war. The second was the Europeans' repudiation of religion as a just cause for war. For all their secularity, nineteenth-century Europeans actually still rationalized colonial conquests by advocating the spread of Christian civilization and the need for evangelization of the "heathen" - who could be animists, Buddhists, Hindus, or Muslims.

The older crusading zeal of Christians against the Muslim infidel remained a factor primarily in Orthodox Russia's and Catholic Austria's wars against the Ottoman Turks, but most historians insist that the underlying cause for these wars came either from Europeans' desire for more territory or Christian ethnic groups seeking to create independent states. Russia conquered Islamic kingdoms in the southern Caucasus, intervened in the Balkans allegedly to protect Christians, and on occasion practiced ethnic cleansing of Muslims who might support the Ottomans during war.[1] The British and French voiced concerns about the Ottoman treatment of Christians but did not protest oppression of Muslims either by themselves or Russians.

The Arabs' experience of modern European nations occurred first while they remained subjects of the Ottoman Empire and then later when they were

---

[1]Russia forced over one million Caucasians to migrate to Ottoman lands between 1862-65 and forced Muslims to leave Bulgaria to secure a Christian majority in 1877-78. Kemal Karpat, *The Politicization of Islam: Reconstruction Identity, State, Faith and Community in the Late Ottoman State* (2001), 31, 209.

ruled by colonial powers. The appetites of Britain (for Egypt) and France stymied the potential development of independent Arab Muslim states in the nineteenth century. Egypt, which retained its own king, became subordinate to British influence in 1882, soon after the building of the Suez Canal. Italy seized Libya (1912), and France took over Algeria (1830), Tunisia (1881), and Morocco (1912). The British ruled non-Arab Muslims in the Indian subcontinent, and the Dutch assumed this role in Indonesia. Only Turkey, as successor to the Ottomans, by being successful at wars with its immediate neighbors, managed to remain independent after World War I. Under League of Nations mandates, France and Britain exercised spheres of influence over Iraq, Syria, Trans-Jordan, the Emirates, and Lebanon. Persia, never part of the Ottoman Empire, retained self-government under the influence of Russia and Britain.

The Arab states succeeded in throwing off colonial domination only after World War II. Except in Turkey, the process of transformation from kingdoms into independent nation states, which in Europe took centuries, occurred in the Muslim world in the last fifty years.

This chapter seeks to show the effects of this rapid transformation on traditional Islamic norms of war. It will first briefly summarize the traditional norms as applied by the Ottomans, and then look at post-World War II developments. Muslim states remain in a state of hostility to Israel, but have never made war against each other since 1920, with two exceptions. Iraq attacked Iran in 1980, and Iraq invaded Kuwait in 1990. The war between Iran and Iraq was a direct result of the revolution in Iran in 1980 in which the Shah was overthrown and Khomeini came to power. A primary focus in this chapter will be on why Iran had an Islamic revolution and then a war with Iraq. The following chapter is about Iraq's invasion of Kuwait and the response in Muslim and Western nations.

I. Muslim Empires and War

Until the twentieth century, the juristic norm or official theory in the

Muslim world was that one universal Islamic government should have primary responsibility for the protection and fostering of the only true religion. The model for statecraft remained Muhammad's revelation (the *Qur'an*) and practices (the *Sunna*) as well as the policies of the first four caliphates and, to a lesser extent, of the Umayyad dynasty (661-750). The caliph, like the Prophet, was supposed to combine in his person political and religious authority. He alone could declare an offensive war or *jihad* to expand the realm of Islam. He also had the responsibility to proclaim *jihad* against heresies within the *dar al-Islam.*

However, for centuries under the Abbasid dynasties (750-945), the theory of perpetual *jihad* to expand the realm of faith remained more an ideal than reality. In practice, disunity over religion within the *dar al-Islam*, considerable autonomy for different regions under rulers who professed loyalty to the caliph who dwelt in far away Baghdad, and even wars (*qital)* among Muslim principalities characterized Islam. Umayyad and Abbasid caliphs accepted long periods of truce with enemy states like Byzantium, and considerations of state rather than religion determined foreign relations, practices that would also characterize the Seljuk and Ottoman Turks.

The realm of Islam contained several schools of Sunnism and a variety of Shi'a, growing autonomy for different regions and rulers, and wars among rulers. In the tenth century, the rulers of the Shiite Fatimid dynasty in Egypt claimed to be caliphs (that is, claiming to have direct descent from the Prophet), and sought to overthrow or at least dominate the Abbasid caliphs, whose religious and moral authority they denied. Under the declining Abbasid dynasty there was more than one caliph at times, and power came to be divided between the caliph-imam with spiritual authority and sultans who exercised political power, including the Mamluks in Egypt, the Buyids of Iran, and the Almohads in North Africa and Spain. Stymied by Byzantium on the west and the Mamluks in the east, the Abbasids also faced invasion from the Seljuk Turks and later from the Mongols, whose leaders converted to Islam and created dynasties in conflict with the

Mamluks. The kingdoms of Islam spent more effort struggling for power against each other than working together on behalf of their common faith.

From a base in Anatolia (in modern Turkey) in the fourteenth century, the Ottoman Turks, with a zeal reminiscent of the first Muslims to expand the faith, created an empire over the next two hundred years that stretched from Algeria to Iran and included the Balkans. The Turks at first dominated only the periphery of the Muslim world, but took over the Arab heartland including the holy city of Mecca in the sixteenth century.[2] The Ottoman rulers who were not Arabs did not claim descent from the Prophet but received the title of sultan from the caliph in Cairo in 1396, which insured them the loyalty of all Sunni Muslim subjects. After 1500 they also claimed to be caliphs.[3] The Ottoman sultans continued to maintain Sunni orthodoxy against the Shiite Safavid dynasty in Persia and to expand or defend the *dar al-Islam* against Europeans. They also recruited Christian soldiers (mostly by force), at times received the support of Christians, allied themselves with the Byzantines against other Muslims, and even married Christian princesses. Islam was supreme in the Ottoman Empire, but each religious community was allowed to administer its own rules, and the Greek Orthodox Patriarch continued to reside in Istanbul (formerly Constantinople) after the city's conquest in 1453.

In theory *shari'a* law had preeminence throughout the Ottoman realms; however, in practice Muslim law predominated only in the personal realm with Ottoman practices serving as a foundation for public law that, however, was not supposed to conflict with *shari'a*. Religious leaders, the *ulema*, financially supported by the sultan, identified Muslim welfare with the interests of the ruling class and preached against internal religious challenges to Ottoman rule. Infighting for the succession to the throne caused coups but no revolution until 1908. So in

---

[2]The discussion of the Ottoman rulers is based on Bernard Lewis, *The Emergence of Modern Turkey*, 3rd ed., (2000), and Karpat, *The Politicization of Islam*.
[3]A sultan is a political role; a caliph is a leader of the Muslim community. There is no documentary proof for the Ottoman title of caliph. At times, the Ottomans claimed the title because of service to the community or protection of pilgrims going to Mecca. Karpat, 241-43.

essence the *ulema* remained content with a situation in which they controlled spiritual life and the sultan controlled political affairs in an empire tolerating enormous diversity in religious practice not only among Muslims but also among Jews and Christians. The Sunni *ulema* preached the necessity of loyalty to the sultan, which meant that any local leader's demand for a return to the "purity" of Islam could not serve as a basis for a popular uprising justified as a *jihad* against corruption.

The Ottoman Empire was extraordinarily long-lived, enduring from the fourteenth century until after World War I when, in 1924, the sultanate was abolished and Ataturk created the modern secular Turkish state. During its four centuries of ascendancy and long decline (at least as related to the strength of Europe) the Empire's strength rested upon a professional army. Although sultans could proclaim offensive and defensive *jihads* against European nations, for most individuals the Qur'anic requirements for individual service in a holy war had little relevance. The sultan made decisions concerning war and peace, and his authority in such matters was absolute and to be obeyed by all governmental and military officials.

The strength and longevity of the Ottoman Empire meant little questioning in the Muslim world of ideas about the universality of Islam, absolute rule of the sultan, justification for war in the name of religion, and lack of legitimacy for a state defined by ethnic or national unity and with borders defined by nationality. Or, phrased differently, the Muslim world that was generally economically self-sufficient and had little interest in what was going on in Western Europe, changed within the limits of its own cultural matrix. The Ottomans while disdaining Christian civilization had long used European mercenaries and military techniques, as in the utilization of cannon at the siege of Constantinople in 1453.

At the height of the Empire's power, from 1500 to 1700, Ottoman armies enjoyed weapons as good as the Europeans and better logistics and organization. Pragmatism rather than religious belief determined Ottoman foreign policy, and battles, with Europeans and other Muslims, were conducted with civility and in a manner to minimize casualties, even when cities fell after sieges. There were long periods of truces, as with the Habsburgs from 1606-1660. Religion could be utilized for state purposes or to motivate soldiers before battle, but sultans and armies appear to have been motivated more by material factors than by zeal for a *jihad* or Islam.[4]

The Ottomans remained a powerful threat to European nations until the eighteenth century; from then on they were on the defensive. The causes of decline were internal weaknesses and the ignorance by the ruling classes of changes in Europe.[5] After a series of defeats, the Ottomans began copying post-1789 French military practices because the Revolution was anti-Christian and militarily successful, and so adopting French science and technology need not jeopardize Islam. Sultans Selim II and Mahmud III (r.1789 -1839) sought to utilize western military techniques as a means of stopping the expansion of Austria and Russia. The modernization campaigns continued, but without an industrial base, the Ottomans could not keep up with the rapid changes in European weaponry and by the 1880s the survival of the Empire seemed doubtful.

Previously the Ottomans had relied upon political/military power to defend their territory and had shown only slight interest in the welfare of Muslims on the periphery. Sultan Abdulhamid II (r.1876-1909) emphasized his position as caliph to assert that the political bond of the Ottoman state was Islam and that he was caliph of the entire Islamic world. Muslims in India, North Africa, and Afghanistan appealed to the caliph as their defender and Western imperialists (incorrectly) saw Ottoman caliphs as instigator of the Sepoy rebellion in India (1857), Seyh Samil guerrilla wars against the Russians in Caucasus and Chechnya

---

[4]Rhoads Murphy, *Ottoman Warfare 1500-1700* (1999), 108, 143-146.
[5]Stanford J. Shaw, *Between Old and New: The Ottoman Empire under Sultan Selim III 1789-1807* (1971), 4-5. Shaw describes Ottoman government as "nepotism, inefficiency, dishonesty, and anarchy in all parts of the empire." Seventeenth-century reformers who remained ignorant of Europe sought to return to techniques that had brought earlier success, but were now doomed to failure. Shaw notes a general hatred of the infidel, but nowhere indicates that any of the many wars he discusses was viewed as a *jihad*.

(1830s-1860s), the Sanusiyya movement in Algeria and Tunisia (1870-80s), and Colonial Urabi Pasza in Egypt in 1882 against Britain. In actuality Abdulhamid made certain that popular Islamic revivalist movements did not threaten his political absolutism at home and used the spiritual authority of the caliphate to quell complaints in Iraq and Syria about the corruption of Ottoman administrators. In his role as defender of Islam, the Sultan could counter both those who saw the only salvation for the Empire as either complete Westernization or a return to an idealized past of early Ottoman practices. For Abdulhamid, reform need not threaten political absolutism. Only once, against Greece in 1897, did the Sultan declare a war a *jihad*.

Arabs in North Africa with no help from weak sultans in Istanbul sought to maintain cultural pride and political autonomy by utilizing Islam and the teachings of *jihad* against European intruders.[6] Historian Kemal Karpat argues that in the nineteenth century there were twenty-four or twenty-six Muslim revival movements, virtually all occurring in areas outside of Ottoman control. The revivalists saw the falling away from traditional Muslim culture as the cause of European successes. Many of the movements began as Sufi spiritual revivals but became political and military. Indigenous tribal authorities had no political or religious authority to proclaim a *jihad*, but the *Qur'an* specified that all male Muslims had a duty to resist an attack upon the *dar al-Islam*. There was also a tradition among indigenous leaders, such as the Berber Almohads, of proclaiming the necessity of returning to pure Islamic practice and using military force to cleanse a dynasty that was violating *shari'a*. Weak Muslim rulers who cooperated with Europeans could be seen as hopelessly corrupt and in need of a *jihad*.[7]

---

[6]Jacques Waardenburg, "Islam as a Vehicle of Protest," in *Islamic Dilemmas: Reformers, Nationalists and Industrialization* (1985), 22-48, is a perceptive essay showing how Islam was used for "self-defense against outside domination," or as a "direct form of religious protest within Islam," or as an indirect form of religious protest as in mysticism or modernism. He distinguishes between forms of protest common to all religions and traditions unique to Islam.
[7]Elizabeth Sirriyeh, *Sufis and Anti-Sufis: The Defence, Rethinking and Rejection of Sufism in the Modern World* (1999), 27-42, shows the complexities in the Islamic response. Resistance could strengthen Islam but also on occasion so could collaboration with the colonial powers. The

To counter British and French expansionism in North Africa, charismatic Muslim leaders like the Mahdi in the Sudan and Al-Fouriki in Algeria, proclaimed *jihads* against Western imperialists. Because these tribal leaders had no political authority from the sultan in Istanbul and no religious authority from the *ulema*, Muslims used an empirical test to determine whether this military resistance had Allah's blessing. These leaders' eventual defeat by the Europeans' superior weapons proved that they were not imams (or ghazis).[8] Muslims accepted that Allah who determined all events had punished them for their moral failures.

To the colonizers, the Muslims' invoking of *jihad* proved their lack of modernity, and only a few pacifists and opponents of imperialism argued that the slaughter caused by machine guns showed the barbarity of conquerors who supposedly reserved civilized restraints in war for conflicts among white Europeans. Cultural chauvinism blinded the West to the accomplishments of Muslim civilization.[9] Russia and Austria stirred up ethnic nationalist feelings to annex lands and create client states, and Britain concluded that Muslims should not be allowed to rule Christians. The sultans concluded that Europeans would not be satisfied with only the carving up of the Empire, but they never solved the problem of how to blend Islam with selected elements of European culture.

The Young Turks who emphasized nationalism and de-emphasized Islam overthrew the Sultan in 1908 and created what would become after World War I the modern secular nation state of Turkey. The new government took the Ottoman Empire into the war on the German side in World War I, because Russia and Britain appeared greater threats. During the war, the Allies played on local discontent with Ottoman rule to win the allegiance of Arab leaders. Defeat allowed the Allies at the 1920 San Remo conference to impose arbitrarily the

---

intense opposition to Sufi orders by the Wahhabi is an example of a reform movement within Islam.

[8] James Turner Johnson, *Holy War Idea in Western and Islamic Traditions* (1997), 19, 35, 144-55, 157ff.

[9] Edward Said, *Orientalism* (1979), documents the tendency of Western scholars to see Islam as unchanging and inferior. A critique of *Orientalism* is in William M. Watt, *Muslim-Christian Encounters: Perceptions and Misperceptions* (1991), 108-11.

borders of the modern Middle Eastern Arab states and to install nominally independent rulers - many of whom had only a slight relationship to the areas they ruled. Instead of a large Arab state, which is what the British had promised, there emerged Iraq, Syria, Lebanon, Trans-Jordan, Palestine, and several small Gulf states like Kuwait and the Emirates. Before the war, the British debated creating a rival caliph against the Ottomans from the Hussein family, descendants of the Prophet who was Amir (*serif*) in Mecca. Members of this family would become kings of Saudi Arabia, Iraq, and Transjordan.

The Arabian Peninsula with its two holy cities would be conquered in 1927 by the Saudi family supported by adherents of the Wahhabi movement. Unlike the other reform movements that used earlier traditions to come to terms with new conditions, the Wahhabi, who originated in the eighteenth-century, were fundamentalists seeking to return to a primitive Islam. The Wahhabis' austere version of the faith opposed many of the practices of popular Islam, including veneration of saints, chanting prayers, mysticism (the Sufis), and the interpretation (*ijitihad*) of the saying of the Prophet to apply to new circumstances. They distinguished the teachings of the Prophet from his person and destroyed shrines at his tomb as well as those of the first caliphs.[10] Intolerant of other interpretations of Islam, the Wahhabi declared a *jihad* against other Muslims in Iraq and opposed Ottoman rule of Mecca and Medina. In the late nineteenth century, the Saudi family sought to enlist the support of the British in order to gain power over the holy places. The new dynasty gained the support of Wahhabi clerics by making its laws reflect their teachings.

In Syria, the French quelled a rebellion and expelled the Arab-British candidate for the throne. Iran retained its independence, but Russia and Britain created spheres of influence, leaving its Shah (king) to balance his policy of modernization between them and the Shiite *ulema*. The new kingdoms had ethnic minorities like the Kurds who sought autonomy or even independence from Iraq,

---

[10]Elizabeth Sirriyeh, *Sufis and anti-Sufis*, 3-4, 22-24.

Iran, and Turkey. The kings who ruled these states gained or retained authority through loyalty and service to colonial powers and dared not displease the European nations whose primary interest became the economic exploitation for their own benefit of newly discovered oil reserves in Iran, Iraq, small Gulf states, and after 1938, Saudi Arabia. Long accustomed to being ruled by Turks who shared their religion and upheld the prestige of Islam, the Arabs, even when governed by Muslim kings, were now dominated by Christian nations that did not hide their contempt for Muslim beliefs and practices.

Independent Arab States

When the Arab nations successfully escaped from direct and indirect colonialism after World War II, leaders of revolutions in Egypt, Syria, Iraq and Algeria invoked the premises of nationalism and socialism rather than a revival of Islam. The new presidents, often former army officers, favored modernization which meant fostering westernization and economic development, while traditional Islam - used largely as a means of rallying support against colonial authorities - seemed either irrelevant or a hindrance to industrialism. When political theorists invoked Islam, they stressed its compatibility with socialism, communism, and/or democracy. Still, the ideal of a unified Islamic realm or Pan-Arabism continued under the secularist Ba'athist Party influential in Egypt led by Gamal Nasser, in Syria under Hafiz Assad, and in Iraq under Saddam Hussein. Each of these leaders sought to be the leader of all Arabs. These presidents professed a goal of Arab unity, but - except in their united opposition to Israel - their states espoused nationalism, pursued policies for self-interest and, as general disapproval of Iraq's invasion of Kuwait showed, most Arab countries accepted the boundaries imposed by outsiders. Whether conservative Islamic rulers like the Saudi royal family or secular Ba'athists, all the regimes in the Middle East and North Africa crushed internal opposition whether it came from Westernized students demanding democracy and political rights or fundamentalists seeking Islamization of society.

All modern Arab states experienced essentially the same conditions: anti-Western sentiment derived from the experience of foreign domination, oppressive government, endemic corruption, ethnic dissatisfaction from minorities, nationalism and pan-Islamic sentiments, rapid movement of rural population to cities and urban poverty, and a newly literate lower middle class with few opportunities for economic advancement. The oil revenues of a few accentuated the differences between have and have-nots among and within nations.

In spite of experiencing all of the above conditions, Iran in the early 1970s appeared a model of stability in an otherwise turbulent Middle East, the state least likely to have a revolution. Shah Reza Pahlavi's government (1942-1979) had a powerful army, a brutally efficient secret police, revenues from oil, and the support of the United States. The Shah was also committed to a policy of modernization, industrialization, and westernization and succeeded in making Iran a major regional military and economic power. Religious differences between Sunni and Shi'a help to explain why a revolution succeeded in Iran while Arab states had coups d'état.

II. The Revolution in Iran

Iran has long been a unique Muslim nation: its people consider themselves Persians and not Arabs, its primary language is Farsi and not Arabic, and eighty-five percent of its people are not Sunni but Shiites. The history of Shiism shows that from its original inception there was a distrust of government and belief in a revolutionary leader.

Shiism originated in a dispute over whether only the direct descendants of the Prophet Mohammad had the right to succeed him as caliph, i.e., the political and religious ruler. Shi'a recognized only the fourth caliph, Ali ibn Abi Taleb, as the legitimate caliph. Assassinated in 661, he had been a friend, cousin, and son-in-law of the Prophet. Ali's son (through Fatima, the daughter of Muhammad) Hasan died, probably by poison, in 669, and his younger son Hussein was killed along with his family and servants after the battle of Karbala in 680.

Hussein, who refused to recognize the legitimacy of the Umayyad dynasty and was killed by treachery, became to the Shiites a kind of cosmic intercessor who could forgive sins. Today, in popular Shiism, during the month of religious mourning, believers ritually reenact Hussein's martyrdom in elaborate ceremonies of mourning (*Muhrin*) and even use self-flagellation as a means of atoning for the sin of non-support at Karbala. So for the Shi'a there is a kind of symbolic shedding of blood for Islam and recognition of the need of martyrdom. Participating in this ritual also serves as a way of obtaining the divine intercession of Hussein.[11] A secondary tradition of the Shi'a viewed both Mohammad and Hussein as bringing justice to the oppressed.

Iranian Shi'a are often called Twelvers because of their belief that, beginning with Ali, there were twelve Imams descended from him, with the last Hidden Imam entering into a state of "lesser occultation" from 874-940 in which he communicated his wishes through four deputies. (Occulation is a kind of sleep or trance allowing the Imam not to die, but to be not present.) In 940 the Imam entered into a state of "greater occultation" which will endure until his messianic return to establish the legitimate kingdom of God on earth. There is much popular calculation as to when the Imam will come. Shiite eschatology or millennialism expects that the world will be restored to a golden age comparable to the rule of the Ali only with the return of the Imam or al-Mahdi, the "rightly guided one."[12]

For the Shiites, the Imam is a sinless leader, and only he has a correct understanding of the hidden teachings and message of Islam because it has been transmitted to him through evoluted initiation by a previous Imam. The Imam is the only legitimate political and religious successor to the Prophet. However, because such an Imam has been absent since 940, in theory all political power in Iran is questionable and there is no moral leader of the state. (Remember, however, for the Shi'a and Sunnis an imam is also one who stands in front of the

---

[11]Heinz Halm, *Shiism* (1991), 139-44.
[12]Henry Munson, *Islam and Revolution in the Middle East* (1990), 26

congregation and leads in worship and prayer; any pious man can be an imam. Imam is also a title for the caliph.)

The Shi'a denied to any living ruler the right to be a caliph (literally, the "successor" to Muhammad), because the Imam was the successor. So all the Sunni caliphs, originally chosen by the consensus of the oligarchic leaders of Islamic community and later by heredity, were, to the Shi'a, illegitimate. The Shi'a endured as a minority and a sometimes persecuted opposition movement until the sixteenth century when the Safavid dynasty in Iran officially adopted Twelver doctrines and gradually converted the country. The Shi'a, rarely revolutionaries, have normally practiced a quietistic acceptance of the government, but there was always potential friction with any ruler because they viewed worldly authority as temporary at best, or as a usurpation of the true ruler, who could only be the twelfth Iman.[13]

Individual religious leaders have greater prestige in Shiite as contrasted with Sunni practice. For the Sunni, any scholar of the tradition is an imam, in the sense of communal leader, and the shared authority and agreement of the *ulema* or the community of religious scholars is crucial. Glorification of any saintly teacher is generally discouraged. Shi'a, by contrast, place more emphasis upon a leading figure, a *muqallid* whose interpretations are binding because he serves as a deputy of the Hidden Iman. High-ranking *muqallid* are given the honorific *ayatollah* or "sign of God" and, at any given time, there can be several ayatollahs to whose interpretations others should defer. These ayatollahs propagated their independent interpretations of the hidden wisdom of the *Qur'an* and the *shari'a* by teaching in holy cities, and their pupils who became *mullahs*, leaders of local congregations and Muslim courts, carried their masters' teachings to distinct areas. In 1975 there were seven ayatollahs, most of whom were apolitical. Shi'a exalt

---

[13]Abdulaziz Sachedina, *The Just Ruler in Shiite Islam: The Comprehensive Authority of the Juristic Imamite Jurisprudence* (1988); for an alternative view, see William Flour, "Revolutionary

the status of the ayatollahs as sacred deputies of the Hidden Iman. In contrast, strict Sunni Muslims remain skeptical of exalting any individual as taking away the authority of Allah and Muhammad, and dislike any shrines other than Mecca and Medina. Shi'a venerate past and present holy men and they have major shrines and holy cities, including Kum in Iran and Karbala in Iraq. Shiite shrines, cemeteries, and holy cities traditionally served as sanctuaries for those fleeing the government. Religious opponents of the Shah had a safe haven, and army encroachment at such places would infuriate the populace.

Unlike the Sunni religious leaders whose financial support comes from the government, Iranian Shiites pay a religious tax to the local mullah who sends part to the ayatollah who taught him for distribution to the poor. (The theory is that the ayatollahs are collecting on behalf of the Twelfth Imam.) So Shiite ayatollahs have a certain amount of economic independence from the government. Ayatollahs and mullahs derive additional income from court cases and from rents on lands belonging to religious foundations; so they were not an economically deprived class and had a financial interest both in preserving *shari'a* courts and opposing land reform. In Iran in the 1970s, the people could learn of Ayatollah Khomeini's teaching either through mullahs' preachings or widely distributed cassettes. Such a mixture of tradition and modernity characterized the Iranian revolution.

On at least two occasions, the Shiite ayatollahs had represented the people in grievances against the Iranian government. In 1892 the Shah Nasir al-Din, under pressure from foreign governments, sold a monopoly on the sale of tobacco to an Englishmen. The monopoly would have hurt the livelihoods of bazaar merchants, so the ayatollahs decreed a ban on using tobacco, making the monopoly worthless. The Shah cancelled the contract. Between 1905 and 1911, in opposition to the increasing tyranny of the Shah, the ayatollahs mobilized the people against him,

---

Character of the Ulema: Wishful Thinking or Reality," in Nikki Keddie, ed., *Religion and Politics in Iran* (1983), 73-77.

but the result was a Western-style constitution and parliament that seemed to some, but not all Shiite leaders, to undercut Islam.

Between 1921-24 Colonel Reza Khan suppressed revolts, unified the country, undermined the constitution, and became Shah, though he still had to maneuver carefully between British and Russian advisers. During the 1920s the Shah tried to imitate the policies of Ataturk through a policy of modernization, restricting the authority of *shari'a* courts, and outlawing wearing the *chador* (the covering of women). Because the Shah appeared pro-Nazi and the British, Americans, and Russians wanted to make sure they controlled Iranian oil and ran the country, the Allies deposed the Shah during World War II in 1942 in favor of his young son, Muhammad Reza (1919-1980). When a nationalist revolution under Prime Minister Mussaddiq overthrew the new Shah and in 1951 nationalized the Anglo-Iranian Oil Company, the American Central Intelligence Agency organized a coup restoring the Shah to power, believing this to be a way to forestall communism and preserve Western control of Iranian oil. Shah Reza Pavlavi would rule until 1979. In 1952 the Shiite authorities did not support Mussaddiq, because they distrusted his secularism and feared communism. In addition, the *marjautaqil* (supreme ayatollah, literally, one who should be emulated above all other ayatollahs) from 1947 until 1961 declared that the *ulema* would not intervene in politics.

The Shah enjoyed good relations with the *ulema* until after 1959 when he enacted land reform and enfranchised women. When there were demonstrations, the Shah used military force to quell the opposition with force. The Shah's program of forced Westernization included industrial development, mass education, restricting the jurisdiction of *shari'a* courts, and exalting the tradition of Persian identity while downplaying the role of Shi'a Islam in Iranian history.

Massive revenues from oil brought wealth for a few, but the newly educated members of the lower middle class and rural peasants who flocked to the cities found little opportunity. There was also widespread resentment of the corruption of the ruling classes, the secret police who arrested potential opponents of the Shah, the selling of oil to Israel, and the close relationship between the Shah and the American government seen as the prime supporter of Israel. Many Iranians disliked the spreading influence of what they saw as the supposedly immoral and materialistic American civilization and resented as neo-colonialism the special privileges enjoyed by 30,000 Americans living mostly in Teheran.

The revolutionary potential in Shiism is clearer in retrospect than it was at the time. Shiism engendered a distrust of government, had a tradition of identifying Hussein with revolution against oppressive government, and in Muharrin observances inculcated the value of martyrdom. It allowed a single venerated leader to creatively adapt the teachings of the Hidden Iman and its mosques, schools, and cemeteries became sanctuaries for mobilizing the people. Also, the clergy had independent income and so were less dependent on the government. Because there was widespread dissatisfaction with the Shah's government, Khomeini could make Twelver Islam a vehicle to restore pure Islam.

In 1962 Ayatollah Khomeini emerged as an open critic of the Shah's corruption, oppression, and deference to the West. Exiled from Iran, he continued to teach in Iraq and, after Iraq expelled him at the request of the Shah, from France. With the Shah's secret police stifling all opposition in Iran, Khomeini became the focus of a wide-ranging movement of those seeking change in Iran, some of whom favored Western-style democracy. Most of the other ayatollahs remained non-political. Khomeini became the leader of a mass popular uprising with contradictory aims, with many students committed to creating a democracy and others seeking to return Iran to what they saw as traditional Muslim norms. There was also a small pro-Marxist labor movement. Even Westernized educated women protested laws forcing them not to wear the *chador* by wearing scarves. Until it achieved power in 1979 with a suddenness that surprised the Shah's government, his military, the U.S., and perhaps even Khomeini, the popular movement was essentially a massive nonviolent protest with demonstrations in the streets as well as in sanctuary areas like cemeteries and at shrines. The Shah, who was dying of cancer, followed an erratic policy of force and conciliation, perhaps because he feared a negative reaction from an American government committed to human rights. Khomeini symbolized and led the opposition movement with authority derived from his reputation for piety and incorruptibility. He opposed any compromise with the Shah, who eventually went into exile.

Khomeini became the supreme ayatollah and in popular belief was seen as at least the deputy of and perhaps even the Hidden Iman who was to restore the golden age of early Islam. At any rate, he became Allah's spokesman and his interpretation of the *shari'a* became binding. Events would show that Khomeini did not accept democracy, religious tolerance, and human rights and was willing to countenance violence against real or alleged opponents of the new Muslim society. His discourse echoed a paranoid style endemic in Iranian political discourse before and after the revolution in which all ills were blamed on outside forces symbolized by the United States, Israel, and later Saddam Hussein. What had begun as a nonviolent revolutionary movement against tyranny, once in power, became a clerical tyranny as the new government imprisoned or executed opponents and allowed young armed militants to suppress dissenters.

The label fundamentalist applied by journalists and scholars to many contemporary Muslim insurgent movements distorts the enormous differences between these uprisings and ignores Khomeini's creative reinterpretations of Shi'a doctrine and practice before and after the revolution. A more accurate interpretation describes Khomeini as preaching a liberation theology, Islamic style.[14] The Ayatollah condemned, for example, not industrialization per se, but the ways in which the Shah's government promoted economic development so

---

[14]Ervand Abrahamian, *Khomeinism: Essays on Islamic Republic* (1993). Marvin Zonis and Daniel Brumberg, "Shiism as Interpreted by Khomeini: an Ideology of Revolutionary Violence," in *Shiism, Resistance, and Revolution*, ed. Martin Kramer (1989), 54-57.

that only a few profited and the masses were left in poverty. Ignoring the traditional exegesis of the *shari'a*, so important to Muslim scholars and religious dogmas in general, Khomeini, before 1979, stressed social and political issues and denounced oppression and corruption. He reinterpreted the Shiite founding myths by making Hussein a revolutionary against an illegitimate regime; so that those killed by the Shah's forces would be likened to the martyrs of Karbala. Such symbolism would later be applied to Iranian offensives against Iraq, with clear connotations of holy war and the virtues of dying for the faith.

The new Iranian government and society resembled neither Western nations, nor traditional caliphates, nor other modern Islamic states. Iran now functions with a written constitution, parliamentary system, elections, women's suffrage, mass education of females and males, clerical supervision of laws, and participation of the ayatollahs in political decisions - none of these were part of the Shiite tradition. (Saudi Arabia, by contrast, dominated by the conservative Wahhabi sect, does not allow women to drive cars or vote or become educated, and has no written constitution. Its parliament lacks power. Saudi Arabia, far more than Iran, deserves the title of Muslim fundamentalist.) Iran's holding U.S. diplomats hostage was also a clear violation of the practice of other Islamic nations. After coming to power, Khomeini purged his opponents while defying the U.S. and warring with Iraq.

With the sanction of voters, Khomeini created a new form of Islamic government, one aiming to restore the political-religious harmony of early Islam. A crucial innovation, with almost no precedent in Muslim history, was giving the clergy political power through "the rule of the jurisprudent." The constitution created a Guardian Council composed of twelve jurists and ayatollahs to veto all legislation passed by the Parliament. The Guardian Council would be appointed by the Leader, the *muqallid taqtid* (the supreme ayatollah, in this case Khomeini), who had full authority over the armed forces, the right to declare war and to make peace, and to approve all candidates for the Presidency. By revolutionizing Shi'a practices, Khomeini became the clerical dictator in a theocracy based upon a constitution. (The election in 1997 of a moderate ayatollah as President and in 2000 of a large, reformist majority in Parliament shows that, unlike all other Arab countries, elections in Iran can result in a change of policy, even though the power of the Guardians remains supreme. (There is a continuing struggle for reform against conservative clerics willing to use legal and extralegal measures.) The power of Khomeini and his successor Khamenei to approve or veto laws and control foreign and domestic policies transformed the political practices of Islam. The Iranian revolution was a fundamental challenge not only to the Shah and the West but also to Sunni and earlier Shi'a understandings of religion and politics.

III. The Iran-Iraq War

The Iran-Iraq war surprised western political analysts who had concluded that economic, political, and strategic rivalries far outweighed religious differences as a primary cause of war in the twentieth century. But in the Iran-Iraq war religious animosities helped start and fuel a struggle that lasted over seven years with deaths conservatively estimated at over 367,000 and 700,000 wounded.[15]

Iraq was ruled by Saddam Hussein, who had come to power through the socialist and nationalist Ba'athist Party and who retained power by eliminating his opponents and escaping assassination attempts. Iraq has no tradition of a peaceful transfer of power. The Ba'athist government was secularist, advocating both separation of politics from religion and religious toleration. Saddam Hussein came from a small Alawite clan (an offshoot of the Isma'ilis which itself is a separate form of Shiism), and Tariq Aziz his foreign minister was a Christian. Hussein's dictatorial rule was based upon patronage of his clan and of the Sunni minority from the northwest. He had shown an ability to divide opponents with favors before turning against them and a willingness to betray any or all ideologies in his quest for power.

---

[15]Dilip Hiro, *The Longest War: The Iran-Iraq Military Conflict* (1991), 250. Charles Tripp, *A History of Iraq* (2000), 223-247, is the best short history.

Iraq, like Iran, had embarked upon a program of industrialization and military build-up, financed by the increased oil revenues gained through the rise in prices brought about after the Iranian Shah initiated an OPEC (Organization of Petroleum Exporting Countries) boycott following Israel's victory in the 1973 war.

Iraq and Iran had long disputed their border, with the Shah able to dominate because of his superior military force. Each had sought to exploit the other's Kurdish minority to seek independence while oppressing Kurds at home. The Iraqi population consisted of 20% Kurds, who wished independence or autonomy, with nearly 80% of the majority Arab population being Shi'a. As an Alawite, Hussein had no religious tie with any major group of the Iraqi people.

Khomeini opposed national states. He aimed at restoring a unity of all Muslims and territorial boundaries between nations appeared to him as a divisive element imposed by colonial powers to weaken Islam. He viewed the secularist Ba'athist party and Saddam Hussein as enemies of Islam. He also wanted to replace what he saw as corrupt monarchies in Saudi Arabia, Kuwait, and the United Arab Emirates. He viewed these kings as oppressing their peoples and serving as lackeys of Western powers. The logical place to spread the revolution was Iraq, whose Shiite majority he expected to rally to a purified Islam. Khomeini also anticipated support from Sunni Muslims, believing that the unity of Islam would override traditional differences. He underestimated Sunni opposition to exalting the status of a religious leader, reinterpreting the *shari'a*, and involving clerics directly in politics.

Saddam Hussein feared the export of the Iranian revolution to Iraq, even though the Iraqi Shi'a consider themselves Arab and speak Arabic while the Iranian Shi'a are Persian and their language is Farsi. A small guerrilla movement of Iraqi Shiites sought to overthrow the Ba'athist government by employing terrorist tactics, including an attempt to assassinate the foreign minister. An ayatollah living in Iraq publicly welcomed the Iranian revolution. To the shock of

Khomeini, Saddam Hussein had this ayatollah executed and ruthlessly suppressed any politically dissident Iraqi Shiites while bestowing economic largess on areas where the Shi'a dominated in order to retain their support.

Iraq at first counted on opponents of the revolution within the Iranian military who disliked the purges Khomeini authorized. Hussein also hoped the U.S. would succeed in its efforts to destabilize the regime during the hostage crisis. The failures of both a military coup by officers still loyal to the Shah and of the U.S. hostage-rescue effort prompted Hussein to conclude that now was the time to strike. Iran appeared weak with internal opposition to Khomeini from Westernized democrats and the army, its society in turmoil because of economic boycott, its military forces weakened and unable to gain re-supply from the U.S., and its isolation from both the U.S. and the USSR (over a strong condemnation of the Soviet invasion of Afghanistan). Saddam Hussein concluded that a surprise attack would allow the normally weaker Iraq to overcome Iran's advantages in population and resources. Iraq had plentiful oil revenues, a powerful military, and grievances. Saddam Hussein believed that, in a few weeks he could seize the disputed border areas, control significant areas of oil production, and create a morale problem so great that Khomeini would be overthrown. In August 1980 he staged an invasion of Iran, expecting to obtain his objectives in a few weeks.

Both nations began with limited objectives but expanded their goals as the war dragged on. Iraq sought to gain support from the Arab minority within Iran and to annex lands or create an autonomous state in oil-producing areas. Hussein soon became committed to overthrowing Khomeini. Iran began seeking to defend its territory, but soon its war aims expanded to include destroying Saddam Hussein's regime. Young radical revolutionaries saw the war as a *jihad* to capture holy sites like Karbala and then to use Iraq as a springboard to liberate Zionist Jerusalem. Khomeini did not declare an official *jihad,* because only the Hidden Iman had that right.

Both Iraq and Iran justified the war as a struggle for Islam. Hussein declared the war a *jihad* against Persian infidels. He told his soldiers to "strike powerfully, because you are truly Allah's sword on earth. The necks you are striking are those of aggressor Magians, collaborators with the lunatic." (Magians refer to non-Muslims including Zoroastrians; the term was highly derogatory.)[16] Iraq sought to enlist the support of its Sunni and Shi'a clergy. During the war the Ba'athist regime played down its secular origins and emphasized that this was a war for Islam. Hussein cultivated Iraqi's Shi'a, most of whom supported Iraq throughout the war - a clear indication of the power of Arab identity and nationalism. The Iraqi Shi'a had never previously identified with Iranian culture. All but one of the Shi'a ayatollahs living in Iraq kept silent about the war. However, Hussein was disappointed that Arabs living on the frontier in Iran did not support Iraq. By contrast, Iran did have success in utilizing the Kurds who continued their quest to create an independent state in the north of Iraq. Hussein presented himself as a pious Muslim going regularly to worship and utilized Islam to justify and rally support for what was originally an aggressive war against another Muslim state.

The Iranians also saw fighting the war as a religious duty but did not vilify the Iraqi people, seeing the sole villain as Saddam Hussein, described as "a perpetuator of corruption": "We are religiously bound to protect and preserve Islam ... This was the same logic we pursued in our fighting against the corrupt Pahlavi regime ... Islamic teachings were going to be eradicated and Islamic principles erased, therefore we were bound by our religion to resist as much as we could." Hussein was identified with the killers of Karbala.[17] So Khomeini labeled Hussein an "infidel" out to "destroy Islam." Iraq's attack upon Iran was a war against a true "government of God." Because Saddam personified evil, there could be no question of discussion of a truce while Iraq occupied any Iranian soil.

Initially Iraq held the initiative, but within two years Iran had regained most of its land. By July 1982 Iraq was on the defensive and now sought a cease-

---

[16]Quoted in Hiro, 44.
[17]Ibid., 46.

fire. For Khomeini and the leaders of Iran, the goal of the war expanded to drive Saddam Hussein from power and to export revolutionary Islam.[18] Throughout the long war, Iran had little difficulty in mobilizing its population. A Revolutionary Guard imbued with ideological fervor believed that morale alone would bring victory, and poorly trained troops were rushed to battle. Conflict with the military hampered early efforts, but Iranian commanders and people ignored any reservations about Khomeini's policy in a unified effort to drive out the invader. Later, the clerics entrusted the waging of the war to the professional military, whose tactics in the watery swamps of the disputed lands compensated for the Iraqi supremacy in weaponry, but at a heavy cost in casualties. (Commanders allowed barefoot children to walk through mine fields and promised them martyrdom if they died.)

At the onset of the war, the eventual shape of the revolution in Iran was still amorphous. The conflict allowed Shi'a clerics to gain control of all branches of the state and to eliminate all internal opposition, insisting that the resulting form of government in Iran was god-given and divine.

Even before the tide of battle turned against it, Iraq had difficulties with morale. There were many more Iraqi prisoners of war than Iranians, perhaps because the Iranians saw religious significance in dying while fighting for their faith. Fearing a loss of support for the war, Saddam Hussein tried to cushion the cost by fighting a defensive war from entrenched positions, making use of his superiority in tanks and guns. He financed the war through loans and grants, primarily from Gulf State neighbors like Kuwait and Saudi Arabia, which feared Iran. (Iraq ended the war with staggering debts that would serve as a cause of Hussein's attempted annexation of Kuwait.) Iraq had no difficulties in obtaining arms throughout the war from Russia, France, and the United States - all of which officially supported the UN embargo on the sale of arms to both sides. Even so, Iran found ways of circumventing the boycott through contacts with Syria, Libya,

---

[18]Ibid.

China, and North Korea. Western governments diverted their attention when their companies sent arms to third parties that were transshipped to Iran. The Reagan administration strongly supported a boycott of Iranian arms both before and after the public learned that it had traded arms for hostages in Lebanon and used the proceeds to fund the Contras in Nicaragua.

The West and Soviet Union initially sought to make sure the war did not spread beyond the original participants and worked through the UN to end the war with a return to pre-1979 borders. After 1982 Iraq accepted the UN offer and portrayed itself as seeker of peace, but Iran continued to refuse outside offers of mediation. (Iran did demand a UN investigation of the beginning of the war, because it was clear that Iraq had attacked first.) For the next five years, Iran staged a variety of offensive efforts that resulted in heavy casualties and minimal conquests. The forces of Iraq regularly used chemical weapons (poison gas), but Khomeini who regarded such weapons as immoral forbade the Iranian forces to reciprocate. Both sides, but primarily Iraq, which had more planes and could obtain spare parts, used air power against civilian targets, but with little military effect. The UN did declare an arms embargo, negotiated truces in air attacks against cities, investigated the gas attacks, and visited POW camps in both countries.

For years Iraq sought to involve the U.S. and European powers in the war. Iraq regularly but unsuccessfully sought to disrupt Iranian oil shipments that were carried by tankers from the Persian Gulf. (Iraqi oil was shipped by pipeline; when manpower shortages led to reduced oil production in Iraq, Saudi Arabia made up the shortfall.) When Iran sought to punish Kuwait in 1987 for supporting Iraq, the U.S. intervened by putting its flag on Kuwaiti tankers and sending its warships. To punish Iran's placing mines in the Gulf, the U.S. destroyed some Iranian offshore oil installations, sank some small gunboats, and on July 3, 1988, in a mistake, shot down an Iranian Airbus with 290 civilians onboard. These events convinced Khomeini that the U.S. would not allow Iran to win the war. So, reluctantly, two weeks later, he accepted the cease-fire as necessary to preserve the successful revolution in Iran.

The fighting ended in August with a truce. The result was essentially a stalemate with boundary issues still unresolved and the leaders who had begun the war still in power. When Khomeini died on June 3, 1989, the massive outpouring of grief from the Iranian people showed that his Islamic revolution had endured. The future of the revolutionary thrust and of the dictatorial powers of clerics that Khomeini imposed upon the Shi'a remain uncertain and will depend upon events in Iran.

The war had succeeded in localizing the Iranian revolution, and the fundamentalist movements today, often financed by Saudi Arabia, do not seek to imitate Iran. The differences between Sunni and Shi'a Islam meant that at the time there was little support in the Arab world for a Khomeini-led revolution. The Iranian revolution's greatest impact may have been in persuading dissidents elsewhere in the Arab world that their struggles against Western-backed authoritarian governments could be successful. In all Arab governments today, radical movements using the terminology of *jihad* seek to improve the quality of life by re-instituting Islamic governments.

In 1980 Iran and Iraq mobilized their peoples to fight successful defensive and offensive wars over borders. For Iraq, the war began for secular reasons, but was justified as a *jihad.* For Iran, the war was initially a defense of its borders but soon became an attempt to expand a religious revolution. Within Iran, spiritual fervor sustained the war for eight years, but any heritage of Shiite unity paled against a tradition of ethnic rivalries and the ability of Saddam Hussein to sanctify his country's nationalism as a defense of Islam.

XXI.
The Gulf Wars against Iraq

The invasion of Kuwait in August 1991 took the world by surprise, partially because when earlier queried about the significance of positioning an army on the border, Iraq's Foreign Minister lied as to his nation's intentions to several leaders including Egypt's President Hosni Mubarak.[1] Iraq had staggering debts incurred during the war with Iran and, arguing that the war had also benefited Kuwait and other Gulf Emirates, sought for forgiveness of $10 billion in loans. The price of oil had fallen, hindering Iraq's ability to pay its debts or rebuild its economy, and Hussein blamed Kuwait for allegedly selling more oil than its OPEC quota allowed and secretly drilling sideways under the border to tap Iraqi oil. (Kuwait countered that Iraq had been drilling sideways.) [2]

Great Britain had set the border between the two countries after World War I, and in 1961 Iraqi leaders had sought to rectify it or to annex Kuwait. So critics of the West found some legitimacy in Hussein's argument that this was a conflict about imperialist control of Arabs. (However, Iraq showed no sympathy for the Kurds who complained about an arbitrary border in the North.) Iraq had officially recognized and had diplomatic relations with Kuwait; in fact, had been engaged in discussions over grievances without success.

Hussein's motivation for the invasion was clear: Kuwait was wealthy, and a quick victory would allow wiping out some debt, add enormous oil reserves, and demonstrate that Iraq rather than Egypt was the military power in the Arab world. Faced with an invading army, the Kuwaitis offered little resistance and the Emir and his family and 300,000 Kuwaitis fled. Iran won a victory in twenty-four

---

[1]John Stoessinger, *Why Nations Go to War* (1993), ch. 7, is a good introduction to events leading to the war.
[2]Charles Tripp, *A History of Iraq* (2000), 251-53 argues that the invasion was a sign to all the Gulf emirates and Saudi Arabia that Iraq should be forgiven its $40 billion in loans. Iraq may have contemplated using Kuwait as a kind of bargaining chip in its negotiations.

hours and in its aftermath troops pillaged the country and committed numerous atrocities against the inhabitants. Hussein proclaimed that the area was now a province of Iraq.

President Bush denounced the Iraqi invasion as an act of aggression against a sovereign state taken in defiance of international law, and a threat to world order by a ruthless dictator. The United States saw the invasion as an attempt by Hussein to gain control of nineteen percent of the world's oil reserves and to threaten Saudi Arabia. (At the time world oil reserves were estimated at Iraq 9.9%, Kuwait 9.8%, Saudi Arabia, 25.2% - total for all Gulf states, 64.5%.[3])

The United Nations Security Council, with all of the big five nations agreeing, condemned the invasion and called for the immediate and unconditional withdrawal of Iraqi troops. Jordan's King Hussein, invoking the traditions of Arab solidarity, sought for a peaceful withdrawal; President Bush allowed 48 hours for this negotiation and sought the consent of Saudi Arabia to station American troops on its soil as a deterrent to invasion by Iraqi troops.[4] The UN imposed and the U.S. and UK fleets enforced economic sanctions on Iraq (food was at first exempted but later added). Iraq rebuffed attempts to mediate, and the United States began sending troops, insisting that Hussein must agree to all UN resolutions (including reparations to Kuwait) and the restoration of Kuwaiti independence. The United States sought troops from allies in Europe and Arab nations and authorization from the United Nations in creating a multinational military force whose purposes - whether to protect Saudi Arabia, bring pressure on Iraq to withdraw, or to free Kuwait in war - were left ambiguous.

Though the invasion's initial justification by Iraq and critique by the U.S. and UN did not involve religion, the conflict soon acquired religious overtones as Hussein, Muslim clerics and lay peoples in the Islamic world debated an ethical

---

[3]Peter Custer, "The Gulf Crisis and the World Economy," in *The Persian Gulf War: Views from the Social and Behavioral Sciences,* ed., Daniel Blumberg (1994), 164. This volume contains a twenty-page chronology of the events.

response. Sensing his international isolation (publicly supported only by Libya, Sudan, the PLO, and Yemen), Hussein sought to enlist popular opinion in the Muslim world. Iraq declared the war a *jihad*, inserted the words *Allahu akhbar* (God is great) onto the Iraqi flag, and convened a conference of Muslim scholars who pronounced the invasion justified and condemned the stationing of American troops in Saudi Arabia as a violation of Qur'anic prohibitions and a desecration of that holy land. By cooperating with the U.S., the government of Saudi Arabia had forfeited its rights as protectors of Mecca and Medina.

Hussein insisted that the enemy was an imperialistic West that with its lackeys in Saudi Arabia sought to control the Muslim world. Allegedly, the U.S. had long wanted bases in the area to control oil, and its unholy alliance with Saudi Arabia was now public. Iraq contrasted the U.S.'s concern with the territorial integrity of Kuwait and obeying UN resolutions with its ignoring of Israeli occupation and settlements on the West Bank and repeated violations of UN resolutions. Picturing its leader as a new Saladin devoted to unifying the Arab world to repel another invasion by Christian crusaders, Iraq insisted on the linkage of all issues in the Middle East (including Syrian and Israeli forces occupying land in Lebanon) and called for an international conference to settle issues in Israel, the West Bank, and Kuwait. The struggle, Hussein insisted, was really about Islam.[5]

II. Responses to the Iraqi *Jihad*: The "Moderates"

Many Muslim political and religious leaders remained skeptical that this was a *jihad* or that Iraq sought the re-Islamization of society. After all, the Ba'athist regime in Iraq had earlier espoused the divorce of the faith from politics and Hussein's regime had often persecuted its Shiite majority. Convocations of leading Muslim scholars in Saudi Arabia and Egypt condemned the invasion as violating the Qur'anic prohibition of making war against other Muslims and

---

[4]Bob Woodward, *The Commanders* (1991), 241-246, 253-256, 260-273, while un-footnoted, has the advantage of being based upon interviews of significant American political figures. It will remain the best account of American actions until archives are opened.
[5]James Piscatori, "Religion and Realpolitik: Islamic Responses to the Gulf War," in *Islamic Fundamentalisms and the Gulf War Crisis* (1991), 1-2. 110-11.

708

weakening the unity of Islam. These clerics denied that the invasion of Kuwait was a *jihad* in either the classical or modern sense. Traditionally, a military *jihad* sought to extend or to protect the faith against unbelievers. Kuwait was an Islamic society, less secular than Iraq. The pillaging of Kuwait and the oppressive nature of Iraqi rule there also violated the classical rules of how a Muslim enemy was to be treated. So this conquest was not a *jihad* requiring the support of all Muslims; rather the invasion was a *qital* or secular struggle. In addition, since the nineteenth century Islamic scholars, relying upon the *Qur'an* but also new understandings of society, had re-interpreted the *jihad* as a defensive war.[6] Here again, clearly Hussein was the aggressor and had violated teachings about a *jihad*.

The moderate Sunnis dealt with the issue of Muslim vs. Christian in two ways. The clerics defended the stationing of non-Muslim troops in Saudi Arabia as allowable for a limited time because the *Qur'an* allowed military force to protect an Islamic government. In addition, the participation of soldiers from Egypt, Morocco, Syria, and Saudi Arabia meant that the division was not the West versus Islam, and in time troops from the West would be replaced by forces from many Muslim nations. The secular government of Turkey, most of whose inhabitants are Muslim, closed its border with Iraq, shut off the oil pipeline, and allowed American planes to refuel at its bases. Moreover, the clerics insisted that the coalition intended to convince Iraq to withdraw and to restore the legitimate government, not to wage aggressive war. Not until January did the leading Wahhabi cleric of Saudi Arabia declare the battle against Iraq a *jihad* and welcome the role played by non-Muslims in defeating "the enemy of God."[7]

The so-called moderate Sunni clerics supported Saudi Arabia and Kuwait but also expressed veiled disapproval of the United States, condemned the Iraqi actions, and criticized Israel - particularly after Israeli security forces opened fire during a disturbance on the Temple Mount in Jerusalem and killed seventeen unarmed men, wounded 150, and imposed a curfew keeping one million

[6]Kelsay, *Islam and War* (1993), 48.
[7]Ibid., 3, 7-10, 219.

Palestinians in their homes. Throughout the crisis the anti-Iraqi coalition feared that Arab rage at Israel would break up the allies or lead to revolutionary protests if the crisis were not speedily resolved.

It is, of course, doubtful whether there was enough political and religious freedom in any Arab state for a conference of Muslim clerics to oppose publicly their governments' policy. There was also no Sunni tradition of a separation between mosque and state that would legitimate an independent check on rulers by the *ulema*. The modern role of the *ulema* in Arab states is analogous to the role of the established Christian churches in Germany, Britain, and Russia before 1914 in which the clergy preached the necessity for a revival of religion in the society but in a crisis supported the state.

III. Response to the *Jihad*: Radicals

Iraq's linkage of Kuwait with Israel and anti-imperialism reached a sympathetic audience in much of the Middle East, particularly among the Palestinians on the West Bank and in Jordan whose major grievance was alleged Israeli oppression. Jordan's King Hussein showed sympathy to Iraq and for the first time allowed members of the radical Muslim brotherhoods into his cabinet. Saudi Arabia, by contrast, expelled Palestinians who had previously constituted a substantial percentage of the work force, but who could not become citizens and had few political rights.

Iran's Shiite ayatollahs, who dominated the government, shared the distrust of Western imperialism and disliked the Arab sheikdoms. During the crisis, Hussein restored all lands seized from Iran in the eight-year war in an effort to win support. However, Iran's memory of the war and Iraq's earlier persecution of the large Shiite community (60% of the population) meant there was no desire to strengthen its old enemy. The revolt of Iraq's Shi'a at the end of the war showed that Hussein's espousal of Islam did not convince his own peoples, let alone his Iranian neighbors. So Iran criticized both the invasion of Kuwait and the presence of an international army on sacred soil while increasing its anti-Israeli propaganda in an effort to deny Iraq pre-eminence on this issue. Officially neutral, Iran provided to Arab Emirates copies of Iraqi communications. At the end of the war Iran cooperated with the Allies in taking care of refugees fleeing after the unsuccessful revolutions. Iran's official silence had the effect of giving maneuvering room to Syria (whose dictator Assad had supported Iran during the war with Iraq, to weaken Iraq rather than for religious reasons) and to pro-Western Arab governments, while weakening so-called popular or "extremist" Muslim brotherhoods in other states.[8]

The Muslim brotherhoods and opposition movements that western journalists label "fundamentalist" also showed ambivalence in dealing with the crisis. These Muslims despised Israel, the United States, and what they regarded as the immoral and anti-Islamic influences coming from the West. They shared a desire to reform and unify Arab nations in conformity with the *shari'a,* but were not opposed to industrialism provided it could be made to improve the living conditions of the poor. The Muslim brotherhoods remained suspicious of the close relationship between the West and the Emirates and resented the enormous wealth of the Gulf States and the lifestyle of members of their royal families. They contrasted the poverty of most of the Arab world with the affluence of the oil states and believed that their wealth should be used for the benefit of all Arabs. Yet they also were aware that Iraq was far less an Islamic society than Saudi Arabia, whose Wahhabi-dominated government used the *Qur'an* as a basis for law. In addition, their movements had been supported by subsidies from Kuwait and Saudi Arabia whose governments favored the Islamic revival and had earlier refused to allow foreign troops on the Arabian Peninsula.

The brotherhoods' ambivalence meant that, although in spite of popular resentment of the U.S. and admiration of Iraqi's defiance of the West, there was also support for a negotiated end of the crisis so that the Arab world could unify against Israel. The Muslim brotherhoods, who wished to overthrow most of the

---

[8]Amatzia Baram, "From Radicalism to Radical Pragmatism: The Shi'ite Fundamentalist Opposition Movements of Iraq" in *Islamic Fundamentalism and the Gulf Crisis* (1991), 28-51.

pro-western governments of the Arab world including Egypt, Morocco, and Algeria, put a check upon too belligerent official support of the U.S.-led coalition against Iraq, but their lack of power meant they could not reverse the policies their governments followed in the Gulf crisis.[9]

IV. The U.S. Debate: What Is a Proper Response?

Within the U.S. there was virtual unanimity that, even if the Iraqis had legitimate grievances, the invasion was unjust and Iraq's treatment of the Kuwaiti citizens, pillaging of its treasures, and holding diplomats and foreign nationals as hostages were war crimes. No one argued that the new status quo should endure. So the debate became one of policies to be followed, because all agreed that there was a fault, an unjust action taken by Iraq.

As in the Arab world, pre-existing dispositions influenced how many but not all Americans approached the crisis. Those who saw Iraq as threatening the security of Israel supported the uncompromising stand enunciated by President Bush and favored a military response. Most American Jewish organizations, evangelical Protestants like Jerry Falwell, and conservative columnists like the *New York Times'* William Safire and A. M. Rosenthal backed the administration's policies. Two prominent scholars of the Just War traditions, Georgetown University's George Weigel, a Catholic critic of a so-called pacifist theme in *Pacem in Terris*, and Rutgers University's James Johnson, a student of and later supporter of Paul Ramsey's perspective, defended Bush's policies; but the conservative pro-Reagan Catholic journalist Patrick Buchanan opposed the administration policies as too favorable to Israel, for which he was labeled anti-Semitic.[10]

---

[9]This section is based upon essays by Jean-Francois Legrain, Beverley Milton-Edwards, Gehad Auda, Hugh Roberts, and Mumtaz Ahmad on the response of the Muslim brotherhoods in Egypt, Jordan, Algeria, and Pakistan, in *Islamic Fundamentalism and the Gulf Crisis* (1991).

[10]James Turner Johnson and George Weigel, *Just War and the Gulf War* (1991), parts 1 and 2. The main text of the book contains a selection of the relevant documents of major Catholic and Protestant church groups and leaders whose dovish tone was opposed by the editors. David E. Decosse, ed., *But was it Just: Reflections on the Morality of the Persian Gulf War* (1992) has essays by Walzer, Weigel, Elshtain, Nusseibeh, and Hauerwas using and critiquing Just War theory as applied to the conflict.

The most vocal critics of Bush's policies earlier had opposed the U.S. invasions of Grenada and Panama to replace hostile governments, thought unnecessary the arms build up and Star Wars missile defense system under Reagan, and disliked what they insisted was the militaristic bias in American foreign policy, as exemplified by aiding the Contras in Nicaragua and the government of El Salvador. These opponents included the spokespersons of most liberal Protestants in the National Council of Churches, Roman Catholics who approved of declarations of Pope John XXIII and Vatican II on war and the American bishops' statement on nuclear weapons, and religious and secular pacifists. Of course, there was no penalty for disagreeing with church leaders, and polls showed that many parishioners were more hawkish than the clergy.[11] The dovish pronouncements of religious leaders often appeared to be directed at members of their congregations rather than political leaders and had little influence on the President and the small circle of his advisers who made policy. Proponents and opponents of the war utilized Just War theories. Pacifist John Howard Yoder insisted that Just War theory was obsolete, because it required honest counselors for a king. The public now took this role, but government manipulation of information meant that it was now impossible to accurately discern the facts.

The divisions within the religious community echoed those in political parties and the military. For example, in testimony before Congress several previous members of the Joint Chiefs of Staff and former Secretaries of Defense saw enormous dangers in going to war and advocated allowing time for the economic blockade and sanctions to work. This was later reported to have been the position of General Colin Powell, Chairman of the Joint Chief of Staffs, who kept his reservations to himself while implementing the President's policies.[12] Teachers at the military war colleges, defense analysts, and political scientists also

---

[11]*Christian Century*, Nov., 14,1991, 1058; Dec. 5, 1126-28, Dec. 12, 1156-57; Feb. 6, 1991; 134; March 13, 1991, 295-98.
[12]Woodward, 298-303.

reached no consensus on appropriate policies. Partisan politics played a role, with most Democrats advising caution and Republicans backing the President. Estimates varied widely from six months to years on how long it would take sanctions to impede the Iraqi war machine and bring its economy to a standstill. Even supporters of sanctions worried that such economic penalties hurt civilians more than the Iraqi government or military. Polls showed that the public wanted Iraq out of Kuwait, favored sanctions if they would work, and detested any strategy that could be labeled appeasement. Virtually everyone wanted to avoid war, and even strong supporters of the military buildup hoped a show of force would by itself be sufficient.

The most intensive debate over U.S. foreign policy and conventional military tactics since Vietnam lasted from August until January. Unlike Vietnam, in which the debate occurred after the fighting started and the issue was whether to seek a limited victory or accept defeat, the debate over Kuwait/Iraq began over the scale of the military build-up, then changed into the advisability of waging war or allowing sanctions more time, and finally centered on the tactics used in what turned out to be a short war but a continuing struggle with Hussein.

The controversy over policy on Iraq illustrates the complicated interactions between strategic and moral considerations in modern America because, in a country in which institutional religion and the state are separated, religious commitment influences political discourse through ethics. The debate also showed the difficulties for citizens to shape foreign policy on the basis of morality when attitudes to war intersect with economic interests, past policies, imperialism, Israel, domestic politics and even concern over the well-being of Iraqi citizens who were perceived as being victims of a dictator. Church leaders and politicians intermingled moral and strategic arguments because they believed that the final decision would cost many lives and, remembering Vietnam, feared that an unnecessary war would threatened the unity of America.

In the debate over Kuwait, politicians and theologians used the categories of justified war. The main differences came not in their conclusions or even the way they analyzed issues, but because theologians, who were aware of differences of pre-and post-Vatican II interpretation of Just War thought, added to their ethical standards citations of biblical verses, examples from church history, and the necessity of prayer. Politicians, whose knowledge of Just War theories came from common discourse rather than wide reading, often blurred the line between strategy and religion. A year earlier the Bush administration had termed the invasion of Panama to overthrow dictator Manuel Noriega operation "just cause." During the Kuwaiti crisis the President discussed his own conversion experience and prayer life. Bush spent the evening before the land war began with the Rev. Billy Graham, who had since the 1950s served as the unofficial chaplain to U.S. presidents. As an Episcopalian who attended church regularly, Bush publicly sought to assure the people that his course was morally right. In his speeches, Bush personalized the struggle as between himself and an evil Hussein and insisted that right must prevail.[13] In spite of the prevalence of secular realpolitik among members of the military and foreign policy establishments in America, the President's conscious invocation of religious values and the ambivalent responses within the American religious communities resembled the divisions in the Muslim world among moderate political leaders, radicals, *ulema*, and the faithful.

The first area of disagreement between the President's defenders and critics was the relevance of history before August 1990.[14] The administration insisted that the debate should concentrate on the invasion, as an illustration of the dangers Hussein's regime posed to the region and to an emergent post-Cold War world order. Critics insisted that a longer perspective helped to understand the invasion. Iraq and Kuwait were arbitrary creations whose borders had been set to guarantee Western control of petroleum, and neither had a democratic government; so this

---

[13]Ibid., 282, 350-51.
[14]The essays in Part II and III of Phyllis Bennis and Michael Moushabeck, *Beyond the Storm: A Gulf Crisis Reader* (1991) represent the anti-war position.

was not a war to defend a democracy or constitutional rights. Rather, one arbitrary government had taken over another. Moreover, the U.S. had supported Iraq in its war with Iran, had continued to build up its military afterwards, and in a conversation with Hussein the American Ambassador had not provided sufficient warning. Hussein had been violating human rights for years, but the administration earlier had shown little concern. So Bush's bashing of Iraqi oppression of its people was hypocritical. In actuality, critics charged, the military power of Hussein was in a sense a U.S.-Soviet creation, an example of the ill effects of following realpolitik. Unfortunately for the critics, whatever the conclusions of this debate over past history, blaming the administration provided no guidance for American policies in the present crisis if the goals were to restore the status quo ante bellum or to give Kuwait a government more attuned to democratic values.

A second debate was about oil. The administration insisted that Iraqi control of 19% of the world's reserves of oil and positioning an army on the border of Saudi Arabia constituted a threat to the economic interests of the West. (The U.S. was in a recession and an increase in the price of oil would be economic disaster.) Under international law and Just War theory, a state could defend property, and it did not matter if the property belonged to oneself or an ally. So opposing Iraq could be defended as good business and good morality. The administration knew it could win the backing of businessmen and believers of realpolitik by discussing oil, but self-interest would not win allies abroad or mass support at home.

Critics wondered whether the U.S. should risk lives by going to war to defend cheap oil rather than adopt conservation policies. The U.S. imported relatively little oil from Kuwait and the nations most dependent, i.e., Japan and Germany, had not sent troops, although they did provide funds. Did the seizure of oil equal just cause, and was all the talk about the sanctity of borders and international law a mask to cover old imperialism?

The administration said that Iraq's invoking of Israel's occupation of Gaza and the West Bank was a red herring designed to divert attention from its actions in Kuwait. Critics agreed but insisted that a conference designed to settle the West Bank issues could also lead to Iraq's peaceful evacuation. The National Council of Churches saw in Iraqi proposals an opportunity to address many ills of the region. Hussein's regime was another example of the pathology of a region that desperately needed reform.

Israel kept a low profile during the fall of 1990, stayed out of the military coalition, and did not even respond militarily to Scud missile attacks during the war, but its restraint did not stop the Israeli assassination of a high-ranking Palestine Liberation Organization official in Tunis during the crisis.

Contrasting interpretations over past U.S. policies, colonialism, oil, and Israel showed that disagreements on whether to concentrate on the long or short-term causes of a conflict hindered Americans' reaching a consensus on what were allowable moral actions. The President focused on the immediate fault, the most recent Iraqi actions, while his critics attempted to broaden the debate to include America's past and present foreign policies. Success in postponing dealing with the long-term problems in the Middle East permitted the President to create an international military force and to mobilize a reluctant people for war, but events would show that the critics were right that a military victory freeing Kuwait from Iraq would cost many lives, not bring peace, and contribute little to a better life for poor Muslims.

V. The Debate: How to Achieve an Iraqi Withdrawal?

During the Iraqi crisis the U.S. rediscovered the United Nations. For years American governments had downplayed the significance of the UN as controlled by Third World Nations that too often sympathized with the Soviet Union or against the industrial powers. Now with Mikhail Gorbachev in power the Cold War was over and the Security Council need no longer be paralyzed by Great Power rivalries. So President Bush from the beginning of the crisis successfully sought to utilize the United Nations' resolutions to legitimate his actions and to persuade its members to endorse U.S. policies. Criticism of the U.S.'s reliance on the UN came from conservatives within the Republican Party, including many members of the Christian right, who had long been suspicious of international agencies and who now insisted that the goal of American policy should be to destroy Hussein's government. Even if Iraq withdrew its troops, the dictator would still be in power and a threat to the region. The UN might succeed in freeing Kuwait, but the Charter forbade interference in the internal affairs of a country. The administration countered that going alone would require the U.S. to risk fighting a major war thousands of miles from its homeland and risk anti-American revolutions in many Arab nations. Because the U.S. needed allies for both troops and money, using the UN was a necessity.[15]

Support for reliance upon a multinational agency came from church groups and individuals who had long wished to strengthen the UN and who hoped that an international organization could depersonalize the battle between Bush and Hussein and offer a face-saving way to end the crisis. After all, China, Russia, and France wanted a non-military solution, and any UN policy would need their consent. However the "doves" feared that a UN-sponsored U.S.-controlled war was just another war, not a method to solve grievances and achieve peace. The U.S. by manipulating the UN into authorizing and waging a war might weaken that body's peacemaking capabilities.

Kuwait added another chapter to the on-going policy debate between advocates of realpolitik and the idealists.[16] Either position was compatible with advocating sanctions only with war as either the last resort or unacceptable alternative. One's conclusions depended on estimating the cost of war in lives versus the benefits of removing a tyrant. The President's language echoed Wilsonian idealism in creating a "new world order" and realism in threatening

---

[15] The U.S. paid only one-third of the cost of the war. Saudi Arabia, the Emirates, Japan, and European allies paid the rest of the $60 billion cost.

force. Hussein was an evil dictator who understood only force and would withdraw only if he faced an ultimatum accompanied by overwhelming military threat. Deterrence was the way to peace. Idealists did not defend Hussein, but stressed his pragmatic or opportunistic past policies and concluded that threats were more likely to make Iraq's leader harden his position than to yield. Even if it was true that Hussein understood only power, the boycott and economic sanctions would eventually bring a change in Iraqi policy. Doves argued that Russia, France, Jordan or the Secretary General could broker an agreement that would save Kuwait without humiliating Iraq and that the U.S. should be flexible. Hawks countered that the Iraqi leader would see compromise as a sign of weakness and that the U.S. was reluctant to fight.

The constant arms build-up by November reached 150,000, an ample amount to protect Saudi Arabia. After the off year election in November, Bush announced that U.S. forces would be increased to 380,000 - a figure that commentators declared would, when added to Allied forces, allow an offensive capability. America's uncompromising stand coupled with an arms build up did not cause Hussein to yield; instead, it led to war. However, the contention is also true that there was no persuasive evidence that continuing the economic boycott or applying the techniques of nonviolent conflict resolution would work with Hussein.

At the heart of the debate over tactics between the President and his critics were contrasting conclusions about the moral acceptability of modern war. The President and Pentagon acted as if war, though a blunt instrument, should be employed as a tool of foreign policy to right a wrong. Modern war was not inherently immoral, at least as compared with the alternative, because a justified war would preserve the international order, a good. Critics countered that the increase in the destructiveness of weapons meant that the war could no longer meet the criteria of proportionality and immunity of civilians. Calculating the

---

[16] There were major divisions within these two camps, with some realists advocating relying on sanctions and some idealists saying American democratic values required military action.

costs of war before it was fought was a risky proposition, because wars were much easier to start than finish and history showed many incorrect estimates of short clean wars. The longer the war, the greater the cost, and the likelihood that the damage would outweigh the benefits. Vietnam showed how in modern war a country had been destroyed in order to save it. The same fate would befall Kuwait. Modern Just War theory had a bias towards peace and battle should only be a last resort.

In addition, critics argued, the history of modern war showed that civilians could not be protected, even if they were not directly targeted. Iraq had a powerful well-trained army of professional soldiers with sophisticated equipment, and had conscripted hundreds of thousands more. Its military had months to target artillery, lay land mines, string barbed wire, and dig motes that were then filled with oil and would be set on fire to slow down a frontal attack. So military casualties would be high. Even though the border area between Iraq and Saudi Arabia was uninhabited desert, fighting would place the civilian population of Kuwait in harm's way. Although the risk of nuclear weapons was remote, the Iraqi government had used poison gas on its own people and the Iranian army and was thought to have some capacity for germ warfare. The military analyst Edward Luttwack, a realist who applied Clausewitzean categories to war, insisted that the capacities of the Iraqi army meant that the war might last a long time and military casualties would be high. Many church leaders concluded that an invasion of Kuwait could not meet the Just War tests of proportionality and civilian immunity.

The Pentagon did not deny that the war might be costly. Instead, attempting to persuade Iraqi's leader to withdraw, Bush insisted that the U.S. had learned the lessons of Vietnam and declared that if war became necessary, the Allies would use overwhelming force. The strategy would seek to minimize Iraqi civilian and Allied military deaths by the use of superior technology and air power, but the army would do what was necessary to restore Kuwait.

The administration declared that the U.S. position fulfilled all Just War criteria: it had declared the fault, specified what conduct would avert fighting, and had submitted its evidence to an impartial international agency, the UN. "Last resort" did not mean postponing indefinitely, and Saddam Hussein had received sufficient time to withdraw. International law, public opinion, economic interest, a potent military, and moral certainty coincided on the same side.

At the same time, the U.S. continued the arms build-up in Saudi Arabia, sought a negotiated withdrawal without compromise on UN resolutions, and planned for a war. The churches prayed for peace while the generals, just in case, sought succor from the God of battles. Bush's constant refrain was that the U.S. did not want war, but that the final decision of peace or war rested not in his but in Hussein's hands.

VI. War and Its Aftermath

The Security Council in December authorized the use of "all necessary means" if there were no withdrawal by January 15, thereby giving Russia one last chance to negotiate within the limits of UN resolutions. Although the President insisted that he did not need formal authorization, a long debate in Congress resulted in narrow victories in both houses for resolutions authorizing "all necessary means." The Congress, like the UN Security Council, used euphemisms that did not endorse but did not rule out military means. Supporters of the President insisted that defeat would weaken his hand in dealing with Hussein. Last minute attempts at negotiations by the Secretary General, the Secretary of State, and the Russian foreign minister failed. In spite of massive pro-peace demonstrations in the U.S., Europe, and the Middle East, four days after Congress voted, the President gave the go ahead for an air war to free a country that in August few Americans would have been able to locate on a map.

The American strategy of massive nighttime air strikes was an immediate success in destroying Iraq's air force and showing the inadequacy of its air defenses. Rigorous control of journalists by the military meant that the public received only images selected to present the Allied air attack in a favorable light. The pictures showed that "smart" precision-guided bombs and missiles destroyed military targets while leaving civilians unscathed. However, later analysis showed that ninety percent of the bombs dropped were conventional; most of these were part of a sustained carpet-bombing of Iraqi conscripts at the front. Air attacks destroyed the Defense Ministry, airports, bridges, oil refineries, chemical factories, power and water purification plants, and suspected nuclear processing sites. After the war, on March 20 a UN report concluded "Iraq has, for some time to come, been relegated to a pre-industrial age, but with all the disabilities of post-industrial dependency on an intensive use of energy and technology."[17]

The intensity of the bombing attack brought massive demonstrations in the Arab world, Europe, and the U.S. and complaints from Russia. No one knew the numbers of civilian causalities, though it was clear that the Allies did not target them. Former Attorney General Ramsay Clark, an administration critic who visited Iraq during the bombings, saw widespread destruction of civilian facilities. Iraq claimed 7000 civilian casualties; a figure the Pentagon denied. In what was widely seen as an attempt to kill Hussein, a missile hit a theater whose basement had been hardened into a shelter where he was thought to have gone, but which was filled with civilians. There were 300 bodies, including 91 children. The U.S. refused to apologize.[18]

In the midst of the bombing, the Russians engaged in a last effort to avoid a ground war. On February 15 Iraq announced that it would accept the UN resolution calling for unconditional withdrawal and promised that it would evacuate Kuwait City in four days and all of Kuwait in twenty-one, leaving all equipment behind. The American ground offensive, scheduled to begin on Feb. 21 was moved back two days. When presented with the plan, Bush denounced it as a "cruel hoax" and called for the Iraqi people to overthrow Hussein. Gorbachev asked for more time, but the invasion began on February 23.

---

[17]Bennis, 70.
[18]*Record of World Events, 1991*, 379-84.

An Allied flanking attack cut off Iraqi troops in Kuwait and the border and led to a complete victory in four days. Immediate post-war estimates of Iraqi military casualties vary greatly; from 35,000 killed with 100,000 wounded, with other estimates from 200,000 to 700,000. Recent estimates are lower, listing the number of war casualties to 10,100. Actually, a range this great shows that no one really knows and that the Iraqi government wanted to conceal the outcome of its leader's disastrous policy. American and Allied deaths were 231, many killed by friendly fire or an Iraqi Scud missile attack on a base well behind the front lines in Saudi Arabia. Americans at the time boasted of the successes of Patriot missiles in destroying Scuds sent against Israel, a claim that was later shown to be false.

For most Americans, whose memories had been shaped by television images from Vietnam, this war was an exhilarating experience, a victory with few body bags, a restoration of Kuwait to freedom, and creation of what President Bush called a "new world order." There were few regrets about attacking Hussein. It was hard to show any sympathy for a leader who had unleashed Scud missile attacks on Israel, released a massive oil flow into the Gulf, set fire to oil wells, and boasted about using germ warfare. His butchery in putting down revolts by the Kurds and Shi'a within Iraq after the armistice made Americans wonder if the war had ended too soon and the terms for the truce had been too lenient. Later analysis proved that Iraq had kept its best and most loyal troops, the Republican Guard, far from the front. Saddam Hussein, more interested in preserving his regime than in defending Kuwait, had sacrificed the conscripts on the front lines.[19] The Guard remained intact and able to quell domestic insurrection.

VII. The Interim

Initially, images of victory overwhelmed any popular misgivings about the causes or conduct of war. President Bush, acclaimed as a great war leader, enjoyed a 90% approval rating, and General Norman Schwarzkopf and the soldiers returned to enormous "welcome home" parades. The celebrations merged

---

[19] Charles Tripp, *A History of Iraq* (2000), 254-55.

patriotism and religious fervor, showing a continuing vitality of American civil religion. The President proclaimed that America's Vietnam syndrome was over.

America won the war and gained strategic advantage. The world was awash in cheap oil; Kuwait and Saudi Arabia continued to allow American troops on their soil; a weakened Iraq could not export war to its neighbors but remained as a counterweight to Iran. Kuwait did not become more democratic. However, the war did not strengthen the United Nations; and the U.S. to show its displeasure remained more than $1 billion behind in its dues until 1999. There was no new world order and the U.S.'s military dominance remained.

In actuality America's war with Iraq did not end, but only changed form after 1991. The U.S. belief that the Iraqi dictator could not survive defeat and rebellion proved wrong. President Bush had called for rebellion, but then did nothing while Hussein's regime suppressed uprisings by the Shi'a in the south and the Kurds in the north; estimates of the number of casualties are as high as 100,000 – more than were killed in the war. In response the U.S. created no-fly zones in north and south and an area near Turkey controlled by the Kurds. A sort of cat-and-mouse game emerged with the Iraqis targeting on radar and often shooting at British and American airplanes patrolling the no-fly zones, with the two allies in response bombing Iraqi guns, missile sites, and radar installations. Over a ten-year period the allies dropped thousands of bombs on military installations (an average of two missions a week) and lost no airplanes, but Iraq gained respect among many Arabs for defying the United States.

As a price for ending hostilities in 1991, the United Nations Security Council required Iraq to agree to dismantle long range missiles and all weapons of mass destruction (chemical, biological, and nuclear) and admit inspection teams. The inspectors found that Iraq had created substantial stockpiles of the first two and was close to making an atomic bomb. They destroyed the facilities needed to build nuclear weapons as well as many chemical and biological weapons, but never claimed to have discovered all stockpiles.

The UN insisted that until Iraq accounted for all its weapons of mass destruction, economic sanctions would stay in place. The UN allowed Iraq to sell limited amounts of oil, with the proceeds being used to purchase food and medicine. Outside humanitarian groups documented widespread malnutrition, particularly among children, because of the sanctions. Estimates of casualties from sanctions imposed in the aftermath of war were in the hundreds of thousands. The first two UN commissioners in charge of the food for oil program resigned in protest, charging that the food and medical supplies were so inadequate that the policy, insisted on by the U.S. and UK, was destroying a generation of children. Church groups and humanitarian observers criticized the sanctions as hurting the civilian population more than the Iraqi leaders.[20] The military clique controlling Iraq profited from smuggling from Jordan, Turkey, and Syria while the people suffered.

After widespread international criticism, in 2002 the UN dropped sanctions on all but militarily useful goods. The Security Council's intrusion into Iraq sovereignty by creating a Kurdish zone, requiring disarmament of offensive weapons, and restricting the amount of oil sold with the UN guaranteeing that the proceeds be used only to purchase food and medicine, was unprecedented. The closest analogy was the Allied occupation of Japan and Germany after World War II, but – unlike them – the Iraqi dictator stayed in power and did all he could to undermine the UN policies. In 1998, Hussein's policy of non-cooperation and the resulting U.S. bombing ended in the withdrawing of all UN inspectors.

---

[20] Anthony Arnove, *Iraq Under Siege: The Deadly Impact of Sanctions and War* (2000); Geoff Simons, *Imposing Economic Sanctions: Legal Remedy or Genocidal Tool* (1999), 169-80. A postwar evaluation concluded that the sanctions weakened Iraq's ability to rearm but strengthened the control of Saddam Hussein over the people. There was adequate food but a general deterioration in living and health standards with the Iraqi people as the real victims of the sanctions. If, as UNICEF claimed, the sanctions resulted in 500,000 deaths, they caused more deaths than the regime's secret police. The general deterioration of the infrastructure was a result of the sanctions. David Rieff, "Were Sanctions Right?" *New York Times Magazine* (July 27, 2003), 41-46.

VIII. Gulf War II

U.S. policy toward Iraq changed after September 11, 2001 following President George W. Bush's (a son of the former President Bush) declaration that any state supporting or giving sanctuary to terrorists could expect military intervention.[21] Critics pointed out that there was no evidence linking Hussein to Al Qaeda, but the administration's frequent linkage of Iraq with terrorists meant that by January 2003 a majority of Americans believed that Iraq had some responsibility for the destruction of the World Trade Towers. Since 1991 conservatives who were now major leaders, including the Secretary of Defense and the Vice President, had advocated using force to overthrow Hussein's government. Even before the defeat of the Taliban, the U.S. began a build-up of military forces in the Emirates. In his State of the Union Address in January 2002 the President denounced Iraq as an "axis of evil" (the religious terminology was consciously adopted) which sought nuclear weapons, but the administration sent mixed signals as to whether it would be satisfied by the destruction of weapons of mass destruction or also required regime change. Under the threat of unilateral U.S. invasion and a unanimous Security Council Resolution, in August 2002 UN inspections resumed. Iraqis reluctantly acquiesced, but the inspectors found no such weapons.

The international debate on the necessity of a second invasion of Iraq showed the isolation of Britain and America. Unlike in 1991, now France, Germany, and Russia opposed military invention, arguing that UN inspections were working. Saudi Arabia, Jordan, Turkey, Egypt, and Syria opposed a new war, and public opinion in the Arab world and in Western Europe was overwhelmingly against. Even after intense American pressure, an offer of a $36 billion aid package, and support from the Turkish government, Turkey's parliament refused to allow American troops to use its land to stage an attack on northern Iraq. In Europe even among U.S. allies in Britain, Spain, and Italy official

---

[21] George W. Bush, "State of the Union Address," Jan. 29, 2002, *Facts on File* (2002), 43. U. S. Congress Joint Resolution, Sept. 14, 2001, *Facts on File* (2001), 705.

support of a war encountered strong opposition from the people. The heads of the UN inspection teams in early 2003 reported that they had found no weapons of mass destruction and asked for more time. The U.S. failed in its attempt to gain a resolution authorizing force from the UN Security Council.

Christian religious leaders spoke out against going to war. The Archbishop of Canterbury, the Pope and the American Catholic bishops, leaders of the National Council of Churches and many so-called mainline denominations (Methodists, Presbyterians, Episcopalians) opposed any war that did not have UN authorization. Support for a war came from conservative evangelicals, some Pentecostals, the Southern Baptist Convention, and those Protestants strongly supportive of Israel. Major Jewish organizations remained divided. Until the battle began, a majority of the American people supported war only with the authorization of the UN.[22] Conservative American Catholics, who normally supported the president, now debated the limits of church authority. A Pew poll on the influence of religion on attitudes to the war showed that members of American churches were more likely than non-members to approve of going to war without UN sanction. Americans seemed to feel that the church was a guide on personal morality but not foreign policy.[23] (Another Pew poll showed that 65% of Americans believed religion was a major factor in causing the war, even though they thought more religious commitment a good thing.[24])

---

[22]The Lehrer Report, *News Hour*, March 3, 2003 found 33% in favor of war, 24% in favor with UN or allies support, 31% opposed. Poll showed the effect of the administration's public relations campaign as it became clear that the UN would not endorse a second resolution authorizing force, but the U.S. would attack soon.

[23]Elisabeth Bumiller, "Religious Leaders Ask if Antiwar Call is Heard," *New York Times*, March 10, 2003, A 16; Laurie Goodstein, "Catholics Debating: Back President or Pope," *New York Times*, March 6, 2003, p. 1, 12; Pew Survey, "Americans Struggle with Religious Role at Home and Abroad." March, 2003; "Religion and Politics: Ambivalent Majority," Sept. 20, 2000 found 64% believed clergy should not discuss politics from the pulpit; 45% said the church should not take political stands, but 70% wanted the president to have a strong religious commitment. Pew Forum on Religion and Public Life, website http://pewforum.org/surveys.

[24]A Pew Survey found that 57% of clergymen spoke on war, but only 21% took a position pro or con. One-third said religion had some influence on their positions, 10% said it was a strong influence – about the same influence as political connection but less than family or friends. Pew Survey "Americans Hearing about Iraq from the Pulpit but Religious Faith Not Defining Opinions." March 13-16, 2003, Pew Forum on Religion and Public Life.

Both sides invoked the norms of Just War theory. According to the hawks, Hussein was a tyrant whose cruelty to his own people and threats to his neighbors made his overthrow moral. The UN was not a sovereign government; so its lack of authorization meant little. Above all, the administration insisted that 9/11 changed the rules of international order and allowed a pre-emptive war. Hussein sought and possessed weapons of mass destruction and would allow terrorists to use them against America. No longer could America wait until after it was attacked. The President used the language of Wilsonian idealism, the U.S. wanted to create a democratic Iraq in Operation Iraqi Freedom, and realpolitik, this dictator could not be coerced by deterrence and it was only a matter of short time until he obtained nuclear weapons. The President in the State of the Union Address and the Secretary of State before the UN Security Council asserted that Iraq already had vast quantities of weapons of mass destruction.[25] Iraq remained a threat to the peace of the region and the U.S. with or without UN sanction would bring regime change.

Like the President, doves mingled the languages of Just War theory and realpolitik.[26] Opponents of the war agreed that Hussein was a tyrant, but insisted that neither the UN nor international law allowed a pre-emptive war. If America could begin a pre-emptive war, so could India or Pakistan or Russia. Just war theory did not allow preventive war unless there was overwhelming evidence of possession of weapons of mass destruction and clear intent to use them. The fact that the UN inspectors found no such weapons and that inspections continued meant that there was no last resort.

In addition, there were worse tyrants, and North Korea with a nuclear weapons program, guided missile delivery system, a large army, and an erratic dictator constituted more of a threat to the peace than a weakened Iraq. If

---

[25]"Several mobile labs, 30,000 munitions, 25,000 liters of anthrax and 38,000 liters of botulism toxin, and eighteen mobile laboratories to produce chemical and biological weapons." These were already deployed in weapons and ready for use. *New York Times*, April 22, 2003, A 29.

America began ousting cruel dictators, it would be engaged in an endless series of wars. If Iraq were such a threat to its neighbors, why were all the surrounding Arab nations opposed to a war? Rather than ending terrorism, a war would more likely increase it. America's recent experiences in nation building in Haiti and Afghanistan did not lead to confidence that it would be willing to make the sacrifices needed to rebuild Iraq, particularly considering the growing deficit. The real enemy was Al Qaeda and militant Islamic fundamentalism, and even bin Laden disapproved of Hussein. 9/11 terrorism was a pretext and not a sufficient reason for this war; the underlying cause was oil.

Neither hawk nor doves doubted that American could win this war; the issue was the wisdom. Would the war end or facilitate terrorism? Would American and British troops encounter biological and chemical weapons? Would house to house fighting in Basra and Baghdad end with many casualties? Could the U.S. after a war impose or facilitate the emergence of a democratic government in an ethnically and religiously divided country? Would defeating Iraq help bring peace to the region and facilitate settling of the Israeli-Palestinian conflict?

The President with a small group of advisers and with the tepid consent of Congress made a decision for war. The strongest ally was Tony Blair, Prime Minister of Britain. Some commentators suggested that the religious faith of both men and their determination to destroy what they saw as an evil regime was a major factor. Once the war began, Bush and Blair received massive public backing by the people, who rallied to support the troops.

The war demonstrated overwhelming American military supremacy in a conventional war. With complete air control and the ability to pinpoint enemy troop movements, the U.S. used precision bombing and missiles to devastate the Republican Guard, followed-up by mobile ground forces that within twenty-one

---

[26]For example, "Iraq and Just War: a Symposium," September 30, 2002, Pew Forum on Religion and Public Life; *New York Times Magazine*, April, 2003. *Nightline* television broadcast, February 28, 2003.

days subdued the entire country.[27] America's "shock and awe" strategy in "Operation Iraqi Freedom" used intensive firepower with a small army. While this proved sufficient to win the battles, the limited number of troops proved inadequate to prevent widespread looting in the aftermath. The number of British dead was thirty-three, and American dead 131 at war's end, but a greater number died in later guerrilla attacks and ambushes. The Associated Press listed 3,500 civilians killed and there are no reliable figures for Iraqi military dead. Iraq used neither biological nor chemical weapons and, except in Basra, did little house-to-house fighting in cities. In fact, the dictator proved to have no real operational strategy to counter American mobility and firepower.[28] The failure to find Saddam Hussein for six months, terrorist violence against UN and Red Cross personnel, and general insecurity made creating a stable government very difficult.

The relative ease of victory did not end the deep animosity for America by the Iraqis or most other Arabs, who saw the war as against Islam and for oil and Israel. They were glad to see Hussein ousted but wanted American troops to go home. Shiite clergy denounced America as an imperialist power and advocated creating a democratic Muslim government. In spite of intensive efforts, the American military uncovered no preparations to build nuclear weapons and no chemical or biological weapons. The rationale for the war now became regime change of an evil dictator and the news media focused on mass graves, most of which dated from 1991.

Gulf War II demonstrated that America's military might is unsurpassed and the nation has the ability to fight a conventional war with precision weapons that cause few civilian deaths and minimal destruction of the infrastructure. Even in Canada, polls showed distrust of America as a threat to peace and a vigorous worldwide peace movement favored military action only after UN approval. Political scientists discussed whether the recent history of the European Economic

---

[27]Unlike Gulf War I where 9% of weapons were "smart," 70% of the bombs used were "guided" and there appeared to have been relatively little collateral damage by missiles missing targets.
[28] Associated Press Report, June 12, 2003.

Community has created a divide between Americans and Europeans over the importance of international cooperation and a distrust of military power.[29] Formerly state subservient churches in Europe demonstrated that they were now free and prepared to speak for peace, whatever the position of the government. Yet in America the clear moral pronouncements on war by religious leaders had little influence on the faithful or those who made the decision for war.

Both Iraqi wars were traditional, with large armies, bombing, few attacks on civilians, and the use of overwhelming force by the victors. The disparity in casualties suggests that few nations without nuclear weapons will be willing to fight the United States in a traditional manner, and this may hasten North Korea and Iran's quest for atomic bombs. Moreover, events in the 1990s detailed in the next chapter suggest that future conflicts will involve terrorism, ethnic/religious differences, and failed states, and in these America's high tech warfare will be of limited use. The overwhelming victory coupled with few Allied casualties makes the Gulf Wars resemble nineteenth-century colonial wars rather than future wars. America is now engaged in creating a democratic government in a country whose population remains suspicious of U.S. motives. Future events in Iraq will determine whether, as Clausewitz recognized 150 years ago, at the moment of victory war becomes an asset declining in value.

---

[29] Robert Kaplan, *Of Paradise and Power: America and Europe and the New World Order* (2003)

XXII.
The Post Cold War World: Religious-Ethnic Wars

The end of the Cold War diminished many conflicts caused by super power meddling, but there were also escalations of old disputes and the creation of new wars. So long as the super power confrontation risked nuclear wars, the disputes of minor powers seemed manageable. Now that restraint was gone, and statesmen had to create new foreign policies for dealing with a world that seemed more chaotic.

This chapter begins by describing the kinds of wars that occurred after 1990, then looks at two interpretations for the roles of religion in causing these conflicts: the rise of fundamentalisms or the clash of civilization. Brief summaries of the important conflicts will illustrate the religious dimensions of modern wars. The second half of the chapter focuses upon peacemaking in the nineties, first, by governments and the UN and, then, by religious groups. Peace groups sought to use perspectives of Liberation Theology and nonviolent conflict resolution in seeking to reduce violence.

I. New Kinds of War

Perspectives gained from the first Gulf battles seemed of little help for those seeking an ethical response to the violence in the 1990s, because traditional ideals of justified war and pacifism seemed so difficult to apply to new kinds of conflict. Few of the wars directly involved the international security of the Great Powers, but all created mass sufferings, refugees, and the need for humanitarian assistance. With so many troubled areas in the world, the United States and NATO - which for the first time in fifty years did not have to consider Cold War implications and had the capability of intervening in many areas - needed to rethink the moral and strategic criteria for participating in unilateral or multilateral peacekeeping operations.

Statesmen found clear guidelines neither in Just War theories, pacifism, nor realpolitik.[1] Just War theory as well as international law assumed the permanence of a sovereign state that enjoys a monopoly on armed force to preserve the internal and external security of its people. Yet in Somalia, Congo, Liberia, Afghanistan, and Sierra Leone, the state essentially disintegrated, and national groups applying an ideal of self-determination in the Balkans killed each other with reckless abandon while practicing ethnic cleansing.

In the past, pacifists generally supported UN peacekeeping operations as humanitarian actions. Now, however, the UN, after the failure of lightly armed peacekeeping forces in Somalia and Bosnia, sent heavily armed U.S. and NATO troops who made threats and used force.[2] Pacifists had to decide if, when humanitarian relief and nonviolent protests did not restore order, it was morally acceptable to rely upon an international army of peacekeepers. Should they support using a multinational military force to prevent ethnic cleansing?

Realpolitik also offered little guidance for politicians. Large-scale military establishments with high-tech weapons proved to be of limited usefulness in civil wars, and neither generals nor the public wished to risk soldiers' lives when there were no exit strategies or clearly defined objectives. Military power could not ease the dangers of nuclear proliferation, as exemplified by Pakistan's and India's testing of nuclear weapons, or the risk of a terrorist group's obtaining the materials for an atomic bomb or biological warfare. Neither the U.S., South Korea, nor Japan wished to use military force against a North Korea dictator who possessed medium-range ballistic missiles and claimed to have atomic bombs.

---

[1]An excellent summary and critique of perspectives is in George Weigel and John Langan, eds., *The American Search for Peace: Moral Reasoning, Religious Hope, and National Security* (1991). John Howard Yoder, *Nevertheless: Varieties of Religious Pacifism* (1992), summarizes pacifist alternatives.
[2]Dennis Jett, *Why Peacekeeping Fails* (1999); William Shawcross, *Deliver Us from Evil: Peacekeepers, Warlords and a World of Endless Conflict* (2000), and David Rieff, *A Bed for the Night: Humanitarianism in Crisis* (2002), are more persuasive because based on first-hand experiences.

In Kosovo, NATO relied upon air power and so-called smart weapons to defeat the Serbian military without unduly risking American pilots' lives or employing ground troops. Intervention occurred only after enormous publicity over Serbian atrocities, a prolonged debate within the UN and NATO, and the failure of negotiations. The initial bombing was a result of Serbia's intensified ethnic cleansing of Albanians. Eventual victory came only after prolonged bombing in Kosovo and Serbia and substantial destruction of the Serbian infrastructure (bridges, power stations), but winning brought no peace. Kosovo now seems destined to require a prolonged UN military presence. Tensions between ethnic groups continue unabated, with the Albanians who were the oppressed majority (over 90%) now persecuting the Serbian minority, and the final status of Kosovo, Macedonia, and Serbia remains ill-defined.

Post-1990 wars did not involve mobilizations of large armies; most were low-tech affairs involving irregular forces armed with rifles. The markets were flooded with army-surplus guns from the former Soviet Union and Eastern Europe that were easy to use and light enough to be carried by children.[3] The Soviet Union in Chechnya, the Serbs in Bosnia, the Taliban in Afghanistan, and the Somali warlords used army equipment left over from the Cold War. With major producers of military weapons facing the prospects of downsizing weapons factories, an intense competition in arms sales emerged with most sales going to nations with undemocratic regimes in unstable regions. America retained its ranking as the dominant maker and exporter of weapons, doing 44% of the business.[4] None of the 1990s wars ended because of a shortage of guns and ammunition.

Except for Iraq - Kuwait there were few clear acts of aggression of one established state against another. Instead, most of these endemic low-scale wars stayed within the boundaries that had once been an empire or state. Some conflicts came from attempts to create new states within the former borders of the

---

[3] The United Nations estimated there were 30,000 children soldiers in 1998.

734

USSR or Yugoslavia and involved friction between newly independent nations; dissidents strove to create a religious revolution in Algeria and Afghanistan. Drug lords and former Marxist guerrillas battled against governments in Peru and Colombia. Neighboring nations overthrew a corrupt dictator and then continued to intervene in the Congo, sparking a war that caused an estimated three million deaths. Poverty, political neglect, and corruption fueled disturbances in Chiapas, Mexico.

For thirty years, the inhabitants of East Timor resisted their forced annexation into Indonesia. Religious and ethnic differences fueled animosity, because the population of East Timor was mostly Roman Catholic and Portuguese-speaking, and Indonesia is 90% Muslim. After a financial collapse brought a revolution against Indonesia's dictator-president Suharto, the new government reluctantly allowed a referendum on independence in East Timor. When the vote went against Indonesia, the military and militia groups went on a destructive rampage brought to a halt only after United Nations' intervention. Elsewhere in the islands of Indonesia, particularly in Aceh, Muslims and Christians who had formerly lived in peace now rioted against each other.

Ethnic/religious issues convulsed Sudan, Northern Ireland, Sri Lanka, Chechnya, Azerbaijan, and Rwanda. Rwanda proved that even a machete could be an effective weapon for genocide, as the Hutu majority massacred 500,000 Tutsi, a group that during colonialism had become the ruling class. Though 80% of Rwandans claimed to be Christians, even churches did not serve as sanctuary.[5] The Western powers, stung by the results in their intervention in Somalia, did little and even denied that genocide was occurring.[6] In addition, long-standing

---

[4]*New York Times,* "News of Week in Review," 9 Aug. 1998, Section 4, p. 2.
[5]Figures of the number of dead in Rwanda range from a few hundred thousand to 800,000. The War Crimes Tribunal indicted three Roman Catholic priests, an Anglican bishop, and a Seventh Day Adventist pastor. One estimate is that 100 priests, pastors, and nuns actively sided with the Hutu militias; nearly 300 clergyman and nuns were slain. *New York Times,* 11 May, 2003, p.11. Alan Ruperman, "Rwanda Retrospect," *Foreign Affairs,* 78 (Jan.Feb. 2000), 94-118, argues that stationing troops as a preventive measure might have stopped the massacres, but logistical issues meant that intervention after the killing started would have been too late.
[6]Samantha Power, *"A Problem from Hell": America and the Age of Genocide* (2002), 329-90.

border disputes involving rival claims to land continued and resulted in violence often approaching war in Israel-Palestine and India-Pakistan.

All of these conflicts exemplified a common post-World War I development: it was more dangerous to be a civilian than a soldier in uniform, because most of the dead were non-combatants. Guerrilla warfare, state repression, terrorist actions, irregular forces sometimes operating in concert with, but more often in opposition to, the regular army, waged undeclared and sometimes unorganized wars with great ferocity. The UN Charter and international law, which forbade intervention in the internal affairs of a state, outlawed aggressive war, and created two distinct conditions, defined as war and as peace, seemed designed for a past epoch. Outsiders witnessing the sufferings of civilians found many villains, but often there was no definitive good party, and joining with one side against another seemed unlikely to bring a truce, let alone long-term harmony.

II. Religion as a Cause of War

Religion was often a factor and occasionally a primary cause in the conflicts of the 1990s, many of which seemed likely to continue for decades. Leaders seeking legitimacy accentuated religious differences to create boundaries between peoples and used the faith of the majority or minority - Buddhism, Christianity, Hinduism, Islam, and Judaism - to justify violence. Not since 1648 had animosity among different sects of the same faith and between adherents of the great religions of the world seemed so worldwide a phenomenon. Scholars began to wonder whether, while they and their governments had remained transfixed by the dangers of the Cold War, religious animosity had been present as a perennial factor.

The Fundamentalism Project, sponsored by the American Academy of Arts and Sciences and the MacArthur Foundation, involved two hundred scholars in five conferences between 1988-1993 and resulted in many publications.[7] Fundamentalism served as a concept to analyze comparatively conservative religious movements in seven religions, even though social and political conditions and distinct traditions influenced the tactics and goals of each movement. Some scholars dislike using the word fundamentalism because it can be seen as derogatory, too American-centered, and simplistic, but there are also weaknesses in alternative descriptions such as ethno-religious nationalism or liberation movements. Whatever name is used, an essential feature of the new fundamentalists is to take ancient symbols and selectively reinterpret them, so that their emphases distort the main teachings of the religion. The result is a new form of religion in which neither novelty nor social and cultural influences are acknowledged.

Our focus is those fundamentalist groups that advocate war and violence. The leaders of some of these movements work through the political system and seek elective office; others disdain politics but work for revolution by terrorist actions. There are also splinter groups, and often religion is combined with ethnicity, as in Afghanistan where, after having toppled the Soviet-backed government, Muslim fundamentalists attacked each other. In general the fundamentalists reject secularism as the basis for government and call for a return to a mythic religious past free from Western materialism, individualism, and democracy. They attack the nation-state and the international system as products of imperialism. Yet their blueprints for a future society are hazy, except that it will be patriarchal.[8]

---

[7]Martin Marty and R. Scott Appleby, eds., *Fundamentalisms Observed* (1991), *Fundamentalisms Comprehended* (1995), *Fundamentalism and the Society* (1993); *Fundamentalisms and the State* (1993), *Accounting for Fundamentalisms: The Dynamic Character of Movements* (1994).
[8]Fundamentalism is "a specifiable pattern of religious militancy by which self-styled believers attempt to arrest the erosion of religious identity, fortify the borders of the religious community, and create viable alternatives to secular structures and processes." R. Scott Appleby, *The Ambivalence of the Sacred: Religion, Violence, and Reconciliation* (2000), 86. Note that fundamentalists can but need not promote violence, and most are peaceful. They claim to know the essence of the religion and reduce the power of "outsiders" who can be secularists, proponents of other faiths, or misguided people in their own faith. Religious violence can come from groups that are not fundamentalists, such as the Irish Republican Army.

Fundamentalists who become terrorists see themselves as warriors caught up in a cosmic war between good and evil. Religion legitimates their violence because their opponents are evil, even subhuman. A terrorist is a soldier for God whose actions receive a blessing from clergy that conveys a kind of sacramental sanction. Because there are no innocent bystanders, religious terrorists tend to kill more people than political terrorists, who consider the impact on public opinion of murdering civilians. There is no guilt for the religious terrorist; instead he or she can become a martyr sacrificing his or her life and others' lives for a holy cause.[9] The goal is to attract attention to a cause, to kill as many as possible, and even to become martyrs. There is a radical disjunction between their actions and any desired political reform. Terrorists wish to inform the world that "we are here" and that anyone is at any time susceptible to violence. Sometimes, as in the two bombings of the New York Trade Center, those responsible do not claim credit - which makes terrorism as a political tactic even more irrelevant.

Fundamentalist movements threaten many governments, but no modern terrorist group has ever led a successful revolution; the Jewish terrorist attacks on the British after World War II, the inclusion of the Sinn Fein in the government of Northern Ireland, and the role of the Palestine Liberation Organization (which unlike Hamas is secular) on the West Bank would be the closest.[10] And these came to power only after renouncing terrorism and now are participating in the international system.

Scholars disagree on the extent of the threat that fundamentalist movements pose for the world order. Some stress that religion became a weapon because of a repressive social system and see the nation/state system as a weak graft onto tribal societies that have never accepted religious toleration, human

---

[9]Bruce Hoffman, *Inside Terrorism* (1998), 91-100. Of the fifty-six international terrorist groups in 1995, twenty-six were religious - examples include Christian White Supremacists (U.S.), Gush Emunim (Jewish), Hamas (Palestinian), and Aum Shinrikyo (Japanese).

[10]The distinction between a terrorist, a guerrilla warrior, and a freedom fighter is often debated. Often the latter two use terror as a weapon in their battles, but of course so do regular armies. Attacks upon civilians (i.e., those serving no direct military function) should be called terrorism, no matter what the justification.

rights, and democracy. They see fundamentalism as a defensive movement against the globalization of Western culture with destruction of traditional societies. Others worry that if the fundamentalists do succeed in undermining existing governments, the terrorist tactics of the minority movements may become widespread.[11] In the aftermath of 9/11 several American conservatives have pictured Islam as a new form of totalitarianism in battle against the West, a new Cold War. Most scholars agree that there are countervailing teachings in all religious traditions and see those espousing violence as a small minority. They stress that many find spiritual solace rather than political power in the fundamentalist religious movements.

A second explanation for religious violence can be summarized with the Hollywood-sounding name "when civilizations collide." Professor Samuel Huntington of Harvard wrote an influential article, later made into a book, in which he saw the past, present, and future fault lines as the places where distinct civilizations that had been shaped by religion had violent encounters: Poland-Russia, the Balkans, Turkey-Greece, the Middle East, the Sudan, and the borders of India-Pakistan. Huntington's thesis was that not just geopolitics but deep animosities between religious cultures caused war. He argued that the influence of the West - in political ideology, capitalism, individualism, pop culture, and Christianity - by undermining traditional society attracted and also repelled much of the world. As global interactions increased among peoples of different faiths, one could anticipate more rather than fewer conflicts.

Huntington saw religions as a cultural artifice and a boundary-setting phenomenon and ignored differences among religions, seeing them as functionally

---

[11]For different perspectives on Muslim fundamentalists, see Tibi Bassam, *The Challenge of Fundamentalism: Political Islam and the New World Disorder* (1998), John Esposito, *The Islamic Threat: Myth or Reality* (1992), and Bruce Lawrence, *Shattering the Myth: Islam beyond Violence* (1998); on Jewish fundamentalists, see Marc Ellis, *Unholy Alliance: Religion and Atrocity in Our Time* (1997); post 9/11 books include Daniel Pipes, *Militant Islam Reaches America* (2002) and Paul Berman, *Terror and Liberalism* (2003); a perceptive review arguing that many recent authors' views of Islam and violence are simplistic is Clifford Geertz, "Islam" and "Which Way to Mecca?" *New York Review of Books* (June 12, 2003), 27-39 (July 3, 2003), 36-39.

equivalent. He provided no analysis of how religions caused violence or shaped civilizations, but emphasized the continuing power of religion as almost a *deus ex machina* to shape behavior: "What ultimately counts for people is not political ideology or economic interest. Faith and family, blood and belief, are what people identify with and what they will fight and die for."[12]

Scholars criticized Huntington's thesis, complaining about vagueness in his concept of civilization, lack of stress on economics and geopolitics, and premature de-emphasis on the state. Equally controversial but less discussed is his understanding of modern religions. For example, in most areas where different faiths intersect, peoples live in peace. For example, Protestants and Catholics fight in Northern Ireland but nowhere else. The Irish Republican Army has for years been officially condemned by the Catholic Church. The Church of England, and Church of Scotland (Presbyterian) oppose the religious intolerance preached by Rev. Ian Paisley and the terrorism associated with Protestant extremists in the Ulster Defense Force. The violence in nations like Afghanistan and terrorism in Algeria and Egypt is Muslim against Muslim. In areas far from the fault line from Indonesia through Southern Eurasia and the Middle East and Maghreb, Islam is used by dissidents as a rallying cry against Muslim-dominated repressive governments that have not brought prosperity and provide no vehicle to redress grievances.

The thirty-year civil war in the Sudan is the best illustration of the Huntington thesis. Sudan, a state whose borders were created by Great Britain with no regard for ethnic unity, is a country approximately 60% Muslim Arab, most living in the northern area, with the 40% living in the South, who are black, divided between 15% Christian and the rest affirming traditional African religions. The best lands and a recently discovered oil field are in the South, but there are more educated people in the North. After independence, the Arab majority in the

---

[12]Samuel Huntington et al, "The Clash of Civilizations? The Debate," *Foreign Affairs* (1993, *Reader* 1996), 67.

North tried gradually through democratic means in the legislature to expand *shari'a* law into the South and to create an Islamic state. After a coup by Islamic army officers ended the power of the Assembly, the military leaders have sought to create a unitary state and to force Islamization of the society. The increasingly heavy-handed actions of the Muslim government in Khartoum generated a civil war in which neither side has been able to prevail. Up to one million people may have died from famine, atrocities, and fighting. At issue is not only whether Arab and African can join in a federated democratic state but also if they can agree upon religious toleration and separation of mosque from state.

The civil war that seems to be evolving into a war of the South for independence is not only Muslim against Christian but a struggle over ethnic factionalism within the South and in the North a debate within the Muslim community as to whether the intolerant Sunni strand of Islam sponsored by the military will lead to suppression of Sufi Muslim brotherhoods. Outside aid from Iran and Saudi Arabia to the North and from neighboring African nations and perhaps the CIA to the South has intensified the war.[13] What at first glance appeared to confirm Huntington's hypothesis on closer examination appears much more complex than simply a war between the worlds of Islam and sub-Saharan Africa.

The Balkans

Even where participants proclaim the primacy of differences in faith, assessing religious influence is difficult. For example, journalists commonly distinguish among Croatians, Serbians, and Muslims in the former Yugoslavia. Two of these are ethnic categories and the third is religious, and all are oversimplified.[14] All Croatians are not Catholic, all Serbians are not Orthodox, and many supporters of an independent Bosnia are not Muslims. The leaders of Croatians and Serbians were ex-communist *apparatchiks*, and before the civil war,

[13] Ann Lesh, *The Sudan: Contested National Identities* (1998).
[14] *War in the Balkans: A Foreign Affairs Reader* (1999) is a good way to read about the unfolding crisis.

present divisions. With provincial governments exerting control of the mass media, politicians created a mythic history of past glories of each community and of oppressions by neighbors. Religious spokesmen, who for years lived in a state hostile to organized religion, now sought to expand their influence. Soon religion became a shorthand marker of ethnic identity.

The traumatic and tragic history of Yugoslavia in the twentieth century - intense sufferings in World Wars I and II, foreign rule, civil war, dictatorships of the right and left - meant that churches and mosques were the only semi-independent institutions that survived. In the absence of alternative institutions, mosques and Roman Catholic and Orthodox churches came to symbolize history and self-identity. So when anarchy threatened after the death of Tito, the communist dictator from 1945-1980, the people utilized religious institutions as a means of preservation.[15]

Acts of terrorism caused neighbors who had lived in harmony for years to fear acts of retaliation and feel a need for protection, and prompted individuals to create or reaffirm a religious/ethnic identity to achieve security. Trust in government as an honest broker eroded, and people turned to militia groups or their co-religionists in other areas to provide protection. In the Balkans, religion became an ethnic marker in ways that had little relationship to the traditional practice of a faith. For rival militia leaders, a religious sanction became useful in convincing fighters that what would have been seen as an atrocity before the war began was now a morally acceptable action. Major Muslim, Orthodox, and Roman Catholic religious authorities initially denounced escalating violence and ethnic cleansing, but the lower clergy often ignored their generalized support of peace. Serbia's President Slobodan Milosevic neutralized church opposition to him. Croatian priests did not obey the papacy's strongly worded cautions. The

---

[15]Michael Sells, A *Bridge Destroyed: Religion and Genocide in Bosnia* (1998) and Paul Mojzes, ed., *Religion and War in Bosnia* show the extent to which the ethnic cleansing originated and was justified as a religious war. Christopher Catherwood, *Why the Nations Rage: Killing in the Name of God* (1997) is valuable because the author was in the area when violence began. Scott Appleby argues that the motivation of the Serbs and Croats was ethno-religious-nationalist rather than

began was now a morally acceptable action. Major Muslim, Orthodox, and Roman Catholic religious authorities initially denounced escalating violence and ethnic cleansing, but the lower clergy often ignored their generalized support of peace. Serbia's President Slobodan Milosevic neutralized church opposition to him. Croatian priests did not obey the papacy's strongly worded cautions. The Bosnian Muslims remained tolerant at first, but the pressure of war increased solidarity, particularly after volunteers and arms came from Iran and Afghanistan.

Bosnia needs to be distinguished from Kosovo because the causes of the conflicts were very different, although the nationalistic exclusivity of the Belgrade government underlay both. In Bosnia ethnic groups dwelt in harmony for years; in Kosovo deep divisions between the Muslim Albanians and the Serbs meant that there had never been a unified society. In addition, the Albanians had a much higher birth rate than the Serbians living in Kosovo, which meant that the Serb percentage of the population had dwindled from one-third to less than ten percent of the population over the last thirty years. Kosovo also contained a shrine of a fourteenth-century battle against the Turks that remains basic to Serbia's sense of national identity.

After the breakdown of Yugoslavia, the Milosevic government attempted to control Kosovo by systematically excluding Albanians from positions of authority. The Serbian Orthodox Church did not condemn Milosevic's policy until after NATO had forced all Serbian troops to withdraw from Kosovo. Like its earlier condemnation of Milosevic's actions in Bosnia, the Church's stand had no appreciable effect. The Serbs both in Serbia and in Kosovo approved of Milosevic's policy, yet few of the Serbs driven out of Croatia (in another example of ethnic cleansing) were willing to settle in Kosovo.

Until the Dayton Accords in 1995, the Albanians had conducted a nonviolent campaign of resistance.[16] When the Dayton Accords, which provided

---

[16]Richard Holbrooke, *To End A War* (1998) tells the story of the negotiations. A critique of U.S., UN, and NATO strategies that lead to the division of Bosnia is Rusmir Mahmutcehajic, *The Denial of Bosnia* (2000).

a solution for Bosnia enforced by the UN, ignored Albanians, the KLA (Kosovo Liberation Army) began a small guerrilla war. Once branded by the West as a terrorist organization, the KLA now claimed to be freedom fighters waging a guerrilla war for independence. Their tactics had not changed, however. In response, the Serbian government became increasingly repressive, although there is a debate as to whether the goal of the increased oppression was to stabilize Serbian control by driving out some Albanians or to engage in a general ethnic cleansing. Outsiders saw an emergent humanitarian disaster with 300,000 refugees. UN Security Council resolutions brought no solution because western governments hesitated to commit forces and Russia backed Yugoslavia. When negotiations failed, NATO began what would become a two-month bombing campaign. In response Serbian armies and irregular forces drove an estimated 850,000 refugees out of Kosovo and killed two or three thousand more.

Kosovo marked a new kind of war. NATO in seventy-eight days of bombing flew 38,000 sorties and lost only two aircraft, and their pilots were rescued. However, the high tech weapons designed to destroy military targets while sparing civilians failed to destroy Serbian armor or to stop ethnic cleansing.[17] Eventually, NATO struck at targets in Serbia, including electric power plants. NATO's threat of a ground invasion also helped persuade Milosevic to withdraw troops.

The aftermath brought a fragile peace. Kosovo still wants independence and ethnic tensions remain high. Milosevic, voted out of office, is on trial for war crimes, but Serbian nationalism remains a political force. Western governments justified the bombing as a post-Cold War humanitarian intervention, but the cost of compliance was so great as to make similar responses less likely.

---

[17]According to Human Rights Watch, there were approximately five hundred civilians killed in Kosovo. The same military strategy was used by the U.S. in Afghanistan where civilian casualties are estimated in the hundreds - at least four hundred. The smart weapons either malfunctioned or were badly targeted. Using smart weapons to spare civilians and to make sure American soldiers run fewer risks is an obvious a way to insure proportionality in war and also good public relations. Some analysts believe these weapons will revolutionize the practice of war. *New York Times,* 21 July 21 2002, 1, 12.

The Middle East

The conflict over the future of the West Bank would be bitter even if there were no religious factor. Jerusalem is claimed by both Israel and the Palestinians as a capital, and the city remains divided between both groups with only minimal interaction between them. The population of the West Bank of the Jordan River, seized by Israel from Jordan during the Six-Day War in 1967, is predominantly Palestinian, but first to a small extent under Labour and then more extensively under the Likud governments beginning in 1977, Israel - in defiance of U.S. and the UN - planted settlements in suburbs around Jerusalem and at strategic locations in what it has claimed were vacant lands.

Although the religious divide among Israelis and Palestinians is deep and all agree that faith is involved, assessing the impact of religious belief on the ongoing conflict becomes difficult because of the varieties of commitment, sectarian differences within Judaism and Islam, and the linkage of the land with faith. The Jewish community in Israel (and in America as well) continues to debate the nature of the state and its boundaries. Is Israel a religious nation defined by Judaism or is it a secular democratic state populated by a people or ethnic group called Jews, who may or may not be religious? What is the role of Palestinians living in the borders of pre-1967 Israel? Should they have full political rights in a Jewish state?

The right-wing parties who support the Likud governments have insisted that the only diaspora Jews welcomed as citizens are those of real faith, i.e., born of an Orthodox mother or converted by an Orthodox rabbi. So the Orthodox parties consider Reform or Conservative Jews as not really Jewish, a belief that infuriates Jews in America where the Orthodox are a small minority. Ultra-Orthodox Jews in Israel insist that the Lord God gave all of Judea and Samaria (the West Bank) to the Jews, with Jerusalem as the ancient and modern capital, and giving up sovereignty over the Holy Land by allowing a Palestinian state would violate the Scriptures.[18]   However, even extremely devout Jews do not agree on policy.   Some Hasidic Jews in America have nothing to do with the modern state of Israel, which they see as a purely secular creation, and argue that the religious restoration of Israel will come only after the return of the messiah.   Other Hasidic Jews support the Likud party and the modern state of Israel even while they await the messiah.   The center of Orthodox Jewish settlement is Jerusalem and for many living there, making all of Jerusalem a Jewish city and reducing the size of the Arab enclave are acts of religious duty.   For the Orthodox, the Temple Mount is still the dwelling place of God, a symbol of God's sovereignty over Israel, and must remain under Jewish control.   The most extreme wish to destroy the Dome of the Rock mosque and rebuild the Temple.

Only a few miles away Tel Aviv's Reform, Conservative, and secular Jewish inhabitants see Israel as a democratic state needing to make peace with its neighbors and define Jews as an ethnic group, some of whom observe the law while others do not.   They mainly support the "land for peace" formula of the Labour Party and resist the Orthodox attempt to impose ritual law on the entire nation.   Religious disagreements are sharpened by ethnic and socio-economic differences between the two groups, with the wealthier, better educated Askenazic Western European Jews more likely to support the Labour Party and Sephardic Eastern Europeans and newly arrived Russian Jews (many of whom are not observant) adhering to the Likud.

In the Middle East extreme religious nationalism is often linked with economic deprivation and/or the failure of regimes to consult the inhabitants. This description does not apply to Jewish settlers on the West Bank, including many who have migrated from America, who wish to expand settlements. These are educated and prosperous people whose religious beliefs impel them to risk living among Palestinians who despise them.   In Hebron, the traditional site of

---

[18]There are settlers who moved to the West Back for religious reasons, but a majority seemed to have been attracted by the subsidies of 70%-80% provided by the Israeli government.   Amos Elon, "No Exit," *New York Review of Books* (May, 2002), 15-19.

Abraham's tomb, for example, 1,200 Jews insist on living in a closely guarded enclave surrounded by 40,000 Palestinians.[19] For the West Bank settlers, religious fervor drives nationalism and occasionally results in acts of terrorism, such as the assassination of Prime Minister Rabin or the killing of Muslims worshiping in Hebron. The right-wing Orthodox are a minority among Israeli Jews, but a closely divided electorate and the system of proportional representation in the Knesset increase their political power in the Likud and Labour governments. One result has been the continuing expansion of Jewish settlements in the West Bank.

In 2000 at the Camp David negotiations, Israel offered to return an estimated 90% of West Bank lands, but no compromise was reached over two difficult issues: the rights of refugee Palestinians and the future of Jerusalem.[20] The Second Intifadah's use of terrorism as a primary weapon, the lack of ability or will of the PLO to stop terrorist acts, and the return to power of the Likud destroyed the momentum for peace. The new Prime Minister of Israel Ariel Sharon opposed the Oslo formula of land for peace, allowed 30 new settlements in the West Bank in his first year in power, authorized assassinations of Hamas' leaders, and used the army to invade the West Bank and Gaza to root out terrorists. However, in the peace initiative started by the U.S. after Gulf War II, the Sharon government accepted the need to establish a Palestinian state with contiguous borders.

For most Israelis the knowledge of centuries of persecution, memory of the Holocaust, loyalty to Judaism as a way of life, consciousness of the hostility

---

[19]Geoffrey Aronson, *Israel, Palestinians and the Intifadah: Creating Facts on the West Bank* (1990), 17-18; unlike many fundamentalist movements like the Taliban whose participants are often ill informed about the variety of traditions of the faith, the Ultra-Orthodox Jews are well educated about theirs.

[20]A series of articles including comments from Ehud Barak and Robert Malley who participated at the Camp David talks, provides information on what was offered and differing perspectives on why the talks failed. Benny Morris, Ehud Barack, Robert Malley, Hussein Agha, *New York Review of Books* (Aug. 9, 2001, June 13, 2002, June 27, 2002). The 90% offer of Israel would have left 200,000 settlers on the West Bank and divided the Palestinian areas because of security corridors for Israel. The negotiations continued after Camp David with Israeli negotiators saying a final agreement was very close.

of Arab nations, and awareness of the smallness of the state of Israel have contributed to a siege mentality and incessant quest for security. Polls show that the public is evenly divided on where and how to establish borders.

Many Muslims in the West Bank and Jerusalem also support a divided land with a Palestinian state with sovereignty over part of Jerusalem and control of holy places in Hebron and Jerusalem. These people are part of a secular coalition, termed the Palestinian Liberation Organization, which officially has repudiated terrorism, recognized the right of Israel to exist, and seeks by negotiation to create a Palestinian state on the West Bank and Gaza with a capital of Jerusalem. Recently Israel and the U.S. have charged that the PLO has tacitly approved of terrorist actions and insisted that its authoritarian structure needs to be reformed. A post-Gulf War II truce failed when the PLO did not disarm radicals, Israel assassinated by missile attacks several Hamas leaders, and Hamas responded with bombings of Israeli civilians. The PLO demands justice for those Palestinians who fled from Israel in 1948 and who seek to return, and the removal of all West Bank settlements. Moreover, most Palestinians (and Muslims throughout the world) regard Jewish control of the Al Aska mosque (Temple Mount), where Muslim traditions assert Muhammad ascended to heaven, as against the *Qur'an*.

Radicals in the "fundamentalist" Hamas, Al Aksa Martyrs Brigade, and Islamic Jihad wish to eradicate the nation of Israel and to re-incorporate the land into the *dar al-Islam*. They view the Jews as Western conquerors and see the new Israeli settlements on the West Bank as creeping imperialism.[21] Citing the responsibility of all Muslims to join a defensive *jihad* when the faith is threatened, Hamas calls for armed struggle that often involves terrorism and will bring the

---

[21]Muhammad Muslih, *Foreign Policy of Hamas*, (Council on Foreign Relations, 1999), 2 argues that Hamas' policies "do not reduce to a rigid doctrine of religious reassertion" and change in response to events. During the Intafadah II, Al Aksa Martyrs Brigade, a part of the PLO coalition, has also engaged in terrorist acts. Some of the terrorists are religiously motivated but not all. Instead, there seems to have been a radicalization of a substantial part of the Palestinian population who approve of terrorism as a tactic and no shortage of young men (and recently a few young women) willing to become suicide bombers.

blessings of heaven upon those who die as martyrs. They see themselves as at war with Israel. Neither Israel, when it controlled the West Bank, nor the PLO, when it was much stronger than it is now, has been able to stop acts of terrorism aimed at disrupting peace negotiations. Hamas and the PLO now compete for the allegiance of the Palestinians who, according to polls, despair of peace and see terrorism as a legitimate response to overwhelming Israeli military power.

The surrounding Arab states and Iran - all of whom fear Israeli military might - help their own security, weaken Israel, aid their suffering Arab brothers and sisters, and show their support of Islam by aiding the Palestinians. Fundamentalist Islamic movements and states which the West terms "terrorist" - Libya, Iraq, Iran, Syria, and the Muslim Brotherhoods - support Hamas; the "moderate" or pro-Western countries including Egypt and Jordan who fear Islamic radicals associated with Osama bin Laden back the PLO.

When two peoples believe land and religion are indissoluble and seek control of the same area, any deepening of religious fervor increases the risk of war. The authorities on both sides have outside critics who seek power by opposing compromise. Today there is enormous disparity in wealth and power between the two communities, with the Israelis relying on their occupation of the disputed West Bank, military power, and aid from the United States. The Palestinians seek help from Arabs and Muslims everywhere and, because of their numerical strength and military weakness, are willing to use many means of protest, including negotiation, the Intifadah, and terrorism.

India-Pakistan

Political leaders often use a religion as a way of seeking power, forgetting that creating a religiously defined national unity always requires leaving someone else out. Gandhi's envisaged *satyagraha* against the British as a political and religious awakening. His vision of the unity of all Indians owed much to Hinduism and occasioned a reaction among Muslims. In the 1930s, Muhammad Ali Jinnah created a Muslim political party against Gandhi's Congress Party and sought Islamic power, though scholars debate whether he wanted power in India or a separate Islamic state. The results were the creation of Pakistan, the most enormous migration in the twentieth-century with eight million people displaced from both countries, a series of massacres of at least 200,000 Hindus, Sikhs, and Muslims, rapes of thousands of women, and the beginning of what have become continuous border disputes.[22] Its Hindu maharajah deeded Kashmir, a province with a Muslim majority, to India in 1947 without consulting the inhabitants. India has refused to allow a plebiscite either on independence, joining Pakistan, or remaining Indian. The example of Pakistan's religious separatism remains India's nightmare and has enforced its emphasis upon a unified but religiously pluralistic state. Pakistan as a result of the migration has become a Muslim state with a desire to incorporate border areas with a Muslim majority.

Muslims in and outside Kashmir have sought to unify the state with Pakistan by force. Kashmir has caused two wars, constant friction on the border, terrorist attacks, and, recently, an occupation of mountain peaks by Pakistani irregular forces supported by the army, resulting in a continuing military confrontation. Compromise over Kashmir is made more difficult because the Indian government fears that changing one border will increase already existing separatist demands elsewhere.[23] Pakistan, politically unstable and militarily weaker than India, is a Muslim state with minorities who have adopted the Taliban's militant Islam and oppose any compromise. Both countries now have nuclear weapons.

In the Punjab in northern India, Sikhs use their religion as a political tool in seeking independence. After Prime Minister Indira Gandhi in 1984 used troops to

---

[22]Gyanendra Pandev, *Remembering Partition: Violence, Nationalism and History in India* (2001), 61, 68, shows how inaccurate the statistics on partition are and how memories of the events have influenced later events in both nations; Ian Talbot and Gurharpal Singh, eds., *Region and Partition: Bengal, Punjab, and the Partition of the Subcontinent* (1999), 106, 209.

[23] Mark Juergensmeyer, *The New Cold War* (1993), 78-109 provides an excellent summary of the religious issues in India, Sri Lanka, and Pakistan. Sumit Ganguly, *The Crisis in Kashmir: Portents of War, Hopes of Peace* (1997), 60-62, 102-30, argues that during the 1965 and 1971 wars the inhabitants of Kashmir sympathized with India, but misrule by India and the taking away of autonomy has increased sympathy for independence or union with Pakistan. The rise of terrorism associated with the infiltration of mujahiddin after the Afghanistan-Soviet war has resulted in the migration of 250,000 Hindus from the Muslim areas of Kashmir.

expel the Sikhs who had seized the holiest Sikh shrine, the Golden Temple at Amritsar, they assassinated her. Her son Rajiv Gandhi then became Prime Minister and was killed by a Tamil Hindu from Sri Lanka who was infuriated by India's intervention in the religious/ethnic war in that country.

In India in 1992, Hindu nationalists occupied and destroyed a sixteenth-century Babri mosque at Ayodhya that was considered the birthplace of the god Rama, even though scholars have demonstrated that the site is not the place identified in ancient texts and the mosque had been sealed as a way of stopping controversy. For many years previously, Hindus and Muslims had shared the place, and Hindu extremists incited and justified violence by creating a mythic past linking Hinduism and India while ignoring the enormous cultural/religious diversity in the nation. As in the Balkans, Middle East, and Sri Lanka, politicians and religious leaders seeking power utilized longstanding religious cleavages that they exacerbated by creating among the majority Hindus a feeling of insecurity, of being threatened by the Muslim minority. In creating a new political-religious party, the Bharatiya Janata (BJP) spokesmen distorted the complicated past history of Muslim-Hindu relations, neglected the tradition of toleration and harmony, and emphasized past victimization and present threat. The BJP controlled the provincial government in Ayodahya and did nothing to restrain the extremists.

The Bharatiya Janata Party came to power in the Indian parliament in 1998 in a coalition government by using Hindu nationalism as a way of creating electoral strength against the multi-religious Congress Party at the expense of Muslims, Sikhs, and other minorities who were allegedly given special legal privileges by a government committed to creating a secular state. Elections in 1999 strengthened the BJP as the dominant political party in India. Before attaining power, the BJP's goal was to make India a Hindu state, but in power its leaders have advocated religious toleration and stressed the common *hindutua* (traditions or culture of India) underlying all religions in the nation.

The success of the BJP has heightened tensions among the plethora of religious groups in the country. Hindu extremists attacked and killed Christian missionaries and laymen and women, and there have been massacres leading to riots between Hindus and Muslims over a train carrying Hindu militants coming from a rally to build a Hindu temple at Ayodhya. In the interest of holding India together and promoting prosperity, the BJP now tries to restrain those whose fervor it created and exploited. Yet its post-riot electoral success in Gujarat came by inflaming anti-Muslim sentiments. There are as many Muslims in India as in Pakistan, and only Indonesia has a larger number. In India, exacerbating religious tensions serves the BJP as a vehicle to attain political power but makes governing more difficult.

Sri Lanka

In Sri Lanka, which gained independence from the British in 1948, the ruling Sinhalese parties began stressing Buddhism as a state religion in order to unify the majority against the Hindu Tamil minority (ca. 18%) who now seek autonomy or independence. The founding myths of Sinhalese, which stressed a visit of the Buddha to the land and a victory of Duttagamini over the Tamils, seemingly legitimated defining modern Sri Lanka as a Buddhist nation. Politicians seeking to unify the state created a fictionalized version of the past and passed legislation discriminating against the Tamils. Buddhist monks, having propagated the simplified history, now justified and even led violent attacks. The Buddhists felt threatened by the close relationship between Tamils in Sri Lanka and those in southern India. The Sri Lankan Tamils, discovering their vulnerability, closed ranks, and extremists among them committed terrorist acts in defense of independence in response to mob attacks and officially endorsed repression by the government. The result was a bloody civil war beginning in 1983 with 55,000 killed and no solution, although peace negotiations continue.[24] When politicians

---

[24]*Washington Post*, 10 Aug. 1998, A9; David Little, "Religion and Ethnicity in the Sri Lankan Civil War," in *Creating Peace in Sri Lanka: Civil War and Reconstruction*, ed., Robert Rotberg (1999), 41-56.

seeking power identify a religious faith with the nation, those who dissent are vulnerable to persecution and may seek revolution.

Afghanistan: The Rise and Fall of the Taliban

Afghanistan's twenty years of war and unstable governments began with the overthrow of the monarchy in 1973, followed by a short-lived republic, and a series of coups by pro-Soviet leaders. In response, an uprising led by Afghani tribal leaders dedicated to Islam and traditional customs seemed on the verge of success when in 1979 Russian invaded to ensure that the communists remained in power. A ten year guerrilla *jihad* followed, fought by the mujahiddin supplied with weapons from the U.S., Saudi Arabia, and Pakistan and aided also by foreign Muslims from many countries devoted to driving out atheistic Russians and creating a purified Islamic culture.[25] The Russians, accepting defeat, withdrew in 1989, leaving a society whose traditional way of life had been destroyed. Afghanistan was now ruled by Muslim warlords, whose main occupations were looting the population, profiting from the drug trade, and fighting each other for power.

The Taliban (meaning "student") was a radical Islamic movement from the Pashtun tribe, an ethnic group comprising about 40% of Afghanistan. Afghani Muslims had traditionally followed the most tolerant school of Islam law and Sunni, Sufi, and Shi'a coexisted. The Taliban, who were not scholars of Islam, were intolerant, viewing their tribal norms as the only truth. They were also influenced (and financed) by the strict Wahhabi movements of Saudi Arabia and by the puritanical Indian Deobandi Muslims, but the resulting synthesis was original. The Taliban had not been a major factor in the war with the Soviets, but in 1994 became powerful after defeating corrupt local warlords in Kandahar. Because they seemed the best hope to bring stability in Afghanistan, the government of Pakistan provided funds, and students from its Wahhabi-financed

---

[25]Robert D. Kaplan, *Soldiers of God: With Islamic Warriors in Afghanistan and Pakistan* (1990, Revised 2001), is a first hand account of the war against the Soviets.

madrasa schools joined the Taliban army.[26] By 1998 due to victories, bribes and alliances, the Taliban controlled 90% of Afghanistan, but the civil war never ended, and only Saudi Arabia and Pakistan recognized the Taliban government.

In power, the Taliban had no political or economic program except Islamization, which in practice meant persecution of Shi'a and other schools of faith, centralizing power in a dictatorship of a few mullahs, outlawing music, dance, and sports, destroying non-Muslim art objects like centuries old rock carvings of the Buddha, and denying women the right to attend school or to earn a living. In essence, the Taliban, using religious police who would beat men on matters as picayune as the length of their beards, created the most restrictive Muslim society ever seen.

The Taliban also provided sanctuary for radical Muslim organizations, including Al Qaeda (meaning "military base"), dedicated to overthrowing allegedly corrupt Arab governments, forcing the withdrawal of American troops from Saudi Arabia, ending Western and particularly U.S. power, opposing Zionism, and creating a pure Muslim society. An Afghan *jihad* now had become internationalized with radical Muslims from many societies being trained and fighting beside the mujahiddin. Osama bin Laden, Al Qaeda's leader, a wealthy Saudi Wahhabi, who had become radicalized by opposing America's war with Iraq, came with two to three thousand followers to support the Taliban. In 1998 Al Qaeda issued a decree (*fatwa*) calling for killing "the Americans and their allies - civilians and military" as "an individual duty for every Muslim." In 1998 Al Qaeda bombed U.S. embassies in Kenya and Tanzania, killing two hundred people, most of whom were Africans, and in 2000 bombed the ship USS Cole in Yemen.

Even before Al Qaeda's hijacking of three airplanes to crash into the World Trade Centers in New York and the Pentagon, the U.S. had focused on the dangers

---

[26]This section is based on Ahmed Rashid, *Taliban* (2001), 86-93, 130-34, 185. The charge has often been made and denied that the CIA provided funding for the Taliban.

from a network of Muslim terrorists and sought to destroy Osama bin Laden. Now President George W. Bush declared "war" against terrorists and those nations that harbored them. When Afghanistan's Taliban government would not hand over Osama bin Laden, the U.S. and Britain with aid from NATO and Pakistan supported the rebel warlords in Afghanistan and easily drove the Taliban from power using high-tech weapons and special forces. Insisting that the war was against all terrorists, the U.S. targeted rebels in the Philippines, Indonesia, Peru, and Georgia, and sympathized with India and Israel in their actions against Muslim extremists. The Bush administration declared that its war was not against Muslims, but terrorists. Still, the mass media reported widespread sympathy in the Arab world for Al Qaeda not from governments but from peoples who remain disenchanted with their poverty and lack of opportunity.

The war destroyed the Taliban government, but this was always the secondary target because there was no evidence that it knew beforehand of the Trade Center bombings. The new government of Afghanistan effectively controls now only the area around Kabul, and Muslim warlords dominate the countryside. Against a pattern of guerrilla warfare by supporters of the Taliban, only minimal reconstruction has taken place. The U.S. has been unable to locate Osama bin Laden, other leaders of Al Qaeda, or Mullah Omar of the Taliban, so the question remains whether America's overwhelming military force will prove an effective long-term weapon against terrorists or only create more enemies. Even more uncertain is whether 9/11 represents the first installment of a continuing strategy of terrorism by religiously inspired men against Western nations or was an aberration of an already failing strategy.[27] Clearly, however, religion played a decisive role in mobilizing a few individuals to sacrifice themselves in terrorist acts designed to kill civilians with no clear political objective.

---

[27]Gilles Kepel, *Jihad: The Trail of Political Islam* (2002), in a new Introduction, 1-20, argues that radical Islam has failed and that the Trade Tower bombing by Al Qaeda is a sign of weakness. The French edition was issued in 2000.

Religiously Inspired Violence

This brief summary of a few of the many incidents of recent religiously inspired violence raises the question as to why such phenomena occurred in some but not all states. Religious violence in the 1990s occurred in new states where elites seeking national unity clashed with ethnic groups who felt threatened. When ethnicity was reinforced by religious diversity, the possibility for fighting increased. A crucial factor seems to have been politically ambitious individuals who played up religious differences in an attempt to gain power. Ethnic/religious violence came in democratic states like India and Sri Lanka and authoritarian nations like Afghanistan and Sudan.

Unlike the U.S., which has created a common nationality incorporating many ethnic groups and diverse religions, most of the states in the world are composed of unassimilated ethnic groups. In mature states, like Great Britain, the mostly Protestant Scots, English, and Welsh exist peacefully together, although the Catholic Irish living on a separate island preserved a distinct culture and achieved independence. In Canada Catholic French-speaking people of Quebec coexist in friction but not violence with the predominately English-speaking, Protestant inhabitants of the other provinces; tiny Belgium is divided between the Flemish and Walloons, who have lived in peace for centuries.

By contrast, in Africa, the Indian sub-continent, and the Middle East, imperialist powers cobbled together in states very different peoples with boundaries set sometimes for geopolitical but often for arbitrary reasons. For example, Nigeria has a north of Muslim Hausa-Fulani peoples and in the south near the coast among the Yoruba and Ibo, a mixture of traditional African religions and Christians; rivalries among them help to explain why that land so rich in natural resources has a history of civil war and military coups. The Organization of Africa Unity, following the UN charter, insists that existing borders created by the colonial powers are inviolable. This mandate now seems unduly rigid and almost designed to cause endemic internal conflict, but the alternative, the breakup of West African states, leads to even more violence.[28]

III. Peace in the 1990s

The 1990s witnessed many forms of peacemaking and a general lowering of international tensions, but organized religion played only a supporting role in those places where politicians brought reductions in organized violence. These include the ending of apartheid in South Africa, negotiating an end to most violence in Northern Ireland, stopping the guerrilla wars in El Salvador and Nicaragua, the strengthening of the European Economic Community, the repudiation of military governments and the return of Brazil, Argentina, and Chile to democratically elected government, and the spread of democracy to Eastern Europe and Russia. The United Nations expanded the number and scope of its peacekeeping operations in Cambodia, Haiti, and Sierra Leone, and the Secretary General negotiated truces in Angola and Mozambique. The UN also monitored elections, established war-crimes tribunals for Bosnia and Rwanda, and created a permanent international court for war crimes. However, it is as simplistic to belittle the role of religion in fomenting war in the 1990s as to ignore its impact on peace.

Religion as Peacemaker

The peace activities directly influenced by religion even before the end of the Cold War came through three forms: Liberation Theology, the prominence of leaders carrying on the nonviolent campaigns of Mahatma Gandhi and Martin Luther King whose spiritual qualities and/or office made them influential, the works and declarations of religious organizations, and actions of people who saw fostering peace by defending human rights and economic justice as part of their faith.

---

[28]Recognizing the weaknesses of the OAU, several African states created a new organization in 2002 called African Union that can intervene and that seeks to promote democracy. Skeptics point out that several dictators helped create the new body.

A theme of this section is that, even while religious leaders publicly spoke out for peace, they found solutions to violence elusive because the causes of war seemed so complex. Was war a ritualized relationship between two sovereign nations seeking to use armed power to achieve certain objectives or was it an extension of a nation's internal cultural orientation originating in violence to women, children, and racial minorities? Was the new global economy a way to share the wealth or a new form of exploitation that would increase the gap between rich and poor? Was internal reform within a country the way to foster peace among nations? In general, religiously motivated individuals made their contributions by working on concrete problems and left the theorizing to academics; the major exception was Liberation Theology.

Liberation Theology

In the 1970s Catholic theologians and priests merged nonviolence with traditional Catholic social thought to create a new religious-political program labeled Liberation Theology. The declarations of Vatican II linking the arms race to Third World poverty provided legitimacy to a theology of liberation that sought to use nonviolent means to bring economic and political freedom for peasants. A selective reading of the *Bible* also provided examples of the special status of the poor and of the necessity for activism against the status quo: the deliverance of the Jews from slavery in Egypt, the prophets' denunciation of political and economic oppression by Israel's kings and priests, and Jesus' condemnation of the rich, praise of the poor, and expulsion of the money changers from the Temple. Too long, said liberation theologians, had the Catholic Church in Latin America, by supporting corrupt oppressive governments, forgotten its biblical mandate to bring social justice.[29]

---

[29]Philip Berryman, *Liberation Theology* (revised edition, 1987), is an introduction first written in the early years of the movement. A balanced assessment of accomplishments and recent setbacks is Michael Lowy, *The War of Gods: Religion and Politics in Latin America* (1996). A prominent theologian is Gustavo Gutiérrez whose thoughts are summarized in James Nichkoloff, ed., *Gustavo Gutiérrez: Essential Writings* (1996). The liberation theologian most concerned with violence was El Salvador's Ignacio Ellacuria whose final meditations upon war are contained

Traditional Roman Catholic Just War theory authorized revolt against tyranny. Using categories derived from Marxist analysis of the class nature of society, liberation theologians saw the extreme disparity between rich and poor in Latin America as reflecting structural violence: that is, a skewed social structure in which the rich monopolized land and the masses lived in such overwhelming misery that they lacked the basic needs for civilized life. The latent violence of the upper class rulers became visible whenever the poor sought to improve their conditions. Structural violence imposed by the upper class was an already existing war that gave people just cause and a God-given duty to resist. God and Jesus used power to break the power of evil. Now priests and Church would identify with the poor in the struggle against temporal evil.

Unlike the situation in the Northern Hemisphere in which people needed conversion, liberation theologians claimed that the peasants of Latin America did not need to be taught the love of God for they already had a deep piety. Instead, the poor through studying the Gospel message would engage in a process of consciousness-raising to appreciate their own value and power. The priest was not a superior to teach or lead the people, but he would learn from the poor as they through *Bible* study and prayer liberated themselves from passivity into an understanding of the Gospel's demand for economic and social justice. The result was that they would no longer accept the status quo as part of an inevitable destiny decreed by God and supported by the institutional Church. Rural peasants and slum dwellers would create Christian-base communities in which they discovered their potentialities and engaged in nonviolent actions for social justice.

In the 1980s Liberation Theology would become a major focus for resistance movements against dictators in Latin America and the apartheid system in South Africa. Blacks and women in the U.S. would use Liberation Theology's

---

in John Hassett and Hugh Lacey, ed., *Towards a Society that Serves Its People: The Intellectual Contribution of El Salvador's Wounded Jesuits* (1991).

postulates to legitimate their quest for social justice. In Nicaragua, Catholic priests and people invoking the categories of Liberation Theology supported the Sandinista movement's struggle against the dictator Somoza. In El Salvador, rightist supporters of the government would assassinate Archbishop Oscar Romero in the Cathedral and soldiers shot six Jesuit teachers at the University of San Salvador who had dared to sympathize with the peasants. In the context of bitter civil wars in these two countries, liberation theologians talked about a "temptation to violence" and refused to condemn armed resistance against right wing governments. Elsewhere, the major thrust of the movement was for creating Christian base communities and nonviolent efforts for social justice.

During the Cold War, supporters of Liberation Theology in the U.S. criticized the Reagan administration's foreign policy of building up the Contras to oppose the Sandinistas in Nicaragua and supporting the government in El Salvador against the guerrillas. The nuns in the Maryknoll Order publicized the atrocities there, before and after government forces raped and murdered six members of the order in El Salvador. The resulting outcry led members of Congress to restrict military aid and to demand reforms. Liberation theologians also criticized the impact of business and multinational corporations as enriching the few and impoverishing the many.

Pope John Paul II embraced the critique of capitalism implicit in Liberation Theology, but opposed its Marxist underpinnings and de facto alliance with radical social movements. In the 1990s, the Vatican silenced the most prominent liberation theologians including Brazil's Adolfo Boffo, and appointed conservative bishops opposed to its emphases. Still, priests and parishioners in many areas in Latin America and students in colleges and universities in North and South America continued to analyze society and to work with the poor using insights derived from Liberation Theology.

Nonviolence and Social Change

Religious commitment motivated the vision and practice of nonviolence pioneered by Gandhi in the quest for Indian independence and by Martin Luther

King in the civil rights movement of the 1960s. Because nonviolence seems not just compatible with but to grow out of the practice of Buddhism, Christianity, and Sufi Islam, religious inspiration has continued to motivate individuals and groups to seek for an alternative to realpolitik and war among nations. Nonviolence as an approach to a disciplined spiritual life and as a method could be used in personal and intrastate conflicts and international affairs. In addition, by the 1980s, nonviolence had become a means of working with the poor as well as a subject of academic inquiry cutting across several disciplines.

In many lands, spiritual leaders sought to promote peace through creating organizations dedicated to nonviolent action on behalf of the poor. In Sicily, Danilo Dolci (1925-1997) and his followers merged Catholicism with Gandhian techniques in seeking to break the hold of the Mafia and to promote economic and social reforms. In India, the Gandhi Institute promoted the study and practice of *satyagraha*. Buddhist Sulak Sivaraksa became a leading critic of the human and environmental cost of industrialization in Thailand, and his organization, *Savrodaya*, sought to promote reconciliation between the Sinhalese and Tamils in Sri Lanka. *Savrodaya* sought to apply Buddhist teachings about nonviolence and peace to politics and economics. Sivaraksa was arrested on several occasions for criticizing the Thai political system.[30] Those seeking a lifestyle of religious sensitivity and political activism dedicated to peace found inspiration and moral exemplars in the life and writings of the Vietnamese Buddhist Trich van Han and Catholic Trappist monk Thomas Merton.

In America, Protestant and Catholic churches created programs for training individuals in the practice of conflict resolution, and participants provided counseling in domestic abuse situations and intervened in many kinds of disputes: landlord/tenant problems, racial incidents, relations between police and community, violence in schools. An Alternative to Violence program worked with

---

[30]Christopher Queen and Sallie King, eds., *Engaged Buddhism. Buddhist Liberation Movements In Asia* (1996) with chapters on India, Sri Lanka, Thailand, and Tibet.

prison inmates, trying to teach nonviolent approaches. Many churches initiated nursery schools or Head Start programs in expectation that children who learned early how to solve conflicts without fighting would retain such skills in adult life. Another form of direct nonviolent action occurred primarily in the Southwest when churches declared themselves "sanctuaries" in order to provide shelter and counseling to legal and illegal immigrants. Involving the faithful in workshops on racism or sexism had a potential for involving congregations in a social gospel congruent with the example of Jesus. To advocates of nonviolence an expanded definition of peace activities would allow significant work to take place on the local level and might also achieve more visible results than lobbying by representatives of church bureaucracies in Washington, New York, London, or Bonn. Having "peace start at home" and letting it "begin with me" proved attractive slogans.

A distinguishing mark of religious groups working for peace was the emphasis upon forgiveness and reconciliation. If religion was a cause of the conflict, then the resources within religious traditions might help to ease tensions. Virtually all religions have procedures or teachings to reconcile individuals and a trained mediator could enable warring groups to use that part of their tradition. Forgiveness was not forgetting, but memory accompanied by moral judgment and some form of restitution. National governments could negotiate peace treaties, but a formal peace without reconciliation at the grass-roots level would be difficult to implement and an admission of religious failure. If real harmony were to emerge, at some stage warring communities would have to acknowledge their faults and take actions to restore justice.

In South Africa, the form of reconciliation came through a government-sponsored Truth Commission presided over by Bishop Tutu. Its emphasis upon confession and repentance clearly had religious overtones. Elsewhere, the International Conciliation Service of the Mennonite Central Committee trained individuals in conflict resolution and conflict management and then sent them overseas to work with groups in conflict. Catholic Relief Services and World Visions initiated similar programs. Where there was already trust in spiritually motivated individuals because of previous work of church groups, as in Central America and Mozambique, the lay people in Communitá di Sant' Egido proved an effective mediator. Northern Ireland was saturated with practitioners of conflict transformation seeking to bridge the gap between the Roman Catholic and Protestant communities.

Within the church communities and also in government agencies like the United States Institute for Peace, there was debate and research on the value of reconciliation versus restorative justice (i.e., war crimes trials). With religion so often a cause of the conflicts, what were the advantages and risks of fostering practices like separation of church and state associated with the West? Promoting the tolerance and acceptance of diversity needed for peace might threaten the fundamentalist program that had fostered the violence. Clearly any peace facilitator would have to know the local culture intimately, move carefully to gain trust, and be willing to make a substantial commitment of time with no guarantee of a favorable outcome. To counter the violent religious militant, he or she would need to be a militant religious peacemaker.

Just as Liberation Theology was studied in universities, so the theories behind and practice of nonviolence became a subject for academic study. Political scientists, anthropologists, sociologists, and psychologists divorced nonviolence from its religious roots and sought to understand whether conflict resolution could be applied in different cultures and what its strengths and weaknesses were in dealing with intra and interstate conflicts. In the university setting, nonviolence became a technique to be analyzed rather than a way of life and a subject to be taught in courses in the new discipline of Peace Studies.[31]

---

[31]Textbooks for peace studies courses, perhaps the best way to see the scope and limitations of the discipline, include David Barash, *Introduction to Peace Studies* (1991) and ed., *Approaches to Peace* (2000); Seyom Brown, *The Causes and Prevention of War* (1987); many publications of the U.S. Institute for Peace are also relevant, e.g. W. Scott Thompson et al., ed., *Approaches to Peace: An Intellectual Map* (1991).

Although a moral perspective may have propelled many of the academic studies, their authors insisted upon divorcing nonviolence from what they regarded as its fuzzy religious overtones. So, for example, political scientist Gene Sharp focused on Civilian Based Defense (CBD) as a way for a small country with a weak military to resist an aggressor state. Starting with Gandhi's insight that the functioning of all governments depends upon the consent of the people, Sharp demonstrated how simple non-cooperation could cause change in policies. Convinced that the conventional teaching of history placed too much emphasis upon wars and military force as instruments for social change, Sharp ransacked the past and found an impressive list of nonviolence techniques that had worked against colonial regimes, dictatorships, and democracies. In recent history, the fall of the Shah of Iran and Ferdinand Marcos of the Philippines and the successful defiance of the Soviet Union by the Solidarity Union in Poland seemed to show the continued power of a united people practicing nonviolence. CBD was essentially a defensive strategy, and Sharp advocated training a civilian people in how to withstand an invasion by a superior military force.[32] Sharp's program rested upon the insight that military force had little success in dealing with the most pressing issues: human rights, dictatorship, poverty, and environmental degradation.

Alternative secular perspectives of the value of nonviolence came from Harvard Professor Roger Fisher who in scholarly and popular books demonstrated that negotiations need not be a zero-sum game and that a correct analysis of disputes would locate meaningful areas for agreement. By isolating factors of benefit to both parties, an intermediary could engage in various confidence-

---

[32]Gene Sharp, *Civilian Based Defense: A Post-Military Weapons System* (1990), and *Making Europe Unconquerable: The Potential of Civilian Based Deterrence and Defense* (1985); *Gandhi as a Political Strategist: With Essays on Ethics and Politics* (1979); Peter Ackerman and Jack Duvall, *A Force More Powerful: A Century of Non-violent Conflict* (2000), provides case studies from the 1905 Russian revolution to the Intifadah.

building strategies throughout a negotiation that would end with a "win-win" situation.[33]

An Australian diplomat turned scholar, John Burton argued that all disputes, from the international to the personal level, exemplified a common structure, and could be solved by focusing on certain needs, like those of security or recognition. Boundary disputes, economic grievances, and political factors grew out of basic psychological needs. For example, both sides in the Arab-Israeli conflict need to escape from fear, to gain recognition of their legitimacy, and to achieve a certain level of prosperity. These goals, common to both sides, could be achieved for all parties through negotiations. Burton advocated creating a private off-the-record meeting lasting several days between influential exponents from two sides and taking them through a structured negotiation so that they could see each others' perspectives, analyze the differences, and then arrive at a creative solution. The end result was not a compromise, or a blurring of issues, but a meeting of the needs of both sides. The object of conflict resolution was not to end conflict or promote brotherly love, but to train people to manage conflicts in ways that would de-escalate tensions, reduce the proclivity to violence, and facilitate working together in the future. Participants could then take insights to political leaders.[34]

For Fisher, Burton, and their followers, conflict resolution was a technique that should be taught in colleges and universities, law schools, and public schools. Diplomats, labor negotiators, businessmen, government officials, and school children needed to learn how to deal creatively with conflict rather than

---

[33]Roger Fisher et al., *Beyond Machiavelli: Tools for Coping With Conflict* (1994); and with Richard Ury, *Getting to Yes: Negotiating Agreement without Giving In* (1983).

[34]John Burton, *Conflict: Resolution and Prevention* (1990), *Conflict Resolution: its Language and Power* (1990). An excellent survey of conflict-resolution theory is Marc Ross, *The Culture of Conflict: Interpretations and Interests in Comparative Perspective* (1993) and *The Management of Conflict: Interpretations and Interests in Comparative Perspective* (1993); a more recent synthesis is Louis Kriesburg, *Constructive Conflict: From Escalation to Resolution* (2003); on the psychology of conflict resolution, see Harold Hall and Leighton Whitaker, eds., *Collective Violence: Effective Strategies for assessing and intervening in Fatal Group and Institutional Aggression* (1999).

threatening lawsuits, coercion, or violence. The new discipline of conflict management was frankly reformist, seeking to transform a world in which war seemed a costly and often unsuccessful way to solve problems and military hardware of little use in dealing with racism and sexual oppression.

The downside of the expanded scope of peace work was that it was easier to assert than to prove that all violence was essentially the same phenomenon and that negotiations over scarce commodities like land and independence could be managed in a way that satisfied both sides. Moreover, if a nation's internal social pathology caused war, then the task of creating peace by macro-reform of the international system, curtailing the spread of nuclear weapons, or promoting democracy was ultimately an exercise in futility. Would it be possible with conflict resolution to create a good strategy for containing tyrants or adjusting international borders so that people like the Kurds or Palestinians could have a state? (Of course, conventional diplomacy and war also had poor track records in dealing with these tasks.) Changing child-rearing practices, undermining machismo, curtailing violence in movies and television, educating for social responsibility, ending racial discrimination, guaranteeing a living wage; in short - creating a culture of nonviolence - all these were necessary to create peace. As described by Johann Galtung, a leading theorist of peace studies, a true peace would occur when the social structure allowed an individual to develop to the limits of her or his capacities. Working for peace had been a Herculean task when the focus was confined to international relations; now, with everything a potential cause of war, creating peace was equivalent to pushing Sisyphus' boulder up the hill, except that the hill was steeper, and there were dozens of rocks and no good way to select a keystone.

As new definitions of peace evolved, it became increasingly difficult to distinguish between moralities based upon religious commitment and humanitarian impulses and those based in secular social science, particularly when all were guided from insights derived from psychology and sociology.

The Individual as Religious Peacemaker

With reputations for moral probity and spiritual sensitivity, Bishop Desmond Tutu and the Dalai Lama used the authority of their offices to influence world opinion against apartheid and the Chinese government's policies in Tibet and for nonviolent solutions to these conflicts. Pope John Paul II spoke out in Cuba and elsewhere about human rights and showed no reticence in lecturing host countries about poverty, economic exploitation, and abortion. But John Paul failed to influence the IRA in Northern Ireland, and neither the Pope nor the Jewish Nobel Laureate Elie Weisel had even minor success in halting the violence against civilians in the Balkans. The Pope's peace-seeking actions in normalizing relations with Israel and offering to journey to Sarajevo were balanced by controversies over his canonizing a Jewish convert to Catholicism later killed in Auschwitz and in declaring blessed (a step toward sainthood) the World War II-era Cardinal Stepanic of Croatia. In the Philippines, Cardinal Jamie Sin, who with his fellow bishops had earlier been influential in persuading dictator Ferdinand Marcos not to use military force against pro-democracy demonstrators, remained a consistent advocate for democracy and against corruption. In Guatemala, Bishop Juan Jose Geraldi Conedera, long a defender of human rights of the Maya Indians, headed a commission that concluded that during its civil war there were 150,000 deaths and 50,000 disappearances, with 80% of the deaths the responsibility of government troops. Conedera was beaten to death with a concrete block on April 9, 1998. A court convicted and sent three military officers to prison for this politically motivated murder; this was the first time a Guatemalan military officer had ever been sent to prison for a political murder.[35] Samuel Ruiz, the senior Catholic bishop in Mexico's Chiapas region, attempted to mediate a possible settlement between the government and the Zapatista rebels until in August 1998 he resigned in disgust after the central authorities initiated a

---

[35]*New York Times*, 9 May 1998, Sec. A, 3; Francisco Goldman, "Victory in Guatemala," *New York Review of Books* (May 21, 2002), 77-79, 82-84.

campaign to discredit him as too sympathetic with the poor. Bishop Carlos Filipe Ximenes Bello of East Timor along with journalist José Ramos Horta received the 1996 Nobel Peace Prize for their defense of the inhabitants of that island against the campaign of suppression conducted by Indonesia's military. Denis Halliday, an Irish Quaker who was the first UN appointee in charge of a program using the proceeds from Iraqi oil sales for food, resigned after he saw the effects of the sanctions on civilians, and led a campaign that in 2002 succeeded in influencing the Security Council to limit sanctions to militarily useful goods and to end restrictions on imports of civilian goods. In 1993 Maha Ghosananda, the chief religious leader in Cambodia, created and led a movement of Buddhists on a peace march joined by 10,000 people that became an annual pilgrimage. Ghosananda at his center worked with NGOs in teaching conflict prevention.[36] Former President Jimmy Carter, a devout Baptist, served as a mediator in international conflicts, including Haiti and North Korea, went as an observer in elections around the world, and established a center for the study and practice of alternatives to violence.

Although the Nobel Committee does not evaluate the religion of nominees, faith clearly was a prime motivation in the work of several recipients of the Peace Prize: Rigoberte Mechu Tum of Guatemala, Oscar Arias Sanchez of Costa Rica, Daw Aung San Suu Kyi of Burma (Myanmar), and Jimmy Carter. Because Nelson Mandela was widely perceived as a man of Christian integrity ennobled by his years in prison, his presence helped ensure that the transition from rule of a white minority to a multiracial democracy in South Africa came relatively peacefully.

Institutional Peacemaking

In the 1990s political scientists rediscovered that religious leaders and institutions have on occasion reduced the threat of violence by serving as trusted intermediaries between opposing factions. The Evangelical Churches of East

Germany, because they had the confidence of both sides, helped make the transition from communist rule a peaceful process.[37] Long a supporter of white rule, the leadership of the Dutch Reformed and Anglican Churches in South Africa in the 1980s supported the dismantling of the apartheid system. No longer could Afrikaner politicians claim a religious sanction for the suppression of the black majority.

British and American Quakers, with a long tradition of political neutrality, have often served as confidential intermediaries between opponents, carrying messages between Israel's Ben-Gurion and Egypt's Gamal Nassar in 1965, between the military leaders in Nigeria and Biafra during the civil war, and between whites and blacks in Rhodesia in 1970. All through the Cold War, Friends sponsored cultural interchanges between Soviet and American citizens, an activity made easier because Russian officials remembered that Quakers provided food to ease starvation after World War I.[38] Like the Quaker UN office, the Church center at the UN provides a space where diplomats can meet in an informal setting for private discussions with no records kept. Formed in the 1960s the World Conference on Religion and Peace brought together in conferences major figures of many faiths to work for harmony among their adherents and to mobilize religious communities to work for peace within and among nations.[39] Older pacifist organizations like the Fellowship of Reconciliation redefined membership to attract non-Christian workers for peace. The Catholic lay organization Sant' Egido expanded its mission for the poor to include work for interreligious dialogue and as a mediator in Bosnia, Algeria, and Mozambique. The Peace Brigade volunteers journeyed to El Salvador and lived with workers threatened with assassination as a way of checking death squads.

[36]An excellent discussion of reconciliation and forgiveness peacemaking is in Scott Appleby, *The Ambivalence of the Sacred*, ch. 4-6.
[37]Douglas Johnson and Cynthia Sampson, eds., Religion: *The Missing Dimension of Statecraft* (1994).
[38]C. H. Yarrow, *The Quaker Experience in International Conciliation* (1979). Elmore Jackson, *Middle East Mission: The Story of a Major Bid for Peace in the Time of Nasser and Ben-Gurion* (1983).

They also moved into Yasser Arafat's headquarters and the Church of the Nativity in Bethlehem during the siege by the Israeli Army in 2002.[40]

Throughout the nineteenth century, churches combined missionary proselytizing with various types of social services: creating schools, teaching hygiene, founding hospitals, sometimes defending the people against rapacious colonial administrators. To these tasks in the twentieth century, churches added various relief activities: feeding the starving, caring for refugees, promoting economic self-sufficiency. Sometimes charitable activities are also attempts to proselytize, and religious organizations have to decide between their responsibilities to promote the truth as they see it and to follow the dictates of their faith to help all the poor. Among those organizations that provide aid based upon need rather than religious affiliations are Lutheran World Service, Church World Service, Catholic Charities, Mennonite Central Committee, and Combined Jewish Appeal. All major Christian denominations now have relief agencies and attempt to coordinate work to avoid duplication. These religiously based relief organizations cooperate with secular humanitarian agencies such as the International Red Cross, Oxfam, and Save the Children - many of whose employees and volunteers see helping the poor as a religious duty. Religious and secular relief organizations assert that fostering peace comes as a byproduct of helping people in distress.

Christian churches do not separate relief work from other social concerns, and all major denominations have lobbies that seek to influence national legislation. There is substantial accuracy in the squib that the social committees of liberal Protestant denominations in America think peace and justice are one word. The same could be said for recent Roman Catholic teachings. However, institutional weakness caused by declining numbers and internal divisions weakened the social testimonies of the so-called mainline Protestant churches that dominated the National Council of Churches in America. The same weakness in number of

---

[39]Homer Jack, *WCRP: A History of the World Conference on Religion and Peace* (1993).

adherents is true for virtually all the churches in Western Europe. At a time when the churches are freer than ever before to criticize the government, declining numbers reduce political clout. In spite of lessened influence, church lobbies in Europe and America retain enormous moral prestige which they use to tell governments that working for peace includes addressing the implications of a global economy, global warming, preservation of endangered species, the rights of women, and the widening gap between rich and poor nations as well as nuclear weapons, arms sales, and the budget for military expenditures.

In America, the countervailing testimonies of fundamentalist, revivalist denominations like the Southern Baptists and political organizations like the Moral Majority and its successor the Christian Coalition mean that Christian religious organizations provide no unified moral perspective on either domestic or international policies. In addition, many evangelical Christians believe that secular peace is a reflection of inward peace and that the most effective strategy for world peace is to convert people. The impact of the growth of Christianity in Africa and elsewhere has meant that the British members of the Church of England are a minority. A similar phenomenon will soon occur to European and American Catholics. In addition, the rapid growth of Pentecostals, Seventh Day Adventists, and Mormons in Africa and South America will change the center of gravity for Protestants. It is too early to predict how the changing demography of Christianity, the rapid expansion of Islam, and the disapora of Hinduism and Buddhism will affect these religions' impact on war and peace.

It is also difficult to assess contributions to peace by individuals motivated by faith in the 1990s because of the proliferation of voluntary humanitarian organizations or NGOs (non-government organizations). Should a person interested in working for peace in Israel support the Jewish organization Peace Now, Amnesty International, the American Friends Service Committee or work through his or her local synagogue? The devout continued to rely on religious

---

[40]Appleby, ch. 4 – 6.

institutions for spiritual nurture, but might also join a secular agency concentrating on one cause. So one member of the Presbyterian Church might join SANE, Common Cause, and the UN advocacy group. Another member in the same local congregation might support the National Rifle Association and a Congressman seeking to cut all foreign aid as wasteful. Since the national denomination had to represent both members, its positions would be a compromise. Seeking greater unity and impact than that found within the church, a Presbyterian peace activist might channel her or his energies through a NGO. Religion might still be the key motivating factor, but statistics would not indicate this. Even when the church's social teaching coincided with the beliefs of an individual, he or she, with a limited supply of funds and time, would need to decide whether a contribution to the Methodist Church for a lobbyist in Washington would be more successful in changing nuclear policy than supporting a lobbyist from the Union of Concerned Scientists. As the world's societies become more pluralistic, the diffusion of religious energy to secular single-issue groups is a tendency likely to continue. Spiritual leaders will have greater freedom from governments in order to evaluate ethical issues of war and peace, but religious institutions will play a smaller role than in the past in fostering and checking violence.

Concluding Reflections:
Religions, Wars, and Peaces

During the researching and writing of this book, I found no easy way to assess the religious factor in a culture. Themes originating in the world views of peoples over time intermingle with their ethnic and national identities in such a way that "religion is the substance of culture and culture is the form of religion."[1] So it is difficult to isolate, let alone evaluate, the roles of religion in preventing, causing, prolonging, and ending wars. A similar case could be made for the problems in examining the roles of a political ideology such as democracy or a particular economic pattern like capitalism or communism in determining issues of war and peace.

As an example of the task involved in defining a religious influence, take the U.S. Christmas celebration as a religious and secular holiday celebrating the birth of Christ, family, gift-giving, love, and commerce. The commemoration of a sacred story underlies the events; so to deny religious beliefs would negate common sense. However, Christianity has so permeated the history and self-identify of Americans, even of non-Christians, that isolating the religious factor for study, even after one defined it, would be a Herculean exercise. A scholar attempting to decide whether an American Christmas is a religious event might conclude that the question is too complex to decide for the entire society.[2] He might conclude, however, that at the micro level it should be possible to arrive at a conclusion using an adequate working definition of what constituted spirituality

---

[1] Paul Tillich, *Theology of Culture* (1959), 2. It should be noted that the point I am making simplifies the complexities in Tillich's understanding of the relationships between religion and culture.

[2] In a 1996 poll, 96% of Americans said they celebrated Christmas but only 40% thought of it as a "strongly religious holiday." Two out of three Americans claim to go to church at Easter. Of those who said they attended church only at Christmas and/or Easter, 20% either misunderstood or "could not even hazard a guess" as to the significance of Easter. George Gallup, Jr., *Religion in America 1996,* 31.

and extensive information about an individual or small group's faith. For example, he could confidently assert that evangelical Christianity causes the Salvation Army's fund raising to support aiding and converting the poor. Generalizations about the motivation of those who drop coins in the Army's kettles would require extensive interviews, conclusions about the reliability of the donors' words, and a determination of whether their conscious motivations told the whole story.

Studying the Salvation Army looks easy as compared to knowing the influences on individuals who exercise power on behalf of the state. Because religious language and ideals are easy to manipulate for ulterior purposes, scholars rarely accept leaders' words on such subjects at face value. For example, every American president since World War II except Ronald Reagan attended church regularly, but he interpreted the *Bible* literally enough to believe in a coming Armageddon, and endorsed the religious themes of the Moral Majority. The presidents came from many Christian traditions: Roman Catholic, Baptist, Southern Baptist, Quaker, Methodist and Episcopal. Since Eisenhower (1953-60), religion has permeated American political discourse, and recent presidents have sought the moral sanctions provided by religion for their policies and have routinely ended speeches with "God bless America." If their faith did not influence their decisions on war and peace, which involved some of the most difficult issues they confronted, then these men consistently misled the people and perhaps themselves as well.

Because religious beliefs are so diffuse in America (as often in Muslim, Buddhist, and Jewish nations as well), biographers of world leaders can rarely ascribe a foreign policy action on the basis of faith. There are too many variables, and one cannot run a regression analysis on the power of prayer or sermons to influence a president's foreign policy. What is true of presidents applies to most non-communist leaders of the world. Except in China, Cuba, and North Korea, few politicians rule on a platform of atheism but their degree of commitment and definitions of what constitutes and should be the role of spiritual values in foreign policy decisions varies greatly. It would be foolish to deny that religion has no role in presidential decisions on war and peace, but it would be presumptuous to try to isolate it from the myriad of other influences.

If we cannot assess accurately the impact of the faith of public persons, there is even less certainty in assaying the role of entire peoples' religions in sustaining peace, avoiding conflict, or in creating and sustaining the wars of the 1990s. The easiest place to begin is to look at the leaders of institutionalized religions, but bishops and mullahs often do not speak for many of the peoples within their faith communities. In the present as in the past, religions encompass and authenticate many voices, reflecting a variety of emphases in their traditions. In modern societies, individuals belong to many voluntary organizations, and religious commitments can be accentuated or cancelled by other activities. In addition, in large portions of Western Europe and America many find spiritual nurture outside of conventional churches. For example, environmental groups draw upon a heritage of Native American spiritual values about nature but rarely with a deep understanding of the Indian sacred cosmos. In the United Kingdom, fewer than 20% are involved with a church, but 80% profess belief in God. What remains clear is that religion is one but not the only or even the most important factor in causing and preventing violence today, and that there is no satisfactory way of isolating the faith variable in a society in order to see its importance.

Caution in drawing conclusions weighing religious influence should not lead to skepticism about the impact on war of the faiths espoused by leaders, soldiers, or civilians. For example, even in modern times, there can be a religious war. A religious war occurs when religion provides the motivation for the conflict, the opponent is selected because of his or her faith, and the priest class blesses the struggle as holy, absolves the warrior of guilt for killing, and promises salvation in case of death while fighting.[3] More commonly, religion should be seen as a part of a cultural package in which the configuration of the parts determines the societies' attitudes towards war. Here it is not necessary to define exactly what constitutes

---

[3] Michael Sells, *Religion and Genocide in Bosnia* (1998), argues that the warfare among Croats, Serbs, and Bosnians fulfilled the criteria for a religious war.

religion or to isolate its impact, but to consider the ideology, the social structures, and functions of faith within communities. In other words, we should study religion like other phenomena.

Religions and Wars: The Variables

What follow are a few conclusions about religion and war:

<u>Religions facilitate wars when</u>:

1. Sacred texts portray violence in an approving manner whether done by a god or by paradigmatic men and women who make war and whose successes the god guarantees. Imitation of such warriors is approved behavior.

2. Rituals and prayers are designed to enlist the help of the god in war, and the blood sacrifices in rituals prefigure the martyrdoms of those fighting for a holy cause.

3. The risk of losing life in war for a holy cause is compensated for by the promise of salvation in the next life. Martyrdom becomes the highest mark of religious devotion.

4. A group defines itself as a holy or chosen people with special obligations and privileges, particularly involving a right to a land. Such chosen people are more likely to war if

    a. socio-political divisions are justified and enforced on religious lines.

    b. the religious group feels persecuted in the present or past and unable to obtain justice.

    c. the religious group is cohesive enough to unify politically and sees the possibility of gaining power to achieve autonomy or dominion.

    d. the land itself is sacralized and contains sites of special holiness.

5. The devotion of the faithful is joined so intensely to nationalism that these seem to be one phenomenon, so that fighting for land and family becomes a religious duty.

6. Political and/or spiritual leaders come from the upper class, share common interests, and see in the religious teachings and institutions a means of gaining or maintaining power.

7. Priests and people are willing to use the political realm to institutionalize and/or enforce correct worship, doctrine, and ethical practices. Such a perspective can justify rebellion against corrupt leaders or suppression of schismatics or heretics.

8. Alternative value systems and institutions are weak or lacking or seem inefficacious.

9. The state fails to provide an opportunity in which minority and/or majority faith communities can obtain political and religious rights and in which there is minimal interaction among religious leaders.

10. People of different faiths live in close proximity but the teachings and practices of their religions seem incompatible.

11. A group sees its truth as universal and is intolerant of other perspectives either within or outside of its religious tradition.

12. A faith's influence is restricted to a "spiritual" realm and its teachings considered irrelevant to a political sphere in which power is the prime consideration.

Religions facilitate peace within and between nations because:

1. Their scriptures and paradigmatic figures proclaim the value of peace, with peace having a heavenly and earthly dimension.

2. They provide a source of ultimate value, often termed a god, beyond the immediate people and culture, who judges or establishes restraints upon behavior.

3. They inculcate ethical norms of love, compassion, honesty, charity, and social justice. These norms apply to rulers and laity.

4. They question the value of transitory worldly goods and political power and rebuke inordinate ambition.

5. They provide spiritual solace helping peoples to endure the ills of the political system, including differences in wealth.

6. They legitimatize the political order by preaching against rebellion and accept the present boundaries of the state as natural or divinely set.

7. They promote forms of devotion that ignore the state.

8. They bring moral perspectives to bear upon the causes and conduct of a war. Religious leaders must have sufficient autonomy so that they are free to speak out in opposition to the state.

Common misperceptions about religions and wars:

1. Religion alone is a major cause of war.

2. Religious wars are among the worst, because religious issues cannot be compromised.

3. The religious factor in war disappeared after the Peace of Westphalia in 1648 only to re-emerge at the end of the Cold War.

4. If all people would take religion seriously, wars would disappear.

5. Extreme religious devotion is a major cause of war. (If this were so, priests, monks, and women would be the primary fomenters of war.)

6. Religious violence is always a subset of other forms of war.

6. Detailed study will make it possible to isolate the importance of religion as compared with nationalism, economics, and ethnicity as a cause of war.

The difficulty in using these generalizations to predict behavior is obvious: virtually all the facilitators and inhibitors of religion and war are present most of the time in modern faith communities that encompass millions and cross national boundaries. Still, these generalizations should provide insight to the question posed in the introduction to this book: why do the religions of the world, all of which advocate living in harmony with one's neighbors and seeking peace, have such a mixed record in fostering peace? Of course, to some extent this discrepancy is a result of misplaced perception, because war as an unusual activity is better defined, more dramatic, and more visible than peace. We know, for example, more about the fifteen years of Nazi rule than about the half-century of reconciliation between Germany and France since 1945. Most people even in violence-prone great powers live in peace most of the time. Still, it is easier for an historian to highlight the role of religions in fostering conflicts - the expansion of Islam, the Crusades, the Thirty Years War, the American Civil War, the partition of India, ethnic conflict in Bosnia, Sept. 11, 2001 - than to discover a conflict prevented or ended by a leader's or peoples' faith.

Religious Ambivalence to War

Religious institutions do not make peace their primary value, because their sacred scriptures accept and even exalt war. The sacred books of religions even while they proclaim the ultimate value of peace also portray violence in a favorable light, thereby establishing a tradition that can be drawn upon in times of stress. So even when the religion teaches peace, it also validates war. God or gods are pictured as intervening to bring victory to favored warriors. Judaism's central heroes - Moses, Joshua, King David, Isaiah - authorized holy wars to create and defend the land of Israel. A major influence of Judaism on Christianity and Islam came from those sections in the Hebrew Scriptures (Old Testament) that emphasized war for land and not from the later rabbinical traditions that emphasized the necessity of peaceful accommodation. The New Testament is permeated with apocalyptic war, and neither it nor the non-canonical writing of early Christians breathes a spirit of tolerance for those who reject Christ, whether pagans or Jews or Romans. After becoming a power in Rome, Christian apologists like Eusebius and Augustine easily grafted a war tradition onto the gospels.

Islam inherited the warring traditions of Judaism, Christianity, and Bedouins on the Arabian Peninsula, to which Muhammad added teachings of the *Qur'an* on *jihad* and the necessity of Muslim rule for justice and peace. Through the example of their engaging in battle, Muhammad and the first caliphs legitimated holy war. From its inception, Islam sought to create in laws an ethical political realm under the rule of God. For Sunnis, mosque and empire should be fused into one entity under a caliph.

In Hinduism, a major theme of the *Vedas* is Indra as a war god, the *Mahabharata* recounts the wars of the Panda brothers, and the *Bhagavadgita* is ostensibly about Krishna's defense of fighting. State Shintoism designed the cult of the war dead to justify war. Of all the religions discussed in this book, Buddhism appears the most likely to lead to peace, because the Buddha never fought, never justified violence, and opposed killing. However, Siddharata Gautama was a son of a prince who accepted the donations of neighboring princes who made war. So while officially denigrating war, later Buddhists found ways to accommodate violence and later warrior-kings in Siam and Sri Lanka could become *bodhisattvas* and samurai become devotees of Zen.

While the linkage between war and religion in sacred stories is not universal, it is certainly widespread, encompassing not only the religions discussed in this book but the myths of ancient Assyrians, Babylonians, Germanic tribes, Aztecs, Native Americans, Hawaiians, Yoruba and Matabele. Thomas Hobbes' insight still remains true: humans are afraid and find fighting a way to create security. Security is identified with peace, and peace with victory is gained through the help of the gods. Unfortunately, victory in war is always problematic, and so religious rites need to be constantly performed as a way to gain the favor of the gods. The blood in the sacrifice is emblematic of the warriors' blood shed for the community. The ties between religion and war and peace in primitive and modern societies are indissoluble.

The Primacy of Spiritual Peace

Within the belief systems and scriptures of contemporary religions are additional reasons for the failure of religious institutions to provide an effective political critique of war. First, when religions pray for shalom, pax, salaam - they are not primarily interested in political peace. Rather, peace is a relationship with ultimate reality, manifested in the Buddha, or in Vishnu, or in God for Judaism, Christianity, and Islam. No political strategy can bring this peace, though most religions including Islam and Christianity have historically placed a high value on the religious responsibility of the state as a reflection of the justice of God. Still, for Christianity and Buddhism the best that politics can provide is an ordered existence so that the church or monastery can do its work. Any political peace will be flawed by *himsa,* or the sinful nature of humanity.

Because a primary function of religion is to bring all men and women to salvation, the devout will seek this goal in almost every political environment, including war. So the religious institutions will seek to accommodate their teachings to war, because to oppose all fighting would jeopardize their missions to the soldiers, to the families on the home front, and to the wider society. The price of seeking influence within the society is accommodation to the norms of the people. When a religion's proselytizing mandate comes in conflict with its desire for peace, seeking converts and helping the faithful normally will dominate.

Outward political peace becomes a symbol for the inward relationship with the sacred, but politics is clearly a secondary interest to religions that have in their history endured dozens of dynasties while constantly proclaiming the necessity of bringing men and women to salvation. To ask that the church, synagogue, ashram, or mosque prevent war is to misunderstand how they function in society. Getting involved in a political debate before, during, or after a war would be to divert attention from the eternal wisdom needed by all.

Religions also distinguish between the sacred and the profane. The spiritual or ultimate reality of religious peace can make it irrelevant to the so-called real world. This bifurcation, designed to preserve the transcendence of the religion, also allowed the devout and the lukewarm to apply religious ethics selectively. Teachings such as original sin or *himsa,* which viewed the peace possible in the political world as at best transitory, reinforced this separation. Although the clergy have often written about conduct in war, generals have rarely consulted them on battle strategy or on the morality of a new weapon. Common today is the secular value system of realpolitik that ignores religious teachings except as an instrument of national power. The men described in this book as realists - Thucydides, Caesar, Kautilya, Ibn Khaldun, Machiavelli, Clausewitz and their modern successors - need not be considered as irreligious just because they saw little application of morality to war. Their *raison d'état* was victory, guaranteeing the survival of the state or dynasty, and a temporary sacrifice of morality because of necessity was a means to desired ends - and the flourishing of a state whose existence was sanctified by religion can be one of those ends.

V. The Captivity of Religious Institutions

Religious institutions endure a Babylonian Captivity that constrains their leaders from speaking out against governments' policies during wars. Religion's captivity in the society is accentuated by its privileged position coupled with financial dependence. It is no accident that religion enjoys the use of some of the world's most beautiful and lavish buildings filled with splendid works of art, all bestowed upon clerics for what in most cases were decidedly mixed motives. Roman emperors, tsars, and kings built churches and monasteries and subsidized the education of clergy. Hindu maharajahs endowed shrines and monasteries. Buddhist kings endowed monasteries, built *stupas*, and gave to monks as part of an attempt to create a *dharma* realm. Religious scholars have always been a dependent class, whose long apprenticeship for studying and then leisure to meditate or think and write is paid for by someone else. The state by direct support of universities and seminaries or by enforcing a tithe or tax marked for religious purposes gave the clergy a financial reason to be loyal. In addition, Christian clergy remained exempted from most taxes and enjoyed legal privileges. In Islam, sultans built mosques, patronized scholars, and subsidized mullahs. Sunni Muslim clerics operated the law courts and received special taxes. The ayatollahs of the Shi'a came from the wealthy classes and enjoyed traditional taxes as well as fees from the courts. In Europe, archbishops, cardinals, bishops, and influential clergy came from the upper classes and shared the same attitudes towards society as the rulers. Enjoying the prestige and support of the aristocracy, the clergy did not have to be coerced into supporting the status quo and condemning peasant rebellion.

After the Reformation, church leaders knew the vulnerability of their institutions to radical changes fomented either by a government seeking wealth or by religious and political radicals determined to rebuild society. Sermons might advocate improving conditions for the poor or the workers, and criticize an exploitative social order, and there was support for reform, but not for revolution. Beginning with the French Revolution, the Roman Catholic Church accurately perceived her vulnerability to republicans, nineteenth-century liberals, socialists, and communists. Only the monarchs, army, and conservative middle class could be relied upon to preserve the rights of the Church. The clergy were not about to bite the hands that fed them.

In the twentieth century, the church looked back in envy at earlier freedoms. Under totalitarian states, Catholics and Protestants had to struggle just to be allowed to worship. The threat of totalitarianism stilled the churches' voice on war in Germany, Austria, and Russia in 1939, and yet in postwar Poland and Hungary the Catholic Church under very repressive regimes managed to make its opposition to communism apparent. Popes called for peace and good will, but opposition to communism brought acquiescence in nuclear deterrence. The Protestant churches in Europe and America equivocated on the morality of nuclear strategy and mostly supported small wars to contain communism, except in Vietnam, and in the 1980s evangelical fundamentalist churches in America approved of increased military expenditures in order to confront the "evil empire."

The Babylonian Captivity of religious institutions to the war-making strategies of democratic regimes is apparent. Here the captivity is both intellectual and financial. The unifying force of democratic states is nationalism, and the clergy, lower and higher, share the mentality of the country. Where the boundaries of the religion and the state are essentially coterminous, as in Indian Hinduism and Japanese Shintoism, the identification of the faith with national aims is easy. Their histories show, however, that neither Islam nor Christianity has provided an effective check upon wars among nations of the same religion. The caliphate, which served as a symbol for a worldwide Islam, no longer exists.

Catholic bishops publicly supported the aims of their respective countries in World War I and II. Only the papacy sought to stand above the fray. Protestant churches have no higher authority outside of a weak ecumenical movement to remind them of loyalty to a transnational peace. In addition, the clergy and church depend upon the good will of the parishioners for financial support. When democratic governments stopped tax support for churches, the tenure of the clergy became precarious. It is easier for the clergy to refrain from political discourse than to oppose the pro-war leanings of the laity. However, since the 1960s liberal Protestants, Catholic bishops, and the popes have emerged as strong critics of military expenditures, nuclear policies, and wars in which civilians are the primary victims. In the United States the pluralistic nature of the religious community lessens the impact of any religious leader or denomination. Political leverage comes only through interdenominational cooperation. In wartime, government pressure to conform, patriotism of the clergy, and chauvinism of the population preclude effective peace work.

For followers of Judaism, Christianity, Buddhism, Hinduism, and Islam in this sinful world, preserving the general welfare of society requires acquiescing in and advocating warfare. For adherents of these religions, Just War theory in its Christian or Muslim garb and warrior codes like bushido and chivalry may not prevent war, but they take more account of humanity's proclivity to war than pacifism and are less immoral than realpolitik. Pacifism becomes a favored option for a spiritual elite in Eastern and Western religions who can accept its rigor, lack of political influence, and call to suffering. Trying to blend pacifism and Just War as in *Pacem in Terris* and the UN has not yet proven to be an effective political strategy to avoid or humanize war. What religions alone cannot now do and could not do in the past is prevent or stop a war, because faith when politicized tends to lose the ability to transcend culture. Clerics often remind people that war is too important to leave to generals and politicians. A lesson to be learned from the history presented here is that it is also dangerous to leave decisions about war and peace to priests, prophets, and preachers. Those of us committed to proclaiming the value of spiritual solace gained through organized religion need to stress constantly the peace-fostering ethics of all faiths. Otherwise, men will, in the future as too often in the past, allow their religions to sanction turning plowshares into swords.

I am sometimes asked: are there any moral exemplars in this story? Yes, many - but most of these worked quietly without political power. The exception and my particular favorite is Gandhi, who transformed Hindu traditions into a vehicle to work for social justice through nonviolent action. He exercised power without compromising peace or the quest for Truth. Religious ethics are formed by a dialogue between a faith community's past and the present environment. As we shape our religious traditions' response to contemporary war, we would do well to remember Gandhi.

Bibliography of Works Cited
and Suggestions for Further Reading

Introduction: The Past in the Present

Bennett, Olivia, Jo Bexley, and Kitty Warnock, eds. *Arms to Fight: Arms to Protest: Women Speak Out About Conflict*. London: Panos, 1995.

Black, Jeremy. *Why Wars Happen*. New York: New York University Press, 1998.

Bramson, Leon, and George Goethals, eds. *War: Studies from Psychology, Sociology, And Anthropology*. New York: Basic Books, 1994.

Campbell, L. B. *Shakespeare's Histories*. CA: Huntington Library, 1947.

Diamond, Jared. *Guns, Germs, and Steel: The Fate of Human Societies*. New York: Norton, 1999.

Ehrenreich, Barbara. *Blood Rites: Origins and History of the Passions of War*. New York: Metropolitan, Henry Holt, 1997.

Elshtain, Jean. *Women and War*. New York: Basic Books, 1967.

___ and Sheila Tobias, ed. *Women, Militarism, and War*. Savage, MD: Rowman and Littlefield, 1990.

Foakes, R. A. *Shakespeare and Violence*. Cambridge, UK: Cambridge University Press, 2003.

Fussell, Paul. *Wartime: Understanding and Behavior in the Second World War*. New York: Oxford University Press, 1989.

Girard, René. *Violence and the Sacred*. Trans. Patrick Gregory. Baltimore, MD: Johns Hopkins, 1977.

Gregor, Thomas, ed. *Natural History of Peace*. Nashville, TN: Vanderbilt University Press, 1996.

Gregor, Thomas and Leslie Sponsel, ed. *The Anthropology of Peace and Nonviolence*. Boulder, CO: Rienner, 1994.

Haas, Jonathan, ed. *The Anthropology of War*. Cambridge, UK: Cambridge University Press, 1990.

Harris, Adrienne and Ynestra King, eds. *Rocking the Ship of State: Toward a Feminist Peace Politics*. Boulder, CO: Westview, 1989.

Hattaway, Michael. "Blood is their Argument: Men of War and Soldiers in Shakespeare and Others." *Religion, Culture and Society in Early Modern Britain: Essays in Honor of Patrick Collinson*. Ed. Anthony Fletcher and Peter Roberts. Cambridge, UK: Cambridge University Press, 1994.

Holinshed, Raphael. *Holinshed's Chronicles As Used in Shakespeare's Plays*. New York: J .M. Dent, 1940.

Howell, Signe, and Roy Willis, eds. *Societies at Peace: Anthropological Perspectives*. London: Rutledge, 1989.

Jorgensen, Paul A. "Moral Guidance and Religious Encouragement for the Elizabethan Soldiers." *Huntington Library Quarterly,* XIII, 1950.
___. "Theoretical Views of War in Elizabethan England," *Journal of the History of Ideas,* XIII (1952): 469-481.

Juergensmeyer, Mark. *Terror in the Mind of God: the Global Rise of Religious Violence.* Berkley: University of California Press, 2000.

Kohn, Carol. "Sex and Death in the Rational World of the Defence Intellectual," in Laslett, Barbara, ed. *Gender and Scientific Authority.* Chicago: University of Chicago Press, 1996.

Lincoln, Bruce. *Death, War, and Sacrifice: Studies in Ideology and Practice.* Chicago: University of Chicago, 1991.

Lorentzen, Lois Ann, and Jennifer Turpin, eds. *The Women and War Reader.* New York: New York University Press, 1998.

Low, Bobbi S. *Why Sex Matters: A Darwinian Look at Human Behavior.* Princeton, NJ: Princeton University Press, 2000.

Lowe, Ben. *Imagining Peace: A History of Early English Pacifist Ideas.* University Park: PA: Penn State Press, 1997.

O'Connoll, John. *The Ride of the Second Horseman: The Origins of War.* New York: Oxford University Press, 1995.

Otterbein, Keith F. *Feuding and Warfare: Selected Works of Keith F. Otterbein.* War and Society Series, I. Amsterdam, Netherlands: Gordon and Breach, 1994.

Pierson, Ruth, ed. *Women and Peace: Theoretical, Historical, and Practical Propositions.* New York: Croom Helm, 1987.

Reyna, S. P. and R. E. Downes, eds. *Studying War: Anthropological Perspectives* War and Society Series, vol. II. Amsterdam, Netherlands: Gordon and Breach, 1994.

Ruddick, Sara. *Maternal Thinking: Toward a Politics of Peace.* New York: Ballantine, 1990.

Saccio, Peter. *Shakespeare's English Kings: History, Chronicle, Drama.* New York: Oxford University Press, 2000.

Smoker, Paul, Ruth Davies, and Barbara Munske, eds. *A Reader in Peace Studies.* New York: Pergamon Press, 1990.

Sponsel, Leslie E. and Thomas Gregor, eds. *The Anthropology of Peace and Nonviolence.* Boulder, CO: Lynne Reiner Publishers, Inc., 1994.

Tanner, Kathryn. *Theories of Culture: A New Agenda for Theology.* Minneapolis, MN: Fortress Press, 1977.

Turner, Paul and David Pitt. *The Anthropology of War and Peace: Perspectives In the Nuclear Age.* New York: Bergin and Garvey, 1989.

I. The Hebrew Scriptures and War

Beale, G. K. *The Use of Daniel in Jewish Apocalyptic Literature and in the Revelation of St. John.* Lanham, MD: University Press of America, 1984.

Blenkinsopp, Joseph. *A History of Prophecy in Israel: From the Settlement in the Land to the Hellenistic Period.* Philadelphia, PA: Westminster Press, 1983.

Burns, J. Patout, ed. *War and Its Discontents: Pacifism and Quietism in the Abrahamic Traditions.* Washington, DC: Georgetown University Press, 1996. Essays by Michael Broyde, Everett Gendler, Yehada Mirsky, and Naomi Goodman.

Christensen, Duane. *Transformations of the War Oracle in Old Testament Prophecy: Studies in the Oracles Against the Nations.* Missoula, Montana: Scholars Press, 1975.

Collins, John Joseph. *Daniel, First Maccabees, Second Maccabees: With an Excursus on the Apocalyptic Genre.* Wilmington, DE: Michael Glazier, 1981.

Craigie, Peter. *The Problem of War in the Old Testament.* Grand Rapids, Michigan: Eerdmans, 1978.

Dozeman, Thomas B. *God at War: Power in the Exodus Tradition.* New York: Oxford University Press, 1996.

Friedman, Richard Elliott. *Who Wrote the Bible?* San Francisco, CA: Harper, 1997.

Jones, G. H. "The Concept of Holy War" in *The World of Ancient Israel: Sociological, Anthropological, and Political Perspectives.* Ed. R. E. Clements. Cambridge, UK: Cambridge University Press, 1989.

Kaiser, Otto. *Isaiah 1 - 12: A Commentary.* Trans. John Bowden. Second edition. Philadelphia, PA: Westminster Press, 1983.

___. *Isaiah 13 - 39: A Commentary.* Trans. R. A. Wilson. Philadelphia, PA: Westminster Press, 1974.

Lind, Millard. *Yahweh Is a Warrior: the Theology of Warfare in Ancient Israel.* Scottsdale, PA: Herald Press, 1980.

Miller, Patrick. *The Divine Warrior in Early Israel.* Cambridge, MA: Harvard University Press, 1973.

Nardin, Terry, ed. *The Ethics of War and Peace.* Princeton NJ: Princeton University Press, 1996. Essays by Michael Walzer and Avierzer Ravitzky.

Niditch, Susan. *War in the Hebrew Bible: A Study in the Ethics of Violence.* New York: Oxford University Press, 1993.

Perdue, Leo G. and Brian W. Kovacs, eds. *A Prophet to the Nations: Essays in Jeremiah Studies.* Winona Lake, IN: Eisenbrauns, 1984.

Rad, Gerhard von. *Holy War in Ancient Israel.* Trans. Marva Dawn. Grand Rapids, MI: Eerdmans, 1991.

___. *Message of the Prophets.* Trans. D. M. G. Stalker. New York: Harper, 1972.

___. *Studies in Deuteronomy.* Trans. D. M. G. Stalker. London: SCM, 1953.

Smend, Rudolph. *Yahweh War and Tribal Confederation: Reflections upon Israel's Earliest History.* Nashville, TN: Abington, 1970.

Stolz, Fritz. *Yahwes und Israels Kriege: Kriegstheorien und Kriegserfahrungen im glauben des alten Israel.* Zurich, Switzerland: Theologischer Verlag, 1972.

Thompson, J. A. *The Book of Jeremiah.* Grand Rapids, MI: Eerdmans, 1980.

Yoder, Perry B. and Willard M. Swartley, eds. *The Meaning of Peace: Biblical Studies.* Louisville, KY: Westminster/John Knox Press, 1992.

II. The New Testament and War

Bammel, Ernst, and C. D. F. Moule, eds. *Jesus and the Politics of His Day.* Cambridge, UK: Cambridge University Press, 1984.

Brandon, S. G. F. *Jesus and the Zealots: A Study of the Political Factor in Primitive Christianity.* New York: Scribners, 1967.

Cadoux, C. J. *Early Christian Attitudes to War: A Contribution to the History of Ethics.* London, UK: George Allen, 1940.

Cassidy, Richard J. *Jesus, Politics, and Society: A Study of Luke's Gospel.* Maryknoll, New York: Orbis, 1978.

___ and Philip Scharper, eds. *Political Issues in Luke-Acts.* New York: Orbis, 1983.

Crossan, John Dominic. *The Historical Jesus: the Life of a Mediterranean Jewish Peasant.* San Francisco: Harper, 1991.

___ and Jonathan Reed. *Excavating Jesus: Beneath the Stones, Behind the Texts.* New York: Harper San Francisco, 2001.

Cullman, Oscar. *Jesus and the Revolutionaries.* Trans. Gareth Putnam. New York: Harper and Row, 1970.

Duling, Dennis and Norman Perrin. *The New Testament: Proclamation and Paranesis: Myth and History.* Fort Worth, TX: Harcourt Brace, 1994.

Ferguson, John. *Politics of Love: The New and Non-Violent Revolution.* Cambridge, U.K.: J. Clarke, 1973.

Fredriksen, Paula. *From Jesus to Christ: The Origins of the New Testament Images of Jesus.* New Haven, CT: Yale University Press, 1988.

Hengel, Martin. *Was Jesus a Revolutionist?* Trans. William Klassen. Philadelphia: PA, Fortress Press, 1971.

Horsley, Richard. *Jesus and the Spiral of Violence.* San Francisco, CA: Harper and Row, 1987.

Kee, Howard. *Understanding the New Testament.* Englewood Cliffs, NJ: Prentice Hall, 1983.

Macgregor, G. H. C. *The New Testament Basis of Pacifism.* London, UK: J. Clarke, 1936.

Mack, Burton L. *A Myth of Innocence: Mark and Christian Origins.* Philadelphia, PA: Fortress, 1988.

Meier, John. *A Marginal Jew: Rethinking the Historical Jesus.* 2 vols. New York: Doubleday, 1991.

Myers, Chad. *Binding the Strong Man: A Political Reading of Mark's Story of Jesus.* Maryknoll, NY: Orbis, 1988.

Yoder, John. *The Politics of Jesus: Vicit, Agnus Noster*. Grand Rapids, MI: Eerdmans, 1972.
Yoder, Perry and Willard Swartley, eds. *Meanings of Peace: Biblical Studies*, trans. W. Sawatsky. Louisville, KY: Westminster/John Knox, 1992.

III.   The Greeks and War

Adkins, A. W. H. *Merit and Responsibility: A Study in Greek Values*. Oxford, UK: Clarendon Press, 1960.
Aristotle. *Politics of Aristotle*. Trans. Ernest Baker. New York: Oxford University Press, 1958.
Aristophanes. *Five Comedies*. Trans. Benjamin Bickley Rogers. Garden City, NY: Doubleday, 1955.
___. *Peace*. Trans. Alan H. Sommerstein. Chicago, IL: Bochazy-Carducci 1985.
Bloom, Harold, ed. *Homer: Modern Critical Views*. New York: Chelsea House, 1986.
___, ed. *Homer's Iliad: Modern Critical Interpretation*. New York: Chelsea House, 1987.
Connor, W. Robert. *Thucydides*. Princeton, NJ: Princeton University Press, 1984.
Diogenese, Laertius. *Lives of Eminent Philosophers*. Trans. R. D. Hicks. Cambridge, MA: Harvard University Press, 1965.
Ducrey, Pierre. *Warfare in Ancient Greece*. New York: Shocken, 1985.
Dudley, Donald R. *A History of Cynicism from Diogenes to the Sixth Century A.D.* London, UK: Methuen, 1937.
Dyer, Gwynne. *War*. New York: Crown, 1985.
Euripides. *The Bacchae and Other Plays*. Trans. Philip Vellacott. Great Britain: Penguin, 1981.
Griffin, Jasper. *Homer on Life and Death*. Oxford, UK: Clarendon, 1980.
Hamilton, Edith. *The Greek Way to Western Civilization*. New York: New American Library, 1960.
Holmes, Arthur F., ed. *War and Christian Ethics*. Grand Rapids, MI: Baker, 1975.
Iliad of Homer. Trans. Richmond Lattimore. Chicago, IL: University of Chicago, 1951.
Inwood, Brad. *Ethics and Human Action in Early Stoicism*. Oxford, UK: Clarendon, 1985.
Keegan, John. *A History of Warfare*. New York: Knopf, 1993.
___. *War and Civilization*. Television documentary shown on Arts and Entertainment Network, Aug 2-5, 1998.
Lipsius, Frank. *Alexander the Great*. New York: Saturday Review Press, 1974.
Mikalson, Jon D. *Honor Thy Gods: Popular Religion in Greek Tragedy*. Chapel Hill, NC: University of North Carolina Press, 1991.

Ostwald, Martin. "Peace and War in Plato and Aristotle," in *Scripta Classica Israelica: Yearbook of the Israel Society for the Promotion of Classical Studies*, ed. Hannah M. Cotton, et al., vol. XV, 1996.

Pearson, Lionel. *Popular Ethics in Ancient Greece*. Stanford, CA: Stanford University Press, 1962.

Plato. *The Republic of Plato*. Trans. Francis Cornford. Oxford, UK: Oxford University Press, 1958.

Pritchett, W. Kendrick. *The Greek State at War*, vol. III. Berkeley, CA: University of California, 1974.

Reckford, Kenneth. *Aristophanes' Old-and-New Comedy* vol. I. Chapel Hill, NC: University of North Carolina Press, 1987.

Reesor, Margaret E. *The Nature of Man in Early Stoic Philosophy*. London, UK: Duckworth, 1989.

Rich, John and Graham Shipley, eds. *War and Society in the Greek World*. New York: Routledge, 1993.

Robinson, Charles Alexander. *Athens in the Age of Pericles*. Trans. Richard Dunn. South Bend, IN: Notre Dame University Press, 1973.

Rubino, Carl A. and Cynthia W. Shelmerdine, eds. *Approaches to Homer*. Austin, TX: University of Texas Press, 1983.

Sommerstein, Alan H., ed. *Comedies of Aristophanes,* vol. V, *Peace.* Chicago, IL: Bolchazy-Carducci, 1985.

Sophocles. *Sophocles*. Trans. Harold Lloyd-Jones. Cambridge, MA: Harvard University Press, 1994, 1996.

Taaffe, Lauren K. *Aristophanes and Women*. New York: Routledge, 1993.

Thucydides. *The Peloponnesian Wars*. Trans. Rex Warner. Great Britain: Penguin, 1959.

Weil, Simone. *The Iliad: A Poem of Force*. Trans. Mary McCarthy. Wallingford, PA: Pendle Hill, 1956.

Whitman, Cedric. *Aristophanes and the Comic Hero.* Cambridge, MA: Harvard University Press, 1961.

Zampaglione, Geraldo. *The Idea of Peace in Antiquity*. Trans. Richard Dunn. Notre Dame, IN: University of Notre Dame Press, 1973.

IV. Rome: Pagan and Christian

Alfoldi, Andrew. *The Conversion of Constantine and Pagan Rome.* Oxford, UK: Clarendon, 1948.

The Ante-Nicene Fathers. Translations of the Writings of the Fathers Down to A.D. 325. Latin Christianity: Its Founder, Tertullian, "Apology" and "On Idolatry," vol. III. *Origen,* "Celsus," vol. IV. Eds. Alexander Roberts and James Donaldson. New York: Charles Scribners, 1899-1903.

Augustine. *The City of God*. Trans. Marcus Dods. New York: Modern Library, 1950.

___. *The Political and Social Ideas of St. Augustine*. Ed. Herbert A. Deane, New York: Columbia University Press, 1963.

Barnes, Timothy D. *Constantine and Eusebius*. Cambridge, MA: Harvard University Press, 1981.

Baynes, N. H. and H. St. L. B. Moss. *Byzantium: An Introduction to East Roman Civilization*. Oxford, UK: Clarendon, 1949.

Bloom, Harold, ed. *Virgil: Modern Critical Views*. New York: Chelsea House, 1986.

Brown, Peter L. *Augustine of Hippo: A Biography*. London: Faber, 1967.

___. *Religion and Society in the Age of Augustine*. New York: Harper, 1972.

Caesar, Julius. *Seven Commentaries on the Gallic Wars*. Trans. Carolyn Hammond. New York: Penguin, 1960.

Camps, W. A. *An Introduction to Virgil's Aeneid*. Oxford, U.K.: Oxford University Press, 1979.

Caspary, Gerard E. *Politics and Exegesis: Origen and the Two Swords*. Berkeley, CA: University of California Press, 1979.

The Church and War: Papers Read at the Twenty-First Summer Meeting and the Twenty-Second Winter Meeting of the Ecclesiastical History Society. Oxford, Oxfordshire, UK: Published for the Ecclesiastical Historical Society by Basil Blackwell, 1983.

Cicero. *On Moral Obligation: A New Translation of Cicero's De Officiis*. Trans. John Higginbotham. London, U.K.: Faber, 1967.

Cochrane, Charles. *Christianity and Classical Culture: A Study of Thought and Action from Augustus to Augustine*. Oxford, UK: Oxford University Press, 1957.

Eusebius, Pamphilus. *The History of the Church from Christ to Constantine*. Trans. G. A. Williamson. Baltimore, MD: Penguin, 1965.

___. *The Life of the Blessed Emperor Constantine*. London: Samuel Bagster, 1845.

Evans, John. *War, Women, and Children in Ancient Rome*. New York: Routledge, 1991.

Figgis, John. *Political Aspects of Saint Augustine's "City of God."* New York: Longmans, Green and Co., 1921.

Harnack, Adolf von. *Militia Christi: The Christian Religion and the Military in the First Three Centuries*. Trans. David M. Gracie. Philadelphia, PA: Fortress Press, 1981.

Harris, William V. *War and Imperialism in Republican Rome 327-70 B.C.* Oxford, UK: Clarendon Press, 1979.

Helgeland, John, et al., eds. *Christians and the Military: The Early Experience*. Philadelphia, PA: Fortress, 1985.

Helgeland, John. "Roman Army Religion," in *Aufstieg und Niedergang der Romischen Welt*, 1470-1505. New York: De Gruyter, 1978,

___. "Christians and the Roman Army from Marcus Aurelius to Constantine," in *Aufstieg und Niedergang der Romischen Welt*. New York: De Gruyter, 1979.

Herrin, Judith. *The Formation of Christendom*. Princeton, NJ: Princeton University Press, 1987.

Hopkins, Keith. *Conquerors and Slaves.* Sociological Studies in Roman
　　History, vol. I. Cambridge, U.K: Cambridge University Press, 1978.
Howard, Michael, et al., eds. *The Laws of War: Constraints on Warfare in the
　　Western World.* New Haven, CT: Yale University Press, 1994.
Kee, Howard, et al. *Christianity: A Social and Cultural History.* New Jersey:
　　Prentice-Hall, 1999.
Livy. *The War with Hannibal.* Trans. Aubrey de Selincourt and ed. Betty Radice.
　　Reading, U.K: Penguin, 1986.
McCormick, Michael. *Eternal Victory: Triumphal Rulership in Late Antiquity,
　　Byzantium and the Early Medieval West.* Cambridge, UK: Cambridge
　　University Press, 1986.
Markus, R. A. *Christianity in the Roman World.* London: Thames and
　　Hudson, 1974.
Mitchell, Thomas N. *Cicero: The Senior Statesman.* New Haven, CT: Yale
　　University Press, 1991.
New Testament Aprocrypha. Gospels and Related Writings. Ed. Edgar Hennecke,
　　et al. Philadelphia, PA: Westminster, 1963,
Origen. *Contra Celsum.* Trans. Henry Chadwick. Cambridge, UK: Cambridge
　　University Press, 1965.
Raaflaub, Kurt and Nathan Rosenstein, eds. *War and Society in the Ancient
　　And Medieval Worlds.* Center for Helenic Studies, Washington, D.C.
　　Cambridge, MA: Harvard University Press, 1999.
Rich, John and Graham Shipley, eds. *War and Society in the Roman World.*
　　New York: Routledge, 1993.
Stevenson, William, Jr. *Christian Love and Just War: Moral Paradox and
　　Political Life in St. Augustine and his Modern Interpreters.* Macon,
　　GA: Mercer University Press, 1987.
Swift, Louis, ed. *The Early Fathers on War and Military Service.* Wilmington,
　　DE: Glazier, 1983.
___. "War and The Christian Conscience. The Early Years," in *Augsteig und
　　Niedergang der Romischen Welt.* New York: De Gruyter, 1978: 835-68.
___. "War as a Moral Problem in the Early Church: The Historian's
　　Hermeneutical Assumptions," in *The Pacifist Impulse in
　　Historical Perspective.* Ed. Harvey L. Dyck. Toronto: University of
　　Toronto, 1996.
Vegetius, Flavius. "The Military Institutions of the Romans," in *Roots of
　　Strategy.* Trans. John Clark. Harrisburg, PA: Military Service, 1940.
Virgil (Publius Vergilius Maro). *The Aeneid.* Trans. W. F. Jackson Knight. New
　　York: Penguin Books, 1984.
Wengst, Klaus. *Pax Romana and the Peace of Jesus Christ.* Philadelphia, PA:
　　Fortress Press, 1987.
Williams, R. D. *The Aeneid.* London: Allen and Unwin, 1987.
Yoder, John Howard. *Christian Attitudes to War, Peace, and Revolution: A
　　Companion to Bainton.* Elkhart, IN: Peace Resource Center, 1983.

V. The Religions of the East: Hinduism

Bandyopadhyaya, Banerjee Narayanchandra. *Development of Hindu Polity and Political Theory.* New Delhi, India: Munshiram Manoharlal, 1980.

Bhagavadgita. Trans. and ed. S. Radhakrishnan. New York: Harper, 1948.

Dikshitar, V. R. Ramachandra. *War in Ancient India.* Delhi, India: Motilal Banarsidass, 1944, reprinted 1987.

Drekmeier, Charles. *Kingship and Community in Early India.* Stanford, CA: Stanford University Press, 1962.

Dundas, Paul. *The Jains.* New York: Routledge, 1992.

Govind Tryambak. *The Art of War in Ancient India.* London, UK: Oxford University Press, 1929.

Gupta, S. P. and K. S. Ramachandran, eds. *Mahabharata: Myth and Reality, Differing Views.* Delhi, India: Agam Prakashan, 1976.

Heesterman, J.C. *The Inner Conflict of Tradition: Essays in Indian Ritual, Kingship, and Society.* Chicago, IL: University of Chicago Press, 1985.

Hiltebeitel, Alf. *The Ritual of Battle: Krishna in the Mahabharata.* Ithaca, NY: Cornell University Press, 1976.

Hindu Scriptures. Trans. and ed. Dominic Goodall. Berkeley, CA: University of California, 1996.

Hopkins, Thomas. *The Hindu Religious Traditions.* Belmont, CA: Wadsworth, 1971.

Katz, Rught Cecily. *Arjuna in the Mahabharata: Where Krishna Is, There Is Victory.* Columbia: South Carolina: University of South Carolina, 1989.

Klostermaier, Klaus K. *A Short Introduction to Hinduism.* Oxford, U.K.: One World, 1998.

The Mahabharata. Trans. and ed. Chakravarthi Narasimhan. New York: Columbia University Press, 1965.

Minor, Robert N., ed. *Modern Indian Interpreters of the Bhagavadgita.* Albany, NY: State University of New York Press, 1986.

The Rig Veda: An Anthology. Trans. Wendy Doniger O'Flaherty. New York: Penguin, 1981

Vettammani. *Puranic Encyclopaedia : A Comprehensive Dictionary With Special Reference to the Epic and Puranic Literature.* Delhi, India: M. Banarsidass, 1975.

Walker, Benjamin. *The Hindu World: An Encyclopedic Survey of Hinduism.* New York: Praeger, 1968

Zaehner, R. C. *Hinduism.* New York: Oxford University Press, 1970.

VI. Religions of the East: Buddhism
Buddhist Nonviolence and Statecraft

A Buddhist Bible. Trans. and ed. Dwight Goddard. Boston, MA: Beacon, 1994 edition.

Demiéville, Paul. "Le Bouddhisme et la Guerre," in *Choix D'Études Bouddhiques 1929-1970.* Leiden: Brill, 1973.

Dialogues of the Buddha. Part 1 in *The Sacred Books of the Buddhists.* Trans. T.W. Rhys Davids. (1899). This edition, London: Luzac, 1969.

Gokhale, Balrisha, G. *Asoka Maurya.* New York: Twayne, 1966.

Gombrich. "The Consecration of a Buddhist Image," *Journal of Asian Studies.* 26 (1966).

___. *Theravada Buddhism: A Social History from Ancient Benares to Modern Colombo.* New York: Routledge, 1991.

Ikeda, Daisaku. *Buddhism: the First Millennium.* Trans. Burton Watson. Tokyo, Japan: Kodansha, 1978.

Ling, Trevor. *Buddhism, Imperialism, and War: Burma and Thailand in Modern History.* Boston, MA: George Allen and Unwin, 1979.

The Middle Length Discourses of the Buddha. The Majjhima Nikaya. Trans. Bhikkhu Bodhi and Bhikkhu Nanamoli. Boston, MA: Wisdom Publications, 1995.

Sharma, Ram S. *Aspects of Political Ideas and Institutions in Ancient India.* Delhi, India: Motilal Barnarsidass, 1959.

Smith, Bardwell, ed. *Religion and Legitimation of Power in Thailand, Laos, and Burma.* Chambersburg, PA: Anima, 1978.

___. *Religion and Legitimation of Power in Sri Lanka.* Chambersburg, PA: Anima, 1978.

Strong, John. *The Legend of King Asoka: A Study and Translation of the Asokavadana.* Princeton, NJ: Princeton University Press, 1983.

Swearer, Donald K. *Buddhism.* Niles, IL: Argus, 1977.

___. *Buddhism and Society in Southeast Asia.* Chambersburg, PA: Anima, 1981.

Thapar, Romila. *Asoka and the Decline of the Mauryas.* Oxford, UK: Oxford University Press, 1961.

The Two Wheels of Dhamma: Essays on the Theravqada Tradition in India and Ceylon, Eds. Gananath Obeyesekere, Frank Reynolds, and Bardwell Smith. Chambersburg, PA: American Academy of Religion, 1972.

Walpola, Rahula. *What the Buddha Taught.* New York: Grove, 1974.

Japan

Berry, Mary Elizabeth. *Hideyoshi.* Cambridge, MA: Harvard University Press, 1982.

Collcutt, Martin. "The Zen Monastery in Kamakura Society," in *Court and Bakufu in Japan.* Ed. Jeffrey P. Mass. New Haven, CN: Yale University Press, 1982, 191-220.

Kraft, Kenneth. *Eloquent Zen: Daito and Early Japanese Zen.* Honolulu: HA: University of Hawaii Press, 1992.

King, Winston L. *Zen and the Way of the Sword: Arming the Samurai Psyche.* New York: Oxford University Press, 1993.

Lu, David J. *Japan: A Documentary History: The Dawn of History to the Late Tokugawa Period.* Vol. I. Armonk, New York: M.E. Sharpe, 1997.

McFarland, H. Neill. *Daruma: The Founder of Zen in Japanese Art and Popular Culture.* Tokoyo, Japan: Kodansha, 1987.

Perrin, Noel. *Giving Up the Gun: Japan's Reversion to the Sword, 1543-1879.* Boston, MA: Godine, 1979.

Turnbull, S.R. *The Samurai.* New York: MacMillan, 1977.

Suzuki, Daisetz T. *Zen and Japanese Culture.* London, UK: Routledge and Kegan Paul, 1959.

Tsunoda, Ryusaku, W. M. T. De Bary, and Donald Keene. *Sources of Japanese Tradition.* Vol. I. New York: Columbia University Press, 1964.

VII. Islam in War and Peace

Adas, Michael, ed. *Islamic and European Expansion.* American Historical Association. Philadelphia: Temple University Press, 1993.

Aho, James A. *Religious Mythology and the Art of War: Comparative Religious Symbolisms of Military Violence.* Westport, CN: Greenwood Press, 1981.

Al-Azmah, Aziz. *Ibn Khaldun: An Essay in Reinterpretation.* London, UK: Cass, 1982.

Blankinship, Khalid Yahya. *The End of the Jihad State: The Reign of Hisham Ibn 'Abd al-Malik and the Collapse of the Umayyads.* Albany, NY: State University of New York, 1994.

Bronner, Michael. *Aristocratic Violence and Holy War: Studies in the Jihad and the Arab-Byzantine Frontier.* New Haven, CT: American Oriental Society, 1996.

Donner, Fred McGraw. *The Early Islamic Conquests.* Princeton, NJ: Princeton University Press, 1981.

Ehrenkreutz, Andrew S. *Saladin.* Albany, NY: State University of New York Press, 1972.

Eposito, John. *Islam: The Straight Path.* New York: Oxford University Press, 1989.

Fischel, Walter J. *Ibn Khaldun in Egypt: His Public Functions and His Historical Research, 1392-1405: A Study in Islamic Historiography.* Berkeley, CA: University of California, 1967

Gauillaume, Alfred. *Islam.* Hammondsworth, UK: Penguin, 1966.

Gellner, Ernest, ed. *Islamic Dilemmas: Reformers, Nationalists and Industrialization: The Southern Shore of the Mediterranean.* New York: Mouton, 1985.

Halm, Heinz. *Shiism.* Trans. Janet Watson. Edinburgh, UK: Edinburg University Press, 1991.

Hawting, G. R. *The First Dynasty of Islam: The Umayyad Caliphate AD 661-750.* New York: Routledge, 1986. This edition, 2000.

Hodgson, Marshall. *The Venture of Islam: Conscience and History in a World Civilization The Classical Age* Vol. I. Chicago: University of Chicago Press, 1974.

Jandora, John W. *The March from Medina: A Revisionist Study of Arab Conquests*. Clifton, NJ: Kingsbury, 1990.

Johnson, James Turner. *The Holy War Idea in Western and Islamic Traditions.* University Park, PA: Penn State University Press, 1997.

Johnson, James Turner and John Kelsay, eds. *Cross, Crescent, and Sword: The Justification and Limitation of War in Western Islamic Tradition.* New York: Greenwood Press, 1990.

Kelsay, John. *Islam and War: A Study in Comparative Ethics.* Louisville, KY: Westminster/John Knox, 1993.

___ and Johnson, James Turner, eds. *Just War and Jihad: Historical and Theoretical Perspectives on War and Peace in Western and Islamic Traditions.* New York: Greenwood Press, 1991.

Kennedy, Hugh. *The Prophet and the Age of the Caliphates: The Islamic Near East from the Sixth to the Eleventh Century.* New York: Longman, 1986.

___. *The Armies of the Caliphs: Military and Society in the Early Islamic State.* New York: Routledge, 2001.

Khadduri, Majid. *War and Peace in the Law of Islam.* Baltimore, MD: Johns Hopkins University Press, 1955.

Khaldun, Ibn. *The Muqaddimah: An Introduction to History.* Trans. Franz Rosenthal. London: Routledge and Kegan Paul, 1958.

___. *An Arab Philosophy of History: Selections from the Prolegomena of Ibn Khaldun of Tunis.* Trans. Charles Issawi. London: John Murray, 1950.

Lewis, Bernard, ed. *Islam: from the Prophet Muhammad to the Capture of Constantinople, Politics and War* Vol. I. Oxford, UK: Oxford University Press, 1987.

Lyons, M. C. and D. E. P. Jackson. *Saladin: the Politics of the Holy War.* Cambridge, UK: Cambridge University Press, 1982.

Mahdi, Muhsin. *Ibn Khaldûn's Philosophy of Culture: A Study of the Philosophic Foundation of the Science of Culture.* Chicago, IL: University of Chicago, 1957.

___. *Ibn Khaldûn's Philosophy of History: A Study of the Philosophic Foundation of the Science of Culture.* Chicago, IL: University of Chicago, 1964.

Partner, Peter. *God of Battles: Holy Wars of Christianity and Islam.* Princeton, NJ: Princeton University Press, 1997.

The Qur'an. The First American Version. Trans. T. B. Irving. Brattleboro, Vt: Amana, 1985.

The Qur'an: Readings in the. Trans. and ed. Kenneth Cragg. London, UK: Collins, 1988.

Rushd, ibn (Averroes). *Jihad in Medieval and Modern Islam: The Chapter on Jihad from Averroes' Legal Handbook 'Bidayat al Mdjtahid.* Trans. Rudoph Peters. Leyden, Netherlands: Brill, 1977.

Shaybani, Muhammad ibn al-Hasan al. *The Islamic Law of Nations.* Ed. and trans. Majid Khaldduri. Baltimore, MD: Johns Hopkins University Press, 1996.

Watt, William Montgomery. "Islamic Conceptions of Holy War," in *The Holy War*. Ed. Thomas P. Murphy. Columbus: Ohio: Ohio State University Press, 1976.
___. *Muslim-Christian Encounters: Perceptions and Misperceptions.* New York: Routledge, 1991.

VIII. Medieval Europe

Adams, Robert P. *The Better Part of Valor: More, Erasmus, Colet and Vives, on Humanism, War and Peace 1496-1535.* Seattle, WA: University of Washington Press, 1962.

Aquinas, Thomas. *Introduction to Saint Thomas Aquinas*, ed. Anton Pegis. New York: Modern Library, 1948.

___. *St. Thomas Aquinas On Politics and Ethics,* ed. and trans. Paul Sigmund. New York: Norton, 1988.

Bainton, Roland. *Christian Attitudes toward War and Peace.* London: Hodder and Stoughton, 1960.

Barber, Malcolm. *The Cathars: Dualist Heretics in Languedoc in the High Middle Ages.* Harlow, UK: Longman, 2000.

Bonet, Honoré. *The Tree of Battles: an English Version.* Ed. and trans. G. W. Coopland. Cambridge, MA: Harvard University Press, 1949.

Brundage, James. *Medieval Canon Law and the Crusader.* Madison, WI: Wisconsin University Press, 1969.

___. *The Crusades, Holy War, and Canon Law.* Brookfield, VT: Gower, 1991.

Cameron, Euan. *Waldenses: Rejections of the Holy Church in Medieval Europe.* Oxford. UK: Blackwell, 2000.

Christiansen, Eric. *The Northern Crusades: the Baltic and Catholic Frontier,* Minneapolis, MN: University of Minnesota Press, 1980.

Christine de Pisan. *The Book of Fayttes of Armes and of Chyualrye.* Ed. A. T. P. Byles. Trans. William Caxton. London: Early English Text Society. Oxford University Press, 1932.

Contamine, Philippe. *War in the Middle Ages.* Trans. Michael Jones. Oxford, UK: Blackwell, 1984.

Copleston, Frederick C. *Medieval Philosophy.* New York: Harper, 1962.

Erdmann, Carl. *The Origin of the Idea of Crusade.* Trans. and foreword by Marshall W. Baldwin and Walter Goffard. Princeton, NJ: Princeton University Press, 1997.

France, John. *Western Warfare in the Age of Crusades, 1000-1300.* Ithaca, NY: Cornell University Press, 1999.

Hall, Bert S. *Weapons and Warfare in Renaissance Europe.* Baltimore: John Hopkins University Press, 1997.

Head, Thomas and Richard Landes, eds. *The Peace of God: Social Violence and Religious Response in France Around the Year 1000.* Ithaca, NY: Cornell University Press, 1992.

Herrin, Judith. *The Formation of Christendom*. Princeton, NJ: Princeton University Press, 1987.

Heyn, Udo. *Peacemaking in Medieval Europe: An Historical and Bibliographical Guide*. Regina Guides to Historical Issues. Claremont, CA: Regina, 1997.

Johnson, James Turner. *Ideology, Reason and the Limitation of War: Religious and Secular Concepts 1200-1740*. Princeton, NJ: Princeton University Press, 1975.

___. *Just War Tradition and the Restraint of War: A Moral and Historical Inquiry*. Princeton, NJ: Princeton University Press, 1981.

___. *The Quest for Peace: Three Moral Traditions in Western Cultural History*. Princeton, NJ: Princeton University Press, 1987.

Joinville, Jean and Geoffroi de Villehardouin. *Chronicles of the Crusades*. Ed. and trans. M. R. B. Shaw. Baltimore, MD: Penguin Books, 1963, reprinted 1977.

Keen, Maurice Hugh. *Chivalry*. New Haven, CT: Yale University Press, 1984.

___. *The Laws of War in the Late Middle Ages*. London: Routledge and K. Paul, 1965.

Knox, MacGregor and Williamson Murray, eds. *The Dynamics of Military Revolution 1300-2050*. Cambridge, UK: Cambridge University Press, 2001.

Lambert, Malcolm. *Medieval Heresy: Popular Movements from the Gregorian Reform to the Reformation*. 3rd edition. Oxford, UK: Blackwell, 2002.

Ladurie, Le Roy. *Montaillou: The Promised Land of Error*. Trans. Barbara Bray. New York: Braziller, 1978.

Lowe, Ben. *Imagining Peace: A History of Early English Pacifist Ideas 1340-1560*. University Park, PA: Pennsylvania State University Press, 1997.

Mayer, Hans Eberhard. *The Crusades*. Trans. John Gillingham. Oxford, UK: Oxford University Press, 1988.

Muldoon, James. *Popes, Lawyers, and Infidels: the Church and the Non-Christian World, 1250-1550*. Philadelphia, PA: University of Pennsylvania Press, 1979.

Murphy, Thomas Patrick, ed. *The Holy War*. Columbus, OH: Ohio State University Press, 1976.

Peters, Edward. *Christian Society and the Crusades, 1198-1229*. Philadelphia, PA: University of Pennsylvania Press, 1971.

Renna, Thomas. "The Idea of Peace in the West, 500-1500," *Journal of Medieval History* 6 (1980).

Riley-Smith, J. S. C. *The Crusades: A Short History*. New Haven, CN: Yale University Press, 1987.

___. *The First Crusade and the Idea of Crusading*. Philadelphia: University of Pennsylvania Press, 1986.

___. *The First Crusades 1095-1131*. Cambridge, UK: Cambridge University Press, 1997.

Russell, Frederick H. *The Just War in the Middle Ages*. Cambridge, UK: Cambridge University Press, 1977.

Shaw, Margaret R. B. *Chronicles of the Crusades*. Baltimore, MD: Penguin Books, 1963.

Theisen, Wilfred. "1022 and All That," *Occasional Paper* 39 (May 2, 1991).

Treesh, Susanna. "The Waldenesian Recourse to Violence." *Church History* 58 (1986): 294-305.

Tyerman, Christopher. *The Invention of the Crusades*. Toronto, Canada: University of Toronto Press, 1998.

Vale, Malcolm. *War and Chivalry: Warfare and Aristocratic Culture in France and Burgundy at the End of the Middle Ages.* Athens, GA: University of Georgia Press, 1981.

Walters, LeRoy Brandt. "Five Classic Just War Theories: A Study in the Thought of Thomas Aquinas Vitoria, Suarez, Gentili, and Grotius." Ph.D. diss., Yale University, 1971.

IX. Splintering of European Traditions

Adams, Robert P. *The Better Part of Valor: More, Erasmus, Colet, and Vives on Humanism, War, and Peace 1496-1535.* Seattle, WA: University of Washington Press, 1962.

Arkaksinen, Timo and Martin Bertman, eds. *Hobbes: War Among Nations.* Brookfield, VT: Avebury, 1989.

Bainton, Roland. *Erasmus of Christendom.* New York: Scribners, 1969.

___. *Here I Stand: A Life of Martin Luther.* Nashville, TN: Abington, 1950.

Baugmgold, Deborah. *Hobbes' Political Theory.* Cambridge, UK: Cambridge University Press, 1988.

Bayley, C. C. *War and Society in Renaissance Florence: The De Militia of Leonardo Bruni.* Toronto, Canada: University of Toronto Press, 1961.

Benedict, Philip et al., eds. *Reformation, Revolt and Civil War in France and the Netherlands1555-1585.* Amsterdam,Netherlands:Koninklijke Nederlandse Akademie van Weternschappen Verhandelingen, 1999.

Bornkamm, Heinrich. *Luther's World of Thought.* Trans. Martin Bertram. St Louis, MO: Concordia, 1958.

Bossy, John. *Peace in the Post-Reformation.* Cambridge, UK: Cambridge University Press, 1998.

Bull, Hedley; Benedict Kingsbury, and Adam Roberts, eds. *Hugh Grotius and International Relations.* Oxford, UK: Clarendon Press, 1990.

Calvin, John. *Institutes of the Christian Religion.* Library of Christian Classics, vol. XX. Ed. John T. McNeill. Trans. Ford Lewis Battles. Philadelphia, PA: Westminster, 1960.

Cargill Thompson, W. D. J. *The Political Thought of Martin Luther.* Brighton, Sussex, UK: Harvester Press, 1984.

Caws, Peter, ed. *The Causes of Quarrel: Essays on Peace, War, and Thomas Hobbes.* Boston: Beacon, 1989.

Clasen, Claus Peter. *Anabaptism: A Social History 1525-1618*. Ithaca, NY: Cornell University Press 1972.

Cooper, J. P., ed. *New Cambridge Modern History, The Decline of Spain and the Thirty Years War 1609-1648/59* Vol. IV Cambridge, UK: Cambridge University Press, 1970.

Daniel-Rops, Henri. *The Catholic Reformation*. Trans. John Warrington. Garden City, NY: Doubleday, 1964.

Davis, Natalie Zemon. *Society and Culture in Early Modern France*. Stanford, CA: Stanford University Press, 1975.

Edwards, Charles. *Hugo Grotius: The Miracle of Holland*. Chicago: Nelson-Hall, 1981.

Erasmus, Desiderius. *The Education of a Christian Prince*. Trans. Lester Born. New York: Norton, 1968.

___. *The Essential Erasmus*. Ed. John P. Dolan. New York: Mentor Omega, 1964.

___. *The Julius Exclusus of Erasmus*. Trans. Paul Pascal. Intro. J. K. Sowards. Bloomington, IN: Indiana University Press, 1968.

Fernández-Santamariá, J. A. *Reason of State and Statecraft in Spanish Political Thought, 1595-1640*. Lanham, MD: University of Maryland Press, 1983.

___. *The State, War and Peace: Spanish Political Thought in the Renaissance, 1516-1559*. New York: Cambridge University Press, 1977.

Fleisher, Martin. *Machiavelli and the Nature of Political Thought*. New York: Atheneum, 1972.

Gauthier, David P. *The Logic of Leviathan: The Moral and Political Theory of Thomas Hobbes.* Oxford, UK: Clarendon, 1969.

Gellinek, Christian. *Hugo Grotius*. Boston: Twayne, 1983.

Gentili, Alberico. *De Iure Bellis Libri Tres* Vol. XVI, pt. 2. Oxford: Clarendon Press, 1933.

Gilbert, Allan H. *Machiavelli's Prince and Its Forerunners: The Prince as a Typical Book de Regimine Principium*. Durham, NC: Duke University Press, 1938.

Gilbert, Felix. *Machiavelli and Guiccardini: Politics and History in Sixteenth Century Florence.* Princeton, NJ: Princeton University Press, 1965.

Grazia, Sebastian de. *Machiavelli in Hell*. Princeton, NJ: Princeton University Press, 1989.

Grotius, Hugo. *De Jure Belli Ac Pacis Libri Tres* Vol. II. Trans. by Francis Kelsey. Oxford, UK: Clarendon Press, 1925.

Hale, J. R. *War and Society in Renaissance Europe, 1450-1620*. New York: St. Martin's Press, 1985.

Hobbes, Thomas. *De Cive. The English Version*. Ed. Howard Warrenden. The Clarendon Edition of the Philosophical Works of Thomas Hobbes. Oxford, UK: Clarendon Press, 1983.

___. *Leviathan*. Introduction K. R. Minogue. New York: Dutton, 1976.

Holt, Mack P. *The French Wars of Religion, 1562-1629*. New York: Cambridge University Press, 1995.

Huizinga, John. *Erasmus.* New York: Scribners, 1924.

Iserloh, Erin, Joseph Glazik, and Hubert Jedin. *Reformation and Counter-Reformation. History of the Church* Vol. V. Trans. Anselm Biggs and Peter Becker. New York: Crossroad, 1986.

Lowe, Ben. *Imagining Peace: A History of Early English Pacifist Ideas.* University Park, PA: Penn State University Press, 1997.

Luther, Martin. *Works of Martin Luther* 6 Vols. Philadelphia, PA: A.J. Holman, 1915-1931.

___. *Luther's Works* Vol. XLVII. Philadelphia, PA: Fortress Press, 1971.

Machiavelli, Niccolo. *The Art of War* (1521). Trans. Ellis Farneworth. New York: Capo, 1965.

___. *The Prince,* ed. Quentin Skinner and Russell Price. New York: Cambridge University Press, 1988.

Mansfield, Harvey C. *Machiavelli's Virtue.* Chicago, IL: University of Chicago, 1996.

Martinich, Aloysius P. *The Two Gods of Leviathan: Thomas Hobbes on Religion and Politics.* Cambridge, UK: Cambridge University Press, 1992.

Muldoon, James. *Popes, Lawyers, and Infidels:The Church and the Non-Christian World 1250-1550.* Philadelphia, PA: University of Pennsylvania Press, 1979.

Parker, Geoffrey, ed. *The Thirty Years War.* 2nd edition. New York: Routledge, 1997.

Ridley, Jasper. *John Knox.* New York: Oxford University Press, 1968.

Sabine, George. *A History of Political Theory.* New York: Henry Holt, 1937.

Scott, James Brown. *The Spanish Origin of International Law.* London: Clarendon Press, 1934.

Skinner, Quentin. *The Foundations of Modern Political Thought* Vol. I, *The Renaissance;* Vol. II, *The Age of Reformation.* Cambridge, UK: Cambridge University Press, 1978.

Strayer, James. *Anabaptists and the Sword.* Lawrence, Kansas: Coronado, 1976.

Suárez, Francisco. *Selections from Three Works. DeTriplici Virtute Theologicca, Fide, Spe, et Charitate,* 1621 Vol. II. Trans. by Gwladys L. Williams. London: Clarendon Press, 1944.

Vitoria, Francisco de. *Francisci de Victoria De Indis et De Ivre Belli Reflectiones.* Ed. Ernest Nys. Washington, DC: The Carnegie Institution of Washington, 1917.

Wedgwood, C. V. *The Thirty Years War.* New Haven, CT: Yale University Press, 1939.

Williams, Peter. *The Radical Reformation.* Philadelphia, PA: Westminster Press, 1962.

Wolin, Sheldon. *Politics and Vision: Continuity and Innovation in Western Political Thought.* Boston, MA: Little, Brown, 1960.

The World of Hugo Grotius. Proceedings of the International Colloquium Organization by the Grotius Committee. 1983. Amsterdam: APA - Holland University Press, 1984.

X. War and Peace in the Age of Reason

Adams, Robert M., ed. *Voltaire, Candide, or Optimism.* New York: Norton, 1966.

Anderson, M. S. *War and Society in Europe of the Old Regime 1618-1789.* New York: St. Martin's, 1988.

Best, Geoffrey. *Humanity in Warfare.* New York: Columbia University Press, 1980.

Bloom, Harold, ed. *Jean-Jacques Rousseau, Modern Critical Views.* New York: Chelsea House, 1988.

Brock, Peter. *The Quaker Peace Testimony 1660-1914.* Syracuse, NY: Syracuse University Press, 1990.

Ceadel, Martin. *The Origins of War Prevention.* Oxford, U.K.: Clarendon, 1996.

Corvisier, André. *Armies and Societies in Europe, 1494-1789.* Trans. Abigail T. Siddall. Bloomington, IN: Indiana University Press, 1979.

Davidson, Robert. *War Comes to Quaker Pennsylvania, 1682-1756.* New York: Columbia University Press for Temple University, 1957.

Frost, J. William. *A Perfect Freedom: Religious Liberty in Pennsylvania.* New York: Cambridge University Press, 1990.

Gallie, W. B. *Philosophers of Peace and War: Kant, Clausewitz, Marx, Engels, and Tolstoy.* Cambridge, England: Cambridge University Press, 1978.

Gargaz, Pierre-Andre. *A Project of Universal and Perpetual Peace.* New York: Garland, 1973.

Gat, Azar. *The Origins of Military Thought from the Enlightenment to Clausewitz.* Oxford, UK: Clarendon Press: 1989.

Hemleben, Sylvester John. *Plans for World Peace Through Six Centuries.* Chicago, IL: University of Chicago Press, 1943.

Jacob, J. R. and Jacob, M. C., eds. *Peace Projects of the Seventeenth Century* comprising Sully's "Great Design of Henry IV," Hugo Grotius, "The Law Of War and Peace," and William Penn, "An Essay Towards the Present and Future Peace of Europe" in The Garland Library of War and Peace. New York: Garland, 1972.

Jacobs, M. C., ed. *Peace Projects of the Eighteenth Century* comprising Charles de Saint-Pierre, "A Shorter Project for Perpetual Peace," Jean Jacques Rousseau, "A Project of Perpetual Peace," and Jeremy Bentham, "A Project of Universal and Perpetual Peace" in The Garland Library of War and Peace. New York: Garland, 1973.

Jennings, Francis. *Empire of Fortune: Crown, Colonies, and Tribes in the Seven Years War in America.* New York: Norton, 1988.

Kant, Immanuel. *Eternal Peace and Other International Essays.* Trans. W. Hastie. Boston, MA: World Peace Foundation, 1914. The Garland Library reprints the 1903 edition by Mary Campbell Smith.

Marietta, Jack. *The Reformation of American Quakerism, 1748-1783.* Philadelphia: PA: University of Pennsylvania Press, 1984.

805

Mekeel, Arthur. *The Quakers and the American Revolution.* York: UK: Sessions, 1966.
Meyer, Henry. "Voltaire on War and Peace." In *Studies on Voltaire and the Eighteenth Century.* Banbury, UK: Voltaire Foundation, 1976.
The Papers of William Penn, Vol. I-IV. Ed. Mary Dunn and Richard Dunn. Philadelphia, PA: University of Pennsylvania Press, 1981-1987.
Rousseau, Jean Jacques. "L'État de Guerre," in *Political Writings of Jean Jacques Rousseau.* Vol. I. Ed. C. E. Vaughan. New York: Wiley, 1962.
Rowe, Constance. *Voltaire and the State.* New York: Octagon, 1968.
Vattel, Emer de. *Le Droit des Gens: ou Principes de la Loi Naturelle, Appliques a la Conduite et aux Affaires des Nations at des Souverains.* Washington, D. C.: Carnegie Institution of Washington, 1915.
Voltaire, Francois-Marie Arouet. *Candide or Optimism.* Ed. Norman L. Torrey. New York: Appleton-Century-Crofts, 1946.
___. *Candide or Optimism, translation, Backgrounds, Criticism.* Ed. Robert M. Adams. New York: W. W. Norton, 1966.
Weddle, Meredith B. *Walking in the Way of Peace: Quaker Pacifism in the Seventeenth Century.* New York: Oxford University Press, 2001.
Weigley, Russell. *The Age of Battles: The Quest for Decisive Warfare from Breitenfeld to Waterloo.* Bloomington, IN: Indiana University Press, 1991.

XI. Revolutions as Just War

Ashley, Maurice. *The Glorious Revolution of 1688.* New York: Scribner's, 1966.
Bailyn, Bernard. *The Ideological Origins of the American Revolution.* Cambridge, MA: Harvard, 1967.
Bartel, Roland, "English Clergymen and Laymen on the Principle of War, 1789-1802." *Anglican Theological Review* 38 (1956).
Bennett, Betty, ed. *British War Poetry in the Age of Revolution.* New York: Garland, 1976.
Best, Geoffrey. *War and Society in Revolutionary Europe, 1770-1870.* New York: St. Martin's, 1982.
Bertho. "Naissance et Elaboration D'une 'Theologie' de la guerre chez les Eveques de Napoleon." *Civilisation Chrétienne.* Ed. Jene Rene Derre. Paris: Editions Beuchesne, 1975.
Chadwick Owen. *The Popes and European Revolution. Oxford History of the Christian Church.* Oxford, UK: Clarendon, 1981.
Chartier, Roger. *Cultural Origins of the French Revolution.* Trans. Lydia Cochrane. Durham, NC: Duke University Press, 1991.
Cookson, J. E. *The Friends of Peace: Anti-War Liberalism in England 1793-1815.* New York: Cambridge University Press, 1982.
Cox, Richard Howard. *Locke on War and Peace.* Oxford, UK: Clarendon Press, 1960.

806

Daniel-Rops, H. *Church in an Age of Revolution 1789-1870*. Trans. John Warrington. New York: Dutton, 1965.
Dansette, Adrien. *Religious History of Modern France. From the Revolution to the Third Republic*. New York: Herder & Herder, 1961.
Doyle, William. *The Oxford History of the French Revolution*. Oxford, UK: Clarendon Press, 1989.
Forrest, Alan. *Conscripts and Deserters: The Army and Society During the Revolution and Empire*. New York: Oxford University Press, 1989.
Gellner, Ernest. *Nationalism*. New York: New York University Press, 1997.
Higgenbotham, Don, ed. *Reconsiderations on the Revolutionary War. Contributions in Military History #14*. Westport, CT: Greenwood Press, 1978.
Hoffman, Ronald and Peter Albert, eds. *Arms and Independence: The Military Character of the American Revolution*. Charlottesville, VA: University Press of Virginia, 1984.
___, Thad Tate, and Peter Albert, eds. *An Uncivil War: The Southern Backcountry during the American Revolution*. Charlottesville, VA: University of Virginia Press, 1985.
Holtman, Robert B. *Napoleonic Propaganda*. Baton Rouge, LA: Louisiana State University Press, 1950.
___. *The Napoleonic Revolution*. Baton Rouge, Louisiana: Louisiana State University Press, 1967.
Hoppitt, Julian. *A Land of Liberty: England, 1689-1727*. New York: Oxford University Press, 2000.
Jackson, John W. *With the British Army in Philadelphia, 1777-1778*. San Rafael, CA: Presidio Press, 1979.
Kedouri, Eli. *Nationalism*. New York: Praeger, 1960.
Kohn, Hans. *Prelude to Nation-States: The French and German Experience, 1789-1815*. Princeton, NJ: Van Nostrand, 1967.
McManners, John. *The French Revolution and the Church*. London: S.P.C.K., 1969.
Paine, Thomas. *Political Writings*. Ed. Bruce Kuklick. New York: Cambridge University Press, 1989.
Palmer, R. R. *Age of Democratic Revolution: A Political History of Europe and America 1760-1800*. Princeton, NJ: Princeton University Press, 1959-1964.
Paret, Peter, et al., eds. *Makers of Modern Strategy from Machiavelli to the Nuclear Age*. Princeton NJ: Princeton University Press, 1986.
Royster, Charles. *A Revolutionary People at War: The Continental Army and the American Character 1775-1783*. Institute of Early American History and Culture. Chapel Hill, NC: University of North Carolina Press, 1979.
Shy, John. *A People Armed and Numerous: Reflexions on the Military Struggle For American Independence*. New York: Oxford University Press, 1976.

Soboul, A. "Religious Sentiments and Popular Cults During the Revolution: Patriot Saints and Martyrs of Liberty," in Jerry Kaplow, *New Perspectives on the French Revolution: Readings in Historical Sociology.* New York: Wiley, 1965.

Tackett, Timothy. *Religion, Revolution and Regional Culture in Eighteenth-Century France: The Ecclesiastical Oath of 1791.* Princeton, NJ: Princeton University Press, 1986.

Wawro, Geoffrey. *Warfare and Society in Europe 1792-1914.* New York: Routledge, 2000.

XII. Religion, Nationalism, and War in the Nineteenth Century

Aron, Raymond. *Clausewitz, Philosopher of War.* Englewood Cliffs, NJ: Prentice-Hall, 1985.

Banner, James M., Jr. *To the Hartford Convention: The Federalists and The Origins of Party Politics in Massachusetts 1789-1815.* New York: Knopf, 1970.

Barclay, David. *Frederick William IV and the Prussian Monarchy 1840-1861.* Oxford, UK: Clarendon Press, 1995.

Beeching, Jack. *The Chinese Opium Wars.* New York: Harcourt, Brace, Jovanovich, 1976.

Brock, Peter. *Freedom from War: Nonsectarian Pacifism, 1814-1914.* Toronto, Canada: University of Toronto Press, 1991.

___. *Freedom from War: Sectarian Nonresistance from the Middle Ages to the Great War.* Toronto, Canada: University of Toronto Press, 1991.

Ceadel, Martin. *The Origins of War Prevention: The British Peace Movement and International Relations, 1730-1854.* Oxford, U.K.: Clarendon, 1996.

Chickering, Roger. *Imperial Germany and a World Without War.* Princeton, NJ: Princeton University Press, 1975.

Clark, Christopher. "The Napoleonic Moment in Prussian Church Policy," in *Napoleon's Legacy*, eds. David Lavid and Lucy Riall. New York: Oxford University Press, 2000.

Clausewitz. *On War.* Eds. Peter Paret and Michael Howard. Princeton, NJ: Princeton University Press, 1976.

Commager, Henry S., ed. *The Blue and The Gray: The Story of the Civil War as Told by Participants.* Indianapolis, IN: Bobbs Merrill, 1950.

Cooper, Sandi. *Patriotic Pacifism: Waging War on War in Europe, 1815-1914.* New York: Oxford University Press, 1991.

Dawson, Jerry F. *Friedrich Schleiermacher: The Evolution of a Nationalist.* Austin, TX: University of Texas Press, 1966.

Dunham, Chester A. *The Attitude of the Northern Clergy Toward the South 1860-1865.* Toledo, OH: Gray, 1942.

Dymond, Jonathan. *An Enquiry into the Acccordancy of War with the Principles of Christianity and an Examination of the Philosophical Reasoning by which it is Defended: With observations on Some of the Causes of War, and Some of its Effects.* London: Longman, Hurst, 1823.

Ellsworth, Clayton Summer. "The American Churches and the Mexican War," in *American Historical Review* 45 (1940).

Eyck. Erich. *Bismarck and the German Empire.* New York: Norton, 1968.

Fay, Peter War. *The Chinese Opium War 1840-1842.* New York: Norton, 1976.

Frederick II, King of Prussia. *The Refutation of Machiavelli's Prince or Anti-Machiavel.* Ed. Paul Sonnino. Athens, Ohio: Ohio University Press, 1981.

Friedrich, Carl J. *Constitutional Reason of State: The Survival of the Constitutional Order.* Providence, RI: Brown University Press, 1956.

Friedrickson, George. *The Inner Civil War: Northern Intellectuals and the Crisis of the Union.* New York: Harper and Row, 1971.

Gallie, W. B. *Philosophers of Peace and War: Kant, Clausewitz, Marx, Engels and Tolstoy.* Cambridge, UK: Cambridge University Press, 1978.

Gat, Azar. *The Origins of Military Thought: From the Enlightenment to Clausewitz.* Oxford, UK: Clarendon Press, 1989.

Gribbin, William. *The Churches Militant: The War of 1812 and American Religion.* New Haven, CT: Yale University Press, 1973.

Groves, C. P. *The Planting of Christianity in Africa* Vol. III, 1878-1914. London, UK: Lutterworth, 1964.

Hayes, Carleton Joseph Huntley. *Essays on Nationalism.* New York: Macmillan, 1926.

Hayes, Sam and Christopher Morris, eds. *Manifest Destiny and Empire: America's Antebellum Expansion.* College Station, Texas: Texas A & M Press for University of Texas Press, 1997.

Hegel, Georg Wilhelm. *Hegel's Political Writings.* Trans. T. M. Knox. Oxford, U.K.: Clarendon Press, 1964.

Howard, Michael Eliot. *Clausewitz.* Oxford, UK: Oxford University Press, 1983.

___. *War and the Liberal Conscience.* New Brunswick, NJ: Rutgers University Press, 1978.

Johannsen, Robert Walter. *To the Halls of the Montezumas: the Mexican War in the American Imagination.* New York: Oxford University Press, 1985.

Kohn, Hans. *The Idea of Nationalism: A Study in Its Origins and Background.* New York: Macmillian, 1946.

___. *Nationalism, Its Meaning and History.* Malabar, FL: Kreiger, 1982.

Levinger, Matthew. *Enlightened Nationalism: The Transformation of Prussian Political Culture 1806-1848.* New York: Oxford University Press, 2000.

Linden, W. H. van der. *The International Peace Movement 1815-1987.* Amsterdam, The Netherlands: Tilleul, 1987.

McPherson, James M. *Battle Cry of Freedom: The Civil War Era.* Oxford History of the United States. New York: Oxford University Press, 1988.

Martin, Kingsley. *The Triumph of Lord Palmerston: A Study in Public Opinion in England Before the Crimean War.* New York: Hutchinson, 1963.

Meinecke, Friedrich. *Machiavellism: Doctrine of Raison d'État and Its Place in Modern History.* New Haven, CT: Yale University Press, 1967.

Miller, Randall, Harry Stout, and Charles Wilson, eds. *Religion and the American Civil War.* New York: Oxford University Press, 1998.

Moorehead, James. *American Apocalypse: Yankee Protestants and the Civil War 1860-1869.* New Haven, CT: Yale University Press, 1978.

Mosse, George L. *Nationalization of the Masses.* New York: Fertig, 1975.

Paret, Peter. *Clausewitz and the State.* New York: Oxford University Press, 1976.

___, Gordon Craig, and Felix Gilbert, eds. *Makers of Modern Strategy: from Machiavelli to the Nuclear Age.* Princeton, NJ: Princeton University Press, 1986.

Perret, Geoffrey. *A Country Made by War: From the Revolution to Vietnam - The Story of America's Rise to Power.* New York, Vintage, 1990.

Rhodes, Anthony. *The Power of Rome in the Twentieth Century: The Vatican in the Age of Liberal Democracies, 1870-1922.* London: Sidgwick and Jackson, 1983.

Rich, Norman. *Why the Crimean War? A Cautionary Tale.* Hanover, NH: Hutchinson and Smith, 1985.

Ritter, Gerhard. *The Sword and the Scepter: The Problem of Militarism in Germany.* Vol. I, *The Prussian Tradition 1740-1890.* Trans. Heinz Norton. Coral Gables, FL: University of Miami Press, 1969.

Royster, Charles. *The Destructive War: William Tecumseh Sherman, Stonewall Jackson, and the Americans.* New York: Knopf, 1991.

Schroeder, John H. *Mr. Polk's War: American Opposition and Dissent, 1846-1848.* Madison, WI: University of Wisconsin Press, 1973.

Sheehan, James. *German History, 1770-1866.* Oxford History of Modern Europe. Oxford, UK: Oxford University Press, 1989.

Slotkin, Richard. *Regeneration Through Violence: The Mythology of the American Frontier 1600-1860.* Middletown, CT: Wesleyan University Press, 1973.

Wawro, Geoffrey. *Warfare and Society in Europe 1792-1914.* New York: Routledge, 2000.

Weigley, Russell. *The American Way of War: A History of American Military Strategy and Policy.* New York: Macmillan, 1973.

Wills, Garry. *Lincoln at Gettysburg: The Words that Remade America.* New York: Simon and Schuster, 1992.

Williams, T. Harry. *A Military History of American Wars: From 1745 to 1918.* New York: Knopf, 1981.

Woodworth Steven. E. *While God is Marching On: The Religious World of Civil War Soldiers.* Lawrence, KS: University Press of Kansas, 2001.

810

XIII. A Civilized Way to Peace

Alonso, Harriet. *Peace as a Women's Issue: A History of the U.S. Movement for World Peace and Women's Rights.* Syracuse, NY: Syracuse University Press, 1993.

Berghahn, Volker Rolf. *Militarism: The History of an International Debate, 1861-1979.* New York: St. Martin's Press, 1982.

Best, Geoffrey. *Humanity in Warfare.* New York: Columbia University Press, 1980.

Bloch, I. S. *The Future of War in its Technical Economic and Political Relations.* New York: Doubleday & McClure, 1899.

Booth, Ken and Moorhead Wright, eds. *American Thinking about Peace and War.* New York: Barnes and Noble, 1978.

Chambers, John W. II. *Eagle and the Dove: The American Peace Movement and United States Foreign Policy.* Syracuse, NY: Syracuse University Press, 1991.

Chatfield, Charles. *For Peace and Justice: Pacifism in America 1914-1941.* Knoxville, TN: University of Tennessee Press, 1971.

___. *The American Peace Movement: Ideals and Activism.* New York: Twayne, 1991.

Chickering, Roger. *Imperial Germany and a World Without War: The Peace Movement and German Society, 1892-1914.* Princeton, N J: Princeton University Press, 1975.

Cohen, Sheldon M. *Arms and Judgment: Law, Morality, and the Conduct of War in the Twentieth Century.* Boulder, CO: Westview, 1989.

Cooper, Sandi E. *Patriotic Pacifism: Waging War on War in Europe 1815-1914.* New York: Oxford University Press, 1991.

Crook, D. P. *Darwinism, War, and History: The Debate Over the Biology of War from the Origin of the Species to the First World War.* Cambridge, UK: Cambridge University Press, 1994.

Davis, Calvin DeArmond. *The United States and the First Hague Conference.* Ithaca, N. Y.: Cornell University Press, 1962.

___. *The United States and the Second Hague Conference: American Diplomacy and International Organization, 1899-1914.* Durham, NC: Duke University Press, 1975.

DeBenedetti, Charles. *Origins of the Modern American Peace Movement 1915-1929.* Millwood, NY: KTO Press, 1978.

Freidel, Frank. *Francis Lieber: Nineteenth-Century Liberal.* Baton Rouge, LA: Louisiana State University Press, 1947.

Gallie, W. B. *Philosophers of Peace and War: Kant, Clausewitz, Marx, Engels, and Tolstoy.* New York: Cambridge University Press, 1978.

Gat, Azar. *The Development of Military Thought: The Nineteenth Century.* Oxford, UK: Oxford University Press, 1992.

Gorrell, Donald. *The Age of Social Responsibility: The Social Gospel in the Progressive Era.* Macon, GA: Mercer University Press, 1988.

811

Gumpert, Martin. *Dunant: The Story of the Red Cross*. New York: Oxford University Press, 1938.

Herman, Sondra R. *Eleven Against War: Studies in American Internationalist Thought 1898-1921*. Stanford, CA: Hoover Institution Press, 1969.

Howard, Michael. *War and the Liberal Conscience*. New Brunswick, NJ: Rutgers University Press, 1978.

Hull, William I. *The Two Hague Conferences and their Contributions to International Law*. Boston: Ginn, 1908.

Marchand, C. Roland. *The American Peace Movement and Social Reform 1898-1918*. Princeton, NJ: Princeton University Press, 1972.

Marrin, Gilbert. *The Last Crusade: The Church of England in the First World War*. Durham, N. C.: Duke University Press, 1974.

Moorehead, Caroline. *Dunant's Dream: War, Switzerland, and the History of the Red Cross*. London: Harper Collins, 1998.

Morris, A. J. Anthony. *Radicalism Against War 1906-1914: The Advocacy of Peace and Retrenchment*. Totawa, N. J.: Rowman and Littlefield, 1972.

Nation, R. Craig. *War on War: Lenin, the Zimmerwald Left and the Origins of Communist Internationalism*. Durham, NC: Duke University Press, 1989.

Tate, Merze. *The Disarmament Illusion: The Movement for a Limitation of Arms to 1907*. New York: Macmillan, 1942.

___. *The United States and Armaments*. Cambridge, MA: Harvard University Press, 1948.

Wank, Solomon, ed. *Doves and Diplomats: Foreign Offices and Peace Movements in Europe and America in the Twentieth Century*. Westport, Ct.: Greenwood Press

XIV. World War I

Bailey, Charles. "The British Protestant Theologians in the First World War: Germanophobia Unleashed." *Harvard Theological Review* 77 (April, 1984).

___. " 'Got mit uns:' Germany's Protestant Theologians in the First World War." Ph.D. diss., University of Virginia, 1978.

Bartov, Omer and Mack, Phyllis, eds. *In God's Name: Genocide and Religion in the Twentieth Century*. New York: Berghahn Books, 2001.

Brock, Peter. *Twentieth-Century Pacifism*. New York: Van Nostrand Reinhold, 1970.

Bussey, Gertrude and Margaret Tims. *Women's International League for Peace and Freedom*. London: George Allen & Unwin, 1965.

Ceadel, Martin. *Pacifism in Britain 1914-1945*. Oxford, UK: Clarendon, 1980.

Chambers, John, ed. *The Eagle and the Dove: The American Peace Movement and United States Foreign Policy 1900-1922*. 2nd edition. Syracuse, NY: Syracuse University Press, 1991.

812

Chatfield, Charles. *For Peace and Justice: Pacifism in America, 1914-1941.* Knoxville, TN: University of Tennessee Press, 1971.

The Church and War: Papers Read at the Twenty-First Summer Meeting and the Twenty-Second Winter Meeting of the Ecclesiastical Society. Edited by W. J. Sheils. Studies in Church History, vol. XX. Oxford, UK: Blackwell, 1983.

Combs, Jerald A. *American Diplomatic History: Two Centuries of Changing Interpretations.* Berkeley, CA: University of California, 1983.

Fussell, Paul. *The Great War and Modern Memory.* New York: Oxford University Press, 1975.

Graham, Robert A. *Vatican Diplomacy: A Study of Church and State on the International Plane.* Princeton, NJ: Princeton University Press, 1959.

Hoover, A. J. *God, Germany, and Britain in the Great War: A Study in Clerical Nationalism.* New York: Praeger, 1989.

Hynes, Samuel. *A War Remembered: The First World War and English Culture.* New York: Atheneum, 1991.

___. *A Soldier's Tale.* New York: Penguin, 1997.

Keegan, Paul. *The Face of Battle.* New York: Viking, 1976.

Kissenger, Henry. *Diplomacy.* New York: Simon and Schuster, 1994.

Kraft, Barbara. *The Peace Ship: Henry Ford's Pacifist Adventure in the First World War.* New York: Macmillan, 1978.

Link, Arthur. *Wilson the Diplomatist: A Look at his Major Foreign Policies.* Baltimore: John Hopkins University Press, 1957.

Marrin, Albert. *The Last Crusade: The Church of England in the First World War.* Durham, NC: Duke University Press, 1974.

The Marshall Cavendish Illustrated Encyclopedia of World War I. Ed. Peter Young and Mart Dartford. Freeport, L. I., NY: M. Cavendish, 1984.

Papal Encyclicals (1903-1939). Ed. Claudia Ihm. Raleigh, NC: Consortium: McGrath, 1981.

Piper, John J., Jr. *The American Churches in World War I.* Athens, Ohio: University of Ohio Press, 1985.

Pierard, Richard V. "John R. Mott and the Rift in the Ecumenical Movement During World War I," *Journal of Ecumenical Studies.* (1986): 22.

Power, Samantha. *"A Problem from Hell": America and the Age of Genocide.* New York: Basic Books, 2002.

Stoessinger, John. *Why Nations Go to War.* 6th edition. New York: St. Martin's, 1993.

Tuchman, Barbara. *The Guns of August.* New York: Macmillan, 1962.

Wank, Solomon. *Doves and Diplomats: Foreign Offices and Peace Movements In Europe and America in the Twentieth Century.* Westport, CT: Greenwood Press, 1978.

Williams, John. *The Home Fronts: Britain, France and Germany 1914-1918.* London, UK: Constable, 1972.

Winter, J. M. *Socialism and the Challenge of War; Ideas and Politics in Britain, 1912-18.* Boston: Routledge and Kegan Paul, 1974.

XV. Searching for Peace, Finding War 1920-39

Europe and America

Alonzo, Harriet Hyman. *Peace as a Women's Issue: A History of the U. S. Movement for World Peace and Women's Rights.* Syracuse, NY: Syracuse University Press, 1993.

Barnes, Kenneth C. *Nazism, Liberalism, and Christianity: Protestant Social Thought in Germany and Great Britain 1925-1937.* Lexington, KY: University Press of Kentucky, 1991.

Benda, Julien. *La Trahison des Clercs.* Paris: B. Grasset, 1929.

Bilis, Michel. *Socialistes et Pacifistes 1933-1939: Ou L'Impossible Dilemme des Socialistes Francais 1933-1939.* Paris: Syros, (n.d.).

Binchy, D. A. *Church and State in Fascist Italy.* Oxford, U.K: Oxford University Press, 1941.

Biographical Dictionary of Modern Peace Leaders. Ed. Harold Johnson. Westport, CN: Greenwood, 1958.

Blinkhorn, Martin, ed. *Spain in Conflict 1931-1939: Democracy and Its Enemies.* Beverly Hills, CA: Sage, 1986.

Cannistraro, Philip V., ed. *Historical Dictionary of Fascist Italy.* Westport, CN: Greenwood, 1982.

Ceadel, Martin. *Pacifism in Britain 1914-1945: The Defining of a Faith.* Oxford, U.K.: Clarendon, 1980.

Chatfield, Charles. *The American Peace Movement: Ideals and Activism.* New York: Twayne, 1992.

___. *For Peace and Justice: Pacifism in America 1914-1941.* Knoxville, TN: University of Tennessee, 1971.

___ and Peter Van Den Dungen, eds. *Peace Movements and Political Cultures.* Knoxville, TN: University of Tennessee, 1988.

___, ed. *The Americanization of Gandhi: Images of the Mahatma.* New York: Garland, 1976.

Day, Dorothy. *The Long Loneliness: The Autobiography of Dorothy Day.* New York: Harper, 1952.

The Encylopedia of The Third Reich. Ed. Christian Lenter and Friedemann Bedurfig. Trans. Amy Hackett. New York: Macmillan, 1991.

Evans, Ellen Lovell. *The German Center Party 1870-1933: A Study in Political Catholicism.* Carbondale, IL: Southern Illinois University Press, 1981.

Fox, Richard. *Reinhold Niebuhr: A Biography.* San Francisco, CA: Harper and Row, 1987.

Helmreich, Ernst Christian. *The German Churches under Hitler: Background, Struggle, and Epilogue.* Detroit, MI: Wayne State Press, 1979.

Historical Dictionary of the Spanish Civil War 1936-1939. Ed. James W. Cortada. Westport, CT: Greenwood, 1982.

Ingram, Norman. *The Politics of Dissent: Pacifism in France 1919-1939.* Oxford, UK: Clarendon Press, 1991

Johnson, Eric. *Nazi Terror: The Gestapo, Jews, and Ordinary Germans.* New York: Basic Books, 1999.

Keynes, John M. *Economic Consequences of the Peace.* New York: Harcourt Brace and Howe, 1920.

Klejment, Anne and Nancy Roberts, eds. *The Catholic Worker and the Origins of The Catholic Church and Catholic Radicalism in America.* Westport, CN: Greenwood, 1996.

Lannon, Frances. *Privilege, Persecution, and Prophecy: The Catholic Church in Spain 1875-1975.* Oxford, UK: Clarendon, 1987.

McCarthy, Esther. "The Catholic Periodical Press and Issues of War and Peace: 1914-1946." Ph.D. diss. Stanford University, 1957.

McKercher, B. J. C., ed. *Arms Limitation and Disarmament: Restraints on War, 1899-1939.* Westport, CT: Praeger, 1992.

Maehl, William Harvey. *The German Socialist Party: Champion of the First Republic 1918-1933.* Philadelphia, PA: American Philosophical Society, 1986.

Meyer, Donald B. *The Protestant Search for Political Realism 1919-1941.* Berkeley, CA: University of California Press, 1961.

Miller, Robert Moats. *American Protestantism and Social Issues 1919-1939.* Chapel Hill, NC: University of North Carolina Press, 1958.

Muste, A. J. *Essays of A. J. Muste.* Ed. Nat Hentoff. Indianapolis, IN: Bobbs-Merrill, 1967.

Nutt, Rich. *Toward Peacemaking: Presbyterians in the South and National Security, 1945-1983.* Tuscaloosa, AL: University of Alabama Press, 1994.

Oliver, John. *The Church* [of England] *and the Social Order.* London, UK: A. R. Mowbray, 1968.

Passelecq, Georges, and Bernard Suchecky. *The Hidden Encyclical of Pius XI.* Trans. Steven Rendell. New York: Harcourt Brace, 1997.

Piel, Mel. *The Catholic Worker and the Origins of Catholic Radicalism.* Philadelphia, PA: Temple University Press, 1982.

Pollard, John F. *The Vatican and Italian Fascism 1919-1932: A Study in Conflict.* New York: Cambridge University Press, 1985.

Prado, Luis Aquirre. *The Church and the Spanish War.* Madrid: Servicio Informativo Espanol, 1965.

Preston, Paul, ed. *Revolution and War in Spain 1931-1939.* New York: Methuen, 1984.

Rhodes, Anthony. *The Vatican in the Age of Dictators.* London: UK: Hodder and Stoughton, 1973.

Sanchez, Jose M. *The Spanish Civil War as a Religious Tragedy.* Notre Dame, IN: University of Notre Dame Press, 1987.

Socknat, Thomas P. *Witness Against War: Pacifism in Canada 1900-1945.* Toronto, Canada: University of Toronto Press, 1987.

Swanberg, W.A. *Norman Thomas: The Last Idealist.* New York: Scribners, 1976.

815

Will, Herman. *A Will to Peace: Peace Action in the United Methodist Church: A History.* Washington, D.C: General Board of Church and Society of the United Methodist Church, 1984.

Winter, J. M. *Socialism and the Challenge of War: Ideas and Politics in Britain 1912-18.* London: Routledge & Kegan Paul, 1974.

Wolff, Richard J. and Jörg K. Hoensch, eds. *Catholics, the State and the European Radical Right, 1919-1945.* Boulder, CO: Social Science Monographs; Highland Lakes, N.J.: Atlantic Research and Publications; New York, 1987.

Wright, J. R. C. *"Above Parties": The Political Attitudes of the German Protestant Church Leadership 1918-1933.* Oxford, UK: Oxford University Press, London, 1974.

India

Ashe, Geoffrey. *Gandhi.* New York: Stein and Day, 1968.

Bennett, Scott. " 'Pacifism not Passivism:' The War Resisters League and Radical Pacifism, Nonviolent Direct Actions and the Americanization of Gandhi 1915-1963." Ph. D. diss., Rutgers University, 1998.

Bhagavadgita. Ed. S. Radhakrishnan. New Delhi, India: Harper Collins, 1993.

Borman, William. *Gandhi and Non-Violence.* Albany, NY: State University of New York Press, 1986.

Dalton, Dennis. *Mahatma Gandhi: Nonviolent Power in Action.* New York: Columbia University Press, 1993.

Gandhi, M.K. *Satyagraha* [Non-Violent Resistance]. Ahmedabad, India: Navajivan, 1958.

Gupta. S. P. and K.S. Ramachandran, eds. *Mahabharata: Myth and Reality, Differing Views.* Delhi, India: Agam Prakashan, 1976.

Heesterman, J. C. *The Inner Conflict of Tradition: Essays in Indian Ritual, Kingship, and Society.* Chicago, IL: University of Chicago Press, 1985.

Juergensmeyer, Mark. *Fighting With Gandhi.* San Francisco: CA: Harper and Row, 1984.

Katz, Rught Cecily. *Arjuna in the Mahabharata: Where Krishna is, There is Victory.* Columbia: South Carolina: University of South Carolina, 1989.

The Mahabharata. Ed. and trans. Chakravarthi Narasimhan. New York: Columbia University Press, 1965.

Minor, Robert N., ed. *Modern Indian Interpreters of the Bhagavadgita.* Albany, NY: State University of New York Press, 1986. Particularly essays by Stevenson on Tilak, Minor on Sri Aurobindo, and Jordens on Gandhi.

Sharp, Gene. *Gandhi as a Political Strategist.* Boston, MA: Sargent, 1979.

Seshachari, C. *Gandhi and the American Scene.* Bombay, India: Nachiketa, 1969.

Japan

Barnhart, Michael A. *Japan Prepares for Total War: The Search for Economic Security, 1919-1941.* Ithaca, NY: Cornell University Press, 1987.

Bix, Herbert. *Hirohito and the Making of Modern Japan.* New York: Harper Collins, 2000.

Cook, Haruoko Taya and Theodore F. Cook. *Japan at War: An Oral History.* New York: The New Press, 1992.

Fletcher, Miles. *The Search for a New Order: Intellectuals and Fascism in Prewar Japan.* Chapel Hill, NC: University of North Carolina Press, 1982

Hardacre, Helen. *Shinto and the State, 1868-1988.* Princeton, NJ: Princeton University Press, 1989.

Harries, Meirion and Susie Harries. *Soldiers of the Sun: The Rise and Fall of the Imperial Japanese Army.* New York: Random House, 1991.

Holtom, D. C. *Modern Japan and Shinto Nationalism: A Study of Present-Day Trends in Japanese Religions.* Chicago, IL: University of Chicago Press, 1947.

___. *The National Faith of Japan: A Study in Modern Shinto.* 1938. New York: Paragon Book Reprint Corp., 1965.

Iriye, Akira. *Power and Culture: The Japanese-American War 1941-1945.* Cambridge, MA: Harvard University Press, 1981.

Kitagawa, Joseph M. *Religion in Japanese History.* New York: Columbia University Press, 1966.

Mitchell, Richard H. *Thought Control in Prewar Japan.* Ithaca, NY: Cornell University Press, 1976.

Smethurst, Richard J. *A Social Basis for Prewar Japanese Militarism.* Berkeley, CA: University of California, 1974.

Suzuki, D.T. *Zen and Japanese Culture.* 1938. New York: Pantheon, 1957.

Takizawa, Nobulhiko. "Religion and the State in Japan," *Journal of Church and State* 30 (Winter, 1988)

Victoria. Brian. *Zen at War.* New York: Weatherhill, 1957.

Wetsler, Peter. *Hirohito and War: Imperial Traditions and Military Decision Making in Pre-War Japan.* Honolulu: University of Hawaii Press, 1969.

XVI. World War II: The Apotheosis of Barbarity

Bartov, Omer. *The Eastern Front, 1941-1945, German Troops and the Barbarisation of Warfare.* New York: St. Martins, 1986.

Bartov, Omer and Mack, Phyllis, eds. *In God's Name: Genocide and Religion in the Twentieth Century.* New York: Berghahn, 2001.

Bernstein, Barton, "Why the USA Dropped Atomic Bombs on Japanese Cities," in *Proceedings of the Forty-Five Pugwash Conference on Science and World Affairs (1995).* NJ: World Scientific, 1995.

Berry, Paul and Mark Bostridge. *Vera Brittain: A Life.* London: Chatto & Windus, 1995.

Bird, Kai and Lawrence Lifeschultz, eds. *Hiroshima's Shadow.* Stony Creek, CN: Pamphleteer's Press, 1998.

Brill, Norman and Gilbert Beebe. *A Follow-up Study of War Neuroses.* U. S. Veterans Administration Medical Monograph. Washington, DC, 1955.

Brittain, Vera. "Massacre by Bombing," Fellowship. X, No. 3 (March, 1944).

Brown, Seyom. *Human Rights in World Politics.* New York: Longman, 2000

Chadwick, Owen. *Britain and the Vatican during the Second World War.* Cambridge, U.K.: Cambridge University Press, 1986.

Chandler, Andrew. "The Church of England and Nazi Germany 1933-1945," Ph.D. diss. University of Cambridge, 1990.

___. "The Church of England and the Obliteration Bombing of Germany in the Second World War," *English Historical Review* 108 (1993).

Cohen, Marshall, et al., eds. *War and Moral Responsibility.* Princeton, NJ: Princeton University Press, 1974.

Cook, Haruko Taya and Theodore F. Cook. *Japan At War: An Oral History.* New York: New Press, 1992.

Cornwell, John. *Hitler's Pope: The Secret History of Pius XII.* New York: Viking, 1999.

Dictionary of Military History and the Art of War. Ed. André Corvisier. English ed. Julian Childs. U.K: Blackwell, 1994.

Djilas, Milovan. *Wartime.* Trans. Michael B. Petrovich. New York: Harcourt Brace Jovanovich, 1977.

Dower, John. *Japan In War and Peace: Selected Essays.* New York: New Press, 1993.

___. *War Without Mercy: Race and Power in the Pacific War.* New York: Pantheon, 1986.

Dunn, Joe Pender. "The Church and the Cold War: Protestants and Conscription, 1940-1954." Ph.D. diss., University of Missouri-Columbia, 1973.

Dyer, Gwynne. *War.* New York: Crown, 1985.

Ellis, John. *World War II: A Statistical Survey: The Essential Facts for All the Combatants.* New York: Facts on File, 1993.

Encyclopedia of the Holocaust, ed. Israel Gutman. New York: Macmillan, 1990.

Ewing, E. Keith. "The Pacifist Movement in the Methodist Church during World War II: A Study of Civilian Public Service Men in a Nonpacifist Church." M.A. thesis, Florida Atlantic University, 1982.

Falk, Richard, compiler. *Crimes of War.* New York: Random House, 1971.

___. *Reviving the World Court,* Charlottesville, VA: University Press of Virginia, 1986

Fireside, Harvey. *Icon and Swastika: The Russian Orthodox Church under Nazi and Soviet Control.* Cambridge, MA: Harvard University Press, 1971.

Furet, Francois, ed. *Unanswered Questions: Nazi Germany and the Genocide of the Jews.* New York: Schocken, 1989.

Fussell, Paul. *Doing Battle: The Making of a Skeptic.* Boston: Little Brown, 1996.

___. *Wartime Understanding and Behavior in the Second World War.* New
York: Oxford University Press, 1989.

The Gallup Poll. *Public Opinion 1935-1941.* Washington, DC: The Gallup
Organization, 1972.

Goldhagen, Daniel. *Hitler's Willing Executioners.* New York: Knopf, 1996.

Gray, J. Glenn. *The Warriors: Reflections on Men in Battle.* New York:
Harcourt, Brace, 1959.

Hafer, Harold F. "Evangelical and Reformed Churches in World War II." Ph.D.
diss., University of Pennsylvania. Philadelphia, 1947.

Hallie, Philip. *Lest Innocent Blood be Shed: The Story of the Village of le
Chambon, and How Goodness Happened There.* New York: Harper &
Row, 1979.

Hamby, Alonzo. *Life of Harry S. Truman.* New York: Oxford University Press,
1995.

Harries, Meirion and Susie Harries. *Soldiers of the Sun: The Rise and Fall of
the Imperial Japanese Army.* New York: Random House, 1991.

Hastings, Max. *Bomber Command: The Myths and Reality of the Strategic
Bombing Offensive 1939-1945.* New York: Dial Press/James Wade, 1979.

Hersey, John. *Hiroshima.* New York: Knopf, 1946.

Howard, Michael, ed. *Laws of War: Constraints on Warfare in the Western
World.* New Haven, CT: Yale University Press, 1994.

Hynes, Samuel. *The Soldiers' Tale: Bearing Witness to Modern War.* New York:
Penguin Press, 1997.

Irving, David. *The Destruction of Dresden.* New York: Ballantine Books, 1963.

Johnson, Eric. *The Gestapo, Jews, and Ordinary Germans.* New York: Basic
Books, 1999.

Kertzer, David. *The Popes Against the Jews: The Vatican's Role in the Rise of
Modern Anti-Semitism.* New York: Alfred A. Knopf, 2001.

Klemperer, Victor. *I Will Bear Witness: A Diary of the Nazi Years 1933-1941.*
Trans. Martin Chalmers. New York: Random House, 1998.

Koppes, Clayton R. and Gregory D. Black. *Hollywood Goes to War.* New York:
Free Press, 1987.

Lloyd, Roger. *The Church of England, 1900-1965.* London: SCM, 1966.

Lukas, Richard. *Forgotten Holocaust: The Poles under German Occupation
1939-1944.* Lexington: KY: University of Kentucky Press, 1986.

McCarthy, Esther. "Catholic Periodical Press and Issues of War and Peace, 1914-
1946." Ph.D. diss., Stanford University, 1977.

Maddox, Robert. *Weapons for Victory: The Hiroshima Decision Fifty Years
Later.* Columbia, MO: University of Missouri Press, 1995.

Malaparte, Curzio. *Kaputt.* Trans. *Cesare* Foligno. New York: E. P. Dutton,
1946.

Marrus, Michael. *The Holocaust in History.* Hanover, NH: Brandeis
University Press, 1987.

Mayer, O. J. *Why Did the Heavens Not Darken: The "Final Solution" in History.*
New York: Pantheon, 1988.

Messenger, Charles. *"Bomber" Harris and the Strategic Bombing Offensive 1939-1945.* New York: St. Martin's, 1984.

de Montclos, Xavier, et al., eds. *Églises et Chrétiens in Deuxieme Guerre Mondiale.* Lyon, France: Press Universitaires de Lyon, 1982.

Newman, Robert P. *Truman and the Hiroshima Cult.* East Lansing, MI: Michigan State University Press, 1995.

Orser, William Edward. "The Social Attitudes of the Protestant Churches During the Second World War." Ph.D. diss. University of New Mexico, 1969.

Oxford Companion to World War II. Ed. I.C.B. Dear and M. R. D. Foot. Oxford, U.K: Oxford University Press, 1995.

Pagliaro, Harold. *Naked Heart: A Soldier's Journey to the Front.* Kirksville, MO: Thomas Jefferson University Press at Truman State University, 1996.

Passelecq, George and Bernard Suchecky. *The Hidden Encyclical of Pius XI.* New York: Harcourt, Brace. 1997.

Phayer, Michael. *The Catholic Church and the Holocaust, 1930-1965.* Bloomington, IN: Indiana University Press, 2000.

Power, Samantha. *"A Problem from Hell": America and the Age of Genocide.* New York: Basic Books, 2002.

Queen, Edward L., II. *In the South the Baptists Are the Center of Gravity.* Brooklyn, NY: Carlson, 1991.

Rhodes, Richard. *The Making of the Atomic Bomb.* New York: Simon and Schuster, 1986.

Roberts, Walter R. *Tito, Mihailovic and the Allies 1941-1945.* New Brunswick, NJ: 1973.

Robertson, Geoffrey. *Crimes Against Humanity: The Struggle for Global Justice.* London: Allen Lane, 1999.

Schmidt, Hans. *Quakers and Nazis: Inner Light in Outer Darkness.* Columbia, MO: University of Missouri Press, 1997.

Schulte, Theo. *The German Army and Nazi Policies in Occupied Russia.* Oxford, UK: Berg, 1989.

Sherwin, Martin J. *A World Destroyed: The Atomic Bomb and the Grand Alliance.* New York: Vintage, 1977.

Sittser, Gerald L. *A Cautious Patriotism: The American Churches and the Second World War.* Chapel Hill, N.C: University of North Carolina Press, 1977.

Stoltzfus, Nathan. *Resistance of the Heart: Intermarriage and the Rosenstrasse Protest in Nazi Germany.* New York: Norton, 1996.

Taylor, Telford. *The Anatomy of the Nuremberg Trials.* New York: Knopf, 1992.

Terkel, Studs. *"The Good War" An Oral History of World War II.* New York: Pantheon, 1984.

United States Strategic Bombing Survey. *Summary Report (Pacific War).* Washington, DC: U. S. Government Printing Office, 1946.

___. *Japan's Struggle to End the War.* Chairman's Office, 1 July, 1946.

820

Verrier, Anthony. *The Bomber Offensive*. New York: McMillan, 1969.
Walzer, Michael. *Just and Unjust Wars: A Moral Argument with Historical
    Illustrations*. New York: Basic Books, 1977.
Weinburg, Gerhard. *A World at Arms: A Global History of World War II*.
    Cambridge, UK; New York: Cambridge University Press, 1994.
Wills, Gary. "Vatican Regrets." *New York Review of Books* (May 25, 2000).
Wittner, Lawrence. *Rebels Against War: The American Peace Movement
    1941-1960*. New York: Columbia University Press, 1969.
Woetzel, Robert. *The Nuremberg Trials in International Law*. New York:
    Praeger, 1960.
Yzermans, Vincent A., ed. *Major Addresses of Pope Pius XII*, Vol.II. *Christmas
    Messages*. St. Paul, MN: North Central, 1961.
Zaretsky, Robert. *Nimes At War: Religion and Politics in the Gard 1938-1944*.
    University Park, PA: Penn State University Press, 1995.

XVII. The Cold War - I
Conventional Weapons and Wars

Allison, Graham and Philip Zelikow. *The Essence of Decision: Explaining the
    Cuban Missile Crisis* 2nd edition. New York: Longman, 1999.
Anderson, Jervis. *Bayard Rustin: Troubles I've Seen: A Biography*. New York:
    Harper Collins, 1997.
Au, William. *The Cross, The Flag, and the Bomb: American Catholics Debate
    War and Peace 1960-1983*. Westport, CN: Greenwood, 1985.
Blight, James and David Welch, eds. *On the Brink: Americans and Soviets
    Reexamine the Cuban Missile Crisis*. New York: Hill and Wang, 1989.
___et al. *Cuba on the Brink: Castro, the Missile Crisis, and the Soviet
    Collapse*. New York: Pantheon, 1993
Brown, Robert McAfee. *Religion and Violence: A Primer for White Americans*.
    Philadelphia, PA: Westminster, 1973.
Caputo, Philip. *A Rumor of War*. New York: Holt, Rinehart & Winston, 1977.
Clergy and Laity Concerned About Vietnam. *In the Name of Freedom: The
    Conduct of War in Vietnam by the Armed Services of the United States*.
    New York, 1981.
Chadwick, Owen. *The Christian Church and the Cold War*. New York:
    Penguin. 1992.
Crane, Conrad. *American Airpower Strategy in Korea 1950-1953*. Lawrence,
    KS: University of Kansas, 2000.
Cromartie, Michael, ed. *Peace Betrayed?: Essays on Pacifism and Politics*.
    Washington, DC: Ethics and Public Policy Center, 1990.
Cumings, Bruce. *The Origins of the Korean War*. Vol. I, *Liberation and the
    Emergence of Separate Regimes 1945-1947*, Vol. II, *The Roaring of the
    Cataract*. Princeton, NJ: Princeton University Press, 1981, 1990.
De Benedetti, Charles and Charles Chatfield. *The Antiwar Movement of the
    Vietnam Era*. Syracuse, NY: Syracuse University Press, 1990.

Dunn, Joe Pender. "The Church and the Cold War: Protestants and Conscription, 1940-1955." Ph.D. diss., University of Missouri, 1975.

Fitzgerald, Francis. *Fire in the lake: The Vietnamese and Americans in Vietnam.* Boston: Little, Brown, 1972.

Frady, Marshall. *Billy Graham: A Parable of American Righteousness.* Boston: Little Brown, 1979.

Gaddis, John. *The United States and The Origins of the Cold War 1941-1947.* New York: Columbia, University Press, 1972.

___. *We Know Now: Rethinking Cold War History.* New York: Oxford University Press, 1996.

The Gallup Poll. *Public Opinion, 1935-1971.* New York: Random House, 1972.

The Gallup Poll. *Gallup Opinion Index, "Public Opinion and the Vietnam War 1964-1967."* New York: Random House, 1967.

Garfinkle, Adam. *Telltale Hearts: The Origins and Impact of the Vietnam Antiwar Movement.* New York: St. Martin's Press, 1995.

Ginsberg, Robert, ed. *The Critique of War: Contemporary Philosophical Explorations.* Chicago: Henry Regnery Company, 1969.

Goldwater, Barry. *Where I Stand.* New York: McGraw Hill, 1964.

Greeley, Andrew. *The American Catholic: A Social Portrait.* New York: Basic Books, 1977.

Halberstam, David. *The Best and the Brightest.* New York: Random House, 1972.

Hall, Mitchell. *Because of Their Faith: CALCAV and Religious Opposition to the War.* New York: Columbia University Press, 1990.

Harris, Louis. *Anguish of Change.* New York, Norton, 1973.

Hebblethwaite, Peter. *Paul VI: The First Modern Pope* New York: Paulist, 1993.

Herr, Michael. *Dispatches.* New York: Knopf, 1977.

Herring, George. *America's Longest War: The United States and Vietnam 1950-1975.* New York: Knopf, 1979.

Hersh, Seymour. *My Lai 4: A Report on the Massacre and Its Aftermath.* New York: Random House, 1970.

Karnow, Stanley. *Vietnam: A History.* New York: Viking, 1983.

Leffler, Melvin. "Inside Enemy Archives." *Foreign Affairs* (1996), 120-34.

Lewy, Guenter. *America in Vietnam.* New York: Oxford University Press, 1980.

___. *Peace and Revolution: The Moral Crisis of American Pacifism.* Grand Rapids, MI: Eerdmans, 1988.

Lowe, Peter. *The Origins of the Korean War.* New York: Longman, 1997.

McNamara, Robert, et al. *Argument Without End: In Search of Answers to the Vietnam Tragedy.* New York: Public Affairs, 1999.

McNeal, Patricia. *Harder Than War: Catholic Peacemaking in Twentieth-Century America.* New Brunswick, N.J.: Rutgers University Press, 1992.

Meinertz, Midge. *Vietnam Christian Service: Witness in Anguish.* USA: Church World Service, 1976.

Mirsey, Jonathan. "The Never Ending War," *New York Review of Books* (May 25, 2000): 47.

___. "No Trumphets, No Drums," *New York Review of Books* (September 21, 1995): 42.

National Conference of Catholic Bishops. *In the Name of Peace: Collective Statements of the United States Catholic Bishops on War and Peace, 1919-1980.* Washington, DC: National Conference of Catholic Bishops, 1983.

Neuhaus, Richard John. "The War, The Churches, and Civil Religion," *Annals of the American Academy of Political and Social Science* 387 (1970): 128-40.

New Republic. 29 April 1985. (special issue on 10th anniversary of fall of Saigon.)

Nhat Hanh, Thich. *Love in Action: Nonviolent Social Change.* Berkeley, CA: Parallax Press, 1993.

___. *Fragrant Palm Leaves: Journals 1962-1966.* Berkeley, CA: Parallax Press, 1998.

O'Brien, Tim. *Going after Cacciato.* New York: Delacorte Press/S. Lawrence, 1978.

O'Brien, William V. *The Conduct of Just and Limited War.* New York: Praeger, 1983.

Osmer, Harold H. "United States Religious Press Response to the Containment Policy During the Period of the Korean War." Ph.D. diss., New York University, 1970.

The Pentagon Papers: The Defense Department History of the United States Decisionmaking on Vietnam. Boston: Beacon Press, 1971-72.

Podhoretz, Norman. *Why We Were in Vietnam.* New York: Simon and Schuster, 1982.

Quigley, Thomas, ed. *American Catholics and Vietnam.* Grand Rapids, MI: Eerdmans, 1968.

Quinley, Harold. "The Protestant Clergy and the War in Vietnam," *Public Opinion Quarterly 34* (1970): 43-52.

Respectfully Quoted: A Dictionary of Quotations Requested from the Congressional Research Service. Ed. Suzy Platt. Washington, DC: Library of Congress, 1989.

Robinson, Lee Ann. *Abraham Went Out: A Biography of A. J. Muste.* Philadelphia, PA: Temple University Press, 1981.

Schroeder, Steven. *A Community and a Perspective: Lutheran Peace Fellowship and the Edge of the Church, 1941-1991.* New York: University Press of America, 1993.

Schulzinger, Robert. *A Time for War: The United States and Vietnam 1941-1975.* New York: Oxford University Press, 1997.

Small, Melvin and William Hoover. *Give Peace a Chance: Exploring the Vietnam Antiwar Movement.* Syracuse, NY: Syracuse University Press, 1997.

Smith, Tracey Dean. "Agitation in the Land of Zion: The Anti-Vietnam War Movements at Brigham Young University, University of Utah and Utah State University." M.S. thesis, Utah State, 1996.
Smylie, James H. "American Religious Bodies, Just War, and Vietnam, "*Journal of Church and State* 11 (1969): 383-408.
Sorenson, Theodore. *Kennedy*. New York: Harper and Row, 1965.
Starr, Jerold. "Religious Preference, Religiosity, and Opposition to War," *Sociological Analysis*, 36 (1975): 325-34.
Stehle, Hansjakob. *Eastern Politics of the Vatican 1919-1979*. Trans. Sandra Smith. Athens, OH: Ohio University Press, 1981.
Stone, Ronald and Dana Wilbanks, eds. *The Peacemaking Struggle: Militarism and Resistance*. Essays prepared for Advisory council on Church and Society of the Presbyterian Church USA. Lanham, MD: University Press of America, 1985.
Stueck, William. *The Korean War: An International History*. Princeton, NJ: Princeton University Press, 1995.
Tracy, James. *Direct Action: Radical Pacifism from the Union Eight to the Chicago Seven*. Chicago, IL: University of Chicago Press, 1996.
Tygart, Clarence E., "Social Movement Participation: Clergy and the Anti-Vietnam War Movement," *Sociological Analysis* 34 (1973): 202-11.
"Vietnam: A Television History." PBS documentary produced by WGBH, Boston; Central Independent Television, UK; Antenne-2 France and LRE Productions. 13 videocassettes, 780 minutes. 1993.
Weigel, George. *Tranquillitas Ordinis the Present Failure and Future Promise of American Catholic Thought on War and Peace*. New York: Oxford University Press, 1987.
Wittner, Lawrence. *Rebels Against War: The American Peace Movement 1941-1960*. New York: Columbia University Press, 1969.
Wuthnow, Robert. *The Restructuring of American Religion: Society and Faith Since World War II*. Princeton, NJ: Princeton University Press, 1988.
Yergin, Daniel. *Shattered Peace: The Origins of the Cold War*. New York: Penguin, 1990.
Zahn, Gordon. "The Scandal of Silence," *Commonweal* 95 (October 22, 1971): 79-85.
Zaroulis, Nancy and Sullivan, Gerald. *Who Spoke Up: American Protest Against the War in Vietnam 1963-1975*. Garden City, NY: Doubleday, 1989.

XVIII. The Cold War - II
Nuclear Weapons

Boyer, Paul. *By the Bomb's Early Light: American Thought and Culture at the Dawn of the Atomic Age*. New York: Pantheon, 1985.
___. *When Time Shall Be No More: Prophecy Belief in Modern America*. Cambridge, MA: Harvard University Press, 1992.

Byrne, Paul. *The Campaign for Nuclear Disarmament.* London: Croom Helm, 1988.

Chadwick, Owen. *The Christian Church in the Cold War.* London, U.K: Penguin, 1992.

Clark, Grenville and Louis Sohn. *World Peace through World Law.* Cambridge, MA: Harvard University Press, 1958.

Cohen, Marshall, Thomas Nagel, and Thomas Scanlon, eds. *War and Moral Responsibility.* Princeton, NJ: Princeton University Press, 1974.

Commission of the Churches on International Affairs and Pontifical Commission "Justitia et Pax," eds. *Peace and Disarmament:Documents Of the World Council of Churches and Roman Catholic Church,* 1982.

Commission on the Relation of the Church to the War in the Light of the Christian Faith of the Federal Council of Churches of Christ in America. *Atomic Warfare and the Christian Faith.* New York, 1946.

Commission to Study Bases of a Just and Durable Peace of the Federal Council of Churches. *A Righteous Faith for a Just and Durable Peace.* 1942.

Davidson, Donald. G. *Nuclear Weapons and the American Churches: Ethical Positions on Modern Warfare.* Boulder, CO: Westview, 1983.

Dougherty, James E. *The Bishops and Nuclear Weapons.* Hamden, CN: Archon, 1984.

Ellis, Jane. *The Russian Orthodox Church: A Contemporary History.* Bloomington, IN: Indiana University Press, 1986.

Falwell, Jerry. *Nuclear Weapons and the Second Coming of Jesus Christ.* Old Time Gospel Hour, 1983.

Ford, Harold P. and Francis W. Winters, eds. *Ethics and Nuclear Strategy?* Maryknoll, NY: Orbis Books, 1977.

George, Alexander and Richard Smoke. *Deterrence in American Foreign Policy: Theory and Practice.* New York: Columbia University Press, 1974.

Henriksen, Margaret. *Dr. Strangelove's America: Society and Culture in the Atomic Age.* Berkeley, CA: University of California Press, 1997.

Hoffman, Stanley. *Duties Beyond Borders: On the Limits and Possibilities of Ethical International Politics.* Syracuse, NY: Syracuse University Press, 1981.

Kahn, Herman. *Thinking About the Unthinkable.* New York: Avon, 1962.

Kaplan, Fred. *Wizards of Armageddon.* New York: Simon and Schuster, 1983.

Kennan, George. *American Diplomacy 1900-1950.* Chicago, IL: University of Chicago Press, 1951.

Kennedy, Edward and Mark Hatfield. *Freeze! How You Can Help Prevent Nuclear War.* New York: Bantam, 1982.

Krauthammer, Charles. "Morality and the Reagan Doctrine." *New Republic* 8 April 1986.

Lifton, Robert J. and Greg Mitchell. *Hiroshima in America: Fifty Years of Denial.* New York: Putnam's, 1995.

___ and Eric Markusen. *TheGenocidal Mentality: Nazi Holocaust and Nuclear Threat.* New York: Basic Books, 1990

Meyer, David. *A Winter of Discontent: The Nuclear Freeze and American Politics.* New York: Praeger, 1990.

Mujtabai, A. G. *Blessed Assurance: At Home with the Bomb in Amarillo, Texas.* Boston: Houghton Mifflin, 1986.

Murnion, Philip J., ed. *Catholics and Nuclear War: A Commentary on The Challenge of Peace.* The U.S. Catholic Bishops' Pastoral Letter on War and Peace. New York: Crossroads, 1983.

Musto, Ronald G., ed. *Catholic Peacemakers: A Documentary History.* 2 vols. New York: Garland, 1996.

Myers, Frank. "British Peace Politics: The Campaign for Nuclear Disarmament and the Committee of 100, 1957-1962," Ph.D. diss., Columbia University, 1965.

Newhouse, John. *Cold Dawn: The Story of SALT.* New York: Holt, Rinehart and Winston, 1973.

Nutt, Rick L. *Toward Peacemaking: Presbyterians in the South and National Security 1945-1983.* Tuscaloosa, AL: University of Alabama Press, 1994.

Potter, Ralph B. "The Responses of Certain American Christian Churches to Nuclear Dilemma 1958-1956." Ph.D. diss., Harvard, 1965.

___. *War and Moral Discourse.* Richmond, VA: John Knox Press, 1969.

Queen, Edward. *In the South the Baptists Are the Center of Gravity.* Brooklyn, NY: Carlson, 1991.

Quester, George. *Nuclear Diplomacy: The First Twenty-Five Years.* New York: Dunellen, 1970.

Ramsay, Paul. *The Just War: Force and Political Responsibility.* New York: Scribner, 1968.

___. The *Limits of Nuclear War: Thinking About the Do-Able and the Un-Do-Able.* New York: Council on Religion and International Affairs, 1963.

___. *Speak Up For Just War or Pacifism: A Critique of the United Methodist Bishops' Pastoral Letter "In Defense of Creation."* University Park, PA: Pennsylvania State University Press, 1988.

Rhodes, Richard. *Dark Sun: The Making of the Hydrogen Bomb.* New York: Simon and Schuster, 1995.

Rotblat, Joseph and Jack Steinberger, eds. *A Nuclear-Weapon Free World: Desirable? Feasible?* Boulder CO: Westview Press, 1995.

Schell, Jonathan. *The Fate of the Earth.* New York: Knopf, 1982.

Stehle, Hansjokob. *Eastern Politics of the Vatican 1917-1979.* Trans. Sandra Smith. Athens, OH: Ohio University Press, 1981.

Sussman, Glen. "Anti-Nuclear Weapons Activism in the United States and Great Britain: A Comparative Analysis." Ph.D. diss., Washington State, 1987.

Talbott, Strobe. *Deadly Gambits: the Reagan Administration and the Stalemate in Nuclear Arms Control.* New York: Vintage Books, 1985.

Taylor, Richard and Nigel Young, eds. *Campaigns for Peace: British Peace Movements in the Twentieth Century.* Manchester, UK: Manchester University Press, 1987.

Tucker, Robert W. *The Just War: A Study in Contemporary American Doctrine.* Baltimore, MD: Johns Hopkins Press, 1960.

___. *Just War and Vatican Council II.* New York: The Council on Religion and International Affairs, 1966.

United Methodist Council of Bishops. *In Defense of Creation: The Nuclear Crisis and a Just Peace.* Nashville, TN: Graded Press, 1986.

United Methodist Church Commission to Study the Christian Faith and War in the Nuclear Age. *The Christian Faith and War in the Nuclear Age.* Nashville, TN: Abington, 1963.

United Presbyterian Church, USA: The Peacemaking Project Program Agency. "Peacemaking: The Believers' Calling." New York: 1982.

Walsh, Michael and Brian Davies, eds. *Proclaiming Justice and Peace: Papal Documents from Rerum Novarum through Centesimus Annus.* Mystic: CN: Twenty-Third Publications, 1991.

Walters, Philip. "The Russian Orthodox Church." In *Eastern Christianity and Politics* Vol. 1, *Christianity Under Stress.* Ed. Pedro Ramet. Durham, NC: Duke University Press, 1988.

Walzer, Michael. *Just and Unjust Wars: A Moral Argument with Historical Illustrations.* New York: Basic Books, 1977.

Wasserstrom, Richard, ed. *War and Morality.* Belmont, CA: Wadsworth, 1970.

Webster, Alexander. *The Price of Prophecy: Orthodox Churches on Peace, Freedom, and Security.* Washington, D.C.: Ethics and Public Policy Center, 1993.

Weigel, George. *Tranquillitas Ordinis: The Present Failure and Future Promise Of American Catholic Thought on War and Peace.* New York: Oxford University Press, 1987.

Welsby, Paul. *A History of the Church of England 1945-1980.* Oxford, UK: Oxford University Press, 1984.

Wilbanks, Dana and Ronald Stone. "Presbyterians and Peacemaking: Are We Now Called to Resistance?" New York: Advisory Council on Church and Society, 1985.

___, eds. *The Presbyterian Struggle: Militarism and Resistance.* New York: University Press of America, 1985.

Will, Herman. *A Will of Peace: Peace Action in the United Methodist Church: A History.* Washington, DC: General Board of Church and Society of the United Methodist Church: 1984.

Wittner, Lawrence S. *One World or None: The Struggle Against the Bomb* Vol. I, *A History of the World Nuclear Disarmament Movement Through 1953,* Vol. II, *Resisting the Bomb 1954-1970.* Stanford, CA: Stanford University Press, 1993, 1997.

XIX. Religion and War in the Creation of Israel

Almog, Shmuel. *Zionism and History: The Rise of a New Jewish Consciousness.* New York: St. Martin's, 1987.

Almog, Shmuel, Jehuda Reinharz, and Anita Shapira, eds. *Zionism and Religion*. Hanover, NH: Brandeis University Press, 1998.

Avi-hai, Avraham. *Ben-Gurion, State-Builder: Principles and Pragmatism 1948-1963*. Wiley: New York, 1974.

Avishai, Bernard. *The Tragedy of Zionism: Revolution and Democracy in the Land of Israel*. New York: Farrar Straus Giroux, 1985.

Bregman, Ahron. *Israel's Wars: A History since 1947*. New York: Routledge, 2nd edition, 2002.

Cohen, Michael J. *Palestine and the Great Powers 1945-1948*. Princeton, NJ: Princeton University Press, 1982.

"Debate on the 1948 Exodus." *Journal of Palestine Studies*, 21, no. 81 (1991).

Elpeleg, Zvi. *The Grand Mufti: Haj Amin Al-Hussaini*. Trans. David Harvey. London, U.K.: Frank Cass, 1993.

Hazony, Yoram. *The Jewish State: The Struggle for Israel's Soul*. New York: Basic Books, 2000.

Louis, William Roger and Robert W. Stookey, eds. *The End of the Palestine Mandate*. Austin, TX: University of Texas Press, 1986.

Meir, Golda. *My Life*. New York: Putnam, 1975.

Morris, Benny. *The Birth of the Palestinian Refugee Problem, 1947-1949*. Cambridge, UK: Cambridge University Press, 1987.

New Encyclopedia of Zionism and Israel. Ed. Geoffrey Wigoder. Cranbury, NJ: Herzl Press Publication, Associated University Press, 1994.

Peretz, Don, ed. *The Arab-Israel Dispute*. New York: Facts on File, 1996.

Perlmutter, Amos. *Israel: The Partitioned State, A Political History Since 1900*. New York: Scribner's, 1985.

Prior, Michael. *Zionism and the State of Israel: A Moral Inquiry*. New York: Routledge, 1999.

Reinharz, Jehuda. *Chaim Weizmann: The Making of a Zionist Leader and The Making of a Statesman*. New York: Oxford University Press, 1985, 1993.

Rodinson, Maxime. *Israel: A Colonial-Settler State?* New York, Anchor Foundation, 1973.

Rubinstein, Amnon. *The Zionist Dream Revisited*. New York: Shocken, 1984.

Ruether, Rosemary Radford and Herman Ruether. *The Wrath of Jonah: The Crisis of Religious Nationalism in the Israeli-Palestinian Conflict*. New York: Harper and Row, 1989.

Said, Edward W. *The Politics of Dispossession: The Struggle for Palestinian Self-Determination, 1969-1994*. New York: Vantage, 1995.

Segev, Tom. *One Palestine, Complete: Jews and Arabs Under the British Mandate*. Trans. Haim Watzman. New York: Metropolitan, 2000.

Shimoni, Gideon. *The Zionist Ideology*. Hanover, NH: Brandeis University Press, 1995.

Shlaim, Avi. *The Iron Wall: Israel and the Arab World*. New York: Norton, 2000.

Sicker, Martin. *Judaism, Nationalism, and the Land of Israel*. Boulder, CO: Westview, 1992.

Silver, Eric. *Begin: The Haunted Prophet*. New York: Random House, 1984.
___. "Arab Witnesses Admit Exaggerating Deir Yassin Massacre." *Jerusalem Post*, 2 April 1998.
Sternhell, Zeev. *The Founding Myths of Israel: Nationalism, Socialism, and the Making of the Jewish State*. Trans. David Maisel. Princeton, NJ: Princeton University, 1997.
Sykes, Christopher. *Crossroads to Israel 1917-1948*. Bloomington, IN: Indiana University Press, 1973.
Teveth, Shabtai. *Ben-Gurion: The Burning Ground 1886-1948*. Boston: Houghton Mifflin, 1987.
Wheatcroft, Geoffrey. *The Controversy of Zion: Jewish Nationalism, the Jewish State, and the Unresolved Jewish Dilemma*. Reading, MA: Addison Wesley, 1996.

XX. Islam and Modern War: Iran and Iraq

Abrahamian, Ervand. *Khomeinism: Essays on the Islamic Republic*. Berkeley, CA: University of California, 1993.
Adas, Michael, ed. *Islamic and European Expansion*. Philadelphia: Temple University Press, 1993.
Gellner, Ernest, ed. *Islamic Dilemmas: Reformers, Nationalists and Industrialization: The Southern Shore of the Mediterranean*. New York: Mouton, 1985.
Halm, Heinz. *Shiism*. Trans. Janet Watson. Edinbugh, United Kingdom: Edinburgh University Press, 1991.
Hiro, Dilip. *The Longest War: The Iran-Iraq Military Conflict*. New York: Routledge, 1991.
Johnson, James Turner. *The Holy War Idea in Western and Islamic Traditions*. University Park, PA: Penn State Press, 1997.
Johnson, James Turner and John Kelsay, eds. *Cross, Crescent, and Sword: The Justification and Limitation of War in Western and Islamic Tradition*. Westport, CN: Greenwood, 1990.
Karpet, Kemal H. *The Politicization of Islam: Reconstructing Identity, State, Faith, and Community in the Late Ottoman State*. Oxford, UK: Oxford University Press, 2001.
Keddie, Nikki, ed. *Religion and Politics and Iran: Islam from Quietism to Revolution*. New Haven, CN: Yale University Press, 1983.
Kelsay, John. *Islam and War: A Study in Comparative Ethics*. Louisville, KY: Westminster/John Knox, 1993.
Kelsay, John and James Turner Johnson, eds. *Just War and Jihad: Historical and Theoretical Perspectives on War and Peace in Western and Islamic Traditions*. Westport, CN: Greenwood, 1991.
Kramer, Martin, ed. *Shiism, Resistance, and Revolution*. Boulder CO: Westminster, 1987.

Lewis, Bernard. *The Emergence of Modern Turkey*. 3rd edition. New York: Oxford University Press, 2002.

Menashri, David, ed. *The Iranian Revolution and the Muslim World*. Boulder, CO: Westview, 1990.

Munson, Henry, Jr. *Islam and Revolution in the Middle East*. New Haven, CN: Yale University Press, 1988.

Murphey, Rhoads. *Ottoman Warfare 1500-1700*. New Brunswick, NJ: Rutgers University Press, 1999.

Omid, Homa. *Islam and the Post-Revolutionary State in Iran*. New York: St. Martin's Press, 1994.

Roy, Olivier. *The Failure of Political Islam*. Trans. Carol Volk. Cambridge, MA: Harvard University Press, 1994.

Shaw, Stanford J. *Between Old and New: The Ottoman Empire under Sultan Selim III 1789-1807*. Cambridge, MA: Harvard University Press, 1971.

Sachedina, Abdulaziz Abdulhussein. *The Just Ruler in Shiite Islam: The Comprehensive Authority of the Jurist in Imamite Jurisprudence*. New York: Oxford University Press, 1988.

Said, Edward. *Orientalism*. New York: Vantage, 1979.

Sirreyeh, Elizabeth. *Sufis and Anti-Sufis: The Defence, Rethinking and Rejection of Sufism in the Modern World*. Richmond, Surrey, UK: Curzon, 1999.

Tripp, Charles. *A History of Iraq*. Cambridge, UK: Cambridge University Press, 2000.

Waardenburg, Jacques. "Islam as a Vehicle of Protest," in *Islamic Dilemmas: Reformers, Nationalists and Industrialization*. 1985: 22-48.

Watt, William M. *Muslin-Christian Encounters: Perceptions and Misperceptions*. London, New York: Routledge, 1991.

XXI. The Gulf Wars against Iraq

Anderson, Kenneth. "Who Owns the Rules of War?" *New York Times Magazine*. 13 April, 2003: 38.

Arnove, Anthony, ed. *Iraq Under Siege: The Deadly Impact of Sanctions and War*. Cambridge, MA. South End Press, 2000.

Bennis, Phyllis and Michel Moushabeck, eds. *Beyond the Storm: A Gulf Crisis Reader*. New York: Olive Branch Press: New York, 1991.

Blumberg, Herbert and Christopher French, eds. *The Persian Gulf War: Views from the Social and Behavioral Sciences*. New York: University Press of America, 1994.

Bumiller, "Religious Leaders Ask if Antiwar Call Is Heard." *New York Times*, 10 March 2003.

Elshtain, Jean et al. *But Was It Just? Reflections on the morality of the Persian Gulf War*. New York: Doubleday, 1992.

Goodstein, "Catholics Debating: Back President or Pope." *New York Times*, 6 March 2003.

"The Gulf War: Five Years After," *Frontline*, Public Broadcasting Co. 1996.

Hallett, Brian, ed. *Engulfed in War: Just War and the Persian Gulf.* Honolulu: Hawaii: Spark M. Matsunaga Institute for Peace, University of Hawaii, 1991.

Johnson, James Turner and George Weigel, eds. *Just War and the Gulf War.* Washington, DC: Ethics and Public Policy Center, 1991.

Kaplan, Robert. *Of Paradise and Power: America and Europe and the New World Order.* New York: Knopf, 2003.

Kelsay, John. *Islam and War: The Gulf War and Beyond, A Study in Comparative Ethics.* Louisville, KY: Westminster/John Knox, 1993.

The Lehrer Report, *News Hour.* March 3, 2003.

New York Times, New York. April 22, 2003.

Pew Forum on Religion and Public Life, "Iraq and Just War: A Symposium," September 30, 2002.

Pew Survey "Americans Hearing about Iraq from the Pulpit but Religious Faith Not Defining Opinions." March 13-16, 2003.

Pew Survey "Americans Struggle with Religious Role at Home and Abroad." March, 2003.

Pisatori, James, ed. *Islamic Fundamentalisms and the Gulf Crisis.* Chicago, Ill: The Fundamentalism Project of American Academy of Arts and Sciences. USA, American Academy of Arts and Sciences, 1991.

Rieff, David. "Were Sanctions Right?" *New York Times Magazine* 27 July 2003.

Smock, David. *Religious Perspectives on War: Christian, Muslim and Jewish Attitudes Toward Force After the Gulf War.* Washington, DC: U. S. Institute of Peace, 1995.

Stoessinger, John. *Why Nations Go to War.* 6th edition. New York: St. Martin's Press, 1993.

Tripp, Charles. *A History of Iraq.* Cambridge, UK: Cambridge University Press, 2000.

Vaux, Kenneth L. *Ethics and the Gulf War: Religion, Rhetoric, and Righteousness.* Boulder, CO: Westview, 1992.

Woodward, Bob. *The Commanders.* New York: Simon and Schuster, 1991.

XXII. The 1990s: Religious-Ethnic Wars

Abrams, Irwin. *Nobel Peace Prize and Its Laureates: An Illustrated History 1901-1987.* Boston: G. K. Hall, 1988.

Ackerman, Peter and Jack Duvall. *A Force More Violent: A Century of Nonviolent Conflict.* New York: Palgrave, 2000.

Appleby, R. Scott. *The Ambivalence of the Sacred: Religion, Violence, and Reconciliation.* Carnegie Commission on Preventing Deadly Conflict. Lanham, MD : Rowman & Littlefield Publishers, 2000

___. *Religious Fundamentalisms and Global Conflict.* Headline Series, no. 301. Foreign Policy Association.

Aronson, Geoffrey. *Israel, Palestinians, and the Intifadah: Creating Facts on the West Bank.* New York: Kegan Paul and Institute for Palestinian Studies, 1987.

Barak, Ehud, Benny Morris, Robert Malley, and Hussein Agha. "Camp David and After: An Exchange." *New York Review of Books.* 9 August, 2001: 13; June 2002: 42-47; 27 June 2002: 47-48.

Barash, David. *Introduction to Peace Studies.* Belmont, CA: Wadsworth, 1991. Press, 2000.

___, ed. *A Reader in Peace Studies.* New York: Oxford University Press, 2000.

Berryman, Philip. *Liberation Theology: Essential Facts about the Revolutionary Movement in Latin America-and Beyond.* Philadelphia, PA: Temple University Press, 1987.

Breadun, Deaglan de. *The Far Side of Revenge: Making Peace in Northern Ireland.* Wilton, Ireland: Collins, 2001.

Brown, Michael and Richard Rosecrance, eds. *The Costs of Conflict:Prevention and Cure in the Global Area.* Lanham, MD: Rowman and Littlefield, 1999.

Brown, Seyom. *The Causes and Prevention of War.* New York: St. Martin's Press, 1987.

Burton, John, ed. *Conflict: Human Needs Theory.* New York: St. Martin's Press, 1990.

___. *Conflict:Resolution and Prevention.* New York: St. Martin's Press, 1990.

___. *Conflict Resolution: Its Language and Process.* Lanham, MD: Scarecrow Press, 1996.

Catherwood, Christopher. *Why the Nations Rage: Killing in the Name of God.* London, UK: Hodder and Stoughton, 1999.

Davis, Scott, ed. *Religion and Justice in the War over Bosnia.* New York: Routledge, 1996.

Destexhe, Alain. *Rwanda and Genocide in the Twentieth Century.* Trans. Alison Marschner. New York: New York University Press, 1996.

Ellis, Marc H. *Unholy Alliance: Religion and Atrocity in Our Time.* Minneapolis, MN: Fortress, 1997.

Embree, Ainslie. *Utopias in Conflict: Religion and Nationalism in Modern India.* Berkeley, CA: University of California, 1990.

Esposito, John. *The Islamic Threat: Myth or Reality?* New York: Oxford, 1992.

Fisher, Roger et al. *Beyond Machiavelli: Tools for Coping with Conflict.* Cambridge, MA: Harvard University Press, 1994.

___ and William Ury. *Getting to Yes: Negotiating Agreement Without Giving In.* New York: Penguin, 1983.

Goldman, Francisco. "Victory in Guatemala." *New York Review of Books.* 21 May 2002: 77-79, 82-84.

Gopal, Sarvepalli. *Anatomy of a Confrontation: Babri-Masjid-Ramjanmabhumi Issue.* New York: Penguin, 1991.

Gourevitch, Philip. *We Wish to Inform You that Tomorrow We Will Be Killed with Our Families: Stories from Rwanda.* New York: Farrar, Straus, and Giroux, 1998.

Ganguly, Sumit. *The Crisis in Kashmir: Portents of War, Hopes of Peace.* Cambridge, UK: Woodrow Wilson Center Press and Cambridge University Press, 1997.

Geertz, Clifford. "Which Way to Mecca." *New York Review of Books.* 12 June 2000: 27-29; 3 July 2002: 36-39.

Hassett, John, Hugh Lacey, and Leo J. O'Donovan, eds. *Towards a Society that Serves Its People: The Intellectual Contribution of El Salvador's Wounded Jesuits.* Washington, DC: Georgetown University Press, 1991.

Hoffman, Bruce. *Inside Terrorism.* New York: Columbia University Press, 1998.

Holbrooke, Richard. *To End a War.* New York: Random House, 1998.

Huntington, Samuel, et al. "The Clash of Civilizations? The Debate." 1993 *Foreign Affairs Reader.* New York, 1996.

Ignatieff, Michael. *The Warrior's Honor: Ethnic War and the Modern Conscience.* New York: Metropolitan, 1998.

Jack, Homer A. *WCRP: World Conference on Religion and Peace.* New York: World Conference on Religion and Peace, 1993.

Jett, Dennis C. *Why Peacekeeping Fails.* New York: Palgrave, 2001.

Johnson, Douglas and Cynthia Sampson, eds. *Religion: The Missing Dimension of Statecraft.* New York: Oxford University Press, 1974.

Juergensmeyer, Mark. *The New Cold War: Religious Nationalism Confronts the Secular State.* Berkeley: CA: University of California Press, 1993.

___. *Terror in the Mind of God: The Global Rise of Religious Violence.* Berkeley, CA: University of California Press, 2000.

Hall, Harold and Leighton Whitaker, eds. *Collective Violence: Effective Strategies for Assessing and Intervening in Fatal Group and Institutional Agression.* Boca Raton, FL: CRC Press, 1999.

Kaminer, Reuven. *The Politics of Protest: The Israeli Peace Movement and the Palestinian Intifadah.* Brighton, UK: Sussex University Press, 1996.

Kepel, Gilles. *The Revenge of God: The Resurgence of Islam: Christianity, and Judaism in the Modern World.* University Park, PA: Penn State University Press, 1994.

___. *Jihad. The Trail of Political Islam.* Trans. Anthony Robert. Cambridge, MA: Harvard University Press, 2002.

Kriesberg, Louis. *Constructive Conflicts:From Escalation to Resolution.* Lanham, MD: Rowman and Littlefield, 2003.

Lawrence, Bruce. *Shattering the Myth: Islam Beyond Violence.* Princeton, NJ: Princeton University Press, 1998.

Lesch, Ann. *The Sudan: Contested National Identities.* Bloomington, IN: Indiana University Press, 1998.

Lowy, Michael. *The War of Gods. Religion and Politics in Latin America.* New York: Verso, 1996.

833

Mahmutcehogic, Rusmir. *The Denial of Bosnia.* Trans. Francis James and
   Marina Bowder. University Park, PA: Pennsylvania State
   University Press, 2000.
Mojzes, Paul, ed. *Religion and the War in Bosnia.* Atlanta, GA: Scholars Press,
   1998.
Muslih, Muhammad. *Foreign Policy of Hamas.* New York: Council on Foreign
   Relations, 1999.
Pandev, Gyanandra. *Remembering Partition: Violence, Nationalism and
   History in India.* Cambridge, UK: Cambridge University Press, 2001.
Power, Samantha. *"A Problem from Hell": America and the Age of Genocide.*
   New York: Basic Books, 2002.
Prunier, Gerald. *The Rwanda Crisis: History of a Genocide.* New York:
   Columbia University Press, 1995.
Queen, Christopher and Sallie B. King, eds. *Engaged Buddhism: Buddhist
   Liberation Movements in Asia.* Albany, NY: State University Press of
   New York, 1996.
Rashid, Ahmed. *Taliban: Militant Islam, Oil, and Fundamentalism in Central
   Asia.* New Haven, Yale University Press, 2000.
Rieff, David. *A Bed for the Night: Humanitarianism in Crisis.* New York: Simon
   and Shuster, 2002.
Rotberg, Robert, ed. *Creating Peace in Sri Lanka: Civil War and Reconciliation.*
   Washington D.C: Brookings Institution, 1999.
Ross, Marc H. *The Culture of Conflict: Interpretations and Interests in
   Comparative Perspective.* New Haven, Yale University Press, 1993.
___. *Management of Conflict: Interpretations and Interests in Comparative
   Perspective.* New Haven, Yale, 1993.
Ruperman, "Rwanda Retrospect." *Foreign Affairs.* 78 (2000): 94-118.
Sells, Michael. *The Bridge Betrayed: Religion and Genocide in Bosnia.*
   Berkeley, CA: University of California Press, 1998.
Sela, Avraham and Moshe Ma'oz. *The PLO and Israel: From Armed Conflict to
   Political Solution, 1964-1994.* New York: St. Martin's Press, 1997.
Sharp, Gene. *Civilian Based Defense: A Post-military Weapons System.*
   Princeton, NJ: Princeton University Press, 1990.
___. *Gandhi as a Political Strategist: With Essays on Ethics and Politics.* Boston,
   MA: Sargent, 1979.
___. *Making Europe Unconquerable: The Potential of Civilian-Based
   Deterrence and Defense.* Cambridge, MA: Ballinger, 1985.
Shawcross, William. *Deliver Us From Evil: Peacekeepers, Warlords and a
   World of Endless Conflict.* New York: Simon and Schuster, 2000.
Talbot, Ian and Gurharpal Singh, eds. *Region and Partition: Bengal, Punjab
   and the Partition of the Subcontinent.* New York: Oxford University
   Press, 1999.
Thompson. W. Scott et al., eds. *Approaches to Peace: An Intellectual Map.*
   Washington, DC: U. S. Institute of Peace, 1991.

Tibi, Bassam. *The Challenge of Fundamentalism: Political Islam and the New World Disorder*. Berkeley, CA: University of California Press, 1998.

Van der Verr, Peter. *Religious Nationalism: Hindus and Muslims in India*. Berkeley, CA: University of California Press, 1994.

Weigel, George and John Langan, eds. *The American Search for Peace: Moral Reasoning, Religious Hope, and National Security*. Washington, DC: Georgetown University Press, 1991.

Yarrow, Clarence. *The Quaker Experience in International Conciliation*. New Haven, CN: Yale University Press, 1978.

Yoder, John Howard. *Nevertheless: Varieties of Religious Pacifism*. Scottsdale, PA: Herald Press, 1992.

Zimmerman, Warren, et al. *War in the Balkans*. A Foreign Affairs Reader. New York, 1999.

Index

*Individuals, movements and countries mentioned only once in the text are often not indexed.

eighteenth-century, 317;
Erasmus, 272;
French Revolution, 358,
  360-61;
Grotius, 303;
Hindu, 151;
Islam, 198, 211, 213, 223;
Locke, 342;
Medieval Europe, 236, 243,
  247-49;
Mexican War, 393;
Rome, 107-08;
Suarez, 295;
Vietnam, 595, 599;
World War I, 442, 443, 445,
  449;
World War II, 521, 523-27,
  546, 550, 551, 554, 557,
  560, 562;
See also Just War theory,
terrorism.
Non-violence (*ahimsa*), 157-58,
  164, 257, 289, 479, 497-502,
  516, 718, 731, 732, 742, 759-66;
  See also Bible, Buddhism,
Gandhi, Jains, pacifism, peace
movements.
North Africa, 681, 684, 685.
Nuclear Freeze, 628, 632, 645-47.
Nuclear Pacifism, 617, 625, 633,
  646.
Nuclear Strategy,
  first use, 613, 618, 625, 646;
  counter force, 700;
  deterrence, 618, 631, 635, 639,
    642, 646, 648, 783;
  graduated response, 620;
  international control, 614-16;
  massive retaliation, 611, 618,
    635;
  mutual assured destruction, 611,
    621, 641;
  proliferation, 732;
  See also Atomic bomb,

hydrogen bombs, nuclear
  weapons.
Nuclear Testing, 625-27, 640, 641,
  647.
Nuclear Weapons, 19, 522, 559-61,
  577, 583, 584, 587, 589-91, 599,
  725, 727, 729;
  Amarillo, Texas, 629-31;
  churches on, 621-27;
  debate on atomic bomb, 561-66,
    583-84;
  See also Atomic bomb,
  weapons of mass destruction.
Nuclear Winter, 643.
Nuremburg, 539, 569-73.

Oil and war, 693, 697, 698, 699, 702,
  705-708, 714-16, 722, 724, 728,
  729.
Oppenheimer, Robert, 560, 612.
Ordeal by combat, 230, 248.
Ottomans, 218, 221, 224, 225, 273,
  274, 308, 368, 371, 372, 405,
  408, 438, 446, 447, 457, 653,
  659, 679-87.

"Pacem in Terris," 636, 638, 640.
  See also Roman Catholics, John
  XXIII.
Pacifism, 16, 50, 75n, 84, 126;
  Absolute, 478-79, 514, 515, 517,
    518, 617;
  Anabaptist, 289, 291, 298, 308;
  between the Wars, 474-89, 512-
    18;
  Cold War, 600, 604, 607, 617,
    624-26, 634-40;
  conscientious objectors (COs),
    283, 285, 334, 436, 451,
    484-85, 522, 527, 533-35,
    639, 640;
  defined, 408;
  early Church, 115-18;
  Erasmus, 273;

STUDIES IN RELIGION AND SOCIETY